GOOD GAME

GOOD GAME

CHRISTIANITY AND THE CULTURE OF SPORTS

SHIRL JAMES HOFFMAN

BAYLOR UNIVERSITY PRESS

Cover Design by Zeal Design Studio

Cover Image © Bruce Lonngren, 2007

Library of Congress Cataloging-in-Publication Data

Hoffman, Shirl J., 1939-
  Good game : christianity and the culture of sports / Shirl James Hoffman.
    p. cm.
  Includes bibliographical references and index.
  ISBN 978-1-932792-10-2 (pbk. : alk. paper)
  1. Sports--Religious aspects--Christianity. 2. Sports--Moral and ethical aspects. 3. Sports--Social aspects. I. Title.

GV706.42.H65 2009
306.4'83--dc22

                        2009029958

Printed in the United States of America on acid-free paper with a minimum of 30% pcw recycled content.

For Claude

CONTENTS

ACKNOWLEDGMENTS

This book had a gestation period extending over several decades. The trail of those who helped along the way tracks far back—so far, in fact, that in attempting to thank those who helped, I am almost certain to omit somebody's name. James Sire asked me to do a book on the topic thirty years ago. Although I didn't finish that assignment, I hope that in some small way, this effort confirms his vision for the book. Mary Duquin, Richard Swanson, and Nick Watson read chapters at various stages of development and made helpful comments. Tom Krattenmaker, Jim Mathisen, Richard Mouw, Stuart Weir, Lowrie McCown, Valerie Gin, Nick Watson, John White, Jack Higgs, Joe Price, Doug Hochstetler, Bud Williams, Dick Swanson, Dennis Hiebert, Roland Renson, Chris Stevenson, and David Naugle kindly loaned or gave me materials. Several people took time out of busy schedules to talk at length. I am especially appreciative to Richard Mouw, Bryan Stone, Sharon Stall, Teresa Clarke, Jennifer Beller, John White, Greg Linville, Richard Wood, Ken Ferraro, and Don Lawrence. I am indebted to Athletes in Action for including me in a weekend of stimulating conversation with a group of academics and others working in sports ministry. Special mention should be made of Gary Wicks' hard work in organizing the Second International Conference on Sport and Religion at St. Olaf College and to Nick Watson and Mark Resti of the Centre for Sports and Spirituality at York St. John University for inviting me to lecture at the Centre's inaugural conference. Both experiences were helpful in clarifying my ideas about aspects of the relationship between sport and religion. The University of North Carolina at Greensboro provided me with a research leave that helped lay the foundation for the book, and the staff of the Jackson Library Department of Interlibrary Loan fulfilled their duties efficiently and with good humor. A special debt of gratitude is owed to Carey Newman, Director of Baylor University Press, and his associates for their enthusiastic support of the project and for their patience with an author who seemed always to miss deadlines. T. J. McLemore deserves special recognition for his painstaking review of the manuscript.

Most authors thank their spouses for putting up with them, realizing that while they were hunkered down in their studies the demands of the household were shouldered by their loved one. Far from merely tolerating her husband's commitment to this project and the absences that it entailed, Claude Mourot enthusiastically supported me, managing to say just the right words at the right time. "Tu es ma joie de vivre," Claude.

Preface

As the son of a Baptist minister growing up in western Pennsylvania, I experienced firsthand the peculiar way Americans mix sport with religion. Almost all of my memories of my teenage years are framed in the context of either religion or athletic competition. Football, basketball, and track and field filled out the entire academic year, interspersed with Sunday morning, Sunday evening, and Wednesday evening services. There was little time for much else. For me religion was a seamless part of sports. My older brother and I (nicknamed "Big Preach" and "Little Preach," respectively) were always called upon to offer the pregame prayers at football games and the invocations at year-end athletic banquets. My parents attended most of my competitions, my father sometimes making known his displeasure of referees' calls. A new basketball coach—something of a legend at a local college—was hired my sophomore year. He took basketball to a new level of seriousness, rejecting any notion that the game could or should be fun and insisting on complete and utter dedication to winning. He was a growly, gorilla sort of man known for his profanity and mean-spiritedness, yet he always made sure the team had recited the Lord's Prayer before taking the court. Whether it was the result of praying or his technical genius, we won the county championship my senior year and the coach was

celebrated as a hero, only to be fired a few years later as his intensity
and commitment to winning got the better of him.

When the basketball coach changed the time of practices from afternoons to evenings, I experienced a struggle between faith and sports for
the first time. Although my father was generally enthusiastic about my
involvement in sports, he immediately saw that the revised practice schedule would make it impossible for me to attend midweek prayer service
on Wednesday evening. Since the coach demanded attendance at every
practice and my father was equally insistent on my attending Wednesday
prayer services, I prepared to wean myself from basketball. Sensing my
disappointment, Dad decided to pay the coach a visit, thinking that he
could change the coach's mind. I waited outside the coach's office for what
seemed like an eternity as the two talked. I never asked what transpired in
the conversation or what the coach said to convince my father to allow me
to attend practice. I only know that in this confrontation between sport
and religion in my early life, sport won hands down. Of course, neither I
nor my father could appreciate then that this seemingly insignificant episode played out in one small gymnasium in an obscure part of Pennsylvania was a reenactment of what had been playing out on a much larger
scale for centuries. When religion runs up against sport, it is usually religion that gets shoved out of the way.

Because sports had played such a central role in my young life, it
seemed only natural that I would decide to major in physical education.
When I was designated winner of the Athletic Award at graduation, I was
sure of God's calling to a career in sports. I enrolled in a small evangelical
liberal arts college in New York where I had the good fortune to have as
a coach Norm Wilhelmi, who provided a blessed contrast to the mon-
strous coach I had labored under in high school. For the first time in my
life I saw that sports could be fun. Laughter abounded alongside effort
and commitment. While we won more than our share of games, losing
didn't bring us to the brink of self-loathing. As it rarely had before and as
it rarely has since, sport nudged up against play.

Still, I came to appreciate, as I hadn't up to that point, the two worlds
that evangelicals inhabit: the daily world of commitment and earnest
application of their faith, and the world of sports in which faith seems
to lose its referential power in the face of fierce partisanship. If faith
had any noticeable effect on the way Christians played and organized
their games, it escaped me. After a particularly bitter game against a
rival Christian college from New England marked by fistfights between

players and depressingly rude behavior by spectators, I tacked a letter to the student bulletin board, suggesting that sports at Christian institutions should be played free of the ugliness that had taken place the night before. While the letter sparked many comments, it didn't have the effect I had intended. In fact, daring to criticize sports had rendered me something of a curiosity, made even more curious by the fact that I was an athlete. Some thought it brash that I would dare to criticize sports at all. It was then that I first realized how reticent the Christian community was to think critically about sports or to explore seriously how the sporting culture intersects with the spiritual path Christians claim to follow.

I spent five years coaching college basketball; photos in my study remind me of what a fine time I had. But my heart was stolen by the love of scholarship, and I moved on to an academic career that allowed me to study not only the science of human performance, but the curious relationship between sport and religion. Moving from being an active sportsman to being an academic provided the distance essential for critical analysis. Nevertheless, I have never wavered in my belief that sport offers Christians unique opportunities for tapping dimensions of their religious lives. That our society has converted sport into gaudy spectacles that snuff out any light the experience has to shed on our spiritual graces is a tragedy. An even greater tragedy is that the Christian community seems not to care.

Obviously, how one goes about analyzing the relationship between sport and faith is at least partly a function of one's own religious perspective and life experiences. In my case, it has meant approaching the analysis from an essentially evangelical perspective. Although some of my evangelical friends and colleagues might be more comfortable if I described myself as being on the fringe of the evangelical circle or perhaps not an evangelical at all, I would resist any other categorization. My sense is that the terms "evangelical" and "evangelicalism" have become so mired in the definitional swamps, and the movement has become so transdenominational, so transdoctrinal in its scope, that the appropriate metaphor may be not a single circle of evangelicalism but a series of overlapping, interconnected circles, perhaps a woven cord. Somewhere in this increasingly complex cord of evangelical theology and ethical practices, my own theology and ethical practices have taken shape.

INTRODUCTION
EVANGELICALS AND THE RUSH TO SPORTS

In Warren St. John's *Rammer Jammer Yellow Hammer*, a fascinating account of the lunacy that is University of Alabama football fandom, he describes a conversation with a Mr. and Mrs. Reese in their $300,000 motor home purchased exclusively for traveling to the Crimson Tide's games. The couple, it turns out, had missed their daughter's wedding because it had been scheduled on the same day as the Alabama-Tennessee game. They pointed out that they had managed to make the reception and told St. John that they had specifically asked their daughter not to schedule the wedding at a time that conflicted with the big game. Asked why he did it, Mr. Reese could only shake his head and respond: "I just love Alabama football, is all I can think of."

In 2004, 79-year-old George Sumner, an avid Boston Red Sox baseball fan, was battling to survive a long bout with cancer as his beloved Sox vied for their first World Series championship in 86 years. His family had expected him to die before the series began but he hung on, drifting off to sleep during commercials but not before instructing his family to wake him when the commercial was over. When the game had finished and the Sox had won the series, he whispered "Yippee!" closed his eyes, and went to sleep. Another bedridden Sox fan, the Reverend William Bourke, didn't last the series. He died after Game 2 and was buried the day after Boston won the series. A commemorative Sox baseball and that morning's newspaper were tucked into his casket.

In 2005, a man was arrested for running onto the football field during a game between the Philadelphia Eagles and the Green Bay Packers. Christopher Noteboom carried a plastic bag, leaving behind him a cloud of fine powder. When he was apprehended he told police he was spreading the ashes of his recently deceased mother who had been an ardent Eagles fan. "She'll always be a part of Lincoln Financial Field and of the Eagles," said Noteboom.[1]

Most sports fans take their sports less seriously. They may settle for painting their faces the colors of their favorite team, donning team jerseys, or wearing bizarre hats. Some furnish their homes with team memorabilia; others settle for a team logo on their automobile. But to deny the power of sport to invade our lives, rearrange our priorities, and transport us to an alternate reality is to deny why we care so much about sport. Whether carving out time from their busy schedules for golf, tennis, or skiing, or frittering away entire weekends watching a smorgasbord of televised sports, Americans are consuming sports on a scale unprecedented in history. The ancient Romans, long considered the gold standard for how sports-crazed a culture could become, were mere dilettantes compared to hardcore sports fanatics of the twenty-first century. The Romans could squeeze 50,000 spectators inside the Colosseum for gladiatorial contests, a quaint assemblage compared to the 107,000 seats regularly sold out for University of Michigan or Penn State home football games. Nearly 260,000 Romans watched the chariot races at the Circus Maximus. Today, more than that watch the Indy 500 race at Indianapolis each Memorial Day weekend, and almost as many attend the Coca-Cola 500 NASCAR race held later on the same day.

In 2007, over 2.5 million fans watched sports in person on a typical fall weekend; tens of millions more watched them on television. Sports are talked about at coffee shops, at the office water cooler, and on hundreds of sports-talk radio stations. They are the perfect topic for sparking conversations at social gatherings. Sports magazines take up prime space on the shelves of book dealers; the granddaddy of them all, *Sports Illustrated*, sells as many copies in a month (13.2 million) as *To Kill a Mockingbird* has sold since its publication in 1960.[2]

The gluttonous appetite for sports far exceeds our tastes for most other cultural activities. In 2005, Americans spent over $89 billion on the purchase of sporting goods, over double what they spent on books

($42 billion). More than 7.6 billion admission tickets were sold at spectator sports events, a billion more than were sold at motion picture theaters. As attendance at symphony concerts declines, cities tear down still-serviceable stadia to make room for larger, more elaborate ones. At this writing, the New York Giants football team awaits a new $1.6 billion (and rising) stadium for which fans must pay between $1,000 and $20,000 simply for a PSL ("Personal Seating License") that will earn them the right to purchase season tickets costing from $80 to $700 per game. Two years before the stadium was completed, 130,000 people were on the waiting list to buy a PSL.[3]

Mass media grant far more coverage to sports than to any other aspect of our culture. *USA Today* allocates approximately one-fourth of its pages to sports. More than a tenth of the *World Almanac* is devoted to sports, more than is allocated for business, science, and politics combined. Publisher Houghton Mifflin's recent American history text for fifth graders treats the Depression and the presidency of Franklin Roosevelt in thirty-three lines, but devotes two full pages to baseball star Cal Ripken Jr.[4]

CHRISTIANS JOIN THE PARADE

The Christian community, which only a century ago was still ambivalent about whether sports were legitimate leisure pursuits for believers, has long since joined the parade. While the affinity for sports in the Christian community has been thoroughly ecumenical, evangelicals have had the most voracious appetite for sports, especially in harnessing them to their religious purposes. Thus, most studies of sport and Christianity are, in effect, studies of sport and evangelicalism. Statistical breakdowns of the religious orientations of the 97 million viewers who watched Super Bowl XLII are not available, but many had likely attended worship at an evangelical church that Sunday morning. Their minister may have alluded to the spectacle in his sermon, relying on it or on some of the Apostle Paul's athletic metaphors to underscore key points about Christian discipline, stewardship, or commitment. Perhaps their church followed the lead of a New Jersey congregation that staged a special football service in which women in the church dressed up as cheerleaders, the choir and pastor dressed in numbered jerseys, and a banner proclaiming "Christ: He Gave His All for the Team" was strung across the sanctuary.[5]

Some congregations mark Super Bowl Sunday by scheduling the evening service a few hours early (or canceling it altogether) to give members an opportunity to kick back in front of their TVs for the 6:30 p.m. kickoff. Some meet in the sanctuary or fellowship hall to watch the big game on over-sized television screens, a practice that the NFL, citing copyright laws, once threatened with legal action. Ultimately the defendant, Fall Creek Baptist Church in Indianapolis, was allowed to continue to show the game provided they didn't project it on a screen larger than 55 inches. A congregant at the church told a skeptical reporter: "This is one way the church can reach out and help people come to the understanding that this does not need to be a competition between God and materialistic things of the world."[6]

Watching professional sports broadcasts in church is a relatively recent development; playing sports in church is not. Gymnasia made their first appearance in liberal American urban churches before 1900. Today the size and amenities of sport and fitness facilities installed in some churches rival those at small or medium-sized colleges. The 45,000-member Second Baptist Church of Houston's Woodway Campus Family Life Center houses three basketball courts, three racquetball courts, an indoor walking track, and elaborate exercise facilities complete with sauna and steam rooms. "Sports ministry" is a fast-growing specialization in Christian colleges and Bible colleges designed to prepare staff for church recreational programs. Even churches lacking plush facilities can offer church league sports where ardent souls can go head-to-head on the softball diamond against the Methodists and Catholics across town.

Intercollegiate sports play an increasingly vital role at evangelical schools and colleges, often overshadowing the institutions' spiritual and academic missions. Some years ago an advertisement for a Christian college in the Chicago area that had hired a former Chicago Bears star to coach its football team carried the lead "Play With the Pros" and reminded young men, "If you're in high school and want to play for a pro in college, call Trinity College, a four-year liberal arts college, today."[7] Athletic programs at many such schools are affiliated with the National Christian College Athletic Association, a kind of evangelical NCAA whose one hundred member institutions vie for national championships in twenty different sports. Other college athletic departments opt for a more highly competitive, media-intensive stage. Wheaton College in Illinois and Calvin College in Michigan, for example, compete at NCAA Division III. Larger institutions such as Baylor University have waded into the murkier waters of NCAA Division I, hoping to attract the athletic talent and the publicity that comes to those who manage to survive the dog-eat-dog world of big-time athletics.

Like most other parents, Christians can become locked into a weekly schedule of car pooling kids to youth league soccer, football, swimming, basketball, gymnastics, martial arts or other sports. If a child happens to be athletically gifted, it's a good bet that his or her family's social life revolves around practice, game schedules, and traveling long distances to watch the child compete; some parents may serve as volunteer coaches or officials. Some manage to "keep it all in perspective"; others live out their unrealized aspirations for athletic stardom through their kids, pressuring them to compete and to win.

But it isn't only sports that have invaded Christian culture; Christian culture has also invaded sports. Professional football has become a heady mixture of toughness, violence, and evangelicalism—vicious collisions coupled with after-touchdown genuflections, trash-talk mixed with heaven-directed index fingers, anger and aggression interrupted by prayers, and riotous celebrations as backdrops to postgame, nationally televised testimonies of faith by athletic stars. In Super Bowl XLI (2007), coaches of both teams had established public reputations as Christian gentlemen. The next Super Bowl brought more of the same. Before the game, standout Arizona quarterback Kurt Warner seemed to be everywhere declaring his faith, as did many players on the Pittsburgh Steelers. A Baptist Press online feature article about Troy Polamalu, the ferocious defensive safety for the Steelers, described him in these enigmatic terms: "While he may be known as a silent killer for his soft voice and hard hits . . . there was nothing quiet about Polamalu's witness for Jesus Christ during the annual media day prior to the Super Bowl."[8]

The symbols and language of Christianity aren't paraded onto our sport fields merely to be part of the show. Deep in the bowels of the stadium, below the braying crowd, players and coaches—most of them no doubt sincere in their faith—gathered in the locker room for a team prayer and to listen to "chaplains," ministers sympathetic to the violent and hypercompetitive world that the players inhabit. Before taking the field many would privately "take a knee," asking God to preserve their bodies in the tumult of the game, perhaps to help their team win, and to use the mayhem that was about to follow to "bring glory to him." Some of them would trace their conversion to representatives from sport-faith organizations such as the Fellowship of Christian Athletes, Athletes in Action, or Pro Sports Outreach, which have spearheaded the infiltration of evangelicalism into professional, college, and high school sports.

If evangelicals of an earlier generation for whom sports were not only a waste of time but an enticement to sins of all kinds could see all of this, they would be appalled. Many fundamentalist denominations that had been sport's worst enemies in the late nineteenth and early twentieth centuries are now its closest friends. Of course, evangelicals' views toward many social practices have softened over the past century, but the sea change in attitudes toward sport from skepticism, cautiousness, and even radical opposition to an equally radical endorsement has been so dramatic in its sweep that it can hardly be accounted for simply by a general loosening of moral restrictions. Evangelicals may view extramarital sexual relations, alcohol consumption, marijuana use, and vulgar language a bit more liberally than they did a few decades ago, but as yet they haven't conscripted such practices into religious service as they have sport. In this respect, the evangelical rush to the sports stadium may be a singular phenomenon in defining evangelicals' accommodation to modern society.[9]

It is tempting to chalk this up to simple cultural accommodation, the willingness of evangelicals to cede moral ground in an effort to remain culturally relevant. Few things, after all, are more culturally relevant than sports. But the massive invasion of Christian athletes and coaches into big-time sports (especially football), the importance placed on sports by churches in their social programs and evangelistic efforts, the extraordinary emphasis intercollegiate sports are given in evangelical schools and colleges, and the rapid expansion of evangelical organizations thematically organized around competitive sports would seem to point to something deeper in the evangelical psyche than simply a quest for cultural relevance. Perhaps sport's painstakingly enforced, unambiguous rules relieve conscientious Christians from the shades-of-gray ethical decisions they face in real life. Perhaps sport's emphasis on discipline and self-control and striving are themes easily harmonized with the gospel. Perhaps religion scholar Randall Balmer had it right when he described the evangelical fascination with sport as "an attempt—albeit a clumsy attempt—to reclaim a powerful, triumphant God of an earlier era," a God "who has no trouble distinguishing right from wrong, good from evil. God the avenger. The Almighty as Arnold Schwarzenegger or Reggie White."[10] To literature scholar Jack Higgs, the attraction comes at least partly from a mutual concern with numbers and growth, the endorsement of competition between teams and denominations, the certainty of apocalypse, and a sense of theater and entertainment.[11]

Sports in Gomorrah

There are many less complicated reasons for evangelicals to play and watch sports. They are fun and exciting and, when played well and in healthy contexts, can be constructive leisure pursuits that make lives richer. But with what seems like depressing regularity, sports are showing their darker sides. The sports pages sizzle with stories about athletes, coaches, and spectators that can shock the most calloused sports watchers. Not long ago, a fight between players and fans at Detroit's Palace came on the heels of an ugly brawl between players from the University of South Carolina and Clemson, a less publicized assault by a Nebraska tackle on a member of the Oklahoma spirit team, and an incident in which Texas Rangers pitcher Frank Francisco threw a chair at a spectator who was heckling him. Major League Baseball and the United States Olympic Committee struggle to control rampant drug and steroid abuse, which has tainted the reputations of some of our most famous athletes. Michael Vick, once one of the most talented and highly paid players in the NFL recently earned his release from Leavenworth prison, where he was sentenced to 23 months for his role in a dogfighting ring.

The famed Tour de France has been in the headlines more in recent years for the doping scandals among its elite performers than for the competition. Noted sportswriter George Vecsey thought it so bad that he facetiously recommended that "a mob of citizens should pick up wooden pitchforks and run the scoundrels out of town." The French newspaper *France Soir* published an obituary for the tour, and an editorial in the newspaper *Libération* complained that "this procession of cyclists has been transformed into a caravan of ridicule." In 2000, sprinter Maurice Green earned the title of fastest human being by breaking the world record in the 100-meter dash at an international event. Before he had caught his breath he had wrapped himself in a huge flag, not of the United States but of his own management group—a fitting gesture, perhaps, for an athlete whose Mercedes bears vanity plates "Mo Gold" and who sports T-shirts that proclaim him "Pheno-Mo-nal." Green's record was smashed in the 2008 Olympics by Usain Bolt, who also made us cringe with his braggadocio.[12]

With astonishing frequency the name of higher education is sullied by the crimes and indiscretions of players, coaches, and alumni; administrators seem oblivious to the way their sports programs have tarnished their school's images. Higher education no longer pretends that its sport programs are about education; they are quite simply about money. Public pressure for entertainment, not educational service, has its grip on the power centers in colleges and universities, and when winning is all that matters, there is an undeniable logic to players and coaches cheating and to administrators looking the other way. When a large southern public university signs its football coach to a contract that pays him in *one week* an amount that exceeds the average *annual* household income for a family of four in that state, and its chancellor (whose salary is one-seventh the football coach's) tells reporters that the coach's salary "doesn't reflect misplaced priorities," you can be sure it is money that is doing the talking.[13]

Gambling on college sports is a major growth industry that poses serious threats to the integrity of games, often making athletes targets of organized crime. Best estimates are that in 2007, $6 billion was bet *illegally* on games during March Madness, the curious name assigned to the NCAA basketball tournament held each March. Legal betting on college and professional basketball doubled from $96 million in February to $195 million in March, an indication of the way the tournament attracts gamblers. So disturbing are the inroads gambling has made in sports that the NCAA has partnered with two other organizations in sponsoring a sports gambling curriculum designed to make high school athletes aware of its dangers. Sport has become the perfect example of what evangelical writer Os Guinness called "'the commodification' of everything, the reduction of the human to the economic, behavior to self-interest, wisdom to 'cost-effectiveness,' success to 'productivity,' society to 'an arena for competitive individualism,' public life to the 'market place,' and human beings to 'consumers' and 'maximizers.'"[14]

Lovers of college sports, by and large, aren't fazed by revelations of skullduggery or egregious excess in the athletic ranks; it seems to be the toll we are willing to pay for a bit of excitement on Saturday afternoons. Some scoff at criticism, arguing that the corruption is much less serious than critics claim. But as those close to the scene will tell you, the glorious spectacles we love to watch on television cover a multitude of sins: "friendly faculty" who design faux independent study courses to keep athletes eligible, tutors who write term papers for athletes, coaches and alumni who pay athletes under the table, schemes to manipulate the psyches of athletes, and boards of trustees whose allegiances lie more with athletics than academics. (Those who doubt things are as bad as I suggest are referred to professor Murray Sperber's excellent book *Beer and Circus*.)[15]

When athletic departments establish reputations for slippery ethics and for glorifying violence, we shouldn't be surprised when that culture spills over to the dormitories, streets, and nightclubs of the community. A recent lacrosse team scandal rained down national criticism on Duke University. Although the players were unjustly accused of rape by a stripper who performed for their team party, the incident opened a window on a sleazy subculture that emphasizes "playing hard and partying hard." "Need a team update?" asked a cynical sports reporter before cataloging a long list of criminal conduct of university football players over a scant two-day period: "[Then] check the police blotter." Until its successful 2008 season, the once squeaky-clean Penn State University football program and its famous coach Joe Paterno suffered through a string of dismal seasons and an embarrassing assortment of crime-related headlines involving many of its players. Between 2000 and 2008, ESPN reported that 46 Penn State players were involved in or charged with 146 crimes including fights, rape, driving under the influence, underage drinking, and assault. Accusations by ESPN reporters that the Penn State athletic department applied pressure on the university's Office of Judicial Affairs to prevent the athletes from being expelled reached a climax when Paterno, after fumbling through an on-air interview, dismissed two players from the squad.[16]

The once sedate and pastoral sport of college baseball also has been plagued by fights. In 1998 profanity-laced taunts by Indiana State fans prompted several Wichita State players to charge into the stands and pummel the hecklers. A few weeks earlier, a Northern Iowa coach had his nose broken and face cut by an Oklahoma player during a bench-clearing brawl. "Shame on us that we in college sports have allowed this to happen," commented the league commissioner. "Shame on administrators everywhere if we keep allowing it to happen."[17]

College coaches have been equally complicit in undermining the ethical foundations of college sports. The indecorous conduct of recently retired basketball coach Bobby Knight during stints at the University of Indiana and at Texas Tech University furnished sportswriters with sensational copy for decades, but Knight's case is hardly unique. Former UCLA basketball coach Jim Harrick, for example, led his team to the national championship in 1994–1995; shortly thereafter he was fired for lying to university investigators about irregularities on his expense account. Next he was hired by the University of Rhode Island, where a former female assistant in the basketball office filed a sexual harassment lawsuit and charged Harrick and his coaches with arranging to have players' grades changed and term papers written for them. The university reportedly settled for $45,000. Harrick was then hired by the University of Georgia, where he was suspended and later resigned when widespread academic fraud was discovered in the basketball program. A basketball scandal at St. Bonaventure University in 2003 that led to the firing of the coach, the athletics director, and the president of the institution later claimed the life of the chairman of the Board of Trustees, who committed suicide. He left a letter saying that he had let his colleagues and university down and apologized to his family. Tragic episodes like these haven't caused universities to blink. The quest for athletic supremacy continues unabated; so does the arms race for more expensive and ethically facile coaches to lead programs in which coaching effectiveness is measured wholly by win-loss records.

The behaviors of spectators at both the college and professional levels have made a bad situation worse. Each season seems to offer new lows of decorum; it is a classic example of what the late Senator Daniel Moynihan called "defining deviancy downward." After a 1998 win over their archrival, the University of Oregon, Oregon State players were spat upon by children and adults as they made their way to the locker room. When Oklahoma fans rained oranges down on the Nebraska bench during a 2004 game, Nebraska coach Bill Callahan directed a profane outburst at the Sooner contingent. At Giants Stadium, officials struggle to curtail the behavior of hundreds of men who gather on the spiral ramps at Gate D and demean women by chanting for them to bare their breasts. Joe Kay, who played for the Tucson High basketball team in 2002, no doubt wishes the crowd could have behaved better when, after his game-winning dunk, delirious supporters crushed him in their celebrations, compressing his carotid artery and causing a stroke which left him paralyzed on the right side of his body.[18]

Excess and mean-spiritedness are infecting sport at the lowest levels. Games that should be played for the pleasure of participation are hijacked by coaches and parents bent on turning them into something seen week in and week out on television. When a father in California is sentenced to 45 days in jail for beating and berating a coach for taking his son out of a baseball game; when a dentist sharpens the face guard of his son's football helmet so that he could slash opposing players; when a police officer pays a pitcher $2 to hit a 10-year-old Little League opponent with a fastball during a game; and when the father of a 12-year-old hockey player beats his son's coach to death outside the hockey rink—oddly enough because he thought the coach was encouraging rough play—it is fair to conclude that youth sports, like those played at a higher level, have lost their way.

THE DEAFENING SILENCE

One need not be an experienced social critic to see the wide chasm separating the Christian worldview and that perpetuated by the popular sports culture.[19] Sportswriter and social critic Robert Lipsyte called the worldview taught by the athletic culture "SportsWorld," "a grotesque distortion of sports" that has "turned our best athletes into clowns," "made the finish more important than the race," and "extolled the game as that William Jamesian absurdity, a moral equivalent to war."[20] Variously described by those inside it and outside it as narcissistic, materialistic, self-interested, violent, sensational, coarse, racist, sexist, brazen, raunchy, hedonistic, body-destroying, and militaristic, the culture of sports is light years removed from what Christians for centuries have idealized as the embodiment of the gospel message. The Christian worldview is based on an absolute, immutable, justice-loving God. The worldview of sports is based on material success. How Christians, and especially evangelicals, have managed to live in these two diametrically opposed worlds, even to the point of harnessing one to serve the other, is the focus of this book.

There have been modern-day Jeremiahs speaking out against the ills of sports, questioning the public's unexamined embrace of them, but they are mostly sportswriters, social critics, and neo-Marxists arguing for reform based on principles of common decency, not evangelicals arguing from deeply rooted religious convictions. The evangelical community has been eager to lead the charge in the culture wars but has remained largely uncurious about sports. Surveys suggest that 90 percent of evangelicals believe that public school instruction should include Christian views of history and science, but there is no indication that they expect the same of the athletic programs in their schools. If 77 percent of evangelicals believe that the mass media are "hostile to their moral and spiritual values," one wonders why they haven't also sensed that hostility in media-bloated competitive sport contests.[21]

Christians frequently voice criticism about the violence in video games, but the violence of sports such as football and hockey, which involves their children more intimately and dangerously, rarely is questioned. Christian conscience has prompted two former professional wrestlers to speak out against the sport's more outrageous aspects, but few Christian commentators seem to have noticed. Instead, the evangelical community has rushed to harness all that testosterone for the Lord. Hence we have the Christian Wrestling Federation, Christian Wrestling Entertainment, and Ultimate Christian Wrestling, all of which promise spectators the same violence, the same celebration of power, the same grotesque images and freak-show ambiance—even some blood—but not, its promoters are quick to point out, cursing or women parading in skimpy costumes.[22]

The institution of sport has been so intricately woven into the fabric of American culture, and thus into the Christian culture, that criticism of sport or suggestions that sports be given a closer look often are viewed as cranky complaints by prigs who don't know good fun when they see it. The person who dares to ask whether the competitive ethic as celebrated in modern sports might conflict in important ways with the Christian worldview risks being labeled a "sport hater." At the dinner table, believers may enthusiastically share opinions about the fortunes of their favorite teams; but turn the conversation to the weightier matter of how they reconcile their devotion to popular sports with devotion to their faith, and silence ensues, often followed by indigestion.

In his masterful book *God in the Stadium*, Jack Higgs wondered why "modern sports, with their celebrated abuses, have been able to escape the evangelical passion."[23] His question echoed words uttered over thirty years ago by *Sports Illustrated* senior writer Frank Deford, whose three-part series on evangelicalism and sports stands as one of the most lucid and penetrating analyses written on the topic. Deford marveled that "no one in the [evangelical sports-faith movement] . . . speaks out against the cheating in sport, against dirty play, no one attacks the evils of recruiting, racism, or any of the many other well-known excesses and abuses . . . . Religion seems to have become a support force for athletics, like broadcasters, trainers, cheerleaders, and ticket-sellers." The ensuing thirty years haven't sharpened the evangelical conscience. The silence is deafening.[24]

To be fair, there is a natural tendency to avoid asking too many questions about something that one has come to know and love. But the reluctance to think critically about sports may reflect something more deep-seated in the evangelical community: what historian Mark Noll called "the scandal of the evangelical mind." The scandal is the failure of evangelicals to "think like a Christian about the nature and workings of the physical world, the character of human social structures like government and the economy [and we might add the social institution of sports], the meaning of the past, the nature of artistic creation, and the circumstances attending our perception of the world outside of ourselves."[25]

Understanding sport, like understanding popular culture in general, isn't something easily done. It requires one to recognize and evaluate its implicit ethos, to look beyond the immediate excitement of the game. Sport, like popular culture generally, "is always about something other than itself."[26] The sports we watch and play help orient us in the world; they furnish templates for how we should relate to and feel about one another. Sports hold captive our imaginations and interpret for us what it means to be successful, devoted, and fair. Religion scholar Catherine Albanese put it this way: "sports have helped Americans fit a grid to their own experience in order to define it and give it meaning."[27] Not being willing to wrestle with the difficult task of understanding sport and its relationship to their faith, evangelicals have lost their influence in the world of big-time sports. They have been left on the sidelines of important debates about the topic when they should have been at the center of the field.

Unless Christians in the athletic and academic communities develop a healthy curiosity about the relationship of sports to faith, they are likely to continue bouncing between two different worlds framed by two different worldviews. Those who believe that sport will eventually be reclaimed for the Christian worldview when enough Christian athletes and coaches have invaded sports would do well to reflect on the enormous numbers of evangelicals already involved in sports. If indeed they are committed to redeeming this fallen institution of society as part of God's cosmic process of redemption, their efforts over the past half-century could be fairly graded an abysmal failure.

THE COST OF SPORTIANITY

Intellectual neglect rarely leads to anything good. In this case it has had three unfortunate effects: the evolution of an improbable sports theology that has stifled prophetic voices; a well-defined trend for evangelicals and their institutions to fall into the same ethical quagmires that have trapped others in the sports community; and the failure of the Christian community to extract from sport the spiritual riches that it offers, opting instead to settle for superficial sport shows and spectacles that, even in their best moments, can stifle the real benefits that sport has to offer.

In the vacuum caused by the reluctance of the Christian community generally, and the evangelical community in particular, to think seriously about sports, a folk theology offered as an explanation for the relationship between sport and the faith has emerged. Viewing it as not quite Christianity, Frank Deford labeled it "Sportianity"—a concoction of triumphal evangelism blended with worldly Darwinian competition, and crafted to appeal to those for whom a love of athletics frames their lives. It combines locker room slogans, Old Testament allusions to religious wars, athletically slanted doctrines of assertiveness and sacrifice, and a cult of masculinity, backed up by cherry-picked Bible verses pre-screened to ensure that they don't conflict with sport's reigning orthodoxies. Sportianity is not the result of haphazard or sloppy theologizing. Neither is it confined to the locker rooms of the NFL, the NBA, or Major League Baseball. Its fundamentals have been rationalized, systematized, and vigorously promulgated by sport evangelism organizations. It is taught with remarkable consistency to high school, college, and professional athletes. Sportianity also explains the meaning of sports to thousands of ministers, laypeople, and the religious press. In fact, at present there are few alternative systems of thinking about sports and faith in the evangelical community.[28]

Professors Tony Ladd and James Mathisen have identified five essential elements of this folk theology: 1) valuing sport for its pragmatic utility; 2) belief in a meritocracy; 3) belief in the virtue of competition; 4) high regard for heroic models; and 5) sermonizing that combines pop psychology with biblical allusions as a way of improving athletic performances.[29] To these we should add that it is largely a product of the athletic mind. Sportianity is Christianity that has been vetted by the athletic community. It avoids asking prickly questions that challenge the presumptions of the sports world; instead, it overlays them with evangelical rhetoric, something that can result in a strange confusion of symbols. As I've described it elsewhere, "sport, which celebrates the myth of success, is harnessed to a gospel which consistently stresses the importance of losing. Sport, which symbolizes the morality of self-reliance and teaches the just rewards of hard work, is used to propagate a theology dominated by the radicalism of grace. The first shall be last and the last first, but not in big-time sports."[30]

Sportianity is harshly ascetic, thriving on biblical images of Christ's suffering, the Apostle Paul's endurance, and the Israelites' military success. The preferred self-image of the athlete is as a warrior, no matter how difficult that might make it to reconcile sports with the faith. Asked by a reporter how Christian athletes could submit their bodies to the ravages of football, a representative from a sport evangelism organization replied: The athlete "is living by a different set of rules, not playing by a different set of rules." He pointed to Mike Singletary, a former star on the Chicago Bears and now the coach of the San Francisco 49ers, noting that he was a mild-mannered guy when he preached in the pulpit, "but he's broken 13 helmets on the playing field and he will tell you that he plays football to the best of his ability because Christ wants him to." In the theological haze that is Sportianity, broken helmets become stars in the Christian's crown, and Christ becomes the author of brutality.[31]

In spite of its theological conservatism, Sportianity preaches a very worldly theology. The concrete trumps the symbolic; doing, accomplishing, and struggling are favored over mystery, joy, feeling, transport, and spiritual insight. Hard work and pain are core elements for articulating sport with the faith. When effort, struggle, and sacrifice become the preferred spiritual offering, joyous play can seem an unworthy offering. One Sportian put it this way: "When the Apostle Paul says 'I press on,' he doesn't need to explain. It is the process of faith, life, and competitive sport . . . Fun? No. Anyone in the affirmative is a masochist. Why does one endure? There are reasons, but fun is not one of them."[32] In the dialectical, serious-but-not-serious world of play, Sportians tip the scales decidedly in favor of the serious, made even weightier by the evangelistic mission they load on sports. In the process, sport played purely for joy, sport that illuminates and spiritually enriches, sport that is serious but also festival and fantasy, gets short shrift. Far beyond the Sportians' horizon is the possibility that the athlete can be an "imitator of the Logos, the Heavenly Wisdom who plays upon the earth, the co-fashioner with God."[33]

EVANGELICALS AS IMITATORS

Christians who have operated close to the sport scene have been largely followers rather than leaders, adopters of the dominant sports ethos rather than trendsetters. Their lack of interest in fairly applying the implications of their theology and hesitancy to criticize the ills paraded under the banner of sports has mired many of them in the same swamps that have bogged down other athletes and coaches who have made no special claims about the transforming power of their faith. There is no shortage of examples.

Several years ago, the president of a small Southern Baptist university allegedly ordered a failing grade to be stricken from the transcript of the school's basketball star, thereby preventing him from being dropped from the team. Later that year the young man played a key role in his team's winning a national championship. When the incident came to light, it received bold coverage in national and international sports pages and on radio and TV, and led to on-campus protests by faculty and students. Trustees hired an Atlanta law firm to investigate; the faculty voted no confidence in the president. Two presidential assistants who criticized the president were demoted. Eventually the president was dismissed. The curiosity of the press was piqued, not so much because yet another school was found trying to skirt the rules in order to ensure a winning season for its basketball team, but because the act stood in sharp contrast to the values the school claimed to believe and teach. The school advertised itself as a Christian college ("committed to serving God and humanity"), the president was an ordained minister for whom the school's graduate divinity school is named, the tournament the team won (thanks to the altered transcript) was the National *Christian* College Athletic Association championship, and the failing grade in question had been earned in a religion class.

Those who lived through the Jim and Tammy Faye debacle, not to mention the Jimmy Swaggart and Ted Haggard embarrassments, might shrug this off as simply more of the same, but I think this case is different. The act wasn't committed, as so often religious scandals are, as a way of lining the pockets of a charismatic leader, to abet a profligate lifestyle, or to ensure a larger share of the television audience. In this case deceit grew out of something much more mundane: a simple desire to field a championship basketball team and thereby win a bit of recognition for a college. The disgrace was wrought not by perverting something serious, but by perverting what many would consider to be one of the least serious of human pursuits: sports. That an esteemed man at a good college would risk both his and his institution's reputations to secure victory on the basketball court underscores not only the strong grip sports have on the Christian community but the severe liabilities of not clearly understanding how sport fits within the Christian life.

Frank Deford had predicted such calamity in his classic article in *Sports Illustrated*. A year later he agreed to an interview by staff of the Fellowship of Christian Athletes. Asked if he still believed that "sport has had a greater impact on religion than religion has had on sport," Deford said that he did: "The bad things about athletics have rubbed off on religion," he said. "Religion is like the tar baby—it's gotten stuck and the more it struggles, the more tar it gets on it. There's the danger when anything moral plays with anything as public, as notorious, as celebrated as sport—you get stuck."[34]

All things being equal, a college coach's success in attracting talented athletes is the prime determiner of his or her team's athletic success. Because competition for attracting athletic talent is fierce, recruiting often gets out of hand, prompting some critics to call it "the cesspool of college athletics." Here again, some evangelical institutions, Bible colleges, and Christian high schools, far from staking out a higher moral ground, have shown that they can get down in the mud and wallow with some of the worst of the scoundrels. When big-time basketball programs recruit athletes who lack the academic requirements for admission, the athletes are sometimes farmed out to smaller two- and four-year schools where sympathetic faculty can be counted on to boost their grade point averages. Christian schools repeatedly have been among those identified in NCAA investigations as having willingly served as diploma mills.

Christian high schools have been implicated in some of the most egregious violations of sportsmanship. A Christian high school in Tennessee, which describes its mission as "dedicated to nurturing and challenging the whole person—body, mind, and spirit—to the glory of God," has developed into a perennial football powerhouse in the nation, but its rise to power has been accompanied by suspicions about its recruiting tactics. When the school was fined by its athletic conference for numerous violations, the unrepentant school adopted a defiant attitude, took the athletic conference to court and won, not because the court concluded the charges were false, but on grounds that the athletic association had violated the school's First Amendment rights. A lawyer for the conference called the court's action "a sad decision. The [athletic conference] makes sure that kids are treated like kids. There are some unscrupulous people out there, and this decision doesn't keep them away." In the opinion of *Sports Illustrated*'s editors, "this isn't one step away from the insanity of college recruiting: it's the same thing."[35]

Even in the cold, cruel world of big-time sports, running up the score on unmatched opponents is regarded as the epitome of arrogance and insensitivity and is roundly criticized by most coaches. During his long career, Billy Tubbs, the former basketball coach at two major institutions, earned the scorn of his colleagues for his practice of intentionally running up the score on hapless opponents. Similarly, when a high school coach in Camden, New Jersey, kept his star player in the game so he could set a record by scoring 100 points, even though his team succeeded in

humiliating the opponents by the lopsided score of 157–57, he incurred
the wrath of commentators everywhere. The player's record didn't last
long, however. Shortly thereafter, Heritage Christian Academy in Cleveland, Tennessee, trounced its opponents 178–28. The coach also kept his
star player in the game so that he could score 101 points.[36]

The best evidence of Christians' failure to mark out a distinctive path
for athletics comes simply from watching them play. Far from being the
kind of life-affirming, faith-affirming events that they could be, games
played in Christian college gymnasia and athletic fields too often end up
as mockeries of the faith statements given prominence in the schools'
mission statements and websites. I have listened to referees complain
about having been assigned games between Christian college "rivals"
where the intensity of the players and the rudeness of the spectators
makes it difficult to keep the game under control. More than one col-
league has told me that some of the worst displays of sportsmanship they
have witnessed were in games between Christian colleges or in church-
league softball and basketball games.

A number of years ago I had the good fortune to lecture on sport and
ethics to the student bodies at two midwestern Christian colleges—traditional rivals in things athletic—on two succeeding days. A basketball
game, which I was unable to attend, was scheduled between the schools
for the following evening. My hope, of course, was that my words would
have worked some magic, helping all involved to keep the game in perspective. I later learned that the crowd had grown so ugly that the coaches
had to stop the game and threaten to empty the gym. On another occasion, when I had finished lecturing on sports at an "Integration of Faith
and Learning" conference sponsored by another Christian college, I was
met at the podium by a psychology professor who, with a wry smile,
handed me a scrap of paper on which something was written. "I thought
you would like to see our school's favorite cheer at football games," he said.
On the paper was the slogan: "Kill, Kill, Blood Makes the Grass Grow."

Church members tolerate ignominies in their church athletic league
games that they would never countenance elsewhere, relying on the
dubious assumption that sports deserve an especially wide berth when it
comes to ethics. Nothing may be on the line except bragging rights, but
contests between softball and basketball teams from different churches
can be far from healthy. I have talked to a man who finally quit playing
in church-league softball games when, during a heated on-field argument, he landed a nasty haymaker on the jaw of the opposing pitcher.

Surely this was a shameful act, but maybe not quite as shameful as what happened in a church league game in Tulsa when a player who had been ejected from the game attacked the referee and choked him unconscious with his whistle lanyard, or the youth minister who allegedly kicked a 16-year-old boy in the groin after he was struck in the head by the ball during a dodgeball game.[37]

All of this follows in a line with the results of a recent survey of students attending a Christian college. The survey solicited the students' opinions about church sport leagues; 64 percent of those who had never participated in church league sports, and 32 percent of those who had, believed that church league sports "have a bad reputation" and that "winning is overemphasized." Perhaps more instructive was the finding that 86 percent of respondents who had played said they did so without any instruction from their churches regarding how Christians should play sports. We can be encouraged that some Florida church leagues continue to honor teams with the "Most Christ-like Award" for good sportsmanship. On the other hand, we can continue to worry that players in many other churches continue to play like the devil.[38]

MISSING THE POINT

The saddest consequence of the Christian community's not having thought carefully about sports may be that they have missed out on the true riches that sports have to offer. Like all sport enthusiasts, Christians find sports compelling on a number of levels: they offer refreshing release from worrisome troubles, they bind communities in fierce loyalty, they offer a stage for demonstrating human excellence, and they inspire dramas acted out in real time. But as Dutch historian Johan Huizinga pointed out in his classic *Homo Ludens: A Study of the Play Element in Culture*, most of our presumptions do not get at the real reason why people play; they can't account for play's "power of maddening." "The fun of playing," said Huizinga, "resists all analysis, all logical interpretation." In the final analysis, he said, play is based on a "certain imagination" of reality and the important thing is to grasp the significance of this imagination to understand how play works in human civilization.[39]

Christians are possessed with a most distinct "imagination" that colors all that they are and do. Christian philosopher Arthur Holmes described humans as not fundamentally *homo faber* (man the worker) or *homo ludens* (man the player), but as *homo religiosis*, underscoring the point that it is the religious nature of Christians that gives purpose and meaning to their work and play. If Holmes and Huizinga are correct, the question of how play might help shape and give life to the Christian imagination supersedes all questions about its practical and mundane benefits. Thinking Christianly about sport means locating it not in the body or in the aims and purposes of institutions, or even in evangelism, but in the Christian imagination, a point far removed from its typical placement in the arsenal of instrumentally useful things. The intellectually curious Christian will find himself or herself engaged at a level not commonly reached when thinking about sport: the symbolic, the aesthetic, the ritualistic, and the religious. This engagement means remaining open to the possibility that the human experience of sport can have religious significance, manifesting the reality of God and of humanness in a way that ordinary life usually does not. But sport's spiritual benefits are not guaranteed. Realizing the best that sport has to offer is highly conditional upon human enactments that, in their intent and expressiveness, symbolize the spiritual realities toward which they point.[40]

Unfortunately, the Christian quest for sport's relevance to the spiritual life—to the extent one could call it a "quest" at all—has stopped far short of reaching this religiously significant terrain. As a result, the Christian community has missed the point of sport. They have come to the banquet, eaten the appetizer, and left, not knowing what sumptuous delights may have awaited them. This has had enormous consequences for how they organize, play, and experience sport. Without a collective *Christian* imagination to guide their thinking and approaches to sport, they have settled for a host of other imaginations: *consumer imaginations* that value sport only as it can advance the financial or public relations interests; *military imaginations* that conceive of sports as battles between armies pledged to fight to the death; and *therapeutic* and *propaganda imaginations* that value sport only as a tool for achieving some practical end. The result is that sport played by Christians isn't different in any substantive way from sport that is taught, celebrated, sold, and used in popular culture, and it is far different from holy play, a rehearsal, as Hugo Rahner called it, "of that Godward directed harmony of body and soul which we call heaven," an expression of "man's hope for another life taking visible form in gesture."[41]

FRAMING THE PROBLEM

The problem for the Christian community, then, is that having launched a rudderless boat into the roiling waters of popular sport, they are adrift, possessing neither a clear sense of what they want out of their sport experiences nor a coherent philosophy to guide them in achieving it. Their blind replication of the model of sport reinforced by popular culture has failed to bring them any closer to understanding how sport and play might complement their religious lives or how sport relates to the outward expression of their spirituality. More importantly, replicating what passes for sport in the broader culture has not enabled them to draw on sport's enormous fund of emotional and spiritual wealth in ways that affirm and celebrate their own worldview.

The sport-faith problem is far from new. From its inception, the church has struggled to define its beliefs and practices in relation to the public's insatiable appetite for sports, sometimes in learned and insightful ways and at other times in arbitrary, even silly ways. In some historical eras the church managed its relation to sport better than in others. At some junctures theological opinion prohibited sports entertainment; at others it sought to discipline it, while at other times it coddled it. But for most of its history, the church remained interested in testing the public sports of the day against its theology. This practice ended by 1950, when the Christian community no longer felt the need to monitor trends in sport as it made the transition from critic to avid supporter.

The story of the church's efforts to make sense out of sport within the context of the Christian life can be instructive, especially for those who, in the twenty-first century, are interested in taking up the challenge of adding to the story. Chapters 1–5 in this volume trace Christianity's dance with popular sports over the past two millennia— a history of fits and starts, peppered with idiosyncrasies and a lot of dead ends. Even so, I believe this history can help frame modern thinking about sports and faith. To those who doubt that sport is worthy of serious examination, these chapters offer ample evidence of great theological minds having been bent to the task. To those who appreciate sport's worthiness as an object of serious examination, the history offers illumination and perhaps hope.

Sport may be a topic neglected by Christian intellectuals, but this has not kept in-the-pew Christians from forming deeply held beliefs and notions about sport and its relationship to the Christian life. These find expression in a kind of layperson's Sportianity, a set of presumptions that are guaranteed to surface when Christians discuss sport and faith. These include beliefs that competition is sacred, that sport "builds up the temple of the Holy Spirit," that sport aids spiritual development through character education, that praying at sport events assures God's blessing and involvement, and that sport's value to Christianity is best measured in the ways it can be used to spread the gospel. Chapters 6 through 10 dissect these arguments, hold them up to the light of empirical and anecdotal evidence, and show why they are in need of reexamination if evangelicals are to mount a serious integration of sport and faith.

My intent in writing this book was not to diminish the motives or the good and valuable work of people in the evangelical sports community or in Christian colleges and churches, for whom I have great respect. I also have tried to remain sensitive to the different worlds inhabited by the academic critic and the practitioner. Critics can level their guns, fire, and retreat to the comfy confines of their studies, but for the coach and the player there is always the next practice, the next game to be played. Though I have been long removed from the role of coach, I have continued to play a part in the preparation of teachers and coaches throughout my professional life. In my nearly forty-year association with sport, first as an athlete, later as an official and a college coach, and finally as a professor, scholar, and administrator in higher education, I have never fallen out of love with sport. That love has shaped my high view of its potential, a higher view, I would argue, than is held by many who might think of me as a sport hater. I suppose I do hate what we have allowed sport to become, the feeble uses to which we try to put it, and the ugly social contexts in which we insist on inserting it; I do hate its distortions and abuses. But my love of the "essence of the sport experience" should not be in doubt.

This book is about reclaiming sport for the Christian imagination. Yet it is only a prelude; it is far from a fully developed Christian perspective on sports. I leave it to better minds and talents to extend, rebut, or modify my arguments. At the same time I recognize the responsibility that a critic has to accompany criticisms with recommendations. Therefore, the final chapter of this book puts forth some basic principles upon which such a philosophy might be built and ventures some suggestions for constructive change. In making these recommendations, I have been guided by the principles and arguments made in other sections of the book, choosing not to be restrained by anticipated protests that my sights for the renewal of sport have been set too high.

1

SPORTS AND THE EARLY CHURCH

The story of evangelicalism's dance with sports begins, appropriately enough, with the dawn of a faith that made its appearance in the context of sports-crazed societies. In the towns and cities where the gospel was first preached, athletics and sporting spectacles were woven into the fabric of civic life; they symbolized not only urban life, but what it meant to be Roman or Greek. French historian Henri Marrou characterized the Greek conception of life as a type of athletic struggle in which winning was one of the most significant aspects of the Greek soul. "There is no doubt that the Homeric hero and hence the actual Greek person of flesh and blood was really only happy when he felt and proved himself to be the first in his category, a man apart, superior."[1] Cities sought identities, not merely through the exploits of their idolized athletes, but by vying with each other in building bigger and better sports and entertainment facilities. Wealthy politicians and entrepreneurs, anxious to display their power and prestige, staged increasingly elaborate and expensive athletic shows at enormous personal expense. If the intensity of a cultural practice is reflected in years of assimilation, both the Greeks and Romans were far more steeped in the ethos of competitive sports than are sport enthusiasts of the twenty-first century. While American football and basketball date back a little over one hundred years, Greek athletics and chariot racing, by comparison, had been around for over six hundred years and the gladiatorial shows had been part of Roman culture for over two hundred and fifty years when the first generation of Christians moved among their fellows.

The peculiar ethical demands of the newly formed faith fomented enormous cultural clashes with the societies in which it was being nurtured. The Christian community was forced to ask itself not only how being a practicing Christian was different than being a practicing Jew, but how being a Christian should modify believers' approaches to all aspects of culture, including athletics, gladiatorial contests, and chariot racing. In his treatise *Dialogus de Oratoribus*, Tacitus, a first-century historian and Roman senator, found the rage for sports among the masses inexplicable and a corrupting force in society: "A passion for horses, players, and gladiators seems to be the epidemic folly of the times. The child receives it in his mother's womb; he brings it with him into the world; and in a mind so possessed, what room for science, or any generous purpose?" (29.3). The pagan religious ceremony, as integral to sport spectacles as "The Star Spangled Banner" or the seventh-inning stretch is to American baseball, was a continuing source of uneasiness, but that wasn't all. The single-minded obsession with self-aggrandizement, fame, and glory that characterized Greek athletics and the smothering ethic of excess and obscene delight in human cruelty that found expression in Roman sports were problematic for the early Christians too. These impulses and the sports competitions that celebrated them represented an inhospitable backdrop for a new religion that emphasized love, sympathy, self-denial, soberness, and meekness. However, given the fact that most early Christians were products of the socializing effects of popular sports, it would be naïve to imagine that their conversions brought swift and sweeping changes in their view of sports. It took time for them to sort out the implications of their faith in a world permeated with time-honored pagan customs and patterns of thought and action. Christianity's conflict with heathenism may have begun, as one writer has noted, "in the arena of the people's play," but it was certainly not a war to the death.[2]

For first-generation Christians, informal play was never a live religious issue. Drawn largely from the lower classes, early converts probably lacked the time and resources required for indulging in sports and games, and when time was available, the constant threat of persecution no doubt robbed them of the inclination. Christian children living in the Hellenistic eastern part of the Roman Empire, where some of the earliest churches began, probably joined in many of the popular forms of informal play: tumbling and acrobatics, juggling, playing with tops and yo-yos, swinging on swings, and playing on see-saws. Perhaps they joined their Greek friends in playing an invasive team ball game (*episkyros*), but on the whole the Greeks had little interest in team sports. They were indoctrinated with *arête*, the Greek ideal of excellence, expressed through a constant testing of their talents against each other, not only in sports, but in music, poetry, rhetoric, even in contests of surgery, kissing, drinking, eating, and beauty. But *arête* was a value centered in the individual; it was difficult, if not impossible, to display *arête* while part of a team. Thus, the massive system of organized youth sports of our day had no corollary in the early Christian era.[3]

The Christian scriptures do not provide a detailed account of Christian social life in the apostolic age and tell us virtually nothing about how Christians spent their leisure, but as British theologian J. G. Davies has pointed out, "they do enumerate principles which were to be applied even more extensively as the centuries passed." Scripture neither explicitly condones nor endorses informal play, implying that the New Testament authors considered it to neither confer special advantage nor pose a substantial threat to the spiritual vitality of early adherents to the faith. The congregations at Ephesus and Corinth may not have competed against each other in a church *episkyros* league, but it wasn't because they viewed physical activity or informal sports as inherently evil.[4] But the public sport shows of the day—glittering, gaudy contests designed to entertain pleasure-starved, hero-worshipping audiences—were an entirely different matter. Although not singled out for condemnation in Scripture or denounced in the very early years of Christendom, public athletic and gladiatorial shows eventually were vilified by a litany of early Christian leaders. As a rule, it was as a form of entertainment, not as a system of education or informal leisure, that sport was problematic for the earliest of Christians.[5]

SPORTS OF THE DAY

Public sport spectacles in early Christian society were shaped by both Greek and Roman influences. The games of the ancient Greeks emphasized the ideals of agon—competitive struggle aimed at sorting out the best from the merely mediocre. The Greeks valued athletics as military training experiences and thus regarded them as an appropriate activity for the masses. The Romans also invoked a military rationale, especially for some of their crueler sports, but for the most part athletics weren't of great interest to the early Romans. To them, the hours spent by Greeks in the athletics of the gymnasia and palestras had been a leading cause of their enslavement and degeneracy. Romans preferred to watch sport spectacles.

At the same time, the line between Greek and Roman sports of the time was not always clear-cut. The spread of the Roman Empire into Greece and its surroundings, for example, brought with it a Roman-like love of gladiatorial contests and chariot racing and for athletics made cruel and barbarous by modifications that appealed to public taste. Once threatened with extinction by the Roman conquest, the ancient Greek athletic contests had recovered by 12 BC, thanks largely to an endowment from Herod that reinstituted the Olympic Games. Thus athletics, gladiatorial contests, and chariot racing all flourished in the eastern Hellenic section of the empire around the time and in the places where Paul and his fellow missionaries labored.

ATHLETIC CONTESTS

Sports entertainment at the time of the early church assumed three different forms: the athletic games of the stadium, the gladiatorial shows of the amphitheater (and theater), and chariot racing. In the eastern part of the empire where the church had its vital roots, the main sports attractions were the race at the hippodrome (circus) and athletics at the stadium. There were four primary athletic events of national interest, ancient equivalents of the World Series or the four "major" tournaments in golf or tennis: the Olympic games at Olympia and the Nemean games at Nemea, dedicated to Zeus; the Pythian games at Delphi in honor of Apollo; and the Isthmian games at Corinth in honor of Poseidon. Athletes who had been victorious at least once at each of these games were accorded special honors and usually a great deal of money. Although these were the most popular, they accounted for only a small portion of the athletic contests of the day. Local games also permeated societies of the Mediterranean world. By the first century the sports craze had begun to spread, even to the point where separate competitions for women participants were being held in various cities. Watching these events wasn't for the fainthearted. Spectators often suffered blazing heat, and cramped quarters, were subject to almost unbearable commotion, and were constantly tormented by flies drawn to the huge quantities of blood and red meat spilled at the altars.[6]

The major athletic contests took place in the context of a grand sacred festival. Huge crowds arrived days before the events to revel in an ancient form of tailgating. Street philosophers lectured passersby, poets and artists presented their latest works, and fortune tellers, magicians, and peddlers of food and souvenirs pestered tourists who walked the streets. The "pregame warm up" began with a procession of over one thousand athletes, officials, and spectators from nearby towns that stopped at appointed places along the way to offer sacrifices and for the athletes to be sprinkled with pig's blood, a ritual purification. The modern equivalent, says one writer, would require the Olympics "to be combined with Coney Island, Carnival in Rio, mass at the Vatican, and a U.S. presidential election."[7]

On the first day of the games, the athletes gathered for administration of the sacred oath in front of a statue of Zeus Horkios (Zeus of the Oath). In contrast to the modern practice of collecting blood and urine samples to weed out dishonest athletes, Olympic participants swore on the flesh of wild boars that they would do nothing evil against the games. The five-day festival started with a competition for trumpeters and heralds at the grand altar; the winners served as the ancient equivalent of a public address system. The remainder of the day was taken up by the offering of animal sacrifices, especially by horse owners who sought divine assistance for the chariot races, the first event scheduled for the hippodrome. The next day at dawn, a procession led by priests of Zeus, clad in purple and carrying switches to punish athletes who committed a foul, visited some sixty-three different altars to various gods. The skies were darkened with smoke from the altars, made even worse by private sacrifices arranged by affluent spectators who hired flutists, dancers, and priests to perform.

The first event was the four-horse chariot race, followed by the horseback race and the two-horse chariot race. The next day the scene shifted to the stadium for the pentathlon: the discus, javelin, long jump, wrestling, and the 200-meter sprint. Victory celebrations and parties went long into the night. On the same night (or perhaps the next), contestants and spectators gathered for a sacrifice at the great altar of Zeus, standing seven meters high and ten meters in diameter. Sacrifices continued through the following morning after a large procession in which one hundred oxen made their way to the altar of Zeus. After the sacrifice large portions of the meat were roasted and distributed to crowds, who spent the rest of the day recovering from the feast. It is significant that spectators saw no line separating athletic competition from worship; they were seamless rituals. And if some evangelical sports aficionados are to be believed, the Apostle Paul was there, watching, eating, mingling, clearing the smoke from his eyes, and discussing the fortunes of his favorite runner or fighter.

The following day featured footraces (*gymnikoi agones*). The afternoon brought the "heavy events": wrestling, boxing, and the *pankration*, a brutal form of no-holds-barred street fighting. Boxers wrapped their fists with leather thongs which served as a cutting edge; some Roman fighters took this practice one step further by weaving spikes into the thongs. Combat continued until one of the competitors surrendered. In a particularly sensational fight, a *pankratist* named Arrachion dislocated his opponent's toe, forcing his opponent to surrender, but by then his opponent's leg scissor hold had suffocated Arrachion; thus a corpse was proclaimed the winner. These athletic contests, says ancient sport expert Michael Poliakoff, involved "a level of officially sanctioned violence and danger that the modern Olympics would never tolerate," even though such violence was fiercely banned in civic life outside the arena.[8]

Romantic notions of ancient Greek athletics as honorable and pure, limited to amateur competitors and infused with a sporting spirit that valued "not winning, but taking part," are hardly consistent with what is known about them. To the Greeks, sports were all about winning. Losers were publicly mocked and humiliated. According to Pindar, the losers went "skulking down back roads, hiding from their enemies, bitten by their calamity."[9] British historian E. N. Gardiner, one of the foremost authorities on ancient sports, said that "few . . . realize how corrupt and degraded were Greek athletics during St. Paul's lifetime." Almost from their ancient beginnings they were about money. "Purists who refused to mix money with sport did not exist in the ancient world, and victors boast of success in the cash competitions as openly as they boast of victory in sacred contests."[10]

Much like modern critics of sport, early Roman commentators resented the enormous sums paid to athletes. Historian Stephen Miller, for example, has estimated that as early as 476 BC a boxer and *pankratist* named Theagenes won the equivalent of $44 million throughout his career. A trainer and medical technician for one athlete signed a contract for $132,000 in today's currency only to be hired away the next year by a rival for $242,000.[11] According to Pindar, the Olympic victors were given lifetime pensions which gave them "sweet smooth-sailing" for the remainder of their lives. They paraded triumphantly through town in four-horse chariots. "Long before the first television endorsement," notes history writer Tony Perrottet, "they made fortunes from cameo appearances at lesser games in Asia Minor and southern Italy; or they embarked on lucrative careers in politics. One wrestler, Marcus Aurelius Asclepiades, became a senator in Athens, anticipating wrestler-cum-Minnesota Governor Jesse Ventura by some 20 centuries."[12]

Scandals, bribery, and cheating plagued the athletic contests of the east. Athletes traveled the stadium circuit, hoping to fatten their wallets at each venue. Many invoked powers from the darker side to help them defeat their opponents and bragged about their athletic exploits in the Greek spirit of unbridled self-assertion. The deadly seriousness with which the Greeks took sport is evident in the *Iliad*, where a boxer named Epeios warned his opponent that he would "smash his skin apart and break his bones on each other" and advised him to arrange to have "those who care about him wait nearby in a huddle to carry him out, after my fists have beaten him."[13] Athletes, particularly those who fought in the "heavy events," were peculiar physical specimens, depicted in art and literature as hulking toughs with torn ears, massive skulls, and tiny brains whose epigrams boasted of the blood they had spilt—"perhaps after all," as one historian mused, "not so very far removed from the gladiators as one might have imagined."[14]

GLADIATORIAL CONTESTS

Athletic contests never really captured the public imagination of Romans, whose sensibilities had been seared by the realities of incessant war. Something more titillating than footraces, javelin-throwing, and wrestling was required. Even the brutalities of the *pankration* and boxing failed to generate much enthusiasm. Romans found what they were looking for in the ancient Etruscan custom of forcing prisoners of war, slaves, and other unfortunates to fight each other to the death. By adding a few pagan embellishments and incorporating the contests into lavish and highly marketable spectacles, the thrill of athletic competition was blended with the sadistic lure of ultimate defeat. The casual acceptance of these brutal shows continues to puzzle modern historians.

Moderns tend to associate the games with the 50,000-seat Roman Colosseum built in AD 80, but in reality, gladiatorial amphitheaters were widely distributed throughout the empire and apparently were enjoyed by the Greeks as well as the Romans. At Pompeii, for example, the amphitheater was large enough to seat the entire city of 20,000. Like Greek athletics, the gladiatorial games were part of a ritual complex incorporating the imperial cult of the emperors, Celtic cult practices, and the cult of Nemesis.[15] Statues of gods surrounded the arena, their faces often covered to spare them some of the bloodiest scenes. When a gladiator had fallen, a man dressed as Charon, ferryman to the underworld, entered the arena and, striking the head of the corpse with a mallet, announced his ownership of the body. He was accompanied by another playing the part of Mercury, who represented the guide of souls to hell. After he had stuck the body with a red hot iron, he escorted the corpse-laden stretcher from the arena.

The games followed various plans, but usually the first event of the morning show featured animal fights: bulls against elephants, lions against leopards, and rhinoceros against buffalo. During Nero's reign, scores of elephants and bulls were said to have been attacked by four hundred tigers in a single day's program. The fights were followed by circus acts, including boys dancing on the backs of elephants and trained tigers and bears, some dressed as gladiators. Animals that managed to survive were usually killed in the hunt, which was the third part of the morning program. Sometimes relatively harmless animals such as deer, ostriches, and donkeys were herded into the arena and killed. Lunchtime often featured executions of criminals and Christians which were carried out in elaborate mimes and crucifixions. Some were set afire; others were killed by lions. In a particularly popular innovation, a pair of victims was brought to the arena, one armed and the other defenseless. The defenseless man was chased around the arena and eventually killed by the armed man, who then surrendered his weapon and, in turn, was chased and killed by the next prisoner.[16]

But it was the gladiatorial fights that drew the most attention. Gladiators were skilled athletes in one sense and trained professional killers in another. Masters of hand-to-hand combat, they engaged in what were perpetual "sudden death overtimes": winners lived, sometimes to reap fame and fortune and to fight another day, while the bodies of losers bled into the arena sand. The contests were infused with religious overtones. Upon entering the arena, gladiators swore sacred oaths that put their lives "on deposit" with the gods of the underworld.[17] If a fighter put on a good show yet lost the battle, his fate rested in the hands of the crowd and, if he were in attendance, the emperor. Historians remain divided over whether it was a thumbs-up, a thumbs-down or some other gesture that determined whether the gladiator could live to fight another day or whether his opponent's dagger would be driven through his midsection. Few gladiators survived more than three years. Although some enjoyed longer lives and were celebrated as heroes and idolized by women, they were despised as humans and deprived of access to elite social functions.

With the passage of time the popularity of the games grew, as did the thirst for increasingly brutal, elaborate, and spectacular shows. The Romans did not have 24-hour telecasts on ESPN, but they watched a lot of gladiatorial games. In the fourth century, 177 days a year were designated as public holidays, with 10 full days given to gladiatorial contests, sixty-six to chariot races, and the rest of them devoted to the theater. Contests were held on many other occasions as well, at sites reaching across the Roman empire. The games required huge expenditures of private and public money. Emperors and aristocrats vied with each other to present the most colossal spectacles. In the early first century, Augustus sponsored dozens of shows that were estimated to have required 10,000 gladiators; the birthday of Vitellius (AD 15–69) was said to have been marked by gladiatorial contests in all 265 districts of the empire. When conventional one-on-one battles failed to excite, promoters offered grander spectacles featuring infantry and cavalry; arenas could be flooded for colossal naval battles. Caesar once sponsored a show featuring gladiators, chariot races, athletic competitions, a naval battle, and five days of wild beast hunts. It ended with a battle between two armies each consisting of five hundred infantry, twenty elephants, and thirty cavalry. In their search for even more sensational entertainments, promoters arranged torch-lit battles featuring women against men, women against women, women against dwarfs, blind against blind, and women fighting from chariots; even combats between aristocrats became popular forms of titillation for frenzied crowds.[18]

Scholars have attributed deep and complex motives to the Roman love for gladiatorial games. Some have identified important connections of the games to military and political life while others have seen the attraction to the games as a way of compensating for the "excruciating feeling of humiliation and insecurity" that faced the Romans in their daily lives.[19] Some believe that the games' popularity was due to the sense of reassurance that the crowds felt upon seeing disasters inflicted on others and not themselves. Others have claimed that by enjoying vicariously the violence of the arena the Romans were purged of aggression and hostility, though this view was certainly untrue in the case of Nero, who is said to have kicked Empress Pompaea to death because she scolded him for his late return from the Circus Maximus. However one dresses up the ritualized torture and unspeakable violence of the arena in sociological theory, it still remains an unprecedented variation on sports. It represents what historian Crane Brinton rightly called "a special case of moral history." One has only to probe the underbelly of bullfights, Acapulco cliff diving, daredevil shows, and auto racing to appreciate that the specter of death and violence is intrinsically fascinating to a large percentage of the population, but only in Rome was the urge satisfied by ritual slaughter.[20]

CHARIOT RACING

Chariot racing in the hippodrome had been part of ancient Greek athletics long before Christ, reaching its ascendancy in the first few centuries of the Roman Empire, not only in Rome but also in the eastern cities where many of the earliest Christian churches were founded. It may be impossible to exaggerate the addictive power of racing in Greco-Roman life. For the average Roman, said a commentator of the age, "the Circus Maximus is temple, home, community center and the fulfillment of all of their hopes." The racecourse, along with forums, fountains, theaters, temples, and the public baths, was regarded as an essential hallmark of a classical city. Although not as brutal as gladiatorial contests, chariot races combined frenzy and fury to create a spectacle that was unexplainable in its grip on the Greek and Roman conscience. Hundreds of thousands packed the massive Circus Maximus to witness spectacles which, in their day, rivaled those of modern-day Super Bowls. The Circus Maximus stretched more than three football fields long (335 meters) and one football field wide (80 meters), an area large enough to hold up to 250,000 spectators. Most races were seven-lap events; twenty-four races were run each day, although history records as many as forty-eight being run on special occasions. Intermissions might include gladiatorial contests, acrobats, boxing, wrestling, and even wild beast hunts.[21]

It is not stretching the historical record too thinly to describe chariot racing as the forerunner of modern-day auto racing in which daring, speed, and the possibility of death on the track combined with ribaldry and drunkenness in the stands. Charioteers tended to be small and their chariots, unlike the bulky ones pictured in the movie *Ben Hur*, were lightweight and designed for speed, enabling them to race at speeds exceeding those possible on a mounted horse. Drivers wore protective uniforms to limit injury in case of a crash. Driving styles were aggressive and ruthless. Cutting across the path of a rival and trying to force his chariot aside and up against the barrier was considered legitimate; hence spectacular accidents, often involving several teams, were accepted as part of the race. All in all the tactics used in these ancient races weren't a great deal different from the "aggressive driving" and "bump-drafting" that have plagued NASCAR in recent years. When asked by reporters what he needed to do to improve his performance, NASCAR idol Jeff Gordon told them that he needed to be aggressive and "jump back in that throttle and carry that corner speed," expressing a sentiment that only his fellow competitors and ancient charioteers could have appreciated.[22]

Although modern race car drivers move at much faster speeds, the chariot races were much more dangerous, to the horses as well as to the men. A fifth-century poem written by Sidonius Apollinarius speaks of the "sweat of drivers and flying steeds," "the hoarse roar from applauding partisans," and at the end, describes the absolute horror: "[Your competitor] shamelessly made for your wheel with a sidelong dash. His horses were brought down, a multitude of intruding legs entered the wheels, and . . . the revolving rim shattered the entangled feet; then he, a fifth victim, flung from his chariot, which fell upon him, caused a mountain of havoc, and blood disfigured his prostrate brow." One of the saddest inscriptions embossed on a Roman tomb was placed there by a charioteer named Polyneices. The tomb contained the body of his son, who died in a racing accident: "Marcus Aurelius Polyneices, born a slave, lived 29 years, 9 months and 5 days. He won the palm 739 times: 655 times for the Reds, 55 times for the Greens, 12 times for the Blues and 17 times for the Whites."[23]

Fierce partisanship ruled the day and the disposition of crowds was a mixed bag: spectators delirious with joy might be seated close to those seething with anger and disappointment. Young vandals with a special talent for crude and incendiary taunts riled both the competitors and the spectators. The "factions"—fan clubs or sport associations with distinct political ties and passionately devoted to their "colors"—had especially notorious reputations for violence. Like the hooligans that disrupt modern European soccer, they "fought with their throats in the hippodrome and occasionally with knives in the streets." On at least one occasion, a brawl in the stands left 3,000 Blues dead, killed by Green hoodlums known as "citizen burners," whose morbid mantra of "burn here, burn there, not a Blue left anywhere" was as familiar to circus crowds as "kill the ump" is to modern baseball fans. Spectator riots were not uncommon. Gambling was pervasive, as was drunkenness; more than one drunken fan made the fatal mistake of running onto the track during a race.[24]

Somewhat like modern day athletes, successful charioteers reaped vast fortunes for the risks they took in the circus. One Gaius Appuleius Diocles, who took part in over 4,000 races in a twenty-year career, is reported to have earned nearly 36 million sesterti in his career. The annual pay for a soldier, by comparison, was 900 sesterti. Critics might complain about the outrageous sums earned by drivers, but they, like most of the citizenry, idolized the drivers just the same. One grief-stricken fan is reported to have thrown himself on the funeral pyre of his favorite driver. But eventually the prize money and the elaborate entertainments proved too costly for the promoters. With the passing of time, the ceremonies and ancillary entertainments (cheaper than the races) began to overshadow the actual competitions. By the twelfth century the shows were simply too expensive for anyone to sponsor.[25]

Religious ceremony formed a significant part of the racing spectacles. Elaborate pre-race ceremonies featured a procession of the gods (*pompa circensis*) with hoisted images of Roman deities. In the second century, the Temple of the Sun bordered the racing grounds in honor of the imperial Sun God, who was the patron saint of the circus and chariot races. Religious processions became so important that by the third century they consumed as much time and attention as did the races themselves. Religion and magic were also evident on the track, where they became tools for honing the competitive edge. Many charioteers, desperate for a win, were ill content merely to seek the blessing of their gods; additional insurance was sought on the dark side. An ominous inscription by one charioteer implored sinister forces to "torture and kill the horses of the Greens and Whites, and . . . kill in a crash their drivers Clarus, Felix, Primulus and Romanus, and leave not a breath in their bodies."[26]

From the vantage point of the twenty-first century, gladiatorial contests, heavy athletics, and chariot racing may stand out as obvious targets of moral outrage, but for the Romans and Greeks, eminently reasonable people in their own right, they represented parts of glamorous and glorious traditions, albeit indelicate at times. Even highly cultured individuals such as Cicero and Pliny the Younger defended the gladiatorial games on the grounds that they encouraged bravery and contempt for pain and death, traits which would come in handy on the battlefields. Senses had become so numbed it may have been impossible for the average Roman to feel sympathy for those who suffered and died in the course of furnishing their entertainments. An indication as to how "naturally" the games were taken by ancients can be seen in the letters of Symmachus, a late fourth-century Roman who did not have a reputation for being a harsh person, yet in reporting the suicides of some Saxons he was having groomed to fight in the arena, his letters show only how sorry he felt for himself, not at all for the Saxons. Seneca and some of his contemporaries might have complained that they returned home from the spectacles "more covetous, more ambitious, more self-indulgent . . . crueler and more inhuman for having been amongst my fellow man," but they were clearly in the minority, pointy-headed intellectuals who obviously didn't know good fun when they saw it.[27]

AN AMBIVALENT LAITY

The attitude of the average Christian convert toward sport spectacles has been described as "one of fanatical antipathy," but "ambivalent and irresolute" is probably a more accurate characterization.[28] Surely the Greek admiration for the uninhibited and unbridled assertion of self could not be embraced by early Christians who were in the process of learning how to adapt their lives to the severe teachings of the Sermon on the Mount. Yet it seems clear that early Christians struggled in deciding how much of the old way of life should be left behind and how much could be continued without marring their Christian witness. Judging from the tirades of church fathers, more than a few Christians, especially in the second, third, and fourth centuries, were sneaking off to the amphitheater, hippodrome, and stadium. Gladiatorial contests and wild beast shows may have been, as a historian notes, "a Christian's worst nightmare," yet it must also be remembered that the early faith attracted people from all walks of life, including many who no doubt were accustomed to attending athletic events and gladiatorial shows. Some may have been sport promoters, athletes, gladiators, and charioteers prior to their conversions. Just as some early Christians volunteered for the Roman army with its long calendar of pagan sacrifices, so too we must suspect that some remained patrons of the sport spectacles. "We should allow once again," says historian Robin Fox, "for Christians who were ready to compromise to a degree which their leaders' moral sermons would not contemplate."[29]

Thus, opinions about the sports of the day varied among the Christian laity. New converts felt pulled in one direction by cultural traditions and the excitement of the arena and in another direction by the stern warnings of Christian ecclesiastics about attending the games. St. Augustine of Hippo, who regarded the gladiatorial contests as "licensed cruelty," tells of his friend, Alypius, who gave up the games when he became a Christian but on one occasion was enticed to the arena by friends. Overcome by guilt, Alypius put his hands over his face and refused to look. Yet before long, the atmosphere got the best of him and soon he was shouting and roaring with the crowd. Surely Alypius was not alone.[30]

But aside from the struggles experienced by hardcore fans, there is little question that the Christian community had acquired a reputation as a detester of spectacles by the end of the first century AD. In a brief play written by a second-century Roman lawyer and apologist named Minucius Felix Marcus, the heathen Caecelius accuses Christians of being dullards by saying, "you have no concern in public displays; you reject the public banquets and *abhor the sacred games*" (emphasis added). Octavius acknowledges the claims and explains that Christians object to the games on two grounds: the pagan worship associated with the games, and the fact that the games "purvey and stimulate immorality."[31] "The world hates the Christian," said the second-century author of the *Epistle to Diogenes*, "though it receiveth no wrong from them, because they set themselves against its pleasures." The early Christian apologist Tertullian from whom we will hear more later, also thought abstaining from popular sport spectacles was the hallmark of a believer.[32]

For some Christians, ridding their lifestyles of sporting spectacles was a defining moment in their religious lives. Thascius Cyprian, a third-century lawyer who became a Christian in mid-life (he called himself "a born-again Christian") gave up his practice and sold most of his property to help the Christian poor. Looking back on his life, he was able to identify the change in his moral convictions as having been provoked by his shunning of displays of riches and the gladiatorial shows. In some cases this change in conviction happened so quickly that it raised suspicions, as for example when early church father St. Jerome observed that the converts who were "yesterday in the amphitheater, [were] today in the church; [who] in the evening [were] at the circus [are] in the morning at the altar."[33]

A HOSTILE CLERGY

Although some of the laity continued to struggle with the issue of sports, there was little doubt where Christian leaders stood on the issue. Preachers and apologists consistently thundered against "the circus, the race-course, the contest of athletes . . . which the Devil introduced into the world under the pretext of amusement, and through which he leads the souls of men to perdition."[34] In the authoritative words of historian Ernest Renan, "one of the most profound sentiments of the primitive Christians, and one too which produced the most extended results, was detestation of the theater, the stadium and the gymnasium—that is to say, of all the public resorts which gave its distinctive character to a Grecian or Roman city." Another historian notes that "actors, musicians, dancers, and athletes were ranked with prostitutes, astrologers, and diviners by Christian thinkers and rejected outright as representatives of the immorality, idolatry, depravity, and inhumanity characterized by such entertainments."[35] The Apostolic Constitutions compiled in the fourth century urged Christians to avoid "indecent spectacles such as the theater and public sports" and forbade baptism, church membership, and communion to those who frequented the amphitheater. Gladiators and fencing masters who taught how to kill were not to be baptized into the faith until they promised to give up their professions, and the canons of the Council of Arles in AD 314 specifically forbade Christians to associate with gladiators or charioteers.[36]

Preachers found it especially difficult to imagine newly converted Christians ambling comfortably among the scores of burning altars at the Greek athletic contests or sitting with a clear conscience as the procession of the gods passed by in the circus. Novatian, an early third-century theologian, fired off a stern warning to early Christians who, he was shocked to discover, were unashamedly attending the games. "Sacred Scripture condemns the spectacles," he said, "because idolatry is the source of all the public games. How incongruous it is for a faithful Christian, who has renounced the devil at baptism, to renounce Christ at the games!" But it wasn't only idolatry that bothered Novatian; he was equally critical of the immorality and brutality of the games, the strife and discord that they fomented among spectators, and the immoral climate they spawned, including "wanton licentiousness, public vice, and notorious lechery." These same two themes—idolatry and immorality—figured prominently in the writings of the Apostle Paul, who condemned the Corinthian practice of eating meat that had been sacrificed to idols (1 Corinthians 8:1-13), possibly to Zeus at the Isthmian games that were held at Corinth. Beginning in the last half of the second century, the church fathers preached unremittingly against Christian attendance of the games.[37]

For church leaders, the sport spectacles represented in microcosm all that was wrong with Roman society. They were paradigms of excess and extravagance, shallowness and sensuousness, selfishness and self-gratification. Church fathers often used the incredible story of Kleomedes—a famous Greek athlete who was said to have killed his opponent using an illegal blow that tore open his rib cage—not simply to condemn athletics but to condemn the whole of pagan society.[38] The brutality of the amphitheater was vilified, not simply because of the pain and suffering it caused the gladiators, but because of its pernicious effect on those who watched. There was an abiding concern about the capacity of fanaticism and consumption of violent displays to erode the reasonableness and humility that were seen as hallmarks of Christian demeanor. For example, Cassiodorus, Christian secretary to Emperor Theodosius, viewed the frenzy of the circus as incompatible with the Christian spirit:

> The spectacle drives out sound morality and invites childish factiousness, it banishes honesty and it is an unfailing source of riots . . . most remarkable of all, in these beyond all other spectacles men's minds are carried away by excitement without any regard for dignity and sobriety. Green takes the lead and half the crowd is plunged into gloom. Blue passes him, and a great mass of citizens suffer the torments of the damned. They cheer wildly with no useful result; they suffer nothing but are cut to the heart.[39]

Perhaps no early Christian leader so elegantly and systematically showed how and why sports of the times should be brought into judgment by Christians as did Tertullian, a late second-century ecclesiastic writer, lawyer, and apologist. His *De Spectaculis* stands as the most explicit and harsh denunciation of sports in the early Christian era.[40] In blunt and uncompromising prose, Tertullian considered arguments put forth by some in the Christian community to justify their attendance at the games and rebutted them like the skilled lawyer that he was:

> *The games bring enjoyment. God is not offended by people enjoying themselves, so it is perfectly legitimate to gain pleasure by attending the spectacles.* Tertullian warned of the danger of allowing one's life to be governed by the pleasure principle, pointing out that if pleasure is what God had desired most for his children, the martyrs were foolish to die their terrible deaths in the Colosseum. (chapter 1)

The games are products of God's creation. Since all things are part of God's creation, they cannot be hostile to Him. This includes the horse, the lion, the strength of the athlete's body, and the cement and marble of the stadium. Tertullian reminds Christians that all forms of evil come ultimately from perversion of God's creation; idols are cast from his precious metals, and murder is committed using iron objects fashioned from raw material created by God. These objects of creation never were created "to issue in acts which He condemns, even if those acts are performed by means of what he has created." (chapter 2)

Scripture does not specifically forbid attendance at the spectacles. Tertullian emphasizes the need to examine the spectacles in light of general biblical principles and calls attention to the contrast in passions stirred by the games and the tranquility of the Christian life. He singles out the acrimonious atmosphere of the crowd for special condemnation:

> So it begins and gives to madness, anger, discord—to everything forbidden to priests of peace. Next taunts or mutual abuse without warrant of hate . . . God forbids us to hate even with cause, when he bids us love our enemies . . . but what can be more merciless than the circus where men do not even spare their princes or their fellow citizens? . . . If any of these forms of madness with which the circus rages, is anywhere permitted to saints then it will be lawful in the circus also, but if nowhere, then neither in the circus. (chapter 16)

God looks on the games and is not defiled, neither will Christians be defiled merely by watching. Tertullian shows where such reasoning leads: since God is looking on the entire universe, all things— even the most evil things—would be legitimate. Would they, he asks, applaud the same acts of cruelty, frenzy, and spite which they witness inside the arena if it were performed on the streets of the city? Of course not! A brawl in the middle of town would be broken up or at least looked on with disfavor by Christians, but, he says, "in the stadium you applaud fights far more dangerous" (chapter 21). "Do you really suggest," he asks, "that outside the circus as well as inside we should practice frenzy? Outside the stadium as well as inside give the rein to bad manners, to cruelty outside as well as inside the amphitheater? . . . No where and never is that permitted which is not permitted always and everywhere." (chapter 20)

Although he was something of a polemicist, Tertullian possessed keen insight into the nature of sports of his day, a perception shaped, no doubt, by many years of attending the shows prior to his conversion in middle age. When such blasts from the pulpit proved ineffective in stemming the public craze for sports, more extreme action was taken. In one of the more grisly protests of this sort, an obscure Syrian monk named Telemachus traveled from the desert to Rome in the early fifth century, where he attempted to halt the gladiatorial shows single-handedly. He managed to make it to the floor of the Colosseum, where he thrust himself between two battling gladiators and commanded them to stop "in the name of Christ Jesus, King of Kings and Lord of Lords." Incensed by the rude interruption, the spectators stoned him to death.[41]

Again, Tertullian didn't speak for all Christians of his age, and especially not for those in succeeding centuries. The large-scale Christianization of society in the late third and fourth centuries would dull the sharp distinction between the attitudes and lifestyles of believers and pagans with respect to many aspects of popular culture. "The question of what it was that defined a Christian had never been easy to answer," says historian R. A. Markus, "but it had become especially troubling in an age when Christianity seemed to have become so easy." A small minority of Christians may always have attended the games and races, but with the passing of a century or two, visiting the circus and arenas became more accepted in Christian circles. How else is one to explain a Phrygian inscription dating to the third century that tells of a wealthy Christian who paid for the expense of city games, or records showing that in Eumenia there lived a Christian athlete named Helix who had won prizes in pagan games extending from Asia to southern Italy, or the Christian emperor Constantine's decision to allow the inhabitants of a town in Italy to honor him by sponsoring sport spectacles?[42]

And there is the curious story of Hilarion, the third-century charismatic Christian ascetic who lived as a hermit in the desert and was said to have performed miraculous faith healings. According to Jerome, this pillar of the faith not only healed a charioteer's neck that had been stiffened by racing: he agreed to bless the racing horse of a prominent charioteer in Gaza whose opponent was said to be amassing wins by using a sorcerer to curse his opponents. According to Jerome (the only historical source), Hilarion gave a blessing to the horses, their stables, and the racecourse and the next time out they romped home to resounding Christian cheers. "The decisive victory in those games and many others later," said Jerome, "caused very many people to turn to the faith." If these records are indeed true, history may duly record Hilarion as the first Christian chaplain to sports and his protégé charioteer as the first athlete evangelist.[43]

The ultimate demise of Greek athletics probably occurred not so much as a result of Christian condemnation as of a declining economy and the waning of interest in the religion with which they were associated. The chariot races continued well into the eleventh century, long after Christians had assumed political power and engineered feeble attempts to Christianize them (see chapter 2). There is no doubt that by five centuries after Christ, Christianity had impacted the races, but despite the protests of ecclesiastics, it never brought down the final curtain on them. In the end, the spectacles simply became too costly to sponsor. And while Christian influence no doubt played a significant role in the eventual demise of gladiatorial shows, there also is reason to believe that even against this most outrageous of sports the church proved to be a weak moderator of public opinion. One indication of this is the fact that wild beast shows continued to be popular even under the rule of some Christian emperors. Constantine banned gladiatorial games in AD 325, but three years later they were held in Antioch as usual, and in AD 333–337 Constantine's sons were still granting towns in Italy permission to hold gladiator shows.[44]

WAS PAUL A SPORTS AFICIONADO?

In the minds of many modern Christians, Paul's use of rich athletic imagery suggests that he may have not been as critical of sports as were his successors of the second and third centuries. The evangelical athletic community has been especially attracted to Paul's heavy reliance on athletic metaphors, viewing them not only as an apostolic blessing on the sports and games of his day, but as justification for their involvement in popular sports today. It is not uncommon, for example, to see Christian athletes sporting T-shirts emblazoned with athletic imagery from Philippians 3:14 ("I press toward the mark for the high calling of God in Jesus Christ") or 2 Timothy 4:7 ("I have fought a good fight, I have finished my course, I have kept the faith").[45]

Citing Paul's use of athletic language in order to justify involvement in sports is hardly an invention of modern Christianity. Third-
century church leader Novatian was dismayed at the way some of his
contemporaries marshaled flimsy evidence from Scripture to justify
their attendance at the games. For example, they questioned why they
shouldn't be allowed to attend the races at the hippodrome when Elijah
had driven a chariot. And if the Apostle Paul "paints for us the picture
of a boxing match and of our own wrestling against the spiritual forces
of wickedness . . . Why then should a faithful Christian not be at liberty to be a spectator of things that the divine Writings are at liberty to
mention?" But Novatian tells his readers that the apostle's references are
merely exhortations to practice virtue, "not concessions to attend pagan
spectacles and enjoy base pleasures," and goes on to wonder whether
"it would have been far better for such people to lack [any] knowledge
of the Scriptures than to read them in such a manner." But this doesn't
answer the question of why Paul would have used these athletic figures
of speech unless he, in contrast to the church leaders that followed in his
wake, were a proponent of popular sports.[46]

First, a quick review of the athletic passages in Paul's writing.[47] The
most elaborate applications of this athletic language refer to the events
of the stadium, especially running. In 1 Corinthians 9:24-26, where Paul
urges his readers to exert greater effort in running "the race," he draws a
parallel between the self-renunciation required in his ministry and that
required of athletes who compete for prizes in the stadium. In verse 27,
he shifts to the metaphor of boxing using the technical term *hypopiazo*
("fist blow under the eye") to make the point that his own desires are
not to stand in the way of the spiritual war. In Philippians 3:12-14, the
apostle, again in the context of an apology for his ministry, uses the
athletic metaphor of a runner to illustrate the critical importance of the
goal for which he is striving in his ministry. In other passages he speaks
of having finished his race and adhered to the course set for him by
God (Acts 20:24; 2 Timothy 4:7). In Romans 9:16, Paul reminds readers
that salvation comes not merely by wishing or running, but by mercy
bestowed by God. A reference to running in Galatians 2:2 mentions his
not having run in vain, and again in Philippians 2:16, Paul notes that
he "did not run or *labor* in vain," where some scholars believe the word
used for labor refers to an athlete's training.[48] In Galatians 5:7, he mentions that although he has been running well, someone has broken the
rules, fouled him, and caused him to stumble, and in 2 Timothy 2:5 he

urges Timothy to endure hardships and to keep from becoming tangled in worldly affairs, reminding him that a man (athlete) is not crowned unless he runs according to the rules.

Other metaphors employ language referring to the training done by athletes (e.g., Acts 24:16) and to umpires that supervised competition, urging believers to let the peace of Christ "umpire" in their hearts (Colossians 3:15). Paul contrasts athletes' corruptible crowns with the much more enduring crowns of righteousness for believers (1 Corinthians 9:24-25). In Philippians 4:1, the thought of reward is prominent where Paul describes the Philippians as "the wreath" with which he himself will be crowned if they stand firm, for they will be living proof that he had neither run nor trained in vain. In 2 Timothy 4:8, he uses terms for both reward and umpire in stating that "there is laid up for me [as on the ivory and golden table at Olympia] a wreath of righteousness, which the Lord, the umpire who makes no mistakes, will award me on that day." Chariot racing, not running, is thought to be the sport envisioned in Philippians 3:13-14, where Paul talks of forgetting what has gone on before and "straining forward" to what lies ahead, saying, "I drive on toward the finishing line."[49]

The gladiatorial contest forms the basis of yet other metaphors. In 1 Corinthians 15:32, Paul claims to have fought wild beasts in Ephesus, reminding his readers that he would not have done so if he didn't believe in the promise of eternal life to believers. He appeals to Philippian Christians to "stand firm" in one spirit, "contending together" as one for the faith of the gospel, in a passage (Philippians 1:27) that some believe to be a clear reference to gladiatorial shows. Like those thrown into the arena to face the beasts, Christians are condemned to fight for their lives (or their faith). In Philippians 1:30, Paul describes himself engaging in a "contest" with his readers, and again in 4:3, speaks of certain women who had once fought side by side with him in the cause of the gospel. These passages are all thought to be drawing on gladiatorial imagery. Commentators have also pointed out subtle references to gladiators in Philippians 1:28, Romans 3:6 and 15:30, and 2 Corinthians 4:8-9.[50]

On the basis of Paul's plentiful athletic metaphors, it is tempting to assume not only that he was predisposed to the sports of his day but also that the sources for these athletic metaphors were his own experiences playing or watching sports. This is unlikely to have been the case. The definitive work on the topic remains Victor Pfitzner's *Paul and the Agon Motif*, a painstakingly thorough examination of the literary, historical, philosophical, and theological context in which Paul's athletic language was used. Pfitzner points out that the athletic terminology had been in use by Greek philosophers long before the dawn of Christianity and that by Paul's day it had lost any direct association with athletic contexts. Like contemporary athletic metaphors used in everyday speech ("Make sure you touch base with me" [baseball], "I struck out on the exam" [baseball], "do an end run around the committee" [football], "go an extra round" [boxing], and "take a rain check" [baseball]), those used by Paul had lost their original connotations and references as a result of popular use. It is quite likely that the apostle would have grown up with them or acquired them in his discussions with street-corner philosophers who roamed the Mediterranean world or perhaps in his many contacts with Greek-speaking synagogues. The metaphors were so common, claims Pfitzner, that "it is not hard to imagine that any Hellenistic Jew could have either written or understood them without himself having gained a firsthand knowledge of the games from a bench in the stadium." Because the metaphors Paul used had long been dissociated from actual athletic experience, along with Paul's background as an educated Pharisee who identified with the Palestinian Jews' "deep-lying abhorrence [of] Greek athletics and gymnastics as typical of heathendom," Pfitzner concludes that "one must question Paul's so-called love for, and familiarity with Greek sports!" Even more problematic was how Paul could have blended an image that glorified the Greek ideal of *agon*, with its spirit of self-assertion and human achievement, with a theological system that repeatedly underscored human insufficiency and divine grace.[51]

It is possible, even likely, that Paul played sports informally in his youth. It is conceivable, though highly improbable, that he maintained an interest in some of the public games during his ministry. However, given what is known about the gladiatorial contests and chariot races it is much more likely that Paul's use of images from these shows was not based on his experiences as a spectator. Neither is it likely that Paul was a fan of the Greek athletics of his day. The pagan religious ceremonies that were an integral part of the contests, and the sharp contrasts between the ethos of the competitions and Paul's exhortation to the spiritual life, make it quite likely that he shared the largely negative views of influential church leaders who followed in his wake. Historian Richard DeVoe allows that Paul's denunciation of "debauchery, idolatry and witchcraft . . . drunkenness, orgies, and the like" as behaviors that will bar people from the

kingdom of God (Galatians 5:19-21), Paul's warning to the Corinthians not to indulge in pagan revelry (1 Corinthians 10:7), and Peter's
warning against living in debauchery, lust, drunkenness, orgies,
carousing, and detestable idolatry (1 Peter 4:3) all might have been
aimed at the popular games.[52]

CONCLUSION

In summing up the story of Christianity's first encounter with popular
sport, it should be emphasized that the historical record contains no evidence of early church authorities having condemned sports played informally; the essential acts of moving, striving, contesting, and developing
skill for purposes of enjoyment never came under attack. Early Christian
children and perhaps adults may have played an assortment of informal games and sports. But sports that were part of grand entertainment
spectacles were another matter entirely. To those in the vanguard of the
faith, the major sport palaces of the day were testaments to a culture
into which Christianity fit only obliquely; therefore they were shunned
by most Christians. Early Christian leaders were not nearly as concerned
about the effects of sport on the participants (since most were not Christians) as they were its effects on the minds, souls, and dispositions of the
Christians who watched. They were careful, critical observers of sport,
arguably more critical than the Christian community is today. They saw
how sport spectacles so often appealed to baser human instincts and
softened Christian resolve against not only pagan religious sentiments
but also the underlying worldview that defined the essence of Greek and
Roman culture. To the early fathers, watching the games risked blurring
the lines that distinguished the new faith from the old religion.

Secondly, the church took seriously its stand against sport and other
public entertainments. Because the sports offered by Greco-Roman society were difficult to fit into a Christian conception of upright living, how
believers positioned sports with regard to their lifestyle represented a kind
of litmus test for measuring Christian commitment. "It is above all things
from this," said Tertullian, "that they [the pagans] understand a man to have
become a Christian, that he will have nothing to do with the games." Third,
from the beginning popular sport proved to be a divisive issue, not only
in setting Christians apart from their pagan neighbors, but in fomenting
dissention within the Christian community as well. Early Christian leaders
may have been united in the belief that the sport spectacles of the day were
incompatible with the teachings of Christ, but many rank-and-file believers

weren't so sure. Thus, in taking a position against sport, clerics and church authorities set themselves apart not only from the secular sports promoters but from part of the early Christian community as well. Almost from the outset it was clear that the church and the laity would be locked in a long battle over sports, and given the public's unquenchable thirst for sport spectacles, it was a contest the church was destined to lose.

2

Proscribing, Controlling, and Justifying Sport

During the first three centuries of its existence, the church operated in the shadows of a pagan society, forced to define itself in contrast to the traditions, customs, and practices of a largely hostile culture. In drawing its boundaries, the church positioned public sport spectacles outside the parameters of a Christian lifestyle. With the conversion of Constantine in the fourth century and the gradual transition of Christianity from a minor persecuted sect to the official religion of the empire, the church continued to be faced with the puzzling question of how much of the surrounding culture it could absorb without losing its spiritual purity and vitality. Particularly problematic was discerning what behaviors and allegiances should distinguish that which was clearly pagan and deserving of rejection from that which was merely "secular" or "indifferent" and worthy of the church's blessing. There was hardly a uniform opinion across the body of believers. From the tone of Augustine and his contemporaries' sermons, it is clear, says historian Carol Harrison, that "conversion did not—could not—bring about a final and decisive break with [the] past, but rather that it lingered on in popular superstitious practices and customs and especially in enthusiasm for pagan festivals and the games." This was an important, even critical time in the evolution of the relationship between sport and Christianity, for the church's resolve began to wither during the Middle Ages.[1]

With the decline of the Roman gladiatorial contests and the waning of professionalized Greco-Roman athletics, sport as spectacle for the masses was slowly put to sleep, but it never expired. Despite the clergy's continuing uneasiness with sports—whether it was the crude town games of the villagers or the more sophisticated hunts and jousting tournaments of the nobility—the public clamor for sports couldn't be squelched. Ultimately, the church proved ineffective in controlling an epidemic that had infected not only those outside the Christian community but many of those inside it as well. Higgs and Braswell would seem to have it right in likening the role of the church in the Middle Ages to the enforcement division of the NCAA in modern times, pointing out that "like the bans of that secular organization, those of the church were ineffectual and not permanent."[2]

Although the church resisted the spread of play and sport during this period, it would be wrong to describe either resistance or acceptance of play as the consistent position of the church, in either pre-Reformation or post-Reformation Europe. In the third century and beyond, some congregations continued to be subjected to sermons condemning the circuses, shows, games, and theater that preachers like Augustine called the "pomp of the Devil." Other congregations were led by religious figures who had a more relaxed and tolerant attitude toward sports. If it is possible to broach an overarching theme that captures the church's stance toward popular forms of play during this period of history, it would be a tripartite one: a continuing ambivalence and uneasiness toward sport coupled with periodic efforts to banish it from the lives of believers; when this proved impossible, undertaking feeble efforts to control it; and, when the church was unable to control sport, overlaying it with Christian symbols and ceremonies, hoping to squeeze from it whatever gloss it might lend to its message and mission.[3]

Efforts to accommodate sport came early, as, for example, in the church's handling of chariot racing. Unlike the gladiatorial games and Greco-Roman sports, whose demise was abetted (though not entirely wrought) by Christian criticism and political action, chariot racing, especially in the eastern reaches of the empire, remained part of the cultural landscape, coexisting with institutionalized Christianity well into the eleventh century. The pagan flavor of the circus had always made Christian ecclesiastics nervous, if not apoplectic, and some degree of hand-wringing continued to hold sway about the violence of the races and the frenzy of the crowd long after serious pagan ceremony had disappeared from the races. By the fifth century, the masses had won the day. In one of most unvarnished examples of how pragmatism guided the church's position, Christian Emperor Theodoric, while readily acknowledging the polluted atmosphere of the races, claimed he was "compelled to support the institution by the necessity of humouring the people who are mad on it. The mob," said the emperor, "is drawn to whatever it has found to dispel care, so we must be generous to racing and must not always rule Our gifts by Our judgment. It is prudent sometimes to relax from severity so that in this way We can keep control of popular entertainment."4

Thus, as pagan trappings gradually withered, the chariot races, like much of the rest of society, were Christianized or "Constantinianized." There may be no more striking illustration of the "Constantinianization" of the empire than the way Christian symbols were woven into the elaborate celebrations that were part of the chariot races. Historian Alan Cameron paints the scene: the emperor would enter the hippodrome and greet his subjects with the sign of the cross, after which the crowd "would hail him as God's earthly representative, and the factions would sing hymns. The chants from the crowds were explicitly religious: 'Glory to God who strengthens the orthodox. Glory to God who casts down the deniers of the Trinity, Glory to God who destroys the deniers of the Mother of God.'" Following the races, winning charioteers would drive their teams to the nearest church to give thanks for their victories. Fans were divided not only in their allegiances to race drivers but by political and even doctrinal differences as well. The Blue faction held to a hard Trinitarian line, while the Greens espoused Monophysitism, claiming that Christ was one composite nature.5

There is no indication that the chants and hymns had any effect on the races themselves. Religion was largely a thin patina layered over a hysterical, dangerous, hypercompetitive spectacle; the brutality, drunkenness, and mania that were abhorred by earlier generations of Christians remained. The ceremony may have helped mollify feelings of guilt among more sensitive Christians who, despite their better judgment, chose to attend, but the races and the emotions of those who watched remained under the sway of sentiments far removed from the Apostle Paul's teachings. Faced with the reality of its impotence in the face of sports mania, the church hardly could hope for more.

TOURNAMENTS

Nothing more poignantly defined sport in the Middle Ages or better symbolized the church's ambivalence toward sports than the jousting tournaments that formed a central part of aristocratic life during the twelfth through fourteenth centuries. The tournament was a vestige of Roman sport-combats dating back to the sixth century, a consummate blend of athletic skill and military purpose. All competitive sports share something with war, but in the tournament, says historian Allen Guttmann, "the line between tournament and battlefield, between mock and real warfare, was thin and often transgressed." Knights, armed with blunted swords and long lances, attempted to knock opponents from their horses and, if they found themselves unseated, would continue the contest on foot. Often "mêlées" involving hundreds of knights stretched out over many acres. Most jousts were sponsored by royalty for the amusement of their guests (in fact, the enormous expense severely limited the number of nobility who could host such events). Sometimes they were part of Easter and Christmas festivities or featured at Shrovetide, the often licentious carnival ("farewell to the flesh") festivities that preceded Lent. From their "sky boxes" perched high above the cramped seats for lower classes, nobility could get a clear view of the pageants financed by their largesse.[6]

What had originated as an informal contest for honing the military skills of knights eventually became part of a grand sporting spectacle designed purely for entertainment. Tournaments were shaped by the tastes of those who paid and those who watched. A blast of the trumpet and the sound of as many as twenty or thirty horses charging from opposite ends of the lists, the sound of crashing lances and armor, and the cries of anguish from the wounded created an exciting Romanesque atmosphere. By the sixteenth century the tournament had become a victim of excess; French and German knights introduced more deadly weapons to make the contests more dangerous and titillating. "Jousting bums," professional competitors who traveled the jousting circuit and were less interested in upholding chivalric ideals than in winning prize money, heightened the violence and lowered what modest standards had existed to constrain violence at the contests. Sponsors of the tournaments responded to the demand for entertainment much like the Romans, offering increasingly showy and vapid pageants. It may be hard to imagine a tournament involving thousands of knights and lasting three weeks, but such events are part of the historical record in sixteenth-century France and England.[7]

Much like modern sport spectacles, the tournaments were a potent blend of erotic and dramatic elements, a trend that continued until their status as a contest of skill and courage was almost obliterated. Women took on roles resembling cheerleaders and became central figures in the tournaments, described by one fourteenth-century writer as arriving on horses "splendidly adorned . . . and in such manner they spent and wasted their riches and injured their bodies with abuses and ludicrous wantonness." Dressed in jewelry and high fashion, they served as hostesses at social functions, awarded prizes, led competitors into the lists with threads of gold and in the fourteenth century performed between jousts. Ultimately, tournaments took on the qualities of a staged drama and the contests themselves faded into the background in favor of "medieval tailgating"—pre-event, weeklong parties, banquets, dances, and other frivolities. Galleries, tents, and pavilions were packed with spectators decked out in silk and gold. Concessions sold food and trinkets. Colorful banners hung from the scaffolding. The sixteenth-century tournament, says Guttmann, was something like a vulgar Rose Bowl parade, featuring floats that were a "phantasmagoria of dwarves, giants, wild men, mountains, and allegorical animals (including a unicorn who, quite conventionally, laid his head upon a virgin's lap)."[8]

The tournament might have lacked the raw brutality of the Roman games, but it was a fierce and dangerous sport nonetheless. Sometimes it was difficult to say whether it was war or a sport. Prize money and defense of personal reputation coupled with personal feuds and the spirit of revenge heightened the emotional pitch. Knights often lost their tempers; some resorted to cheating by substituting sharp weapons for duller blades. The mêlées violated the civil peace, frequently ranging across the countryside where they would mangle farmers' vineyards and orchards and other personal property. Although the intent usually was not to kill an opponent, deaths frequently occurred, as did serious injuries. At least sixteen knights were killed in Saxony in 1179, and at a tournament at Nuys near Cologne in 1240, sixty-eight knights died, many having suffocated in the heat and dust.[9]

The tournaments were considered sufficiently dangerous to personal and community interests to earn the scorn of the church and civil authorities. By the eleventh century, the church councils had laid out a well-defined opposition, banning them from Monday to Friday and on feast days. In 1130 the Council of Clermont, unsure of exactly what these new contests should be called, issued a blistering edict: "We firmly prohibit those detestable 'markets or fairs' at which knights are accustomed to meet to show off their strength and their boldness and at which the deaths of men and dangers to the soul often occur. But if anyone is killed there, even if he demands and is not denied penance at the viaticum, ecclesiastical burial shall be withheld from him." Many early churchmen regarded deaths of this kind as accidental in one sense, yet as acts of homicide and suicide in another. The Dominican John Bromyard preached fire and brimstone sermons against the tournaments, envisioning in bold detail the future of knights in hell, where they would take sulfurous baths in armor that is nailed to their bodies and, in place of the embraces of "wanton young women," they would be lavished with the affections of toads. But the aristocracy had a difficult time viewing the tournaments in the same dim light; after all, Elizabeth I, the titular head of the church, was a big fan.[10]

To complaints about violence was added the charge that the tournaments showcased displays of prowess, strength, and aggressiveness that seemed more related to sinful pride than to Christian courage and manhood. Among the thirteenth-century churchmen who damned the tournaments was Jacque de Vitry, bishop of Acre, who accused knights of committing all seven deadly sins: "pride, because of their desire for praise; envy, because they resented greater praise for other 'tourneyers'; anger, because they struck out when tempers became frayed in the sport; avarice, because they desired other knights' horses and equipment and even sometimes refused to ransom each other; gluttony, because of the attendant feasting; sloth, because of the reaction to defeat in combat; and lust, because of the desire to please loose women by wearing their favorite colors in the lists."[11]

Seventy-five years earlier (1312), Pope Clement V had threatened excommunication not only to participants but also to spectators and sponsors of the jousts. His concern was not rooted so much in the moral or spiritual turpitude of the contests as in practical matters: the tournaments were hindering preparation for the crusades by wasting horses and money and by killing and maiming knights. If Clement's actions seemed to reflect a certain exasperation with the tournaments, one could hardly blame him: between 1130 and 1179, the church had issued five separate bans against the tournaments, with little effect. Even local priests ignored the papal ban; after all, many of them were family members of the jousting set and depended upon them for financial support. More than a century later the church continued to offer weak resistance. In 1316, just four short years after Pope Clement had issued his ban on the contests, Pope John XXII ascended the throne and sent up the white flag rescinding Pope Clement's order.[12]

This radical shift in church policy was not hammered out on the anvil of theological debate; it was an entirely pragmatic decision that took into account four relevant factors: (1) the tournaments had become one of the most effective means of elevating popular sentiment for the crusades; (2) collections taken at the tournaments were important sources of income for local churches; (3) by excommunicating knights who defied the papal ban, the church had diminished the pool of knights who were spiritually qualified to participate in the crusades; and (4) other knights were refusing to join the crusade unless they could first practice their fighting skills by participating in the tournaments. "Better to ignore the minor sin of tourneying," said Pierre du Bois, "so as to avoid the major catastrophe of failure against the pagans." Thus, without any discernable change in the nature of contests or the competitive spirit which animated them, the church decided in the fourteenth century that participating in the tournaments wasn't quite so sinful after all, with one important proviso: knights should approach them purely for the instrumental purposes of sharpening their military skills that would be used in the service of the crusades. Having originally been *banned* by one pope in order to preserve resources and improve chances of success in the crusades, the tournaments now were rationalized by his successor on precisely the same grounds, but only if the knights competed with the proper motivational mindset.[13]

In much the same way that chariot racing eventually was Christianized, the tournaments also came to be dressed up in religious ceremony. They had long been supported by a mythology in which knights fought for glory and Christian honor rather than personal profit and gain, even though, says historian Christopher Dawson, in reality the ethos wasn't appreciably different from that which governed the barbarian warriors whom they had replaced. A pledge of honor and fidelity to God was coupled with an unhealthy contempt for death and a "spirit of implacable revenge." Dawson believed that this dynamic militancy, reinforced by supernatural motives and offered in service to religious idealism, brought out "all that was highest and lowest in medieval society." The craving for physical aggressiveness was sublimated in religious idealism; forces of heroic self-abnegation of ascetic, peace-loving monks and the moral ideals of a gospel of grace and humility were set against the equal and opposite forces of aggression and the violent impulses of the Christian warrior. The religious impulse found expression in dramatic testimonies of certain knights who, like modern evangelical athletes, used their fame as a platform to tell of their conversions, which sometimes took place in Damascus road–like experiences while the knights were returning from the fights. The aggressive impulse found expression in the symbolism and pageantry of the tournament itself.[14]

"Trial by ordeal," the deeply engrained notion that God favors those who are brave and strong and just and that he directs the outcome of contests, also found expression in the tournaments. Thus praying that the cosmic odds of sports competition will be tipped in one's favor is hardly an invention of modern sports. Even though expressly forbidden to do so, many priests had been attending the tournaments since at least 1227. Some inhabited the "locker rooms," and, like modern chaplains who tend to the spiritual needs of professional and college sports teams before games, held pregame masses for knights. Jousts were often included in explicitly religious rituals such as christening ceremonies. By the mid-fifteenth century, the fighters were staying in and displaying their armor in religious establishments, and by the early sixteenth century priests were tutoring knights in how to say prayers at critical moments in a joust, not all that unlike former Notre Dame football coach Gerry Faust's efforts to teach his team to say "Hail Marys" at crucial points in games.[15]

By first rejecting the contests, then by seeking grounds for accommodation, and finally by injecting them with frothy religious superficialities, the church set the ground rules for defining its relationship with sport, rules which continue to flavor the relationship in the present day. The church had found itself in something of a joust itself, up against what always has proven to be Christianity's most formidable foe: popular sentiment. The practical difficulties of denying the public unfettered access to an institution that was as deeply engrained in medieval society as baseball is in modern America were painfully obvious. To take too hard of a line on the brutality and arrogance of the superficial displays, or to focus too intently on the contradictions inherent in the code of the knight and the code of the church, threatened to mar the church's standing in the community and to cost the pope political support. Thus, what previously had been sinful was declared permissible; what earlier had been grounds for the severest of ecclesiastical penalties became integrated with Christian symbolism and placed in the service of the crusades. In the end, it was a capitulation based entirely on self-interest. There was no formal ethical or theological recalculation. But the church, as if to convince itself that it still retained a modicum of control over the contests, insisted that their approval hinged on an overriding, albeit whimsical condition: knights who chose to engage in this bloodthirsty sport had to do so without coming under the sway of its violent and revengeful impulses. Given the violent nature of the sport, it was a fanciful and disingenuous stance.

Towns and Villages

While members of the aristocracy reveled in the tournaments or in hunting or hawking on their estates, most peasants settled for less formal, less expensive, less garish, and manifestly cruder forms of play on the village greens and in the countryside. In doing so they managed to wrench from their games a spirit of joy and delight that had escaped their ancestors and would continue to elude their posterity. Contests were incorporated into English religious festivals celebrated during Christmas and Easter. Competitive sports also were played as part of autumn harvest festivals in northern Europe and on saints' days in Italy. Loosely organized church-sponsored festivals in June and July, known variously as May ales or May games, church ales, summer games, or summer plays, also included a range of sports ranging from the sedate to the outright deadly.[16]

In "stoolball," one of the tamer sports of the day, a person defended a milking stool with their hand or a stick while another attempted to knock it over by pitching or rolling a ball. Some consider it to have been the basis of the game of "rounders," which has been credited with being the progenitor of American baseball. In another sport called "bowls," peasants rolled a heavy ball in an attempt to knock over a single pin placed at their opponents' feet. Handball games were popular in England and *jeu de paume* ("game of the palm"), the forerunner of tennis, was played in France. But such leisurely pastimes never captured the imagination of entire villages quite like the boisterous and partisan team sports that set village against village, district against district, single men against married men, and in some cases, church against church. These contests were a far cry from romantic notions of peasants frolicking on the village green, but in their day they were socially approved ways of giving vent to age-old rivalries.

Village life in sixteenth- and seventeenth-century Venice, for example, featured *battagliole sui ponti* ("the little battles on the bridge"), a mock battle for possession of a bridge. These Sunday bridge fights could assume many forms: individual boxing bouts, small-scale brawls, or enormous battles involving sticks and stones played out over several hours before tens of thousands of spectators. Sometimes the contests led to riots; stabbing by knife and dagger was common. Sometimes spectators threw tiles from rooftops at contestants. Far from criticizing them for their frivolousness and lethalness, social commentators of the times deemed these events "memorable and worthy of being seen by kings, cardinals, and the knights of Europe."[17]

The *giuoco del calico*, a free-for-all fistfight, eventually morphed into a ball sport roughly similar to rugby that had a long and bloody history in Italian cities, especially in Sienna. Participants bandaged their heads to soften the blows, but they were brutalized nonetheless. Upon witnessing the black eyes, pale faces, bandaged limbs, missing teeth, and otherwise sorry state of the players, a fifteenth-century writer surmised that it must have been the onlookers and certainly not the players who derived the enjoyment. In the fourteenth century, an annual invitational wrestling tournament was held each year in celebration of St. James Day in London. The bitterness and brutality of the matches would have caused the departed saint to shudder in disbelief. Eventually Henry IV came to regard the matches as sufficiently brutal to warrant their abolition.[18]

The Shrovetide games played the day before Lent were probably the most popular, and of these Shrovetide football (*la soule*) was probably the most violent. The game was described by Sir Thomas Elyot (1531) as "nothing but beastly fury and extreme violence, whereof proceedeth hurt." Historian Dennis Brailsford describes the game as one in which "heads and legs were broken and deaths were not unusual as the sides pushed, hacked and kicked their way through the streets of shuttered shops, through streams and mud, wasteland and fallow. This wild version of football had to be occasional; neither civil peace nor economic stability was compatible with its frequent performance." The contests were fueled by alcohol and age-old rivalries and embedded in a social context that encouraged licentious behavior. They were outrageously destructive. A Frenchman, watching the game for the first time, was said to have commented: "If the English call this play, it would be impossible to say what they call fighting."[19]

The *palio*, a horse race held in towns and cities, was another readily accessible feature of spectator life. *Palio* literally meant "a piece of cloth," referring to the banner which was the tangible prize awarded to the winner. In its earlier iterations, the race was between donkeys and was embedded in a larger, more chilling spectacle held in the public square. Dogs would be unleashed on boars, hares, wolves, and deer held in corrals while spectators watched from behind a fence. Bulls would be tormented ("bullbaiting") by attaching fireworks to their harnesses and then killed with sticks and stones. Men would shoot arrows or thrust spears into animals from the safety of large wooden floats that paraded through the center of town. Such ancillary entertainments were excoriated in the sixteenth century by the Council of Trent and eventually were prohibited by government authorities, but records show that the macabre entertainments were still in vogue sixty-five years later when they were featured as part of the celebrations honoring the elevation of Alexander VII to the papal throne.

Eventually donkey racing gave way to horse racing, which became a regular feature of Italian city life by the mid-seventeenth century. Like most of the village sports, the races were held in conjunction with religious celebrations such as the commemoration of deliverance from an oppressor, the reinstitution of a city after its having been excommunicated, or the arrival of sacred relics. The most famous Florentine *palio* was held in honor of St. John the Baptist, but the most enduring has been the *palio* of Siena. It continues to be a popular tourist attraction in Siena, where two races are run in the *campo* (town square) each summer. One celebrates the Assumption of the Virgin and the other commemorates a reported visitation by the Madonna during a sixteenth-century famine. Residents are not disinterested spectators, committed as they are to the horse representing their own *contrada* or district, each of which has its own churches, traditions, and horse and jockey, along with a passion exceeded only by a centuries-old contempt for some of their rival *contrade*.

A few days before the race, the *palio* banner bearing the image of the Virgin is paraded through the streets and down the aisle of a church, where it is blessed by the archbishop. On the day of the race, jockeys lead their horses to the altars of their respective *contrada*'s chapels, where a priest blesses the horse and jockey in a brief ceremony. The races are chaotic affairs in which jockeys beat their horses and often each other with whips. Injuries and bribery are commonplace. The conclusions of the races bring revelry for the victors, weeping for the losers, and often fighting between them. Members of a losing *contrada* have been known to hunt down their own jockey and beat him if they were convinced he had been bribed or otherwise had not done all he could do to win.

Even patron saints are not granted immunity from the crowd's vengeance. Once, having endured a long losing streak, the *contrada* of Chioccola tossed a statue of the patron saint of horses, St. Anthony, down a well in disgust, earning them the name of "*affograsanti*," literally, "the drowners of saints." Thirty years later the contrada was still without a win to its credit. A group of exasperated women of Chiocciola, sensing a connection between the dunking their ancestors had given St. Anthony and their string of bad luck at the *palio*, rescued the statue from the well. Chiocciola won the next *palio*.[20]

CHALLENGES TO AN AMBIVALENT CHURCH

The church's orientation toward sports in the Middle Ages was the culmination of accommodation that had taken place centuries earlier. Debates over precisely what "conversion" meant in terms of personal conduct had raged much earlier in the fourth century. As historian Ramsey Mac-Mullen describes it: "It [was] not easy to trace the boundaries around behaviors that marked a person as a tolerable member of the church and everything else as alien."[21] Thus, for the conscientious Christian the age-old issue was whether the contexts and festivals in which sports were so frequently embedded could be sufficiently dissociated from their pagan religious overtones to make them acceptable forms of entertainment for Christians, or whether the pagan worldview was so intricately entwined with them that they required wholesale repudiation by the church. Certainly in the minds of some fourth-century Christians, the circus, the horse races, and other festival games were merely secular institutions, indifferent with respect to any specific religion and hence nonthreatening to the underpinnings of the believer's faith. (Historian Ronald Hutton claims that by the dawn of the Middle Ages, Christians who kept these and other customs may have had little notion that by carrying on these activities they were commemorating older deities.[22]) So it was that Constantine and his Christian successors came to the conclusion that it was possible to view festival games apart from their pagan trappings, so long as the schedules of the festivals didn't conflict with those of the church. But others, including the great Augustine, disagreed.

Augustine had a different view. His largely negative opinion of the public sport spectacles seemed to have been shaped in part by the bitter schisms that developed around the issue, dividing not only Christians from non-Christians, but dividing Christians who attended popular spectacles and theaters from those who thought attending sinful. Feelings on the issue ran so high in Augustine's hometown of Carthage that a group of Christians, incensed with the government's accommodation of pagan cultural trappings, rioted, sacking the imperial statues and shaving the regilded beard from a statue of Hercules. The emperor punished the city by closing the theaters and circuses, which John Chrysostom thought hardly punishment at all: "For what is there that is harsh about them [the punishments]? That the emperor has shut the orchestra and forbidden the hippodrome—that he has stopped up these founts of iniquity?"[23]

Apparently Augustine's early position on sports was ambivalent; before the riots he had gently reminded his congregation that festivals "are to be tolerated and not loved," and urged them to "abstain as far as you can, from worthless spectacles." But with the violent disruptions of civil order threatening the foundations of the community (between 399 and 401), he was forced to choose sides. Though mindful of the beneficial ways in which public sport spectacles could, in Markus' words, promote "a cohesion of human wills" and, much like sports in modern times, reinforce a secular sense of community and add a measure of stability to society, he ultimately adopted a hard line on the spectacles in hopes of bringing an end to the civil strife.[24] He accused congregants who were attending the festival games of offending their weaker brothers and being stumbling blocks to pagans who might be searching for the truth. Those about to be admitted to the church were warned that "by going to the shows you will be exposed, O Christian, your cover will be blown, when you profess one thing and do another . . . not keeping faith with your profession." In prophetic tones, he announced that the Lord would come not to bring peace but a sword "which would separate the Christian, not only from his pagan family and friends," but from his "evil habits," and the evil habits included "rejoicing with the impious, drinking, feasting, theatres and spectacles."[25] Later, after the Vandals had invaded Carthage and apocalyptic doom permeated the air, Augustine was flabbergasted that even in the face of imminent destruction Christians continued to be drawn to the circus.[26]

As ascetics gained a foothold in the cities and churches in the fifth and sixth centuries, monastic life, with its emphasis on personal holiness, came to be widely respected as a model for the Christian community. Accordingly, positions on worldly amusements tightened even more. From Antioch, Severus railed against the passions excited by the chariot races and trembled at the specter of Christians employing the voice that they had earlier had used to praise God in church to "utter demonic words at the spectacle." He condemned the luxury and money that was spent on the public shows and games and worried about the partisan feelings stimulated by the races. From Gaul, theologian Caesarius of Arles denounced the "furious, bloody or shameful spectacles," and bade "those who resort to the circus, the theatre or the hunt to dispel sadness or anxiety . . . to turn inward for true divine consolation."[27] Salvian, a charismatic Gallic priest who had renounced his family to live in the desert, heaped scorn on the Roman shows and games, associating them with all forms of vice and all kinds of demons. Salvian was especially revolted that professing Christians were forsaking church services to attend the games.[28]

Yet Salvain, Severus, and Caesarius hardly spoke for the entire church because many congregations remained divided on the issue of the games. One could always find scattered rebukes by seventh- and eighth-century monks and ascetics who believed that dance and play inappropriately glorified corruptible bodies, encouraged idleness, and provoked unjustifiable jest. But to portray the church as unstinting in its loathing of sports, as some have done, ignores the fact that monks in some orders such as the Jesuits were fairly lenient in their appraisals, especially of recreational sport. In Provence, ascetics didn't appear to object to the games so long as Christians didn't miss church services on feast days; yet at about the same time, John of Ephesus was describing a chariot racetrack erected in Antioch as "a church of Satan." While Augustine was warning the newly baptized in his African church to renounce the shows and spectacles, public spectacles were being financed by the Christian Ostrogothic government in Italy. The spectacles eventually died, not because of ecclesiastic disapproval, but because public funds began to be invested in cathedrals and charity work rather than in circuses and games.[29]

By the twelfth and thirteenth centuries, the church was challenged not only by the tournaments but by the games and sports played on the village greens. Pastimes that destroyed property and bodies could hardly be shoehorned into a Christian theological framework. Others were concerned that the atmosphere permeating many of the town sports too often stirred the soul in unchristian ways. One fifteenth-century bishop pleaded for the banning of *la soule* "because of the ill feeling, rancor and enmities, which in the guise of recreative pleasure, accumulate in many hearts, give baleful occasion for hatreds to arise." One of his contemporaries, Florentine Archbishop Antoninus, who tolerated watching athletics (provided they "did not mock religion"), was vehemently opposed to watching violent sports of his day, not simply because they defaced the bodies of participants, but for their insidious effects on the human sensibilities of those who watched—the same reasons that fifteenth-century Spanish Catholic Pedro Covarrubias had condemned bullfighting and Augustine had condemned attendance at hunting outings.[30]

In many ways, the church found it easier to adopt a firm stand against the tournaments than against village sports played by parishioners, if only because many of the village sports were an integral part of medieval church life. Not only did the church sponsor the festivals at which many of the contests took place; its courtyards provided some of the best places to play games as well. In the twelfth century, *jeu de paume* was being played in the cloistered area of churchyards. In fact, some historians credit the rectangular dimensions of the cloistered area as having determined the rectangular shape of the tennis court.[31] In some fifteenth-century French churches, *jeu de paume,* now played with racquets rather than the palm of the hand, became such an important part of church life that congregations incorporated it into annual rituals. At some churches, for example, it was the custom for the bishop each Easter Sunday, after treating the parish to a meal of white pigeon and pastries, to lead a grand procession to his palace, where the congregation in turn would present him with an expensive pair of tennis racquets and some tennis balls. The ceremony wasn't taken lightly. When one sixteenth-century parish surprised the bishop by substituting a cheap pair of batons instead of the regular racquets in the annual rite, the bishop was outraged. He brought suit and won the case.[32]

In many districts, far from being viewed as contemptuous encroachments on religion, sports were accepted as easy companions of Sunday worship. Following the Sunday service parishioners might meet in the churchyards or cloistered areas for ball games or for *la soule* on the expansive venues of church-owned meadows. In some districts church officials were known to vie with noblemen for the right to "put the ball in play" before games, and in some regions, elaborate ceremonies were designed around the presentation of the ball before games were held. Competitions often were arranged between parishes, especially in *la soule;* these competitions were perhaps an early version of church league sports.[33]

These intercongregational contests could spin off into mayhem. In 1222, the seneschal (assistant) of the abbot of Westminster, riled by a defeat of his cathedral's wrestling team by a church from the surrounding district, plotted revenge by arranging a rematch and stacking his team with some "strong and skillful wrestlers, that he might gain the victory." Apparently, the matches weren't going quite the way the seneschal had hoped. The chronicler reports that the seneschal and his henchmen, "who sought revenge rather than sport, without any reason flew to arms, and severely beat the citizens, who had come unarmed, causing blood-shed among them."[34] In retrospect, modern-day ministers who wring their hands at the indignities that so often mar church-league sports can at least be reassured that they are not struggling with a new problem: anger, hostility, and occasional violence in church sports have a long, if not glorious, tradition.

In their official appraisal of the appropriateness of church-affiliated sports, even the more violent ones, clergy were not entirely unbiased because the proceeds from the festivals at which sports were played went directly into parish coffers. In fact, says historian Ronald Hutton, the "summer games," especially those held in the countryside, "were the largest single source of parochial revenue."[35] As a result, local priests may not have been as motivated to reign in Shrove Tuesday football or the mock battles played under the aegis of the church as were their ecclesiastic superiors. Some older, class-conscious priests did denounce what they saw as the sacrilegious custom of freewheeling young clerics who lowered themselves to play with their congregations in the often brutal game of *la soule*. Young priests also were commonly scolded by their ecclesiastical superiors for playing *jeu de paume* "without shame, in their undershirts, not decently dressed."[36]

Despite the pickiness of older clergy, many congregations and priests were supportive of village sports, conscious of their importance in sustaining public sentiment toward the parish. Thus it was that the church became less a critic and more an abettor of sports. Behind even the most sanctimonious and fiery denunciation of sports lurked the thinly veiled acknowledgment that, in the final analysis, public demand, not ecclesiastical edicts, would rule the day.

THEOLOGICAL DISCOURSES ON SPORT AND PLAY

As a rule, the attacks on sports by priests tended to revolve around practical rather than theological issues. Complaints were more likely to center on broken church windows from *jeu de paume* players, shirtless priests sweating with the laity, and noisy disturbances from Sunday morning games that were contested in the churchyard during Sunday mass than on spiritual or moral concerns. Played out against this backdrop of tension between sports and the local church and ecclesiastical authorities—and in a sense, completely independent of it—was a lively theological dialogue spanning the Renaissance that went to core issues about play and attempted to explain how it fit within the Christian life. While there is no indication that this theorizing had a significant impact on Christian conduct, it does offer insight into the thinking of some of the keenest theological minds of the time about the place of sports and recreation in the Christian life. Some of the most influential texts on the topic, for example, were authored by members of the esteemed thirteenth-century Parisian faculty of theology, a barometer of the seriousness with which leading theologians of the day, unlike their modern-day counterparts, took the human experiences of the playground.[37]

Theological opinions in the church formed an arc stretching from Chrysostom's early reminder to his congregation that "it is not God who gives us the chance to play, but the devil," to sixth-century Pope Gregory the Great's labeling of "inane rejoicing" as a vice connected with gluttony, to Thomas Aquinas' thirteenth-century teaching that play, under the right conditions, actually could be virtuous, to the fifteenth-century writings of Spanish Catholic Francisco de Alcocer, for whom playing for pleasure or gain, while possibly a pretext for sin, was not inherently sinful in itself. Bolstered by the Aristotlean notion of *eutropelia* (literally, "well-turning," the mean between playing to excess and not playing at all), theological discourses almost always underscored the importance of moderation. Some begrudgingly gave sport its due, although not without moralistic sniping at the many excesses wrought in its name. Some remained steadfast in their belief that play could never be virtuous because it was too easy; true virtue, they said, required effort. By the mid-sixteenth century, the trend of Christian theologians seemed to lean toward accepting sports, at least those played informally. Indicative of this were two books published by cardinals that afforded sports and games a place in the Christian life, one vigorously rejecting the asceticism of some of the monastic orders in favor of spontaneous open-air exercises such as riding, javelin throwing, and ball playing, and the other suggesting that games could be used to train character and develop "grace of body," although it severely condemned dancing.[38]

Most theologians found little fault with skillful, expressive movement per se. Dance, for example, had been featured in early Christian
liturgies, something evident in the early writings of both Justin Martyr
(AD 150) and Hippolytus (AD 200). In the fourth century, even the stern
Chrysostom, while violently opposed to sport spectacles, instructed his
parishioners to dance to the glory of God as a way of "revealing your
souls to the musical instruments on which the Holy Spirit plays when
he instills his grace into your hearts." This embrace of dance had great
eschatological significance, notes theologian Hugo Rahner, for it was "a
secret preparatory exercise for the object of their longing, the dance of
everlasting life." It was only as the dances became sexually charged that
the church moved to eliminate them from the liturgies.[39]

Along with dance, the metaphor of play also figured prominently in
theological discourse. The act of creation often was referred to as a playful act by God; his creatures were spoken of as his "toys." The pious life
was described as a "playful spirit" or portrayed as a willingness to be "a
plaything of God." Others considered play to be the human experience
most closely resembling the experience of heaven, something hinted
at in the messianic vision of boys and girls playing in the streets of the
eternal city recorded in Zechariah 8:5. A particularly poignant use of the
metaphor was found in the diary written by the martyr Saturus who, in
a vision, witnessed two Carthaginian martyrs, Perpetua and Felicitas,
as they were ushered into heaven. After they had been carried to the
throne flanked by four elders who lovingly stroked their cheeks, they
were welcomed to heaven with the words: "*Ite et ludite*—go and play!"
Then Saturus says to Perpetua: "Now thou hast what thou didst desire,"
and Perpetua responds: "Thanks be to God! I was merry in the flesh, now
here I am merrier still!" Although these saintly visions of play no doubt
helped pilgrims understand their place in the divine plan, there is no
record of them having been used to shape, in any substantial way, Christian thinking on the issue of sport and play in the here and now.[40]

One of the sticking points that prevented large-scale Christian
ecclesiastical endorsement of sport was the seeming incompatibility
between Christian teaching on the need for believers to be good stewards of their time (a godly gift) and carving out blocks of time to engage
in what was considered largely frivolous activity. The ethic of conserving
and investing personal time in worthy pursuits had a long history both
within and outside of the church. Arcangeli notes that far from being a
Calvinistic invention, the notion was prevalent in early monastic orders

just as surely as it was in sixteenth-century English Puritan thinking when William Prynne lambasted the dance and theater as "the prodigall mispence of much precious time," and Puritan Richard Baxter decried "needless and inordinate games" as "thieves or time-wasters to be watchfully avoided."[41] One of the counterclaims used against this line of argument was the more optimistic (yet hardly celebratory) notion that games, sports, and play should be allowed because they distracted attention from more lurid enticements. The more vigorous forms were also thought to dissipate the pool of physical energy that otherwise might have been tapped to indulge in yet more sinful pursuits. Cardinal Giovanni di Domenici, for example, was of the opinion that exhausting sports like football could have a cathartic effect on hormone-ravaged youth by cooling their hot blood.[42]

Whereas the practical consideration of military preparedness had been the church's fallback position on dueling and the public spectacles of jousting tournaments, in time therapeutic and educational benefits became the defense of informal sports and play, thanks in no small part to a flood of writing by Italian renaissance educators who had begun to allow a place for physical education in their curricula. Sport was a very hot topic: between 1450 and 1650, more than eighty books dealing with some aspects of sport were published in Italy. Progressive thinkers such as Vittorino de Feltre and Leone Alberti, inspired by the Athenian ideal of harmonious development of the whole person, preached the importance of a physical education as a way of developing the body. "Games and exercises which develop the muscular activities and the general carriage of the person should be encouraged by every teacher," said Aeneas Sylvius Piccolomini, who eventually became Pope Pius II.[43] In the thirteenth-century, English Franciscan Alexander of Hales reached the conclusion that play and sports were not inherently immoral, arguing that they helped people rebalance their tempers, improve their character, and develop physical strength. Three hundred years later, in a book titled *Introduction to a Devout Life*, Bishop of Geneva Françis de Sales devoted three chapters to sport, recreation, and pastimes, recommending that sports such as tennis and stoolball and games such as chess be given a place in the devout life because they increase the "industrie of the mind" and "nimbleness of the body."[44]

Yet not all theologians thought such arguments were convincing. Seventeenth-century Jansenist theologian Jean Baptiste Thiers, for example, argued that if the purpose of play and games was to refresh and restore people so they could return to their farms and shops with renewed vigor, then it clearly belonged to the sphere of work. And, said Thiers, if work is essential only because of the curse brought on by Adam's sin as described in the book of Genesis, then far from being a divinely implanted impulse to help humans express their relationship to the Creator, "play and amusements have become necessary for us because of sin." Had not Adam sinned in the garden, said Thiers, there would have been no need for sport, play, or entertainment. On the whole, it was hardly a ringing endorsement for the role of sports in the Christian life.[45]

The enthusiasm for justifying sports on these utilitarian grounds may have been a reflection of a medieval theological mind that was impatient with self-indulgence, and playing simply for the fun of it seemed such an outrageously self-indulgent act that it was impossible to ignore completely the obvious joy found in play. Thus, a bevy of theological treatises weighed in on whether or not sports could be played merely for enjoyment, and if so, the form that this enjoyment should take. Laughter, frivolity, and jest were inseparable companions of play and games and many theologians found the line separating the joys of sport and those derived from attending the theater or watching the antics of traveling comedians (which were usually frowned upon) not all that distinct. Others, like Alexander of Hales, one of the earliest clerics to examine seriously sport's effect on the soul, painstakingly distinguished enjoyment derived from play that is therapeutic in its effects (and thus "morally neutral") from enjoyment that derives from a "dissolute disposition of the mind" (always sinful) and the preferred type that springs from "a spiritual mirth of the soul" (such as David's dance before the ark).[46]

Thomas Aquinas, whose career blossomed in the twilight of Alexander's life, addressed the issue in *Summa Theologica*. His conditional approval of play and games as a feature of the Christian life paved the way for an increasingly open attitude of the church on the issue.[47] Not only did he assert that play could be lawful, but he ventured that under some circumstances it could be virtuous. As a devotee of Aristotle, such an assertion put him in a difficult position. On one hand he agreed with Aristotle that play is *autotelic* (self-ending)—that is, that play is something one does only for the pleasure it brings and not for some external end. Yet he also adopted the Aristotelian position that there can be no virtue in an activity that doesn't have an identifiable end beyond itself.[48] If play is an autotelic activity, and autotelic activities cannot be virtuous, how was it possible to hold to a position that games can be virtuous? Using a bit of slick open-field running, Aquinas accepted Aristotle's definition of play (agreeing that pleasure and nothing else is the end of play) while at the same time arguing that this pleasure produces its own extrinsic effects, namely "recreation and rest of the soul." Thus play properly is directed to nothing outside of itself save the enjoyment it brings, but the enjoyment it brings can reap benefits for the soul.

In saying this, Aquinas was stopping well short of suggesting that a game had *intrinsic* virtue, that its spiritual value lay in its capacity to rehearse religious themes or vivify spiritual metaphors. The pleasures of play became redeemable on the strength of their usefulness. Like sleep and other kinds of rest, play and games were lawful because "there was a kind of rest associated with games." Yet it was significant that Aquinas believed that the benefits of play extended beyond the body to restore the soul. Hard intellectual work, even religious contemplation, can exhaust the soul; the remedy "must needs consist in the application of some pleasure, by slackening the tension of the reason's study" (*Summa Theologica*, question 168). In some ways this was a recitation of the therapeutic view offered earlier by Alexander of Hales, but by stressing the connection between play and spiritual refreshment, Aquinas had left ajar the door for contact between the joys of play and spiritual health.

Commentators of the day struggled to distinguish between types of sports and games that could and could not be incorporated into the Christian life, often devising elaborate classification systems to frame their analyses. Most were elaborations on Aquinas' and Alexander's ideas. Many followed what Arcangeli labels the "devil-man-god scheme." In a typical system, the lowest rung (*ex diabolica suggestione*) was occupied by recreations which were intrinsically sinful, such as "indecent spectacles and violent sports" that posed a threat to life, as well as games of chance. The highest (*magna devotione*) included saintly recreations that were religious in character or that could convey a religious message. The middle ground (*humana recreatione*) included all of those morally neutral activities done as a way to relax and refresh or to amuse oneself, including children's games and physical exercise.[49] Most sports fit within the range of "neutral" or "morally indifferent" activities whose sinfulness depended almost entirely on the intentions of the players or the circumstances surrounding their performances.

This notion that sport represented a morally neutral ground provided a vast landscape for spirited debate on its place in the Christian life. Aquinas' view of sports and games had been entirely conditional.

Some forms of play were sinful by their very "species." These included games and amusements that were "discourteous, insolent, scandalous and obscene" and those involving "indecent words and deeds such as are injurious to [their neighbors]."[50] But used to refresh the soul and exercise the body, games could be virtuous. Avoiding excess and bad intentions was the way to avoid turning play into sin. Moral restraint was absolutely essential; games should be played with "an upright mind" rather than a spirit of license or "absolute freedom." Furthermore, the circumstances surrounding play should "befit the hour and the man." Finally, play should be governed by principles of moderation and reason; an excessive attachment to play, such as "when a man prefers the pleasure he derives [from play] to the love of God, so as to be willing to disobey a commandment of God or of the Church rather than forego, such like amusements," is a mortal sin.[51]

Aquinas thus echoed the sentiments of Alexander of Hales and others who worried about the effect of sports and theatrical performances on the dispositions of spectators. Casual forms of watching (*in transitu*) were permissible, said Alexander, but deliberate and persistent watching (*inspection studiosa*) could induce a person to mortal sin. Aquinas did his share of hand-wringing over sex and violence in public performances too, but he didn't condemn attendance at public entertainments altogether; he was content to warn Christians to be careful, reminding them that such occasions represent a risk to Christian conduct and character. By the fifteenth century Antoninus had taken the issue a step further, distinguishing between three categories of spectator entertainments: at one level were spectacles forbidden by law, such as tournaments and duels; at another level were spectacles not expressly forbidden but which included obscenities; and third, spectacles he described as "vain and amusing" (such as watching athletic games) which were not condemned providing they did not "mock religion."[52]

By and large, the discourse was never as tolerant of watching sports as it was of playing them. In a fifteenth-century moral treatise, Alexander Carpenter ranked the impulses associated with watching athletic games no higher than second in a four-category classification of motivations, although sports watching fared better in Carpenter's scheme than did gambling, watching comedians, or attending the dance and theater. Nevertheless, sport lacked the clear and unequivocal blessings given to games driven by the highest impulses, including chess.

The debates continued well into the sixteenth century, when Juan Luis Vives, the Spanish Catholic protégé of Erasmus, penned his universal plea for peace among Christians (*De Concordia et Discordia in Humano Genere*). In it he bitterly opposed violence paraded under the banner of sports. Vives also rejected the notion that sports could be justified as a means of preparing young men for the military. In another pamphlet (*Linguae Latinae Exercitatio*), he set forth six laws that should govern play. Sport for the Christian, said Vives, should aim at refreshing those weary of mind and body and continue until that weariness is dispelled. He approved of sport that risks no "danger of quarreling or fighting," sport that includes an element of skill rather than mere chance (although he allowed for a modest "stake" to increase the zest of a game), and sport in which players win or lose with "absolute equanimity" and in which the players remain throughout the game "companion[s], cheerful, jovial and mirthful" without "any trace of deceit, or sordidness or avarice."[53]

Virtually every endorsement of play was hedged with stern warnings about excess, yet the trend of theological commentary across the Middle Ages was to give play greater and greater latitude. Arcangeli notes that, by the eve of the Reformation, the confessional treatises of the period trended toward justifying sport more than stigmatizing it, something some of the reformers ultimately were to denounce as "typical of Catholic low moral standards." In the fifteenth century, a bishop would urge his flock "not only to participate in the more important acts of worship . . . but also those for relaxation and pleasure." And by the sixteenth century, a Dominican would proclaim that play was not only lawful, but virtuous, and a cardinal would refer to it as "holy."[54]

SPORT AS WORSHIP

As a rule, sports had only tentative attachments to the churches' spiritual missions or to individual or corporate expressions of faith. But for a short period of time in certain regions of Europe, sport-like rituals became part of the liturgy. These attempts to link sports with liturgy and church ceremony appear to have been short lived and had their roots in pagan cults. Some popular ball and stick games, for example, may have originated as Egyptian cultic rites. They were introduced by churches in Spain and southern France and played at Christian Easter festivals. The practice of separating players of *la soule* into opposing teams, each representing separate regions of the area, may have been borrowed from the Moors.[55]

At some point during the Middle Ages, the ball, thought to date back to 2000 BC where it symbolized the head of the Egyptian god Osiris, passed into Christian hands as a symbol of the resurrection and became part of the Easter liturgy in churches. In approximately the same era that the Mayans of Meso-America were symbolically reenacting mythical forces of good and evil on their enormous ballcourt at Chichen Itza, Catholic priests were practicing their own symbolic ball liturgies. In France in the city of Auxerre during the twelfth century, it was customary for the dean of the chapel to perform a sacral ballgame-dance (the *pelota*) on Easter day across the labyrinth of the floor of the cathedral. The ceremony was enacted with great pomp and ceremony. A newly inducted canon would hand a ball to the dean, who, clad in flashy garments and chanting and dancing to a liturgical hymn, would lead a procession down the aisle of the church. During the procession dancers would pass a ball back and forth, all the while keeping step to the music played by the organ. The ritual passing of the ball may have symbolized for pagans the changing course of the sun throughout the year; for the dancing priests it may have represented the course of the incarnate Christ: his death, burial, and resurrection as the Christ-Sun at Easter.[56] Another dance and ball game played by French bishops and clergy on Easter evenings in the choir of the church is thought to have expressed "an attitude towards the immortality of a future heavenly existence." On Easter Mondays, the people would assemble at the archbishop's palace for a meal, where "the tables, having been duly set with allspice, wine, and food, a formal meal was taken, after which the Archbishop threw a ball amongst the assembled people who promptly played a game of ball."[57]

The tradition of liturgical ball games may have begun as far back as the ninth century, when parishioners of Saint Maria Major in Naples were said to have "celebrated every year in this church certain games of ball [*percula*] for the comfort and refreshment of the soul." Not much is known about the games played in Naples, but one historian believes that they were ceremonial, were played in the church edifice itself, and were justified as having a religious or spiritual purpose. Parishioners in some English churches also played a game that was laden with religious symbolism. It involved hurling balls over the roof of the church on Easter day, a practice one chronicler thought to have been Christianized by the church in the hope of transforming it "by appropriation to the divine service, into a symbol of Christ himself, the rising Easter-sun."[58]

To what extent competition played an important part in these ceremonies is not known. What does seem clear is that at one point ball
games were played as a way of reifying certain religious myths, and in
this regard they represent the single instance in the history of the church
in which a significant element in the Christian community accepted
sport-like activities as possessing intrinsic symbolic religious merit. For
ancient pagans, sports had been virtually inseparable from religious
rituals. Perhaps it is better stated this way: the pagan community had
sensed the rather natural way playing games could express and affirm
religious realities. In standing firm against paganism, the early church
defined itself not only in opposition to pagan games but also against
the idea that game playing could be religious expression. As a result, the
Christian community secularized sports early on, separating them from
religion in a way that ancients would not have understood. Thus, this
short-termed medieval appropriation of sport as part of a liturgy represented something of a watershed in the conceptions of the role of sport
in the Christian life, a point at which, given different circumstances, the
church might have welcomed sport as a legitimate means for expressing
Christian faith and belief. The one chance that the church had to embrace
sport and to value it as an adjunct to spiritual expression fell victim to a
variety of cares and concerns that had little to do with sport per se. What
vestiges of sympathy for appropriating play as religious expression that
might have remained were overwhelmingly extinguished by the reformers and Puritans, who ensured that the irrepressible appeal of sports to
the souls and affections of believers always would take place outside the
orbit of the church's influence.

3

BOWLING, BICYCLES, AND OTHER SNARES OF THE DEVIL

The Protestant Reformation severed the relationship that had existed between the medieval church and sports, games, and popular culture. Sports had been so entangled with the liturgical calendar and religious celebration that reformers found it almost impossible to distinguish between the two. For many, rejecting the Catholic festivals of May Day and Carnival, feast days sponsored by trade groups held in honor of saints, and the Sunday afternoon festivities involving gambling and dancing necessarily meant rejecting the sports that were also part of the events. Still, the stereotypical characterization of the reformers as arch-antagonists to all of popular culture—killjoys who engineered a wholesale abolition of sports along with the drunkenness, sexual license, violence, and rowdiness that had played such a part in Catholic holidays and festivals and village recreations—is no longer taken for granted by historians.[1]

Opinion on matters related to sport, pleasure, and the body varied widely among the splintered Protestant sects. Some were more opposed to sports than others, but generally not as opposed as certain Christian humanists who came before (e.g., Erasmus) or as the English Puritans who came after the Reformation. Opinion also was subject to change over time. For example, play was an important feature of life in the Netherlands during the florescence of Calvinism but was banned

73

later. For the most part, reforming sects didn't identify their differences on the basis of their positions on play and amusement; the one possible exception was the rather united position of Lutherans, who "showed a predominant orientation towards the tolerance of popular pastimes." Historian C. G. Coulton may have exaggerated in saying, "when we come across 16th or 17th century clerics dealing with popular sports it would be very difficult to decide on internal evidence whether the writer was on the Roman or non-Roman side," but it is equally unwarranted to speak of a generalized "Reformation" position on the matter of sports.[2]

LUTHER AND CALVIN

In a work of this sort it is impossible to capture fully the variegated opinions on sport during this period. The influential views of Martin Luther and John Calvin, men of exceptional talent and insight who were at the forefront of the theological revolution, can serve as typologies, but again, they probably do not capture the range of opinions held by preachers in the movement.

Luther's rough-hewn character lent itself to sports; in many ways his thinking followed that of earlier Catholic theologians who valued sport only insofar as it could be shown to be useful. Luther was fond not only of music, but of fencing and wrestling as well. The former, he claimed, "drives gloom from the heart and the other gives full development to the limbs." He loved gymnastics because they exercised the lungs and promoted health, essential if the hard work of Christian service was to be realized. But like Cardinal di Domenici, he considered them especially important for their powers of catharsis and distraction. "The ultimate objective [of sports]," said Luther, "is to keep us from lapsing into other activities—drinking, wenching, gambling—as we can already see happening (for shame!) in our courts and cities." It was largely a defensive rather than a celebratory position. If sports are rejected out of hand, he said, other more reprehensible activities will take their place.[3]

Martin Bucer, the brave intermediary between battling reformist sects, also had an open mind on physical recreations, as did the Italian reformer Peter Martyr. Luther's contemporary, Ulrich Zwingli, may have been the most ardent sport supporter among the reformers. In his treatise on the Christian education of youth, Zwingli "allowed" games played with one's companions "provided they are games that require skill and serve to train the body." In Zwingli's view, these included running, jumping, stone throwing, putting the shot, and wrestling, although he urged special caution with wrestling "for some have made earnest of the exercise and have turned it into a fight."[4]

John Calvin, generally regarded as the theological giant of the Reformation, was an austere man who lived a life of self-denial and stern moral discipline. He was a workaholic who began his dictation early in the morning and maintained a hectic schedule of lecturing, preaching, and reading late into the evening. He is said to have slept little and rarely set aside time for relaxation and recreation. His stern theology was used to justify severe punishment for citizens of Geneva who violated his strict ethical and theological teachings. Whatever might have been his considerable personal and ecclesiastic strengths, he could hardly be considered an embodiment of playfulness.

Yet his theology was not one that can be championed by spoilsports. In theory, Calvinism assigned vocational and avocational pursuits to a sphere of life called the *adiaphora*, "the things indifferent," in which the Christian's conscience was to hold sway; discernment was to be guided by general principles gleaned from the Scriptures. At least in its narrow bearing on the issue of sport and play, the *adiaphora* was not appreciably different from the opinions of Alexander of Hales, Aquinas, and other Catholic theologians in concluding that sports and play were "morally indifferent." Calvin taught that Christians were at liberty not only to use but to enjoy the pleasures of the present world, providing no offense was brought to weaker believers and acts were done with a clear Christian conscience for the purpose of bringing glory to God. But many of the sports and recreations of the day furnished indisputable evidence that pleasurable pursuits, even those from the hand of God, could be abused if left unchecked by Christian discipline. To Calvin's way of thinking, the risks of abusing some types of play far outweighed the dangers of infringing on Christian liberty. If he was to err, he would err on the conservative side. Accordingly, the theater was forbidden on grounds that the plays shown there bred adultery. Card playing was prohibited on grounds that it wasted time. The *Laws of Geneva* outlawed "drunkenness, dissolutions, excess, arrogancy, and insolency, plays or games, idle running from house to house . . . dissensions, fighting or brawling, injuring of others." Dancing remained a target of Calvin's preaching until the end of his life.[5]

But as to the quiet playing of recreational games, Calvin had a much more lenient view. Provided they were not abused, some forms of play and sport were permitted, not simply on the Lutheran grounds that they were useful in restoring players for more serious work, but because the mere pleasure of playing was seen as a valuable end in itself. In a departure from medieval theologies that had accepted sports only as they could prove useful, Calvin opened the door to seeing more expressive possibilities in sports and recreation. "In the acceptance of the present life," he said, "we must remember that it is given us not only to use but to enjoy. It is obviously the natural order of things that we should indulge in taking pleasure from those things which God has given us liberally to enjoy." For example, in discussing wine, Calvin said that it was lawful to use wine (indeed, on at least one occasion the Council in Geneva presented him with a barrel of wine as a token of friendship), not only in cases of necessity, "but to make us merry." Although secular music serves enjoyment rather than need, "it ought not to be judged of no value; still less should it be condemned," unless of course it is music "that degrades, that corrupts good manners [and] flatters the flesh."[6]

It was the opinion of Calvin scholar Henry Van Til that "the court of conscience" represented by Calvin's *adiaphora* was sufficiently spacious to accommodate golf and recreational sports in general. Others have noted that Calvin played darts, threw quoits in his garden, and played other games in his living room, although the record shows that "these indulgences seldom proceeded from his own suggestion," and that "always they were briefly enjoyed." Surprisingly, even though he and the Consistory at Geneva meted out severe punishments to those who played sports during the Sunday services, Calvin apparently wasn't against playing on Sunday after services had been concluded. For example, John Knox, the Scottish founder of Presbyterianism, claims to have seen him bowling on Sunday afternoons.[7]

Thus historians such as Dennis Brailsford surely exaggerate when they describe Calvin as "at best suspicious of physical education and could, at worst, be interpreted as almost completely hostile." An oft-cited example of his distaste for sports was his recommendation that the recreation program for the Geneva Academy be organized "in such a way that all silly sports be avoided," but this can hardly be read as a blanket condemnation of sports. In this case Calvin was speaking as a school principal rather than as a theologian, and as modern physical education teachers can appreciate, principals often demand that order be maintained in their gymnasia. In this regard, modern school principals may be no less tolerant than was Calvin of "silly games" (unstructured and unregulated activity) in his gymnasia.[8]

Like all sources of pleasure, sport and play were to be allowed into the Christian lifestyle without unbridled excess and licentiousness on one hand or a rigorous asceticism on the other. Ultimately, the tempering ingredients were to be the Christian's desire to bring glory to God and a mindfulness of eternity. Christians were left to work out the implications of this in-the-world-but-not-of-the-world stance, possessing the good things of this life because they were offered from God, yet being careful not to become possessed by them in the process. In retrospect, Calvin had provided his evangelical progeny with the potential for a healthy and imaginative framework upon which to construct a sensible understanding of sports in culture.

English Puritans

Calvin and his contemporaries may not have been ardent sports enthusiasts, but they remained open to the possibilities of informal play in the life of the Christian. This changed in the post-Reformation era of second- and third-generation English Protestants in which theology and ethics were moved by a torrent of social and political currents. When the Puritans came to power, the fine balance that many reformers had managed to achieve in the duality of glorifying God through the service of work and glorifying him by finding pleasure in the gifts he had freely given was lost as the scales tipped decidedly in favor of work. In the Puritan worldview, the chief (and for some, the only) end of man was diligent pursuit of his calling in productive work. Time spent for no useful purpose was an illegal draft on one's account of God-given hours and minutes. A propensity for wasting time was not merely a character defect; it was evidence of a soul outside of the elect and thus doomed to perdition.

This moral scheme placed play on the opposite pole from work and, in light of work's sanctified status, separated play from that which was considered divine. Provided it could be shown to have physical benefits, play that was physically vigorous (and decorous) might be granted a pass on the question of "idleness"—the more arduous it was, the closer it came to resembling work and hence to being tolerated. Yet even in these cases play was suspect, a sinful distraction from a believer's diligent pursuit of his calling. Most moral critics didn't bother drawing such fine distinctions—all play was tainted with the curse of frivolity and spontaneity, doubly bad in the Puritan view because of the playful, idle lives of their nemesis, the wealthy gentry. "Be ashamed of idleness as thou art a man," wrote one Puritan writer, "but tremble at it as thou art a Christian." Those who gave in to the urge to pursue pastimes, said seventeenth-century Puritan Richard Baxter, were "thieves of time" whose actions signaled "an unsanctified, ungodly heart."[9]

Historian Michael Oriard has described spiritual autobiographies of the day that contained vivid accounts of conversion experiences in which turning away from the frivolity and wastefulness of sport and play was described as an important step in turning toward God.[10] The most famous of these was written by the great Puritan writer and minister John Bunyan, author of *Pilgrim's Progress*. After hearing a sermon on the evils of sports, Bunyan succumbed to the lure of the game of cat (thought to be a precursor to baseball) only to have its sinfulness revealed to him in a Damascus road–like experience of "a merciful working of God upon [his] soul." "Having struck it one blow from the hole, just as I was about to strike it a second time, a voice did suddenly dart from heaven into my soul, which said: 'Wilt thou leave thy sins and go to heaven or have thy sins and go to Hell?'" A vision of an angry Christ convinced him of the utter sinfulness of the game.[11] This epiphany notwithstanding, Bunyan soon fell off the play wagon, only to renounce sports altogether a few months later when he gave them up for service to God. This pattern of renouncing sports and "childish vanities" as part of a sinful, misspent youth, says Oriard, helped to reinforce in the Puritan mindset the sinfulness of sport and play: "If to turn to God is to turn away from play, then play, by extrapolation, is fundamentally sinful."[12]

The Calvinistic nod to enjoyments available through recreation and music as gifts from God was replaced by an emphasis on utility and work. (Obviously, seeds for such thinking had been planted in the writings of the reformers.) Consequently, even the harshest assessments of sport went hand in hand with the realization that most people needed some respite from work and daily stress. Left unexplained even by such prolific writers as pamphleteer Philip Stubbes was precisely how sports could be played "in the fear of God." But valuing sports as "refreshment" didn't necessarily mean that they should be enjoyed. They were an inescapable, regrettable fact of life. Biblical scholar and vicar William Burkitt, for example, wrote that "a wise and good Man perhaps could wish that his body needed no such Diversion, but finding his Body jade and tire, he is forced to give way to reason, and let Religion choose such Recreations as are healthful, short, recreative, and proper, to refresh both Mind and Body."[13]

Even though the Puritans recognized the need for physical recreation, the sticking points were always in the methods and the amount of time, energy, and resources that could legitimately be devoted to it. Burkitt, echoing the sentiments of medieval theologians and many of his contemporaries, taught that recreation should be approached in a spirit of moderation. The Christian also should be careful not to profane the Lord's Day and should avoid recreations such as duels and animal baitings that were inherently sinful. But above all, said Burkitt, the Christian is to ensure that his recreations are consistent with their *divine institution*, which is "the refreshing of the Mind, and Recreating of the Body, to make them both the fitter for the Service of God."[14] Playing was not so much a response to a divine urge or a way of experiencing one's faith in action as it was a divine gift granted for rejuvenating a weary body and assuaging the tiresome effects of labor. According to this line of thinking, if sports have any justification at all in the Christian life, it will be found in their practical utility.

Most sermons about sport and play were broadsides against specific sports, but one brave attempt by a Puritan thinker to lay out a comprehensive philosophy of sport, play, and recreation stood out from the rest. Richard Baxter's wide-ranging *A Christian Directory*, described by contemporary evangelical theologian J. I. Packer as "next to the Bible, the greatest Christian book ever written," lays out a clear and compelling definition of "lawful" sports and recreation. They are "the use of some Natural thing or action, not forbidden us, for the exhilaration of the natural spirits by the fantasie, and due exercise of the natural parts, there by to fit the body and mind for ordinary duty to God." It was unfortunate that in struggling to sketch out the factors that determined the "lawfulness" of recreations, Baxter, like most Puritans of his day, tended to qualify his nod toward sport and play with so many head-shaking restrictions that his more informative and helpful words on the topic tend to be ignored.[15]

First among Baxter's eighteen stipulations was that "the end which you really intend using it [sport and play], must be fit to you and for your service to God," which led him to the curious conclusion that *only Christians* are able to lawfully pursue sport and recreations, since their only moral justification is service to God. Those outside the fold cannot attach such a lofty spiritual goal to their play. Play that involves financial or emotional excess is not lawful, nor is play that mocks and makes "sport of holy things." The Christian's play should not wrong, defame, or reproach others and should not be obscene or entice others to sin. Baxter didn't reject watching sports outright, but bounded his recommendations with the prescription that it should not involve taking pleasure in watching "duelers, fighters, or any that abuse each other." Recreations that were too costly were also sinful. Finally, as a way of underscoring the importance of making even finer distinctions between sports, Baxter set this very high bar: the Christian is responsible for choosing "the most fitting and profitable" recreation among all possible, lawful recreations. Whoever chooses to participate in a sport or recreation, even though it is a lawful recreation, when "a fitter might be chosen," is guilty of sin.[16] It was a subtle yet prodigious tack that thrust what history has shown to be an unbearable load on the Christian conscience: the task of subjecting the nonseriousness of sports and recreations to serious spiritual scrutiny.

The notion that sport could be a legitimate feature of the Christian life only to the extent that it furthered good and practical ends and prepared players for God's service in the divine economy was hardly new, but it became more severe and concentrated in the sermonizing of English Puritans. When the litmus test for sports and play required players first and foremost to be useful in furthering the Lord's earthly ends, playing for mere enjoyment came under a dark shadow. Social historian Max Weber says that when play and sports "became purely a means of enjoyment, or awakened pride, or raw instincts as the irrational gambling instinct, [they were] of course strictly condemned." Baxter had made it clear that sports "used only to delight a carnal fantasy" with no other purposes "than to please the sickly mind that loveth them" were clearly out of bounds for the Christian.[17]

This work-oriented perspective on sports led more astute Puritans to see that if practical benefits were the God-ordained purpose of sports, then the benefits were most important. If the same benefits found in sports could be more efficiently found in other, less morally suspect activities, the Christian could hardly argue for sports on these same grounds. In spite of his lengthy dissertation recommending that sports be accepted into the Christian life, Baxter himself confessed that nobody really *needed* to play games; far better exercises could be found. As for himself, he preferred books and the company of friends for the mind, while he recreated his body with hard labor.[18]

Puritans rightly recognized that sport, like theater productions, novels, and most entertainments, thrived on illusion that took players to another world quite apart from their ordinary lives. With their peculiar rules, customs, and pretenses, sports deliberately manipulated the imagination. In the world of play emotions ruled. Complete surrender to the illusionary world of play, allowing oneself to be separated from the life of everyday responsibility, seemed to Puritans a very dangerous thing for the Christian to do. Games seemed naturally to militate against moderation; they put players' emotions and behavior on an uncharted course. "Now, who is so grossly blind, that seeth not that [some recreations] not only withdraw us from godliness and virtue, but also hail and allure us to wickedness and sin?" asked Stubbes.[19]

Put in modern terms, the Puritan question was how participants could keep the illusionary world of sports from shaping ethical perspective, how players could resist the urge to blow the game out of proportion, a question as relevant in the twenty-first century as it was in the seventeenth. Even those sports not judged to be inherently sinful in themselves posed risks to the Christian conscience. The key to successfully handling this journey into the illusionary world of sports, of course, was to avoid what Aquinas and his contemporaries had called "excess," but specific prescriptions on how this could be done were conspicuously absent from the discourses of the Puritan clergy. In the Puritan mind, the solution was to approach games less with a spirit of release and freedom and more as a tightrope to be walked with vigilance and sternness of purpose, one cautious step following another lest balance be lost and the soul, pushed by the emotional pitch of sports and pulled by the invitation of Satan himself, fall into the pit of hell.

The Puritans needed walk no further than their village squares to gather evidence of the way sports could distort Christian judgment. In the bragging and posturing of village louts just in from the football fields, the Puritans saw prideful arrogance, and they didn't like it. Although some stuffy clergy gave the opposite impression, on the whole Puritans eschewed prideful and arrogant behavior. In spiritual matters they were realists: the life of faith was a struggle and sin was a stubborn fact of human existence. The realization that anyone could fall at any time cultivated a deep respect for humility in social as well as spiritual matters. In John Bunyan's *Pilgrim's Progress*, Christian displayed a mild smile of achievement after exerting all of his strength to be the first to ascend a hill, but he immediately stumbled and had to be helped to his feet by Faithful, whom he had beaten to the top. It was Quaker preacher George Fox's contention that games such as "feasts, may-games, sports and plays trained people to vanity . . . and led them from the fear of God."[20] It may not have been fully developed in any of their broadsides against sports, but there was an underlying suspicion of competitive games on this account: they involved displays of mental and physical prowess which in themselves could become strong temptations to self-glory, boasting, and pride.

There were a litany of other things that rightly bothered the Puritans. A variety of sports that were popular at the time were ripe for criticism. Many were embedded in social contexts that couldn't have demonstrated more poignantly what the Puritans stood against. Jousting tournaments had been replaced by competitions in wrestling, footracing, marksmanship, and dueling, often attended by rambunctious and drunken crowds. Both the nobility and the clergy were known to have been irresponsibly addicted to tennis and handball, playing them when more serious work remained to be done. Although officially forbidden to lower classes, bowling, often associated with gambling and other vices, was played by the common people. Cudgeling—a sport involving fighting with heavy clubs—led to many a broken head. Football games between teams of hundreds of men from the lower classes ranged over vast territories. Historians have described these games as "closer to real fighting than modern sports," citing English society's generally "low threshold of repugnance 'with regard to witnessing and engaging in violent acts'" that held sway in society at large.[21] The so-called "blood sports"—unbearably cruel boxing matches in which men pummeled each other with fists until one of them could no longer stand, animal baiting in which a bull or bear would be chained to a stake and beaten with sticks and clubs by "players" or gnawed on by hysterical dogs, and cockfights and dogfights—all inflamed Puritan passions. Methodists and Quakers mounted especially strong campaigns against animal sports. Yet even after they had been officially banned, such sports remained popular in England until well into the nineteenth century, attracting people from all social and economic backgrounds. Even Elizabeth I was reported to have entertained the French ambassadors with bearbaiting and bullbaiting.

To their credit, the Puritans joined their archenemies, the Anglicans, in condemning the inhumane sports. No Puritan spoke out more bitterly against the Romanesque sports of his day than did Philip Stubbes. In a 191-page, nearly hysterical rant, Stubbes warned against being a party to animal baiting: "Though [animals] be bloody beasts to mankind, and seek his destruction, yet you are not to abuse them, for his sake who made them." He spoke even less kindly about football, which he considered more of "a bloody and murdering practice than a fellowy sport or pastime." "Is this a Christian dealing," he asked, "for one brother to maim and hurt another . . . is this to do to another as we would with another to do to us? . . . *God make us more careful over the bodies of our Brethren!*" (emphasis added). Stubbes conceded that bowling, along with dice and card games, might theoretically be legitimate recreational pursuits for the Christian, provided they were "used" moderately "and in the fear of God," but he couldn't help but warn that "a *good* Christian man will not so idly and vainly spend his golden days" (italics added).[22]

The Puritans may have had a pinched view of the world, but in their sermons and writings they dared to test the intersection of sports and play with the spiritual life. Generally speaking, they positioned sports within broader and more sophisticated frameworks than do modern Christians. A game was never just a game; it was part of a total patchwork of values to be evaluated in light of the faith claims made for life as a whole. The sports people played and how they played them signaled more than recreational preferences; they cut to the heart of their spiritual visions.

SPORTS ON SUNDAY

As much as the blood sports and rowdy entertainments—with their intrinsic cruelty, association with gambling, sordid social contexts, and pagan and Catholic origins—chafed the Puritan conscience, it was the fact that many of them were played on Sunday that really angered the Puritan clergy. In fact, hostility to sports being played on Sunday tainted the Puritan taste for sports in general. By banning sports on Sunday, says Oriard, "Puritan theology set play not just against work, but against piety."[23]

Nothing seems more foreign to the modern Christian community than the notion that sports should not be played or watched on Sunday, but such are the eroding effects of secularism. The idea had its genesis in objections to Sunday labor that reached far beyond Puritanism. Social and economic considerations, more than scriptural interpretation, led to the criminalization of Sunday play, even though the fourth commandment often was cited as a reason. Sunday rest simply made a great deal of economic sense. As the Puritans set out to purify the Church of England by ridding it of its largely agricultural, small-village, popish medieval holidays, they came down hard on the enormous number of Catholic feast days on which work was suspended for play. When these holidays were eliminated, the work week was automatically extended.

Consequently, enforcing Sunday rest not only seemed a humane thing to do, it ensured a more rested and productive work force. It also restrained industrious businessmen, caught up in cutthroat competition, from succumbing to self-destructive urges to work themselves and their employees to death.[24]

On its face, such a work-oriented view of the Sabbath might actually have pried open the door for Sunday sport and recreation. If *work* is forbidden on Sunday, surely its antithesis—*play*—should be welcomed. Some writers came close to reaching such a conclusion, one arguing that Sunday sport should be the right of "tradesmen and husbandmen" who work on the other six days, but these writers were not anxious to extend the privilege to the leisure class, "who for the most part make every day holiday in following sports."[25] Taking the opposing stance were those who argued that if restoration for work was the rationale for Sunday play, that is, if play is "used that men may by it be made more fit to labour," then "recreation belongs not to rest, but to labour," and thus "it must be granted on days of labour, and not on the Sabbath."[26] And if Sunday sports were to be legitimized on grounds that they rested and restored those who took part, then most of the sports of the day clearly failed the standard. The brawls, fights, and competitions that infected the bulk of local sports seemed more likely to dissipate physical and emotional energies than to restore them.

In time, emphasis shifted from honoring Sunday as a day of recuperation and rest to one set aside for meditation and edification, a day in which Puritans "might wholly in soul and in body without all let and interruption attend upon the worship of God." It was to be a day of labor, but "a different kind of labor, for wrestling with God" in meditation. The typical Puritan Sunday was spent listening to two sermons with the remainder of the day spent praying and thinking about and discussing the sermon with family members. "Let no man think that a bare rest from labour is all that is required of him on the Lord's day, but the time which he saves from the works of his calling he is to lay out on those spiritual duties," was the advice of Bishop Lewis Bayley, chaplain to King James I.[27]

This conception of Sunday as a day of worship rather than a day of rest owed in part to Calvin's teachings that the Sabbath was instituted for the purpose of making humans "conformable to the Creator." It wasn't simply a time for ceasing labor, but a day believers should give up all fleshly desires and "activities of our own striving so that, having

God working in us, we may repose in Him." At the same time, Calvin had worried about ceremonial and "superstitious" observances of Sunday, which in his view dangerously elevated the importance of the day. The Sabbath, he reminded, served to keep the church in order and preserved occasions for "hearing the word, the breaking of the mystical bread, and for public prayers." Yet Calvin never let his high and worshipful view of Sunday interfere with his Sunday bowling, a practice that never sat well with severe Sabbatarians, especially when some of the bishops eagerly followed his example.[28]

Calvin might have thought it proper to bowl on Sunday, and sports and festivities might theoretically have fit nicely into a *leisurely* Sunday, but most Puritans saw little room for them in a *devotional* Sunday. The frenzy and devotional enthusiasm that gripped people for sports was incompatible with the Puritan sober-minded vision of Sunday. How could one maintain a worshipful or prayerful attitude, or review in his mind the minister's exhortations, while playing quoits or football or ninepins? When sports and games on the village green began to compete for the congregation's attendance at Sunday services, the Puritan sentiment against Sunday sports and reveling ratcheted up even more, causing one Puritan to lament "that the youth will not by any means be brought to attend the exercises of catechizing in the afternoon; neither the people to be present at the evening service."[29]

In the end, the disjunction that developed between sport and Sunday owed to a number of influences: the pagan fertility origins of many of the Sunday games, the rowdiness and brawling that accompanied them, the tendency of Sunday games to interrupt services and to compete with ministers for the attention of their flock, and the disruptive influence of sports and games on a congregant's spiritual constitution. If the blood sports and ball games, fighting, and cudgeling were bad for the Christian on the weekdays, they were doubly bad when played on a day committed to spiritual restoration. And there also was the matter of "the Book." As Puritan political pressure was gradually brought to bear against Sunday sports, James I, with the support of the Church of England, issued his *Book of Sports* in 1618, which lashed out at Puritan strictures on the Sabbath and expressly recommended sports and dancing and games for parishioners on Sunday following services. When Anglican preachers were required to read the king's declaration from the pulpit, it infuriated the Puritans and sealed dastardly connections between Anglican apostasy, desecration of a scripturally anointed Sabbath, and public sports.

SPORTS IN PURITAN NEW ENGLAND

When the Puritans landed on American shores, their forbearers' antipathy toward sports and play landed with them, but the widespread mania for sports and public amusements that had so frustrated them in England was absent from the societies in which the first generation of settlers found themselves. This, coupled with the fact that the harsh world in which the original Puritans found themselves left them with little time for sports and games, meant that sport wasn't a pressing religious issue for the first one hundred years of the "American experiment." To the extent that sport blossomed in the New England colonies at all, it blossomed, as one historian put it, "like a flower in a macadam prison yard."[30]

With the passing of generations and the influx of immigrants unsympathetic to the Puritan worldview, the tensions that had been so palpable in England began to surface in America. Eventually, the American settlers' misgivings echoed those of their English predecessors. Clerical diatribes against sport and play continued but became more selective in their condemnations. There are few indications, for example, of preachers railing against quiet games and sports played in the privacy of the home. But Puritan resistance strengthened as sports became more popular. Playing sports on the Sabbath and playing to excess continued to be challenged from the pulpit, as did sports or games that encouraged or incorporated betting or were injurious or cruel to animals or humans. The Puritans resurrected their intemperate hatred of football and blood sports. They continued to be suspect of sports considered vestiges of pagan or Catholic games, especially the maypole dances that so irked their Puritan ancestors in the old country. And they continued to abhor sports that encouraged riots and moral license, and in truth there was much in the sports of the day to be abhorred.[31]

Violent sports and especially dueling were targets of Puritan condemnations. In the preface to a famous sermon published by the Reverend Joseph Sewall, a group called "United Ministers of Boston" laid out an impressive argument concerning Christians' duty to protect the integrity of their own bodies. In the ministers' views, deaths from dueling were murder. Though duels might proceed on the basis of an agreement between the two parties who mutually accept the risks involved, a "man's voluntary exposing of his own life to the hazard and opening his body (as it were) to the sword of him that slays him, does not make it otherwise . . . *no man has the power over his own life to lay it down of himself, at his own pleasure, and therefore cannot give power to another to take it away"* (emphasis added). In play as surely as in fighting, Christians were not at liberty to intentionally put their bodies in danger.[32]

Little is known about how much influence the Puritan clergy had on the play life of the people in the pews. By and large the early Americans were a joyous, loving, even playful people, even slightly wicked at times. Judging from the sermons preached from the pulpits of the day, many in the congregations were sneaking off to the bullbaitings and bearbaitings, the cockfights, and other officially decertified sports. Clerical grumbling about the recreational lives of churchgoers might have had some effect on the lives of those in the pew, but as historian William Baker points out, at the height of the great migration (1630–1640) only one in four immigrants was a church member. Still, Puritan preachers' well-articulated stance went a long way toward determining how religious leaders of successive generations would think about sport and play.[33]

In light of the diversity of religious and social backgrounds of the settlers, it is probably inaccurate to speak, as some do, of "a puritanical disposition" toward sports and games. Convictions on the issue varied all the more as the migration to America continued. The Anglicans who came to Virginia were more tolerant in their approaches to sport than the New Englanders and the Quakers in Pennsylvania. Even preachers became divided on the topic. The attitude of most clergy might have edged close to that of the English Puritans, but a diary entry by a preacher named Peter Thacher ("this evening was the first time of our playing nine pins in our alley") suggests that all ministers weren't revolted by sports. In fact, two of the most popular wrestlers in seventeenth-century Connecticut were respected ministers. Even the severe William Prynne, who blasted those who danced, attended the theater, or played games of chance, pointed out plenty of lawful recreations that remained available to them: hawking, hunting, leaping, vaulting, wrestling, and shooting, for example, were described as "harmless."[34]

Prynne's list of permissible sports is noteworthy if only because the skills required for excelling in them closely paralleled those required in warfare, and preparation for war was a significant item on the settlers' agenda. "Neither in England nor in America did the Puritans ever object to martial sports," says Robert Higgs. They were in a constant state of military readiness. With few exceptions, men between the ages of sixteen and sixty met regularly for compulsory military training in the mornings; in the afternoons they engaged each other in martial sports thought to develop military skill. Wrestling was the most popular of these war-training sports, offering, as historian Bruce Daniels says, "the drama of a genuine battle between men, but lack[ing] the dreadful consequences of blood sports such as boxing or cudgel fighting." Yet even in these sports excess could rear its ugly head, as "competitions and rivalries [often went] far beyond the needs of military training."[35]

The stipulation that sports should have productive ends, particularly those important in military exercises, extended the argument the medieval church had mounted to defend the ghastly jousting tournaments. Such rationalization became a prescription for the way sports were to be played, favoring a military model that viewed games as microcosms of battles to be pursued, not just with sternness of purpose, but as symbolic tests of courage, manliness, valor, and ultimately, personal worth. When military might and defense of honor are the goals, light-hearted approaches to sport tend to be suspect, even to be regarded as treason.

THE CASE AGAINST ENJOYMENT

The value of sports for preparing players for war never kept the staunchest Puritans from noticing the insidious way that sports could roil the temperaments of players and insinuate frivolity into the lives of even the most devout. The enjoyment derived from play continued to be a problem for many Puritan preachers. Not since thirteenth-century scholastic theologians constructed their elaborate taxonomies had enjoyment derived from play been subjected to such microscopic theological examination. Macaulay's quip that the Puritans hated bearbaiting not so much because of the pain it caused the bear but because of the enjoyment it brought to the spectators might have overstated the case, but there was little question that the New England Puritans, like their English predecessors, had reservations about playing sports merely for the enjoyment they brought participants. Enjoyment wrung from sports was a synthetic emotion, a poor substitute for the religious joy that Christians naturally should desire.[36]

The soul's unceasing longing for spiritual peace could be satisfied only by God in heaven; until then, it seemed logical that Christians would be attracted to the closest thing to heaven, "the awful mirth of religious rapture." The enjoyment found in prayer, meditation, listening to sermons, and anticipating heaven were far superior to any worldly pleasures that might have been abandoned at the time of conversion. When the congregation sang "religion was never designed to make our pleasure less," it was not suggesting that believers seek pleasure in sports and amusements; it was affirming precisely the opposite. Religion offered all the joy that the earnest soul needed. It was what would come to be known as "sober mirth," a slight variation on what fifteenth-century Franciscan Angelo da Chivasso had labeled *ludus spiritualis* and *ludus divinus* (to be distinguished from *ludus diabolicus*). If sober mirth was the preferred state, it followed logically that the enjoyments derived from sports, games, and amusements were counterfeit substitutes for the genuine pleasure available to the Christian in the devotional life.[37]

The notion of sober mirth received a great deal of attention in a 170-page, three-sermon treatise on sports and play written in 1707 by Benjamin Colman—the only book-length work on the topic of leisure and recreation published in colonial New England. In a scheme not all that different from that proposed by Alexander of Hales and his contemporaries three centuries earlier, Colman sketched out a taxonomy of enjoyment or "mirth." It was the Christian's duty, said Colman, to seek first and foremost "spiritual and religious joy proper to a saint; his rich privilege and his duty to aspire after. It is a joy on spiritual accounts, spiritually *felt* and spiritually *expressed*" (emphasis added). The first sermon established a theoretical case for recreation by acknowledging that people need some recreation. But even sports and amusements pursued moderately for strict purposes of physical and emotional recreation should be "innocent," not lead to injury "to God or our neighbour," and should not "transgress sobriety, holiness, or charity." The desired emotional state was sober mirth, "pure and grave, serious and devout, all which it may be and yet free and cheerful."[38]

While this seemed to be the basis for a reasonable approach to sports, Sermon II gave a more "realistic" examination of the problem, taking back much of what had been given in Sermon I. Once a game begins, the cat is out of the bag. Lurking within the innocent pastimes of "sober mirth," "virtuous mirth," and "profitable mirth," said Colman, are their enemies, "vicious mirth" and "carnal mirth." The dangers were obvious to Colman: once a "licentious manner of expressing our mirth takes over, all possibilities of innocence, neighborly love, or sobriety vanish." Sport had to be contained and, if Colman was to be believed, containment was a formidable challenge.[39]

Even the most honest efforts by these intelligent and well-educated men to give play the benefit of the doubt were so hedged in with concerns about its capacity to erode one's spiritual foundations that it is difficult for moderns, let alone for many Puritans who were sitting in the pews, to know for sure what was being given a green light. Michael Oriard puts it artfully: "Although Puritans played and tolerated play within prescribed limits, at a level below explicit articulation they assigned play to Satan's domain." To paraphrase Colman's warning, "The pretence of restraint may be outwardly maintained but disdain is sneered from the eye and contempt is in the smile; tho indeed envy and spite are under the paint; the look is pleasing enough and gay but tis only a disguise, a forced laugh while a man's galled and mad at heart."[40]

It is tempting to think of the Puritans' suspicion of play as something born of ignorance and an impoverished, backwoods education, but nothing could be further from the truth. The Puritans were, in every sense of the word, intellectuals. Max Weber described them as "steeped in the culture of the Renaissance," people who, "with their reliance upon the Book and their wealth of scholarly leadership, founded the intellectual and scholarly tradition which for three centuries enabled New England to lead the country in educational scholarly achievement."[41] These prodigious thinkers, quite unlike their modern counterparts, took play and sport and recreation seriously, yet concluded that play was of a completely different order than religion, incapable of integration in any meaningful way. Unlike the thirteenth-century priests in southern France who led the ball processions down the aisles of their chapels or participated in sports rituals as part of religious ceremony, the Puritans found it difficult to imagine sport as a spiritually expressive experience or discovering "spiritual mirth" on the playground. Such an orientation toward sports helped widen the divide between sport and religion in the Puritan conscience and to secularize sports, insulating them from any spiritual inspiration and guidance in the centuries that followed.

LEGACY TO NINETEENTH-CENTURY PROTESTANTISM

The wave of immigration in the second half of the seventeenth century materialized the fears that had haunted two generations of Puritans. New people with different cultural and religious backgrounds, different views on Sabbath play, and different standards for amusement, coupled with an expansion of Protestant denominations and the preaching of an escalating liberal theology, encouraged a more relaxed way of thinking about sports and amusements. Cracks in the largely antagonistic view of sports appeared when a small minority of the ministerial elite softened their stance on sport and play and began to recommend the same sports that had been condemned in the 1690s. In the larger society, many sports were gradually sloughing off their tarnished reputations, helped in part by the voices of national leaders like John Adams and Benjamin Franklin, who thought them not only permissible but valuable in the life of citizens.[42]

Yet well into the nineteenth century, Puritan suspicions of play colored the opinions of clergy and religious writers. New England preachers, stimulated by the wave of religious consciousness stemming from the Calvinistic revivals of the mid-eighteenth century, repeated decades-old objections to excesses in all forms of play. Ball and blood sports and spectator games came under fire, as did the questionable settings in which many sports were played. Sport haters had only to look at what had transpired in England after the Puritans lost their political power base to catch a glimpse of where lax standards on sport and amusement might lead. Early eighteenth-century England was marked, says historian Allen Guttmann, by "a shift in emphasis from piety to hedonism," especially noticeable in the form taken by public sports and amusements. It was a period historian Bruce Daniels labeled as "the most raucous, ribald era of English sports history."[43] Without the constraints enforced by Puritan strongmen, sports came to be driven completely by public taste and commercial interests. Games were organized, players were paid, and spectators paid to watch. Contests were advertised, records were kept, sports heroes emerged, betting businesses cropped up, and sports spectacles became increasingly lurid in their staging. The "butcherly sports" were revived; bullbaiting and bearbaiting attracted bloodthirsty crowds from all social classes. Football thrived in popularity largely on the basis of its sensationalism and violence. In a throwback to the Roman spectacles, shows featuring races between scantily clad women or between dwarfs and men with wooden legs were staged during intermissions of races between athletic men. Horse racing went hand in hand with heavy drinking and sexual promiscuity.[44]

Between the eighteenth and twentieth centuries, spectator sports in America flourished as the public flocked to stadia, ballparks, and other athletic venues. In the words of one period theologian, "the parson with the pitchfork of excommunication has not prevailed against human nature."[45] Faced with the prospect of a public gone mad about sports and increasingly uninterested in what they had to say, some Protestant leaders surrendered; some dug in their heels ever more deeply. Reasoned reservations about sports often gave way to passionate irrationality, which drove wedges even more deeply between the church and the public sports of the day. This rich, not always reasonable, anti-sport tradition that was conspicuously at odds with the tastes of an unresponsive laity would flavor Protestantism's relation with sports into the early part of the twentieth century.

To the critics' way of thinking, the conflict was a battle for the minds and souls of the church. An almost palpable fear that sport and play would capture the energy and commitment Christians owed to their churches and lead to lives of spiritual dissolution lay at the heart of many broadsides issued against sports of the nineteenth century. One way this fear showed itself was in clerical opposition to the "bicycling craze" that was spreading across America. Bicycling became a hot button issue for many denominations, especially the Methodists. In a six-part treatise (*Psychology, Hygiene, and Morality of the Bicycle*), the influential Methodist James Buckley weighed the advantages and disadvantages of bicycling and concluded that it was not sinful in itself, but he was careful to hedge his recommendation with observations about its destructive potential for Christians, especially women:

> Many [women] of good family become bold in feature, bearing and gesture, and indulge freely in road badinage and slang. They sit in indelicate attitudes on curbstones, roadsides, and under trees, with young men; they drink and joke at drugstore counters; not a few have become typical hoydens and, when not riding, parade the streets in bicycle costume . . . Wives have taken to the wheel against the expressed wishes of their husbands, and have neglected their family duties . . . The bicycle has figured in divorce cases without number.[46]

Even the circus, by present-day standards an ideal family entertainment, faced tough opposition. "No Christian can follow Jesus and then be found in a circus," trumpeted the editor of a Georgia periodical. Indeed, the discerning Christian could see sin signaled in the very appellations: "cirCUSS" and "CARNival."[47]

The positions taken by some denominations were barely distinguishable from those taken by their forebears. Twenty-first-century Methodists are fond of recalling founder John Wesley's admonition to preachers to exercise by walking in the open air to improve their health, but they forget his famous dictum: "He who plays as a boy will play as a man." And it was Wesley who wrote: "Thou fool! Dost thou not imagine because thou dost not see God, that God dost not see thee? Laugh on, play on, sing on, dance on; but for all these things God will bring you to judgment."[48] Such harsh judgments about sport and play lay behind the banning of "every species of play" in the denomination's Cokesbury College in Maryland in 1790. Wesley's sentiments continued to hold sway over Methodist thinking into the nineteenth century, especially in the southern states. As late as 1890, long after sports had become commonplace in liberal churches, a Texas preacher writing in a Southern Methodist Publishing House booklet continued to advise that "life is short, and no time is to be lost in youth's valuable years . . . Sport, fun and frolic have no chapter in youth's Book of Life in our day; learning and doing fill up the entire volume."[49]

Again, most of the ministerial fire was reserved for the social contexts where sports were played rather than for the sports themselves. Drunkenness, brawling, and gambling were offensive and widespread. Bowling and billiards, along with card games (played with or without gambling), were wrong because of the shady establishments that housed them. It may be impossible to overstate how venomous were the complaints against some of the most popular sporting spectacles. Under a banner headline "Has it About Gone Far Enough?" an 1867 issue of *The Boston Congregationalist Recorder* attacked rowing contests (the premier sport spectacle of the day) because of the pre-race betting and post-race drunkenness in which losers joined the winners "just to show they are not 'soopsey' enough to be beaten without good grace." For the same reason, professional baseball was opposed by many clergy. As far as one Methodist minister was concerned, baseball players were an "idle and shiftless lot," their pay was "ridiculously high" and their games were degraded by fights, injuries, drunkenness, and betting. The national pastime was still taking a beating as late as 1891, when an Arkansas Baptist periodical charged that baseball players could "execute more deviltry, use more profanity, and make idiots of themselves in more ways" than anyone else in society. "Our national game?" cried out a Disciples of Christ writer. He preferred to call it "one of our national curses! Does not every watchman on the wall cry the alarm? . . . Speak out. Keep the boys away from it. Cry with me."[50]

Some of the rhetoric was clearly hysterical. "Can the ball-playing, marble-playing brother go from his [prayer] closet into such exercises?" asked the editor of Georgia's leading Baptist periodical. The answer was an unqualified "no." But some of the rhetoric revealed a measured concern about the effects of physically harmful sports on players' bodies, and in this regard, college football took a beating from the religious press. The popularity of intercollegiate football had soared, as had the number of serious injuries inflicted on players. The editor of the staid Congregationalist *New Englander* clearly had football in mind when he wrote: "The law of God requires that we love our neighbor and seek his good. If then under the pretense of recreation, we contrive to injure our neighbor in any way, or expose him to personal inconvenience or suffering we are no longer excusable, but criminal."[51] Even the liberal Washington Gladden, who had gone far out on a limb to defend sports, found no room for rough and brutal sports like football in the Christian life. Rumblings against football were especially common in the South, especially in Methodist and Baptist circles. In Virginia, the editor of a Baptist journal expressed amazement that anyone could be attracted to "a dirtily clad, bare and frowsy-headed, rough and tumble, shoving, pushing, crushing, pounding, kicking, ground-wallowing, mixed-up mass of players, any of whom might have come out with broken limbs, or be left on the ground writhing with ruptured vitals."[52]

It wasn't simply the physical carnage of football that bothered the early southern evangelicals. The game was a symbol of materialism, fanaticism, modernity, and liberalism; it showered attention on the body and unjustly glorified it. The moral corruption that surrounded the games drew fire as well. In the minds of many southern conservatives, intercollegiate football was "a symptom of the declension that had rotted away the moral and pedagogical foundations of northern universities." In 1892 the Western Conference of North Carolina described football as "a source of evil, and no little evil and ought to be stopped." In 1893 *The Raleigh Christian Advocate* began publishing a series of articles by the North Carolina Methodist Episcopal Church criticizing athletics at Trinity College (the forerunner of Duke University) and reprinted an article that had originally appeared in a New York Methodist journal likening football to the gladiatorial contests of ancient Rome, Spanish bullfights, and "the criminal class in general." Football encouraged gambling and led to disgraceful conduct, including "wild revels, bacchanalian songs and delirious shouts . . . enough to make a stout heart quake." Students at Wake Forest College formed a football team in 1888 but were pressured to discontinue it in 1895. Methodist-sponsored Wofford College in Spartanburg, South Carolina, eliminated football in 1897, and Baptist-sponsored Furman University dropped it six years later. Bowing to pressure from its denomination, Methodist-affiliated Trinity College abolished football in 1895 after firing its northern-rooted president, who refused to heed the board's order to abolish the game. It wasn't reinstated until 1920.[53]

CUTTING TO THE HEART OF PLAY

Behind almost all of the complaints about violence, gambling, drunkenness, and moral looseness was an overriding concern about the play spirit itself. This spirit was the engine that drove all of the evil concomitants. It may not have been articulated as such in most of the writings of the period, but the power of play to entice, corrupt, undermine Christian temperament, and dull spiritual discernment appeared between the lines of criticism. The insidious way this could happen, enticing the believer to seek out increasingly more potent fixes, was a familiar theme in the religious literature. "You engage in what you call a decent amusement now, for the mere pleasure of it, or from motives of self-gratification. But soon you are cloyed with that; it ceases to gratify [and] . . . you must have something of a strong and more stirring character . . . [Eventually] you become a pleasure-hunter of the lowest class."[54]

This domino theory of play-sin-play-greater sin cropped up in assaults on even what would seem to be the most innocuous games. When the country became fascinated with croquet upon its import from England in 1866, it caught churches by surprise, taking some of them four years to ban the game officially. A writer in the *American Christian Review* portrayed it as a dreadful link to the "dancing fever," another craze that was appealing to more and more churchgoers. He showed, in twelve easy steps, how croquet would lead to perdition:

1. a social party
2. social and play party
3. croquet party
4. picnic and croquet party
5. picnic and dance and croquet party
6. absence from church
7. imprudent or immoral conduct
8. exclusion from church
9. a runaway match
10. poverty and discontent
11. shame and disgrace
12. ruin.[55]

It is significant that this protest didn't extend to exercise, the healthful effects of which had by now been recognized. Several early leaders in the physical education movement were model Christians. Charles Beck, generally recognized as the first teacher of physical education in

the United States, was an ordained minister, and the first college professor of physical education, Dr. Edward Hitchcock, was a deeply committed Christian.[56] The exercise regimes recommended by these and other
physical education experts of the day tended to be arduous calisthenics
and heavy gymnastics imported from Europe. Their practical benefits
were as obvious as the pain suffered by those who endured them. It was
easy for the religious community to see how they prepared the believer
for "greater service." They were recreations of the right kind, "not only
permitted to us but enjoined upon us . . . by the authority of our Savior." Most importantly, they were not play. They didn't churn the spirit
or cloud spiritual discernment. There was little danger that believers
would actually enjoy them or become addicted to the pain and torture
that they inflicted. It was on the strength of such reasoning, for example,
that "physical culture" classes were added to the curriculum at Goshen
College, a Mennonite institution, in 1899, yet as late as 1907, a Mennonite leader blasted baseball as "an abomination" on grounds that it is
"esteemed by the world" and that it "excites passions and lusts."[57]

Enjoyment, that quality inherent in play that had bothered the
Christian community since the thirteenth century, continued to figure
in theological commentary on play in the nineteenth. In the late 1800s,
theologians and preachers from a variety of denominations continued
to suspect games that were played for sheer enjoyment. It was difficult
for them not to see that playing games for the sheer fun of it was nothing more than self-gratification, pure selfishness, not to be reconciled
with scriptural passages that admonish believers: "Whatever ye do, do
it heartily as unto the Lord." Play that could be shown to produce clear
benefits to the body yet not entice players by "amusing" them was given
a green flag, but it was never easy to determine a player's motivations.
To make matters worse, what might be divinely ordained recreation one
minute could become sinful amusement the next. A commentator in an
1851 issue of the Congregationalist *New Englander* sought to clarify the
issue this way:

> Very frequently, the same external acts or courses of action
> change their character with a change of motive, and far from
> being recreations, become amusements. Thus a student partici-
> pates in a game of ball, or of quoits, as a recreation. It is needful
> for him, and he has no other object or end in view. But soon he
> becomes attached to the game, and pursues it far beyond the

purposes that recreation requires. He pursues it for the mere pleasure of it. It has ceased to be a recreation and becomes an amusement.[58]

In 1850, Anglican theologian Jeremy Taylor advised readers not to "let your recreations be lavish spenders of your time, but choose such which are healthful, short, transient, recreative, and apt to refresh you; but on no hand dwell on them, or make them your great employment: for he that spends his time in sports, and calls it recreation, is like him whose garment is all made of fringes, and his meat nothing but sauces; they are healthless and useless."[59]

The recreation-amusement dichotomy that surfaced in these and other writings was an ingenious, though flawed, scheme for solving the problem that perplexed nineteenth-century churchmen just as it had Aquinas and his contemporaries five hundred years earlier: how to keep games from spinning out of control and how to ensure that Christians pursue them in moderation. They clearly understood that games were enjoyable, and perhaps only at a tacit level, they knew that enjoyment came only as players approached games with a certain seriousness, surrender of will, and acceptance of an alternate reality represented by the rules and customs of the game. For early Protestants, this risked immoderation, and for them, the price for participation was simply too high.

This was especially important to Calvinists, Puritans, and their Protestant progeny as they strove to bring the entire physical world into a uniform, cohesive whole under the rule of God Almighty. They believed, says Daniels, that "leisure and recreation had to take place within the framework of the moral community; they had to be interwoven with Scripture, workplace, village, meetinghouse, home, family, and all the other parts of godly life that collectively constituted the only acceptable ritual in New England." They failed to understand how this could be done if games were played purely for enjoyment and players (momentarily at least) became physically and psychically detached from the material world, locked into an illusionary existence in which not only attitudes but behaviors and customs of ordinary life may not apply.[60] They never considered the possibility that this illusionary world, with its enthusiasm, mystery, and joy, might represent a unique and important human experience for integrating play and the religious lives of believers.

The solution they proposed was to try to keep play anchored in the real world, strip it of its inherent existential qualities, make it mundane and practical, and cut out its very heart, enjoyment. Not only did they fail to appreciate the insights of Aquinas that, under the right circumstances, play could be spiritual refreshment and perhaps a virtue, they tried to rid it of joy, the quality of play that promises spiritual refreshment. With moderation as the guiding light, they tried to convert play into something that was not play at all.[61] This has proven to be a very durable, very Protestant conception of sport.

4

The Church Heads for the Playground

By the end of the nineteenth century, sport was beginning to stamp its imprint on the American character; the country was on the threshold of an era some historians call "the golden age of sports." The first gloved boxing match was showcased during this period, basketball and volleyball were invented, ice hockey was introduced from Canada, golf was imported from Scotland, tennis was first played on Staten Island and the first public playgrounds were founded. Bicycling was the rage, its popularity mushrooming to astounding proportions in the mid-1890s. Estimates are that in 1896, one out of every eighteen people was a cyclist. In Greece, the Olympic Games were reprised, and the United States, though not especially interested in them, sent a team which won nine of twelve track events. The "golden age" might also have been called "the spectator age." The Amateur Athletic Union, the National Baseball League, and the Big Ten Athletic Conference were inaugurated; Madison Square Garden opened in 1879 with seating for 8,000 spectators. Urbanites were particularly attracted to the sports spectacles: horse racing was an enormous draw (153 major horse races were held in 1839), as was human footracing. Over 30,000 spectators watched racers who competed for a prize of $1,000 offered to any man who could run a ten-mile course in less than an hour. Competitive rowing had also become popular, thanks in part to an early international race (1824) in New York Harbor reportedly watched by 50,000 spectators.[1]

By the turn of the century, more than 20 million fans were attending professional-league baseball games each year. Football mania swept the country. While only 2,000 people watched the first Harvard-Yale game in 1875, more than 22,000 were there when the teams met fifteen years later. By 1893 the annual Thanksgiving Day game in New York City between Yale and Princeton had, in the words of one journalist, become "the greatest sporting event and spectacle combined that this country has to show."[2] Annual football attendance at colleges rose to over 10 million, and by 1920 seating capacities of major college and university stadia had doubled to a total of nearly 2.5 million. The sports-crazed mood of the country was described by one political pundit this way: "Ohio has two contenders [James Cox and Warren Harding] for the presidency of the United States and one contender for the baseball championship of the world. Ask anyone in the state who is going to win and they'll answer 'Cleveland.'"[3]

As a love for big-time sports wove its way into the American social fabric, Protestants began to show signs of shaking off their suspicions, gradually becoming more optimistic about sport's place in the Christian life. In 1851, shortly after Thomas Beecher assumed his pastorate at Park Congregational Church in Elmira, New York, his congregation was taken aback at his obvious passion for cricket and even more stunned when he joined a local baseball club. Yet he was still in the pulpit twenty-four years later when the congregation, apparently won over by their pastor's playfulness, dedicated a new church building complete with gymnasium.

No longer was the Protestant line on sport and amusement dictated by ministers and theologians. By the late nineteenth century, congregations were locked in debate over the extent to which the church should legislate against amusements. In a presentation to the Sixth Annual Baptist Congress in 1887, a Baptist minister told the assembled: "Time was, when we could shut the question out of the church with sweeping prohibitions; wave off its perplexities with some snap-rule of arbitrariness. That time has passed." General principles to guide the Christian's approach to sport were what was needed, said a Presbyterian preacher: "While the Bible lays down great and essential principles to control practical life, it leaves their application to the circumstances of particular persons, the demands of each age, and the judgment of the enlightened conscience."[4]

Protestants had always had misgivings about playing and watching sports on Sunday, but resistance began to erode in the late nineteenth century. In 1900 when a preacher informed the United Presbyterian Ministers Association that the Lord had crippled several players on the Pittsburgh club for playing on Sunday, a sassy sportswriter asked why the Lord hadn't, then, stepped in to help improve the play of the struggling teams of Boston and Philadelphia, which didn't play on Sundays. Around the same time, a Muncie, Indiana, town ordinance forbidding quoits or cricket on Sunday was threatening Sunday baseball. Ultimately a truce was arranged between the local churches and the baseball club: the clubs could play Sunday baseball, but the town band would play sacred music between innings. By 1900 some ministers had even become forceful advocates of Sunday sports. The rector of Holy Trinity Church in New York City, by his own admission hopelessly addicted to golf, urged other addicts to stop by the Sunday services on their way to the golf courses. At the worship hour, he pointed out, while the golfer's mind "is free from the intoxication of the game, it may be that the spirit of the holy place will so steady him that he will go out a better man, will find fuller satisfaction in his game, will treat his caddy with more consideration and will count his strokes more carefully."5

Frederic Sawyer's mid-nineteenth-century essay *A Plea for Amusements*, which lauded the "liberalization of sentiment" toward amusements, foreshadowed a Christian acceptance of sports that Sawyer himself might not have predicted. Before the close of the century, evangelicalism was being blended in popular sport spectacles in some of the most imaginative ways. Following its victory over Yale in the great 1893 Thanksgiving Day game, a journalist reported that the Princeton team, "naked and covered with mud and blood and perspiration," stood in its locker to sing the Doxology "from the beginning to end as solemnly and seriously, as they ever did in their lives." To readers who might have considered such a ritual sacrilegious, the reporter reminded that "any one who has seen a defeated team lying on the benches of their dressing-room sobbing like hysterical school girls, can understand how great and how serious is the joy of victory to the men who conquer."6

Some of the fiercest contests pitted evangelical institutions against each other. After one such interdenominational skirmish between Baptist Wake Forest and Methodist Trinity, a player on the losing team ruefully noted: "To be beaten by a rival sect, Christians though we both were, was more humiliating than to bite the dust before the pagan hordes of the constitutionally unchurched university! Queer that we church people love each other so." The president of Trinity reveled in the fact that his Christian school had defeated the secular University of North Carolina, an accomplishment which, in his mind, would put an end to the "age-long habit of the condescending attitude" of Carolina alumni toward church-affiliated colleges and give Trinity "an indefinable prestige of a general but most effective kind."[7]

In the South, Methodists and Baptists, traditionally among the most recalcitrant in their opposition to sport and play, took longer to adopt a relaxed stance. For years the Methodist *Christian Advocate* had been the denomination's watchdog for sinful and enticing amusements, but in 1924 the same publication was reminding its readers "to capture some of the summer athletics for your church," and the Baptists were taking pains to ensure that young people of the denomination understood that "sports are no longer sinful to this denomination." It was a remarkable reversal: in the span of a half-century, large segments of the Protestant community, long society's self-appointed suppressors of play, had overcome their suspicions and done an about-face on the sports issue. Protestants had always done their share of playing, but usually in back of the barn. But as the twentieth century opened, Protestants in increasing numbers were now playing and watching sports in the open. Even more startlingly, church leaders were enthusiastically endorsing and promoting play as part of church and church-college social programs. Some claimed playing to be an inherent right for Christians; others went so far as to label it a Christian duty.[8]

This "great reversal" owed in no small degree to expedience, something suggested in the fact that theological arguments for sport tended to lag rather than lead the charge to the playground. Facing a gathering stampede to sports events, many churches feared being trampled in the dust and, as historian Florence Cozens suggests, threw up their hands and adopted an "if-you-can't-beat-'em, join-'em" stance. Certainly there are hints of inevitability and surrender in the complaints of some of the clergy of the day. "People will play, thank God!" said Hebert Gates in the introduction to his book *Recreation and the Church*: "We may play with them if we will, and thereby help them to realize the best that this instinct has to offer or we may hold aloof, adopt an attitude of narrow, indiscriminate condemnation or at best of cold indifference, and allow the boys and girls to play on without us and without our sympathetic guidance."[9]

Yet to describe Christianity's reversal on the issue of sport as simply a result of having caved to the secularizing pressures of popular sentiment is to ignore a host of contributing forces, both theological and social, that greased the skids toward accommodation. The nineteenth century gave rise to some of the most interesting and fast-moving developments ever witnessed in the seven centuries of Protestantism's existence. Two theological innovations formed an important backdrop to Protestant evangelicalism's acceptance of sport: a revolution in moral philosophy, and the ideals of perfectionism and post-millennial eschatology popularized in revivalism, which swept the country in the early and mid-nineteenth century.

AN EMERGING MORAL PHILOSOPHY

Prior to the nineteenth century, American Protestants were united in the beliefs that the Scriptures were inspired, that they were the only authoritative guide to life, and that eternal salvation was available only through God in Jesus Christ. It also was widely believed that virtuous acts and generally good character had their source in spiritual redemption. For Jonathan Edwards and his contemporaries, in a world divided into the lost and the elect, virtue was "a fruit of election." There was no universal, natural moral sense; humans could only aspire to virtuous living through the grace of God. "You can't trust too little to yourselves; nor too much to [God]," was the advice of one eighteenth-century Presbyterian theologian. Thus, when it came to sports and other popular amusements, the only possible way their destructive influences on the soul could be resisted was if the person, as an 1802 writer put it, "be brought as a sinner to the mercy seat of Christ to seek pardon and strength. Discerning how amusements fit properly within our lives," he said, "requires that our hearts be right in the sight of God."[10]

By the second decade of the nineteenth century, such thinking had been submerged in the tenets of a new moral philosophy that had gained a foothold at Harvard (Unitarian), Brown (Baptist), Yale (Congregationalist), Princeton (Presbyterian), and other colleges and spread to seminaries and pulpits throughout the land. Known variously as "Evangelical Enlightenment" or "theistic commonsense," this new moral vision emphasized human capacity in ethical and moral living. Increasingly, theologians came to believe that God's "expectations of human beings as moral creatures could be discovered independently of the traditional sources of religious authority, through a close investigation of human nature." According to this moral perspective, the perplexing ethical dilemmas foisted upon Americans by urbanization, westward expansion, and immigration could be resolved more by relying on "universal ethical intuitions" and "commonsense moral reasoning" than ecclesiastical authority. God's revelation could validate itself on the basis of its own inherent reasonableness and practical value. In the words of the conservative president of Princeton University in 1812: "The best reason which anyone can have for believing a proposition is that it is so evident to his intellectual faculty that he cannot disbelieve it." Thus the new moral philosophy elevated the importance of moral effort and moral training and reduced the agency of God, foisting much greater responsibility for ethical behavior on humans themselves. Given the presuppositions of the new philosophy, character education undertaken outside the framework of a Christian theology made a great deal of sense. And few experiences were thought to be more effective shapers of character than sports.[11]

REVIVALISM, PERFECTIONISM, AND MILLENNIALISM

Eighteenth-century Protestantism was rocked by a series of revivals—interdenominational, directed to mass audiences, often featuring theatrical ("heart-touching") sermons—which became a principal force in personal conversions to Christianity. The revival of 1740–1742 that swept New England, commonly referred to as the First Great Awakening, remains the most famous, but the nineteenth century featured periodic revivals as well, especially between 1800 and 1860. Revivalism migrated from the western frontiers, where Methodists, Presbyterians, and Baptists dominated the movement, to New England, where more sedate and intellectually respectable revivals were held among the normally staid Congregationalists. Lyman Beecher, the popular Congregationalist preacher and writer, was originally opposed to revivalism, but as the movement continued to gain popularity he eventually modified his theology and methods of preaching to accommodate the surge. By the mid-nineteenth century, revivalism was the dominant force in American Protestantism, thanks in part to English and European influences but also to the energetic, charismatic, and entertaining preaching of evangelist Charles Finney, arguably the most influential religious personality of the century.

Finney preached a gospel of individual conversion and spiritual perfection: unlike the old-line Calvinists who believed that salvation and moral actions were entirely the province of God, Finney believed that the Christian's own decisions and moral efforts were also vital parts of the salvation process. He also preached a gospel of perfectionism, the notion that conversion could lead to a sanctified and nearly (but not completely) perfect spiritual and moral life. His preaching career coincided with the spread of millennialism, the belief that Christ's return would follow a historical period of a thousand years of peace, social harmony, and Christian morality. For Finney and other revivalists, this vision of a future ideal society became a necessary precondition for Christ's return. Not only did millennialism cast a dark shadow on the problems of the society in which the revivalists lived, it breathed a sense of urgency into crusaders' efforts to bring about the moral reform of society. Christians need not sit idly by and await the glorious return of their Savior; they could hasten his return by helping to improve public morality. Thus, says historian Timothy Smith, "men in all walks of life believed that the sovereign Holy Spirit was endowing the nation with resources sufficient to convert and civilize the globe, to purge human society of all its evils and to usher in Christ's reign on earth."[12]

What this meant for Methodists, the denomination most closely associated with perfectionism, was spelled out in 1854 by Pentecostal William Arthur in his best-selling book, *The Tongue of Fire*. In enumerating the signs of having been anointed by the Holy Spirit, Arthur emphasized a commitment to reclaim society, a radical notion for many Methodists who believed that the gospel was all about "forming a holy community in the world to come, but never in this." But from Arthur's standpoint, "The general renewal of society . . . destroy[ing] all national holds of evil; root[ing] sin out of institutions; hold[ing] up to the view the gospel ideal of a righteous nation . . . is one of the first duties of those whose position or mode of thought gives them any influence in general questions."[13]

Although Finney did not consider himself to be a reformer, his theological dispositions, when coupled with popular notions embedded in the new moral philosophy and abetted by popular liberal theology, fueled an activist, idealistic Protestantism that formed the foundation for a host of nineteenth-century reform movements. Anti-slavery, anti-dueling, child rescue, playground, and temperance movements owed their inspiration to the revivalistic impulse, as did other movements dealing with the pressing problems of the slums, inhuman working conditions, industrial strife, crime, political corruption, and the plight of poor, displaced immigrants. And among the methods and experiences in which reformers, especially those working with young people, placed their greatest confidence were play, sports, and recreation.

SPORT, PLAY, AND THE SOCIAL GOSPEL

A welter of church-related social reform efforts along with a pervasive secular reform movement were incorporated into an amorphous theo-sociological mobilization known as the social gospel. The social gospel wasn't a formal, organized movement as much as it was a network of church-related individuals and organizations committed to ministering to the needs of the whole person, material as well as spiritual. Crusaders, operating on the basis of a loosely knit theology, had an unshakable confidence in their ability to bring about improvements in society. The movement was thoroughly ecumenical, including "evangelical liberals" for whom the revelation of God in Christ was the religious norm but who favored reinterpretation of traditional doctrines in light of human experience and "reasonableness." It also included "modernistic liberals" who regarded Christ as not so much the source as the exemplar of the religious norm, and for whom the values of Christianity tended to be interpreted within a framework of critical scholarship. Some, like the influential preacher-reformer Walter Rauschenbusch, defied theological categorization. The movement's leaders were mostly bright and articulate ministers whose faith in the traditional gospel had been tailored in varying degrees to accommodate advances in science, economics, psychology, and social theory and whose emotions had been sensitized to the plight of the less fortunate strata of society by the boundless examples of social injustice. Perfectibility of humanity, elimination of inequalities, and improvement of society were the fundamental goals of the social gospel, and not infrequently, social reform took precedence over piety, doctrine, and religious identification.

The goals of the movement, coupled with the optimistic view of play and recreation featured in popular social and educational theories, virtually assured that sports would play a prominent role in the practice of the social gospel. Leisure had become an inescapable feature of everyday life for many workers. The advance of industrialization had reduced the average work week from sixty-three hours in 1860 to fifty hours in 1910, but it also had led to overcrowding in the cities, inhumane working environments, and a heretofore unseen frenzy in the marketplace.

In the minds of the social gospel proponents, the tensions of management and the monotony of the assembly line had created a need for diversion and healthy leisure activity. "What is wanted in our busy life," wrote a popular religious writer of the day, "is some means of honest work and healthy recreation for the mind and body, which shall unbend the strained faculties from time to time, and send the toiler back to his duties as a healthier and happier man." Clearly there was a familiar, utilitarian refrain in these conceptions of recreation. The Christian community had always related to play the same way they had related to poetry; as "garden destroyers," they were "more at home with the usefulness of agriculture than the elegance of floral borders."[14]

But the social gospel envisioned a much broader range of therapeutic possibilities for play than simply bolstering the physical body. Mental and emotional release and a host of hypothetical improvements to the player's character were at least as important. The physical benefits of sport are important, said Henry Atkinson, social services secretary for the Congregational Church, but amusement is the gold which gilds the pill of exercise. In one hyperbolic passage in his book *The Church and the People's Play*, Atkinson reminded readers that "to play one game of tiddly winks with zest will do a man more good than to push up a five-pound dumbbell a thousand times." Deep emotional involvement, a red flag for earlier generations of Protestants, was absolutely essential if play was to have its intended emotional and moral catharsis.[15]

Atkinson, like many progressive clerics of the era, believed that opportunities for playing were, like decent housing or humane labor laws, an inherent right of every person regardless of their financial means and that it was part of the church's obligation to ensure that everyone who wanted to could avail themselves of them. Not to provide wholesome recreational relief risked play-starved Christians seeking out less desirable activities. In a novel twist of the Apostle Paul's passage on Christian liberty, Atkinson claimed scriptural support for his position:

> "If eating meat," said St. Paul, "makes my brother to offend, I will eat no meat while the world stands." This position was heroic and splendid in Paul's day; interpreted today, it might be put in these words as expressive of the ideal attitude of each church member: "If failure to provide for the play of the people by means of playgrounds, social centers and other recreational facilities makes my brother to offend, I will exert myself to favor and to work for the establishment of these things."[16]

If trumpet blasts were needed to usher in a new way of thinking about sports as a tool of the social gospel, they came from two eminent Congregationalist ministers, Horace Bushnell and Washington Gladden. Bushnell was an anti-revivalist, anti-conversionist thinker in the vanguard of a group of mid-nineteenth-century liberals who worked tirelessly to free up Protestant thinking from its long-constrained conceptions of sport, play, and amusements. The second edition of his book, *Christian Nurture*, established theological foundations for play, elements of which would surface periodically in the speech of religious leaders who followed in his wake. As if he were anticipating themes in the short-lived "play theology movement" that made a brief appearance in the 1970s, Bushnell saw many similarities between play and religion; in fact, he said, religion is "a form of play." Like religion, play is "impulsive, and inspired rather than driven, joyful rather than disciplined; it is the highest state of mankind."[17]

Few thinkers of his day had such an elevated theological estimation of play as did Bushnell. The mere fact that the play spirit was so evident in children and animals was clear evidence to Bushnell of its divine "appointment." How peculiar it would be, he said, if the instinct so evident in animals was withdrawn from humans, and how even more unusual it would be for God, once "having put the same sportive instinct in their make [to] restrict them to a carefully, practical sober mood." Play was not merely human enjoyment or earthly diversion, said Bushnell, but a symbol and mediator of Christian liberty and a foreshadowing of eternal life.[18]

Although Bushnell clearly thought play appropriate for children, it wasn't at all clear that he approved of play for adults. While he believed that child's play was innocent, free, and spontaneous, there is the impression that he believed adult play was too easily corrupted. Still, adults could find benefit in reflecting on their childhood play experiences that, to Bushnell's mind, held lasting symbolic significance for adults. God has set "the beginning of the natural life in a [playful] mood that foreshadows the last and highest chapter in immortal character." Adults can look back on the natural play experiences of childhood ("the paradise of nature behind us"), claimed Bushnell, and catch "a glimpse of paradise before us." For him, this symbolic reenactment of eternity was the basis for the sanctity of play.[19]

A more pragmatic tone was set five years later by Washington Gladden, a key leader in the social gospel movement. One highly controversial Sunday evening sermon Gladden preached at the First

Congregational Church in North Adams, Massachusetts, and later published so that his comments "would not be misconstrued and left to hearsay," stands as the era's most articulate examination of sports by a Christian leader. Gladden demolished the age-old Christian characterization of sports and amusements as sinful because they counterfeited the emotional satisfaction available only through prayer, devotion, hymn singing, and other devotional pursuits. Followed to its logical conclusion, said Gladden, this line of thinking would condemn almost any attempt to find enjoyment in this world, including the entertainments of literature and art and the endearments of home and family life, as sinful. "Recreation is indispensable to physical health," said Gladden, "and that cannot be a sin which God has made an imperative necessity to our bodily well-being." On this basis Gladden not only endorsed athletics and gymnastics but predicted that one day participation in sports would be enjoined as a Christian duty.[20]

Gladden's endorsement of sports and amusements did not mean that he accepted them unconditionally. Among those he singled out as especially wrong were amusements that led to the infliction of pain on men or animals. Equally sinful were amusements that exposed a player's life to harm or death, no matter how much athletic skill and courage they required. (Gladden thus condemned tightrope walking and "circus feats of all kinds" as morally wrong.) But not all sports were wrong, and Gladden faulted the Christian community for failing to make important distinctions between sports themselves and the abuses committed under the banner of sports. The church, he noted, had rejected many sports which, when viewed apart from their abuses, were innocent, excellent, and inherently good. As an example, he showed how billiards and bowling, "for the most part unhesitatingly condemned by Christian people," are "certainly most excellent gymnastic exercises . . . not only free in themselves from all that is vicious and harmful, they develop skill, physical strength, agility and precision of movement." But simply because they tended to be played in "bad places" and "for the most part by lewd fellows of the baser sort," these games were forbidden to young people by the church. Almost any form of amusement that was good in and of itself could be abused, even baseball, which Gladden noted "has been more orthodox than the rest among Christian people." Yet, he noted, "there are more abuses connected with base ball [sic] than with any other athletic sport in the land." Thus by their own logic, Christians who forbid bowling and billiards should also forbid baseball. Both are surrounded by excess, drinking, gambling, and profanity. Gladden wasn't suggesting that Christians "level [their] anathemas at ball-playing, and prohibit young men from engaging in this pastime," but that they look more carefully at all amusements, being careful to "commend the good and condemn the evil."[21]

For Gladden, the playgrounds of America were important spiritual battlegrounds upon which the forces of good contested with the forces of Satan for ownership of the best sports. When Satan corrupts any good pastime, Christians drop it "in horror, denouncing not only its abuses, but the game itself," so that "all the best amusements have been given up without a struggle to evil men and seducers, and have been used by them as powerful attractions by which to ensnare and ruin our youth." The solution, said Gladden, is not for the church to ignore sports but to rid them of their abuses and to guide them with Christian thinking. "The devil ought not to have the monopoly of the best games any more than of the best tunes. If he has got possession of them Christians should rescue them from his clutches, and surround them with proper safeguards, and guard them against abuses."[22]

Some, like the editor of a Congregational journal, had seen the light some years before. The church's obligation, said the writer, was to "provide, within the circle of Christian propriety and consistency, all the recreation which its adherents need." (Twenty years before Gladden's famous sermon, Moses Coit Tyler, an itinerant gymnast, intellectual, and the first American professor of history, had recommended converting a church sanctuary or two into exercise rooms, an innovation he believed would make people "more prayerful, and more charitable, and more virtuous, because they would have a more regular supply of gastric fluids, and less torpidity in the liver, and fewer obstructions of the intestinal canal.") But Gladden's sermon established the main talking points others would use in the ensuing decades in their efforts to pry open the gates to the playground. Typical were a writer's comments, one year after Gladden's sermon, warning that the church "must not ignore the subject of amusements, nor play the ascetic, nor simply criticize and complain; but it must provide pure, varied, and sufficient recreations, in doors and out of doors, for the daytime and for the evening, for the two sexes, singly and jointly, for mind and body, for those outside of the Church as well as for those within."[23]

SPORTS MOVE INTO THE CHURCH

Soon liberal clergy from many quarters were acknowledging the place of sports in the Christian life. In 1885, Williams S. Rainsford at St. George Episcopal Church in New York City was pressing for "athletic work among the boys and girls in every possible way": gymnasia and athletic fields, running tracks, cricket creases, and baseball fields. In 1891, Jersey City Tabernacle opened a "People's Palace"—a precursor to today's megachurch "family centers"—which included facilities for bowling, billiards, and physical culture classes with a gymnasium. Many nineteenth-century Episcopal parish houses included gymnasia and billiards rooms, facilities popular among the immigrants and laborers served by the houses. Church athletic teams came into existence as early as 1860, and by 1907 church athletic leagues were operating in New York City. A poll taken showed that of twenty-six large urban churches surveyed, twenty-four sponsored athletic teams.[24]

By the turn of the century, social gospel leader Josiah Strong remarked approvingly of a change in church architecture that included social parlors for improvement of social life, reading rooms, and even "facilities for physical culture and recreation—a gymnasium, baths, very likely a swimming pool, and perhaps a bowling alley, which not long since would have been deemed sacrilegious." Such trends were logical outgrowths, he said, for a religion committed to "uplifting . . . the whole man instead of a fraction of him, and to the salvation of society as well as to that of the individual." In triumphant tones, he proclaimed that such changes were critical because religion was increasingly "dealing less in futures and laying more emphasis on the present."[25]

Of the various rationales given to justify building sport facilities in churches, all incorporated Gladden's presumption that sports could work their good only if the church oversaw the way they were organized and played. If the church was to provide a place for the people to play, obviously it had a responsibility to provide the direction of that play. Some considered sport integral to the social life of the church as a way of forging strong bonds of fellowship. For example, in his book *The Church at Play*, Norman Richardson, a professor of religious education, attempted to show how sport could neutralize "criticism, selfish ambition and suspicion" by encouraging "friendliness, loyalty, courtesy, trustworthiness and team spirit." Others took a more pragmatic tack, arguing that church gymnasia were justified because they diverted young people from sin. Renting facilities for billiards, bowling, and ball playing, said one religion writer, "would do more to keep [the church's] young people from the ways of sin than a Sunday school." "If the boys can be kept from the streets and saloons by innocent games, let every church have its gymnasium," said another.[26]

Not everyone who valued sports as a way of luring young people to church held sport in high esteem. In his best-selling turn-of-the-century book *The Boy Problem*, William Bryan Forbush, in a not-very-subtle put-down of sports, envisoned them purely as a way of making contact with youth: "A contact that begins with athletics, walks, physical development and manual training may ripen into the literary, the scientific, the ethical and the religious influences. But it would seem wise to utilize the ruder instincts which are on the surface before reaching down to the deeper ones."[27]

SPORTS FOR CHARACTER

Getting young people off the streets and out of trouble and providing carefree moments of healthy and productive leisure for factory workers and immigrants were important aims of the social gospel movement, but it was the deeper and more significant belief that sports and play could directly and powerfully influence moral development that fueled the reformers' efforts. Their thinking on the topic had no doubt been influenced by the mid-nineteenth-century teachings and writings of Charles Kingsley, who is credited along with Thomas Hughes with founding the muscular Christianity movement in England. "In the playing field boys acquire virtues which no books can give them," said Kingsley, "not merely daring and endurance, but, better still, temper, self-restraint, fairness, honour, unenvious approbation of another's success, and that 'give and take' of life which stand a man in good stead when he goes forth into the world, and without which, indeed, his success is always maimed and partial."[28]

Such thinking resonated with the social gospellers who had an astonishing, if unanalyzed, confidence in the power of sport and play to positively affect lives. The new theology that viewed personal salvation in more humanistic terms was evident in the YMCA's gradual subordination of their charter goal of keeping men from sin to the more modern goal of making them physically and morally fit. Luther Gulick, a liberal evangelical and arguably the most significant figure in the early development of the YMCA, regarded the day he realized that "good bodies and good morals" went hand in hand as a profound turning point in his life. There was, he said, a relationship between physical discipline and moral rectitude; consequently, team games can bring about "direct spiritual results." In 1914 Harry F. Ward, a Methodist known for his radical socialist theology, elevated the importance of sports and games as shapers of character above theology by asserting that "religion is concerned today with character rather than creed, with conduct rather than ordinances, and we are learning from the people who are studying the question that there is no stronger means for building up of character than to take hold of the desire for recreation and use it constructively."[29]

This faith in the character-building power of sports was impelled more by "commonsense" than by empirical data or any well-defined theology. The playgrounds of cities were considered moral and ethical laboratories. Gulick and his colleagues believed that sports, and especially team sports, provided a public sphere in which ethical behavior could not only be tested but molded. He believed that peer pressure would constrain players' behaviors and shape them in socially desirable ways. Obeying the rules, being loyal and willing to sacrifice personal glory to the common cause, graciously accepting defeat, and looking upon victory as a group rather than individual achievement would not only make for good sportsmanship but would carry over to the larger society and prepare young people to be productive citizens.

The connection of this line of thought to theology was never well developed. In fact, efforts to do so often led to imperfect and muddled messages. When renowned philosopher Josiah Royce spoke to the Boston Physical Education Association in 1908 on the topic of group loyalty, he described it as the nexus of morality, and since loyalty must necessarily be expressed through action (muscular activity), sports were one of the best ways of instilling it. Royce said, "When the apostle compared the moral work of the saints to the running of a race his metaphors were well chosen because of this perfectly definite analogy between the devotion of the trained organism to its physical task and the devotion of the self to its cause."[30]

Such hyperbolic musings as to how sports shaped moral character were much in the air, often blurring the boundaries between moral, cognitive, and physical faculties. Many seemed to believe that exercising the body (especially in the context of a team sport) exercised the mind and morals at the same time. Muscle control was seen as the direct link between children's cognitive-moral decision making and their conduct in social settings. This had enormous implications for those oversee-ing sport programs, for the muscles were more accessible and easier to control than thoughts or feelings. As historian Dominick Cavallo put it, the thinking was, "control the muscles and you control the mind and conscience." An official of the American Playground Association put it in more poetic terms: "First the feet begin to keep time, then the whole body catches the rhythm, then the individual forgets his dignity, his pride, becomes a little child and has entered the kingdom of heaven, has joined the dance and has become part of the team."[31]

And what sport could do for players it could also do for spectators. According to Jane Addams, legendary founder of the famous settle-ment house in Chicago and winner of the Nobel Peace Prize in 1931, players and spectators alike "are lifted out of their individual affairs and so fused together that a man cannot tell whether it is his own shout or another's that fills his ears; whether it is his own coat or another's that he is wildly waving to celebrate a victory. Does not this contain a suggestion of the undoubted powers of public recreation to bring together all classes of a community in the modern city unhappily so full of devices for keeping men apart?"[32]

Protestant ministers and religion writers took their cues from play reformers, often proposing majestic benefits that were derived from playing vigorous sports. In 1912, University of Chicago religion professor Allan Hoben published *The Minister and the Boy*, devot-ing an entire chapter to "The Ethical Value of Organized Play." Being careful to first warn of "the danger of erecting a superficial and mere pleasure-seeking ideal of life [in the] revival of play that is sweeping over our American cities," Hoben went on to note many similarities between play and religion. Both were spontaneous, both were expres-sive of the self and free from "ulterior ends," both attract by powers of "semi-intoxication and rhythm," and both prepare for effective living. But the most important religious function of sports, wrote Hoben, was their potential for shaping character. He doubted if anything, even the Ten Commandments, "could compete with a properly directed game in enforcing the fair play principle."[33]

Hoben's assertion made explicit a point often buried in the flow-ery testimonials to play by many theologians: the moralisms in the Sunday morning sermon or in the lessons of Scripture may prick a few consciences or perhaps prepare a few hearts for social reform, but as a laboratory experience guaranteed to instill strength of character, sensitivity to others, and a spirit of justice, the playground was miles ahead of the pulpit. And what play could do for society at large it could also do for the local church. Criticism, backbiting, selfish ambition, and suspicion, deadly enemies of church unity, could be neutralized by the "friendliness, loyalty, courtesy, trustworthiness and team spirit" that came from playing games together. Unable to anticipate the less appealing side of modern church league sport, Richardson theorized that "when church people really play together they cannot help becoming better friends."[34]

BODY REFORM MOVEMENT

Christian perceptions of sport were also influenced by the health and fitness movement that swept the country in the late nineteenth century, thanks in part to the early influences of Sylvester Graham (for whom the famous cracker is named) and Bernarr Macfadden. Graham was an ordained clergyman who achieved widespread attention for his collection of largely misguided theories about nutrition and health. His enthusiasm for health and exercise percolated into grandiose claims for physiology to the point where fitness became more important than orthodox Christian doctrine. "The millennium can never reasonably be expected to arrive, until those laws which God has implanted in the physical nature of man are, equally with his moral laws, universally known and obeyed," spouted Graham. Salvation didn't require conversion or church attendance as much as adhering to "rational laws of health, easily understood by common people, without help from clergy or physicians." He held that the key to salvation was exercising, controlling the sexual appetite, and eating well, which for Graham meant eating a lot of oat bran. Graham's followers continued his health reforms, although with less flourish and more scientifically circumspect rhetoric.[35]

Following in Graham's wake, and contemporaneously with the social gospel, a body reform movement took root, propelled in large part by the writings and preaching of Bernarr Macfadden, a man variously described by biographers as preacher, body builder, faddist, promoter, huckster, sexpot, crusader, and self-proclaimed father of the Physical Culture Movement. The flamboyant Macfadden preached a religion of physicality, describing it as "a religion superior to traditional religion," which he called "prudish" and "repressive." The tendency of both Graham and Macfadden to set the practice of religion at odds with the practice of bodily health was at least partly responsible for a reactionary, evangelical-based body reform movement aimed at reuniting the two. The movement blossomed under the aegis of those whom historian Clifford Putney labeled as "the body-as-temple men." Sermons and writings heralding the sanctity of the body, its importance as the temple of the soul, and the Christian's duty to keep it in good order became the vogue, at least in the more moderate and liberal ranks of evangelicalism. For some of the temple men the body was more than a container for the soul; it was a means of salvation in itself. As historian Harvey Green observes, "perfection of the body was an essential part of Christian morality in this system of thought and was perhaps the most vivid expression of the prewar millennial spirit which had promoted the idea that human action could determine individual and social salvation."[36]

Beyond the basic "body-as-temple" metaphor, explanations of how sport participation and a healthy body redounded to the spiritual benefit of players tended to be long on presumption and short on theology. The most commonly voiced theory pointed to bodily health as a prerequisite for salvation, and since sports were the accepted means to bodily health, they formed the first step in the path to redemption. Sports may not be salvific in themselves, said a turn-of-the-century preacher, but they are "a first cousin to religion" because "refreshment of the body went a long way toward giving the soul a chance." "To be a well man or woman is the first step towards being a religious man or woman . . . in a redeemed world the body must be redeemed as well as the mind," was how an editor of the magazine *Outlook* put it. For Washington Gladden, it was a settled principle: the healthful benefits of play bolstered the soul's defenses against the forces of Satan. Out of the diseased and unfit body came "the cravings for stimulants and narcotics" and much of the "irritability and bad tempers of which men have to repent."[37]

Few in the early twentieth century spelled out the spiritual vision for recreation quite as forcefully or eloquently as did Norman Richardson, who came close to suggesting that it was indispensable for salvation: "Multitudes of men and women exist under such conditions as to make it physically and mentally impossible for them to respond to the gospel message unless that gospel message comes to them in the form of opportunities for recreation." Not only this, said Richardson, recreation can help people "retain the hope, the faith, the love which was theirs before they were caught in the mesh of the modern world's work and care." It was a grandiose vision that captured the imagination of the body reformers unlike any other aspect of theology.[38]

The YMCA played a special role in forging links between the spiritual and the physical. Inspired by the mid-century revivals in Britain, the organization was founded in 1844 as a spiritual ministry to "influence young men to spread the Redeemer's Kingdom amongst those by whom they are surrounded" through Bible studies, prayer, and fellowship. The first American association was begun in Boston in 1851, and other branches followed quickly throughout the country. Although rooted in a strong evangelical mission, the association was ecumenical in its scope, ever conscious of the need to walk a middle course between social Christianity and a more conservative, world-shunning fundamentalism. But as the social gospel movement continued to shed an ever-expanding light on social injustice, poverty, and other ills connected with urban life, the YMCA adopted an increasingly "this-world" conception of the gospel and expanded its outreach to include sports and exercise.

The move to provide for gymnasia in the architectural plans of the early Ys received the enthusiastic endorsements of such theologically diverse ministers as liberal Congregationalist Henry Beecher and evangelist Dwight Moody, although Moody would later question the emphasis placed on social reform and worry that sports had eclipsed spiritual enrichment in Y programming. In the beginning, the gymnasia were viewed primarily as a means for attracting young men to religious programs, but through the efforts of leaders such as Luther Gulick, the gyms were "Christianized" by injecting Bible studies into exercise lessons, often over the objections of some rough-hewn physical directors who weren't entirely sympathetic with the YMCA's religious goals. For Gulick, the gymnasium should be neither "a trap to catch young men" nor something that existed only for the bodies of its members. "The gymnasium belonged to the YMCA," said Gulick, "as a fundamental and intrinsic part in the salvation of man."[39]

Over the complaints of some conservative evangelicals, the YMCA gradually stretched its mission beyond its old custodial rule of keeping young men from sin to include the more progressive goal of character building, and sport played a pivotal role in this revised mission. As early as the 1880s, YMCAs encouraged bowling and billiards and endorsed ball games while many conservative denominations were still denouncing them. The New York YMCA sponsored "Athletic Sundays," which included testimonies by the famous coach Amos Alonzo Stagg, members of the Princeton football team, and Billy Sunday, the converted baseball player who was soon to become the dominant evangelist of the era.

Although the association took a strong stand against some aspects of professional and collegiate sports, especially the "evils of betting, swearing, physical excesses, dishonesty, and a trivial view of the serious things in life," sports reform was hardly the aim of the movement. In the minds of Gulick and others laboring at the Springfield, Massachusetts YMCA Training School (now Springfield College), reform would come about automatically if enough Christian men were trained and infused into the teaching and coaching ranks.[40]

Thus the rise of sport within the YMCA went hand in hand with a gradual separation of the Y's programs from evangelical theology. The mission of saving souls was gradually replaced with a vague sense of character enhancement. Exercise and sport, rather than religion, became valued as the most potent instruments for developing character. The transition of the Y from a spiritual haven to a sport and exercise emporium did not go smoothly. Hard feelings erupted between those who wanted the YMCA to retain its commitment to an emphasis on spiritual development and those who envisioned a worldlier social mission. Eventually the Y and its sport programs were aligned with a liberal theology, which did nothing to improve sport's image in the minds of conservatives who, under other circumstances, might have welcomed athletics, provided it was thoroughly integrated with a New Testament ethos. Increasingly, a liberal vision dominated the organization. By 1923 a distinguished foreign secretary of the YMCA felt free to publicly declare that he had changed his creed from "I believe in God" to "I believe." And in 1930, the *Association Forum* published an article that summarized the Easter message as consisting of the "concepts of sacredness of personality, the duty of service, the reality of fellowship, and the power of self-sacrifice."[41]

With the elimination of the creedal statement ("the evangelical test") that had been long required for membership and the adoption of a broad theology that aimed at "a world-wide fellowship of men and boys united by a common loyalty to Jesus Christ for the purpose of building Christian personality and a Christian society," the organization had virtually separated itself from its initial evangelical moorings. When one of the Y's most popular leaders rose at a national convention in 1931 to complain that sports and other activities were crowding out the Y's religious mission and to urge support for a commitment to belief "in Jesus Christ as a living leader of personal religion and social reform," he found himself roundly outnumbered by those who thought his suggestion too radical. From the viewpoint of Christianity's rocky relationship with sport, he shouldn't have been surprised. Whenever the choices have been for religion *or* sport, invariably the people and their religious leaders have chosen sport.[42]

MUSCULAR CHRISTIANITY

No mention of a religion of physicality in the late nineteenth and early twentieth centuries can ignore the contribution of a broad-based sport and masculinity movement termed "muscular Christianity" that made its appearance as part of the mid-nineteenth-century Christian socialist movement in England. The movement, founded by Charles Kingsley, was aimed at instilling manliness and Christian character in young men through hard and, as some contended, brutal forms of play. Thomas Hughes popularized the connection of godliness to manliness in a series of boy-targeted novels such as *Tom Brown's Schooldays* and *Tom Brown at Oxford*. The manliness preached by Kingsley and Hughes was more than a shade removed from the Victorian ideal of S. T. Coleridge and Matthew Arnold, where to be "manly" was to be mature, responsible, intelligent, and above all, possessing of Christian character. For muscular Christians who thought "effeminacy" was being cultivated in seminaries and sapping the vitality of the Anglican Church, the cultivation of manliness was not merely a means of recasting a pathetic clerical image; it was a spiritual duty. So venerated was manliness in the muscular Christian cult that one critic accused it of redefining a saint as "one who can walk a thousand miles in a thousand hours," while another contended that for Kingsley, "Christian practice seems not seldom to mean little more than being clean and physically well-developed."[43]

For Kingsley, manliness came by participating in outdoor activities, not so much by sports and games as "natural activities" such as hiking rugged trails, climbing trees, taking ice-cold morning baths, and other wilderness pursuits. Hughes, on the other hand, believed resolutely in the inherent value of rough team sport activities and the need to develop what he referred to as "the animal spirits of the young." "Bring 'em up sarcy, Marm," was his advice to mothers, "I like to see boys brought up sarcy." He was fond of team sports such as cricket and soccer because they taught unselfishness, but he was particularly fond of rugby, which he said "was worth living for; the whole sum of schoolboy existence gathered up into one straining, struggling half-hour; a half-hour worth of a year of common life." Even boxing and fistfighting were regarded as "the natural way for English boys to settle their quarrels": "As to fighting, keep out of it all you can, by all means . . . But don't say 'No' because you fear a licking, and say or think it's because you fear God, for that's neither Christian nor honest."[44]

Twenty years after first publishing *Tom Brown's Schooldays*, Hughes wrote *The Manliness of Christ*, in which he enumerated the "tests of manliness" in chivalric terms: contempt for ease, readiness to risk pain or death for the right, loyalty to truth, and self-restraint. But after having a chance to observe sports in America, he expressed regret at the excesses he saw in athletics. Athletic prowess, he concluded, was not proof of manliness after all. "A great athlete may be a brute or a coward, while a truly manly man can be neither." If it was not actually the case, the impression is that Hughes mellowed in his later years and softened his stand on the value of rough and violent play. But if he did mellow, it came long after his and Kingsley's influence had been felt by liberal churchmen in America.[45]

The fingerprints of muscular Christianity and male mythmaking were all over the social gospel conception of play and sport in America, a fact that was especially evident in popular books published in the early decades of the twentieth century. Sport's potential for developing the manly qualities of courage, perseverance in the face of hardship, and mental and physical toughness were character traits many were eager to link with the social gospel. The movement had come under fire for its underlying melting mood of sympathy, compassion, and fellow-feeling and was seen in the eyes of many as a milquetoast religion, appealing to all "that is timid and shrinking rather than that which is courageous and outspoken." Intellectuals of the period—theologians and ministers especially—were often caricatured as wishy-washy, frail and nerdy, and hopelessly inept in physical skills, especially those required in athletics. So emasculated had the clergy's image become, said the Reverend Thomas Wentworth Higginson, that when two sides were to be chosen in a bowling match, the two participating ministers were the last to be picked. As if this were not enough, said Higginson, the man everyone agreed was the best preacher was picked last, the choice being made, said the team captain, on the assumption that "the best preacher would naturally be the worst bowler."[46]

For many in the social gospel, simply exposing boys to virile models in a sporting context and offering some moral tutoring was all that was needed to set boys on the right path. As William Forbush put it, "a man with some slight athletic prowess, a willingness to guide by adaptability rather than by domineering, can do almost anything with a group of boys." Allan Hoben encouraged rural ministers to be available to supervise boys in after-school sports programs; if the boys, said Hoben, "do not get more moral benefit and real equipment for life's struggle in this hour and a half than they are likely to get from a day's bookwork in the average one-room, all-grades, girl-directed country school, it must be because the minister is a sorry specimen." In 1915, the American Sunday School Union published two books that represented first and second prizes in a competition for the best manuscript on the topic of amusements. Both Howard Young's *Character Through Recreation* (first prize) and Robert Whitaker's *Laughter and Life* (second prize) preached the values of sport in developing manly traits. Whitaker's book (with due apologies to the judges) was by far the most perceptive. It was a high regard for manliness that moved Whitaker to imagine a "manly Christ" who was "the Christ of the Playground." Blasting medieval depictions of Jesus as a frail and tortured being in a sickly appeal to "the violent sympathies of untutored minds," Whitaker envisioned a virile, vigorous, fun-loving, and, most importantly, muscular person. "Jesus would be vastly more popular with men if we had not feminized and clericalized half of his maleness away," he said. "We have an urgent need," he said, "to get back to the New Testament type."[47]

The idea of linking masculinity to spirituality had a long history in Christianity. Images of powerful men with bulging biceps voluntarily waiving their manly capacities and humbling themselves before a righteous God had stirred hearts and minds as far back as the thirteenth century, when virile knights strutted arrogantly on the lists after kneeling in pre-match prayers. It was both an alluring and enduring image that linked human fortitude with spiritual discipline in a way the early Calvinists would not have appreciated. By suggesting that health and physical effort paved the way for a sanctified life, the body-as-temple men may have been in sync with tenets of the new theology, but they were miles apart from a historic Calvinism that had preached the utter insufficiency of humans to save themselves. Yet by implicitly incorporating the myth of masculinity into the doctrines of Christianity, a powerful soul-grabbing image was projected: if men of strong might and will still needed to kneel before a righteous God, then to an immeasurably greater degree the weak needed to so! It has been an amazingly durable theme that continues to color the testimonies of modern athlete evangelists to this day.

VOICES IN THE WILDERNESS

The optimism that colored social gospel commentary on sport almost always was a qualified optimism. Religious leaders had sensed the dual potentiality of sport: to shatter character just as easily as it could strengthen it, to teach dishonesty as well as honesty, to degrade as well as uplift players and spectators, and to retard as well as advance the cause of the social gospel. If sport was to help advance the lofty goals of the social gospel movement, Christian direction was essential. "The only way to prevent people from becoming victims of permanently injurious influence," said Richardson, was "to inspire and direct their recreation activities." Without moral leadership, said Atkinson, the craze for pleasure "exercises itself, not in wholesome relaxation from work, but in excitement growing out of the whirl of senseless amusements, which leaves a person bankrupt, physically, mentally and morally." And moral bankruptcy was certain to occur when sports were left in the charge of those whose only interest was financial. We would not think of allowing education and religion to be governed by the law of supply and demand, said Gladden; neither should we allow play to be governed by the same principle. He believed that if supply and demand were allowed to shape public amusements, what sells would soon define community moral standards, and the trend inevitably is downward. In the minds of even the most enthusiastic social gospel preachers, sport and play could work their good ends only when infused with the Christian spirit and guided by the ethics of a social Christianity.[48]

Thus, if the church gymnasium and the church athletic team were expressions of Protestantism's newfound enthusiasm for play, they just as clearly marked an age-old concern for the moral dangers it posed. The need to impress sport with the distinctiveness of the Christian faith— not only church-sponsored sport, but sport on the public playgrounds, in gymnasia, and on the athletic fields of colleges—was taken very seriously. The Christian's duty, said Whitaker, was to "make recreation moral in purpose, fill the whole spirit of it with the sense of God as filling all life." If this happened, he said, "the more mischievous forms of recreation will slough off themselves." One of the few in the movement who hesitated to saddle the church with the burden of organizing and supervising games and amusements, Washington Gladden, thought reform had the best chance of succeeding if dedicated Christians would merely seek positions as recreation leaders in secular agencies. There the "kingdom of amusements," like the "kingdom of industry or the kingdom of politics," could be brought under the empire of Christian ideas and forces. The Christian community, he said, should "enter into them and pervade them and transform them by its own vital energy," even if it meant wresting control from Satan himself. As the Christian community was soon to discover, it was much easier to heed Gladden's admonitions to "enter into" and "pervade" sports than to "transform them."[49]

As described in chapter 3, many evangelical denominations took bold and ferocious stands against football and other sport spectacles, but in their battle to reclaim athletics and Christianize sport, they were pitted against a thriving sports establishment propelled by commercial and egoist impulses that had captured Americans' hearts as well as their pocketbooks. It was a mismatch that the Protestant reformers had almost no chance of winning, but like the good soldiers they were, they stood fast in the trenches, not hesitating to bring under fire any immorality paraded under the banner of sports. And there was much for them to complain about.

By the late nineteenth century, college and university athletic programs were rife with scandal. Administrators had begun to discover that the financial benefits of winning far outweighed the educational benefits of losing, and in the pursuit of victory, shady dealings became matters of course. Seven members of the 1893 University of Michigan football team were found not to have been enrolled as students. Yale was accused of luring a talented athlete by offering him free meals, tuition, a trip to Cuba, a monopoly on the sale of football programs, and a position as agent for the American Tobacco Company. A player known only as "Wood" was one of several Georgia Tech ruffians who played in Tech's 1893 game against Georgia. Alleged to have been invincible, Wood was struck by stones thrown from the Georgia fans as he dragged Georgia tacklers up and down the field. "Wood's response was to plaster the face of a Georgia player with a handful of blood and gore," walk off the field to his hotel room, and stitch up his own wound.[50]

The sheer violence of football prompted calls from many clergy to ban or modify the game. Georgetown University suspended football for two years in 1894 after a player was killed, apparently by being kicked in the back. Twelve years later another Georgetown player was killed, convincing the university that the game should be abolished altogether. "The bloodshed had been altogether out of proportion to the athletic benefit," said the head of the university. Twelve players were killed in

1902 and twenty in 1905. Such brutality offered in the name of sport was anathema to the social reformers who had labored so hard to improve the physical health of the nation. One of the most blistering accusations came from Shailer Mathews, dean of the Divinity School at the University of Chicago, a popular proponent of social Christianity: "Football today is a social obsession—a boy killing, education-prostituting, gladiatorial sport. It teaches virility and courage, but so does war. I do not know what should take its place, but the new game should not require the services of a physician, the maintenance of a hospital, and the celebration of funerals."[51]

Conservative evangelicals, especially those in the South, objected not only to the game's corruption and violence but also to its effect on the spiritual temperament. It released "unrestrained male sinfulness" and "fostered the male passions" that evangelicals had devoted such effort to containing. The brutality of the sport, said the Methodist *Alabama Christian Advocate*, "tends to so animalize the players as to make fighting come naturally." And its effect on fans was not good either, "convert[ing] a crowd of students, inflamed with liquor and excited by loyalty to their institution, into a howling mob of toughs, gamblers and drunkards."[52] But representatives from the religious community were hardly united against football and other rough sports during the period. About the same time Charles Eliot stewed about football at Harvard, Father John Cavanaugh, president of Notre Dame, was telling people, "I would rather see our youth playing football with the danger of a broken collar bone occasionally than to see them dedicated to croquet." With time, churches in both the South and the North softened their opposition to the game, but not as a result of any evident change in their theological or general ethical convictions. Public demand simply won out over clerical outrage. In 1929, during the official dedication of the Sports Bay in the Cathedral of St. John the Divine in New York City, Episcopalian bishop William I. Manning told the assembled: "A well played game of polo or of football is in its own place and in its own way as pleasing to God as a beautiful service of worship in the Cathedral."[53]

Boxing was, in many ways, an easier target for evangelical critics. The Jack Dempsey–Georges Carpentier fight in 1921 was condemned by both the General Assembly of the Presbyterian Church of the United States and the Board of Temperance and Public Morals of the Methodist-Episcopal Church, the latter urging that this be the last fight on American soil. The Methodist-Episcopals objected even more strenuously to

the famous Dempsey-Tunney fight scheduled as part of the sesquicen-
tennial celebration in Philadelphia, calling it "unrepresentative of American life, and a disgrace to the city of Philadelphia." When the general
director of moral welfare for the Presbyterian Church joined the attack,
Pennsylvania's Governor Pinchot came to boxing's defense, pointing to
its importance in preparing for war and citing the improved atmosphere
at arenas where boxing matches are held.[54]

But even a sport that seemed so egregious a violator of the Christian ethic failed to provoke a united front from the religious community.
When a hearing was held at the State House in Albany, New York, on
the Walker Bill, which proposed to legalize boxing and place it under
state regulation, both the leading proponent and the leading dissident
were Episcopal ministers. Speaking against the bill with backing from
the Women's Temperance Union, the Salvation Army, and a representative of the YMCA was the Reverend William Chase, who argued that
the bill would open the door to "brutalized ring exhibitions" and attract
gamblers and gangsters. Speaking in favor of the bill with backing from
military veterans and various sports aficionados was Episcopal rector Dr.
B. W. R. Taylor, who told the group: "For the men who oppose boxing . . .
I say they are lacking in sporting blood and true manly spirit, and I don't
give a fig for anybody without sporting blood." A list of nine hundred
clergymen who favored the bill was presented at the hearing.[55]

In the end, the complaints of morally minded Protestants were little
more than straws in the wind. The church had entered into and per-
vaded athletics, but it never really achieved much in the way of transforming sport. Two out of three wasn't bad, but it was never enough to
keep sports from falling under the sway of an ethos that, in many ways,
has shown itself to be an awkward fit with the Christian gospel. A few
victories could be claimed, but they were small and scattered. Protests
from evangelicals have been credited with bringing about rule changes
that eliminated some of the grosser forms of barbarity associated with
turn-of-the-century football, such as the infamous "flying wedge" that
had led to scores of injuries. Also, some church athletic programs reported
some success in shaping ethical perceptions of play. William Rainsford,
in recounting how successful the athletic program in his parish had been,
pointed not only to his teams' competitive successes, but to their help in
combating what he labeled "the chief danger of American athleticism—
professionalism." Aside from such isolated triumphs, history records no
major impact of the social gospel on the popular conception and practice

of sports. There is no evidence that the high ideals that figured so prominently in the rhetoric of church leaders were ever realized. Instead of sport growing closer to the ideals of the Christian faith, it ultimately moved in another direction, propelled by the forces of public taste and commercial interest.[56]

5

THE RISE OF SPORT EVANGELISM

The progressive philosophy of the social gospel movement would continue to be associated with liberal theology and practice, but its force as a revitalizing and unifying agent for Protestantism had greatly diminished by 1920. The world was not getting better, as Enlightenment evangelicalism had predicted. By the end of World War I, the stage was set for a ferocious battle between conservative and liberal evangelicals, a conflict that would find its full fruition in the "fundamentalist-modernist controversy" in the twentieth century. The ire of fundamentalists was especially provoked by the tendency of many liberals to substitute a concern for social betterment for the singularly important matter of personal salvation.

The impulse for social reform, originally sparked in conservative quarters by nineteenth-century revivalism, had diminished, as had serious ruminations by Protestants about sport and play as part of the divine economy. Ecclesiastical condemnation of big-time sports, common fodder for sermons in the nineteenth century, no longer thundered from pulpits. Vanishing too were learned works on play, sports, and amusements intended to help Christians to position sport in the framework of their religious lives. The liberals had thrown the ball onto the field and conservatives, so to speak, had picked it up and run with it, unfazed by its more troublesome aspects that had so worried the social gospel leaders.

In the stampede to the playground, Robert Whitaker's vision of an "evangelized sport" and his pleas for Christians to work to "make recreation moral in purpose" and to "fill the whole spirit of it with the sense of God" were trampled underfoot. So were Washington Gladden's admonitions to Christians to enter into, pervade, and transform sport. From this point on, the mania for sports would spread with little or no denominational, doctrinal, or religious direction. But sport would continue to capture the imagination of the Christian community, although largely unaffected and unexamined by the ethical derivatives of any theological motif.[1]

It may not be an exaggeration to say that sport came to the defense of fundamentalism. The first three decades of the twentieth century were not good years for fundamentalists. Conservatives steadily lost their grip on mainline Protestant denominations (except for Lutherans and Southern Baptists) whose colleges, seminaries, and outreach organizations had come under the influence of liberal social and theological thinking. Increasingly (and perhaps undeservedly), fundamentalism came to be associated with a lower-middle class, unsophisticated mentality that distrusted intellectuals and popular social trends. In reaction to a steady enlargement of liberal churches and theology, fundamentalists hardened their stance, emphasized their belief in "the fundamentals of faith," and became an embittered minority with a suspect social image. Sport, especially in the form of famous Christian athletes and coaches, promised fundamentalism what it could find in few other avenues of society: social respectability. If liberals could use sport as a means of social reform, conservative evangelicals could use it to polish a tarnished social image. If liberals could co-opt sport to discredit the effeminate reputation often associated with the social gospel, fundamentalists could use it to show that a popular, manly athlete could humble himself to walk the sawdust trail in a tent meeting and publicly kneel at the altar.[2]

For liberal reformers like Robert Whitaker, "sport evangelism" had meant transforming ("evangelizing") sport by changing its tone and methods to conform to Christian thinking. The evangelical form of sport evangelism meant taking sport as society had shaped it and using it as a spotlight to shine on the human need for redemption. Liberals had favored informal sports. They fretted about the sketchy morality of sport spectacles organized for commercial purposes. But for conservatives, the publicity such spectacles promised was the handmaiden of the evangelistic harvest. Informal sports played on playgrounds, sandlots, and even in church gymnasia were important, but they never captured the conservative imagination quite like sports played in the arena. Spectator entertainment and hero-worship, more than sports participation per se, were seen as the keys to unlocking the kingdom. Fandom, long suspect by Protestants, had found a home in the evangelical community.

The impetus for mixing sport with evangelicalism came from late Victorian England, where the myths of athleticism and muscular Christianity, originally propagated as part of liberal-social Christianity, were co-opted by English evangelicals and exported to America. The myth was personified in the Cambridge Seven cricket players, many of whom had been converted at American evangelist Dwight L. Moody's revivals in England in 1884. Not all were from Cambridge, yet all had some identifiable connection to sports. One, C. T. Studd, was considered to be the premier cricket player of his day. Shortly after their conversions, all seven volunteered as missionaries to China and spent their lives in mission work. In the weeks before they departed for the mission field, they were featured in a series of "farewell meetings," part of a barnstorming tour of Scotland and England. The tour was intended to pay tribute to these men who had committed their lives to Christ and to encourage other university students to do the same. Although the men weren't all elite athletes, the evangelical community milked the athletic image, playing up their exploits at meetings and in the press. The vision of young men of decent social class, well-educated, clean-cut, manly, and athletic, sitting on stage at the meetings, singing hymns, and telling of their own conversions and callings to the mission field was, in the words of one writer, "a sight to stir the blood, and a testimony to the power of the uplifted Christ to draw unto himself, not the weak, the emotional, the intellectual only, but all that is noblest in strength and finest in culture." Fifty years later evangelicals were still polishing the athletic image. Studd's biographer, Norman Grubb, titled his biography *C. T. Studd: Cricketeer and Pioneer*, even though Studd had played cricket seriously for only five years or so and had been a missionary for forty-five.[3]

The year after the Cambridge Seven set off to China, a better-than-average American baseball player by the name of Billy Sunday became a Christian. Five years later he retired from baseball, entered the ministry, and between 1896 and 1920 became the most popular figure in American religion, courted by presidents and men of wealth. On one national poll, he was tied for eighth place with Andrew Carnegie as "the greatest man in the United States." Sunday preached an elementary theology he characterized as "the old time religion" and set it against the "deodorized and disinfected sermons" of "evolution-loving liberals" who, he claimed, were making "a religion out of social service with Christ left out." His oratorical antics—handsprings, "sliding into base," standing on stools, arm waving, and other choreographed theatrics—captured the imagination of a public starved for entertainment. Less recognized by historians, however, was Sunday's role in consolidating the link between sport and evangelicalism.[4] He justified his flamboyant and often vulgar style on grounds that it appealed to the masses and added to his harvest of souls. His sermons were sprinkled with baseball analogies and tales from his days on the diamond. Backsliders were chided because their "spiritual batting average[s] were not up to God's league standard." He ridiculed those "who step up to the collection plate at church and fan," depicted lost souls as those "who are dying on second and third base," and urged the Lord to "give us some coaches out at this Tabernacle so that people can be brought home to you."[5]

Sunday called attention to fundamentalism in an age when liberals were getting all the respect and winning most of the battles. By preaching a no-nonsense gospel of equal parts militancy and masculinity, Sunday engendered the respect of the common man. He conjured up a tough, chip-on-his-shoulder Christ. "Jesus was no dough-faced, lick-spittle proposition. Jesus was the greatest scrapper that ever lived." With a violent Christ as the prototype, Sunday urged his crowds to be ready to stand and fight against an "off-handed, flabby-cheeked, brittle-boned, weak-kneed, thin-skinned, pliable, plastic, spineless, effeminate, ossified three carat Christianity." When audiences, especially college men, resisted his altar calls, he appealed to their masculine instincts: "Do you know why you haven't come down here? You're not man enough. I throw it in your teeth. You're not man enough."[6]

Sunday had become a Christian in 1887 and continued playing baseball until 1891. Two years later, in an article titled "Why I Left Professional Baseball," he listed ten reasons why he left baseball, but not before making clear that the profession was agreeable and honest, that he viewed it as "a healthful occupation," and that his retirement had nothing to do with his flagging skills. (He did have reservations about the way the game "developed a spirit of jealousy and selfishness [in which] one's whole desires are for personal success regardless of what befalls others.") Wheaton College professors Tony Ladd and James Mathisen point to Sunday's article as evidence of his rejection of professional sports, arguing that it signaled the dawn of what they termed a growing "disengagement" between fundamentalism and sport.[7] If indeed such disengagement occurred during this period, Sunday was hardly its cause. He remained a fan of the game. His list of reasons for leaving baseball curiously omitted the rampant drunkenness among baseball players—what many ministers of his day found most problematic about the sport—even though he frequently excoriated "the liquor traffic" in his meetings. After he had retired from baseball, he continued to exploit his baseball persona by incorporating baseball metaphors and antics into his sermons. He played in an old-timer's game in Philadelphia and forcefully advocated for baseball in the press. Said Sunday: "When some withered-up, walrus-jawed, limber-legged, gimlet-eyed, pink-tea-blooded old fool of a pessimist comes to me and tells me in a voice like a dying calf and the gurgle of a wheezy cistern pump that the game is crooked as the devil, and that pennants are bought and sold, I feel like knocking his block into the middle of next week."[8]

THE RISE OF THE SPORT EVANGELIST

Sunday certainly wasn't the only Christian ballplayer of his day, nor was he the only advocate of a gospel of evangelical masculinity. His career spanned an age when fundamentalist barriers to a wide range of sports were being lowered, first in northern denominations and later in southern churches; it was an age in which the prototype of the clean, all-American, Christian athlete made its first appearance. Young people began to have paraded before them in the religious press famous Christian athletes who, if not always evangelical in their theology, shared evangelicals' contempt for smoking, drinking, dancing, and carousing. The social constraints on evangelicalism, not always attractive to adolescents, were recast as practical benefits of the faith and held up for admiration by young athletes. Typical was an article that appeared in 1911 in The Amethyst, an organ of the Northern Presbyterian Church, titled "What Baseball Players Think of Cigarettes." Readers were assured that Clark Griffith, Branch Rickey, and "Home Run Baker" didn't think it was right to smoke, and that Walker John, "the world's greatest pitcher, does not drink, smoke, or chew and goes to bed early."[9]

In linking Christian morality to sports celebrity, evangelicals came to appreciate early on that the evangelistic currency of sports hinged largely on competitive success. It was winning, not playing fair, that brought attention. Thus, the image of a champion became more salient in the evangelical cause than either the image of the good sportsman or that of the squeaky clean, upright-living, manly man, although if both came in a single package, so much the better.

In the latter decades of the nineteenth century there were, as Robert Higgs notes, "a virtual army of Christian coaches," the most famous of whom were better models of the athletic than the Christian ethic. John Heisman, the football coach at Georgia Tech who hated fumbling as much as he loathed profanity, had a well-earned reputation for "gaming the system." He illegally signaled plays from the sideline, perfected the "hidden ball play" in which the quarterback would stuff the ball under his jersey while pretending to tie his shoe, and was repudiated by colleagues for running up the score against hapless Cumberland College (222–0) in retaliation for a trouncing Cumberland had given to Tech's baseball team a year earlier. Fielding "Hurry Up" Yost at Michigan regarded his coaching position as "a pulpit" for preaching football as a "sanctified instrument for the good"; he opposed smoking, drinking, and swearing. At the same time, he thought nothing about humiliating unmatched opponents. He is reported to have gloated about his team's thrashing (130–0) of the University of West Virginia in 1904 and having outscored opponents 2271 to 42 in a span of four years. He was a committed Christian, yet was described by Stanford's president as a practitioner of "the kind of corruptions in athletics that colleges should eschew."[10]

But the coach whose career best crystallized the tensions between living the Christian life and establishing a reputation as a winning coach was Amos Alonzo Stagg, arguably the most famous American football coach to walk the sideline. Stagg, a student of theology, described coaching as a kind of Christian service. He was hired in 1892 by the University of Chicago's president, who liked having a man "who could direct athletics and pray" at the same time. Yet Stagg's religion never interfered with his compulsion to win. Guided by his twin philosophies that "the objective of football is to win rather than to play merely for pleasure" and that football is "a game of war within the limitations of the rules and of sportsmanship," he established a remarkable reputation, not only as a winning coach, but as one who helped put college athletics on a win at all cost trajectory. After browbeating the University of Chicago president into agreeing that he "not [be] compelled to explain for what purposes certain money [in the athletic budget] is to be used," Stagg continued to whine that he "was not doing right by myself in agreeing to come to Chicago for so small a salary," even though he was paid many times more than the typical professor. In 1898, he was rebuked by the president for using an ineligible player. He had no qualms about the viciousness that was essential for fielding a winning football team, once remarking to a player that he had picked him for his team "because you can do the meanest things in the most gentlemanly manner."[11]

The success of Stagg's teams owed not only to his managerial genius and flare for strategy, but to on-the-field trickery and deception that barely skirted the line of cheating, prompting his critics to call his coaching style "most unchristian." Stagg was unchastened, writing that while the British honor both the letter and spirit of the rules, Americans honor only the letter, something he thought fine: "If we are smart enough to detect a joker or loophole first, then we are entitled not only in law but ethics to take advantage of it." In an exhaustive analysis of Stagg's career, Peter Iverson reached the disappointing but probably correct conclusion "that football's 'purity man,' willingly stretched and broke the rules to win, while defending the game as a builder of good character." His "opportunistic nature and drive for recognition," says Iverson, "helped fuel his legendary coaching career and myth as a heroic character."[12]

With time, evangelicals came to expect ethically blighted sports as par for the course. More enthused about sharing the spotlight that society shone on sports than scrutinizing picky ethical details, evangelicals were swept into the fold, sensing untold evangelistic riches by identifying with popular sport. The die was cast when a 1947 Billy Graham revival featured runner Gil Dodds, who had set the world indoor record for the mile. Dodds ran a mock race around the stadium against a local athlete before the service and later was invited to the podium, where he asked the crowd, "I wonder how many of you here tonight are doing your best in the race for Jesus Christ?" Dodds set the course for the army of sport evangelists that would follow, crediting the Lord with helping him win and preaching Billy Sunday's "muscularity." "It takes a man to become a Christian," said Dodds, thereby unwittingly barring over 50 percent of the population from heavenly glory.[13]

In the 1950s and 1960s, when evangelicals sought visibility not only in the intellectual marketplace but also in popular culture, sports came to occupy an increasingly significant role in American society, deepening their bonds with cultural and political life. It seemed only logical for Christians to capitalize on their popularity. During this period several athletic ministries were born, including Venture for Victory, Fellowship of Christian Athletes, and Athletes in Action.[14] Famous athletes were ushered to microphones, and evangelical publishing houses published their stories. One such athlete was Bill Glass, a four-time Pro Bowl player for the Cleveland Browns who later established a thriving prison ministry. Glass blended a physically intimidating physique with a genial personality and a violent, tough-man version of the gospel. "Even though I am a Christian," said Glass, "I can play a rough brand of football. In fact, as a Christian, I ought to play an even rougher brand than anyone else." Glass penned a series of books for teenagers brimming with athletic mythology. One such book, containing a foreword by Billy Graham, tells kids: "If you get beat, after the game is over you ought to congratulate the winner . . . Yes, practice good sportsmanship, but when you get in the dressing room and no one is looking, back off about ten yards and run and ram your head into the locker because you hate to lose so badly. Don't ever be a good loser. Be a bad loser. Good losers usually lose." Asked how Christians could play a game that teaches players to "run down the weak, hammer your enemy, gouge him where it hurts and the referee can't see," Glass rebuked those who play dirty, but said he saw nothing unchristian about rough aggressive play. "The weak shouldn't play in the first place," he told his interviewer. Glass's prescription for Christian sport was: "Charge. Charge . . . Dominate your opponent. Dominate him. Fire across the line, overpower him. Feel his body crumble beneath your power."[15]

If Glass was the evangelical establishment's reigning athlete of the 1960s, Tom Landry was its reigning coach. Landry was named the first coach of the Dallas Cowboys in 1960 and continued in that role for twenty-nine years. He was enormously successful, taking his teams to fifteen divisional title games and five Super Bowls. Firm in his faith and stiff in his demeanor, Landry championed a no-nonsense, corporate-managerial approach to football. "Nothing funny," he once said, "ever happens on a football field." Landry's style was vastly different from Glass'. He willingly talked of his faith to those who made inquiries, but hesitated to push it on others. His testimonials to the importance of faith in his personal life reflected a deep and abiding faith. The minister at Landry's church reportedly devoted an entire sermon to a newspaper column that had been written about Landry; the article was clipped, laminated, and disseminated throughout the congregation.[16]

But on the whole, Landry wasn't much more convincing in trying to reconcile the fiery competition and brutality of his sport with his Christian beliefs than were Stagg, Yost, or Heisman. He once told a writer: "If you can't play within the rules and play a tough, punishing type of game, you can't play as a Christian. We try to eliminate the vicious side of the game, but you have to punish the opposition." Sportswriter Skip Bayless' book about Landry (*God's Coach*) is perhaps the most thorough analysis of Landry's career. Bayless recounts players' accusations of Landry's "lying to them and the media in the name of 'business' and hiding behind the Bible." Landry's highest compliment of a player was that "he's a pro," which, said Bayless, "meant that [the athlete] played when he was hurt . . . that he agreed to take painkilling injections . . . that he risked serious or permanent injury . . . that he ignored the doctor's warning and all the screaming signals with which God so wondrously equipped the body." Although the book lauded Landry on many counts, Bayless—a born-again believer—struggled to understand how Landry could work for the team's owners, "who used Landry's godly figurehead to shield what often was an ungodly organization—even to justify their life-styles and ethics."[17]

Both Glass and Landry helped not only to cement the bond between big-time sport and evangelicalism, but to forge evangelical understanding of sport as an experience in which ethical lapse is a normal and understandable reality. They projected dramatically different images. In his glorification of savagery and manliness, Glass seemed at times reminiscent of muscular Christians Hughes and Kingsley, although with a sharper edge. Landry, on the other hand, was more nuanced in his philosophy, more inclined to talk about the celebrated virtues of discipline, hardness, fortitude, and sacrifice than about the unseemly underbelly of the game. If Glass was the violent knight, Landry was the monk; if Glass was the take-no-prisoners toughman, Landry was the hard-driving, Stagg-like CEO. Both images, however, appealed to various segments of the evangelical community: Glass to athletes, Landry to sports fans.

Glass and others precipitated the eventual founding of organized sport evangelism, funded in large part by sports-loving, couch-potato, evangelical businessmen who regarded it as a unique and worthy missionary effort. No longer would sport evangelism be left to the ad hoc, hit or miss personal witnesses of individual athletes. Shaped and nurtured by athletically minded staffs, many of whom had theological training, sport evangelism morphed into a national and international movement, designed and operated according to field-tested methods and intensely honed to produce results. Fawning fans who could not quite make the connections between a gospel of grace and humility and a tough, relentless competitive spirit would be helped to understand.

Not all in the Christian community found the call to sports irresist-
ible. Radical fundamentalists continued to reject sport in the first half of
the twentieth century as they did most aspects of popular culture; many
complained about Sunday sports. Fundamentalist Bob Jones University
in Greenville, South Carolina, for example, still eschews intercollegiate
sports on the grounds that visiting teams may bring drinking, smoking,
and carousing fans to campus. In 1921, Moody Bible Institute's *Moody
Monthly*, the leading fundamentalist periodical of the period, reacted
awkwardly to a reader's question about a church establishing sport
leagues in which only those who attended church could play, but assured
readers that "it is proper for clergyman to mingle with their men and
boys in their sports." A year later, the magazine compared those who
attended the Dempsey-Carpentier heavyweight championship fight to
naked pagan Sandwich Island natives who cheered similar "savagery."
On the whole, however, fundamentalist criticisms of sport were sporadic
and tepid, rarely exceeding in tone or vehemence those offered up by
liberals of the period who rejected sport more on humanitarian grounds
and common sense than because of theological concerns.[18]

THE BONDS TIGHTEN

A full telling of the story of the tightening bonds between evangelicalism and big-time sports from the 1930s to the present day is far beyond
the scope of this book. Readers are referred to the fine book *Muscular
Christianity: Evangelical Protestants and the Development of American
Sport* by Tony Ladd and James Mathisen that describes in great detail the
events, personalities, and organizations that were critical facilitators of
the trend. The evangelical parade to the playground had already begun
to assemble when Billy Sunday became a Christian, but the band didn't
start playing until Olympic runner Eric Liddell, popularized in the book
Chariots of Fire and in the 1981 Oscar-winning film by the same name,
refused to run in the 100-meter race in the 1924 Olympics because the
race was held on a Sunday. A last-minute arrangement permitted Liddell
to run in the 400 meters on a different day, a fact far less embellished than
his willingness to follow the dictates of his evangelical conscience. In his
conversations with fans and reporters, Liddell drew facile comparisons
between faith and running; he described winning as a God-honoring feat
and running as a spiritual obligation, all familiar themes in today's evangelical sport talk.

The seed for organized sport evangelism in America was planted in 1952 when a small group of talented basketball players playing under the banner "Venture for Victory" spent eight weeks in Formosa (Taiwan) holding 160 revival meetings, playing 79 basketball games, and preaching to 65,000 Chinese. In ensuing years, the team would travel throughout the Orient and South America. Two years later, the granddaddy of evangelistic sports ministries was born. The Fellowship of Christian Athletes (FCA) was the brainchild of basketball coach Don McClanen, who dreamed of "harnessing of heroes to reach those who idolized them for a life for the Lord." It has grown steadily in both numbers and influence. The "Annual Impact Report" for the nine-month period of September 2007 to May 2008 claimed 1,759,444 athletes and coaches "reached" through FCA events and 26,652 "faith commitments."[19]

In the 1960s, Athletes in Action, the second most influential of the sport evangelism organizations, was given life through the efforts of Bill Bright, founder of Campus Crusade for Christ, who wanted a "more aggressive evangelism and discipleship training" than offered by the sometimes ecumenical FCA. (FCA insider Gary Warner wrote that his organization did "not produce enough pelts on the salvation barn door to satisfy the Crusade zealots.") AIA has since blossomed into a massive evangelical organization with ministries involving at least nine sports, plus power lifting; it is active throughout the United States, Canada, Latin America, Africa, Asia, and Europe. The organization claims to have a presence on 128 college campuses and an "on-going ministry" with sixteen chaplains serving NFL teams, one NBA team, two major-league baseball teams, and one major-league soccer team.[20]

Around the same time that AIA was getting its legs, the unassuming and very talented second baseman of the New York Yankees, Bobby Richardson, began holding chapel services for interested teammates before Sunday games. His efforts eventually blossomed into the formation of Baseball Chapel, Inc. Today the organization sponsors 400 chapel leaders who lead services before almost all games in big-league and minor-league stadia for home and visiting teams as well as for umpires. A few years later, in the early 1970s, Pro Athlete Outreach was founded "to train professional athletes and their spouses to become leaders for Christ." By this time professional sports had been flooded with players from evangelical protestant backgrounds, so much so that Billy Graham was led to tell a *Newsweek* reporter that "there are probably more really committed Christians in sports, both college and professional . . . than in any other occupation in America."[21] Graham's estimate seemed to be right on target: a few months later, papers carried stories about the 1971 San Francisco Giants baseball team, composed largely of Christians. Reporters, frustrated with all of the religious talk inserted into postgame interviews, tagged the team "The God Squad." "It's terrible," grumbled one writer who had returned from a road trip with the team, "for almost every interview you had to go through ten minutes of religion first." A few years later, humorist Roy Blount attempted to select an "All Religious Team" to compete against an "All Heathen Team" in an imaginary "Christians vs. Lions Bowl" but claimed that he had to abort the project when he couldn't find enough genuine heathens to field a squad. It seemed almost every athlete was a Christian.[22]

Small evangelical colleges began to venture into the deeper waters of intercollegiate sports in the 1950s for the self-professed aim of evangelism. By 1968, the National Christian College Athletic Association was formed "to provide a Christian-based organization that functions uniquely as a national and international agency for the promotion and enhancement of intercollegiate athletic competition with a Christian perspective."[23] The public relations benefits and the perils that can accrue to Christian colleges in big-time sports were discovered firsthand by Tulsa-based Oral Roberts University in the 1970s after it had made a major financial commitment to intercollegiate basketball. Going big time, said founder-evangelist Oral Roberts, wasn't merely to bring attention to the school; it was intended to be a major force for evangelism. Within five years, ORU made it to the NCAA playoffs and shortly thereafter found itself complicit in a national scandal involving their basketball coach.

The late evangelist Jerry Falwell may have come closer to attaining Robert's dream of building a powerhouse football team at an evangelical institution. Fallwell started an athletic program two years after founding Liberty University in 1971, and a few years later told a writer from *The Washington Post* that he wanted to field a football team that would beat Notre Dame. "Winning is very important to us," said Falwell. "I agree with Vince Lombardi; if it's not important then why keep score? We want to win and we cry when we don't win." A star running back chipped in: "Our goal is to be the hardest-hitting team anyone has ever played. We don't want them looking at us as a pansy team . . . Their idea of being a Christian is a little-bitty guy carrying a big Bible. What we do is out-hustle people, knock their heads off and they'll say 'These guys are different.' . . .

Of course it's hard sometimes to show them the love of Christ after we've beat them up and down the field. You say, 'Hey Jesus loves you,' and they don't exactly understand."[24]

Falwell pursued his dream of fielding a national champion by hiring big name coaches and investing substantial funds in pursuit of winning teams. Falwell never masked his outright obsession with fielding winning teams. He fired Moran Hout, the school's stellar football coach, in the same year Hout was named Virginia Division I Coach of the Year simply because former Cleveland Browns coach Sam Ratigliano became available for the position. Head football coach Ken Karcher, his athletic director, and two assistants were fired in 2005 because of Falwell's disappointment in the progress his teams were making toward the goal of moving from Division I-AA to Division I-A. "We're not even playing par I-AA football here, so obviously we have to start over, and that's what we're doing," Falwell said.[25]

The evangelical sport alliance has been abetted by a prodigious output of books and magazines. There is a seemingly limitless market for biographies authored by Christian coaches and athletes. In *Racing to Win*, Washington Redskins coach and NASCAR owner Joe Gibbs claims to call "his plays by the best selling Book of all time." A blurb on the cover of his book assures readers that "his incredible story of triumph and defeat in the high-stakes world of professional sports and in life will make you a believer too." In *From Ashes to Glory*, former University of Colorado football coach and founder of Promise Keepers Bill McCartney tells of his spiritual journey and his rise to the top of the coaching ranks. In *All Things Possible: My Story of Faith, Football and the First Miracle Season*, quarterback Kurt Warner describes how his faith played a role in his nearly miraculous rise from anonymity to become the MVP of the Super Bowl. Men's stories dominate the genre just as men tend to dominate the sport-evangelism movement (partly, it should be noted, because so much of sport evangelism centers on football, a sport that largely excludes women), but books such as *Competitor's Edge*, in which women athletes talk about sports and their faith, have also found a market.[26]

Books written with breathless adoration marketed to fans of college teams are another favorite. If you want to know how faith is incorporated and even demonstrated in the Saturday afternoon exploits of your alma mater, read *Faith of the Sooners: Inspiring Oklahoma Sports Stories of Faith*; *Faith in the Crimson Tide: Inspiring Alabama Sports Stories of Faith*;

and *Lessons From Nebraska Football: Inspirational Stories and Lessons From the Gridiron.* (For the time being, at least, we can set aside memories of scandals that have afflicted all of these programs.) And if you and your fellow believers are having difficulty sorting out Christian athletes from their less devout teammates, *A Sports Fan's Guide to Christian Athletes and Sports Trivia* offers a theologically vetted list of nearly 300 famous athletes who are bona fide Christians. Those who might find it difficult to step outside the sport mentality even for their daily devotions can find athletically slanted devotional books to allow them to do both at the same time. The *Sports Devotional Bible*, a book of general sporting interest, promises to show how "virtues such as character, trust, perspective, discipline, and faith make both great athletes and strong Christians."[27]

Two magazines crafted around the theme of faith and sports deserve special mention. *Sharing the Victory*, a publication of the FCA with a circulation of 82,000, features inspirational stories by athletes, some famous, some not so famous, but almost all with an impressive resume of competitive victories that receive big play in articles. Athletes and coaches tell how their faith has helped them overcome adversity in their off-field lives and how it helps them deal with the stresses of competition. ("Adversity" is a term widely applied to losing seasons as well as to personal struggles.) There is little here to deepen one's understanding of the meaning of sport in the Christian life, nor are there any stories of how an athletes' spiritual calling might put him or her at odds with the dominant ethos of big-time sport. You won't find much in these pages to chasten the sports establishment, but you will find much to whitewash its sins. The magazine's brightest moments come when it encourages young athletes on ethical matters outside of sports and in its upbeat and positive stories on the lives of athletes and coaches.

Sports Spectrum, with a circulation of 25,000, is in many ways a slicker, more interesting periodical. The magazine was launched in 1990 under the auspices of the Radio Bible Broadcast in Grand Rapids, Michigan. It is a sleek, evangelical knock-off of the worldly *Sports Illustrated.* Lively articles describing the accomplishments of Christian athletes from all levels of competition, upbeat takes on the glories of sports, columns on topics of general as well as special interest, exceptionally good photographs of athletes in action and expertly designed layouts, and a limited number of advertisements, all interlaced with punchy devotionals based on athletic analogies, fill its pages. Its editors and writers are obviously fascinated by the world of sports.

Left unmentioned in the pages of the magazine is anything that might reflect unflatteringly on sports. Unlike *Sports Illustrated*'s conscientious coverage of both the good and the bad in sports, *Sports Spectrum* is all about the good. You won't find much mention here about racism, recruiting scandals, ill treatment of athletes, cheating, or the tensions between sports and higher education. Sport, one could easily presume, poses no thorny problems for Christians. Sociologist James Mathisen describes the magazine as holding to "a persisting individualistic moral orientation toward sport—root out individual selfishness and cheating, perhaps, but do not confront the more structural dimensions of racism, sexism, and corporate irresponsibility in education or politics or big business."[28]

Christian intellectuals rarely opine on sports; as a result, the thoughts and language of the general literature on evangelical sports tend to be the thoughts and language of athletes, coaches, and Christian sports promoters. It is not difficult to see the powerful socializing effects of sports at work helping to form mindsets in readers that not only disarm but disable their critical faculties. Since most of these books and magazines are intended for a young athletic crowd with little or no theological training, perhaps the goofy analogies and mangled metaphors should be given a pass as simply well-intended efforts of sports nuts to share their faith and their love for sports. But that would seriously underestimate the significance of this literature in helping frame sports in the contexts of readers' religious beliefs. For better or worse, the thinly veiled sports worship that graces these pages validates it for impressionable young people, if for no other reason than that much of it is printed by publishers and organizations representing a powerful segment of the evangelical publishing industry. If a prophetic voice is to be heard from the evangelical community on the matter of sports, it is very unlikely that it would come from one who has gorged on a steady diet of this literature.

BEHIND-THE-BLEACHERS SPORT EVANGELISM

The publicity-conscious evangelical invasion of sport has been concentrated for the most part in high-visibility athletic spectacles, but it has inspired less hyped but arguably more defensible grassroots, "behind-the-bleachers" athletic competition as well. Informal and amateur sports were the preferred choice of liberal social gospellers who felt that keeping the profit motive out of sport and downplaying the symbolic significance of winning were the surest paths to realizing the life-changing goals they envisioned for participants. In the 1920s, some conservative denominations began to recognize the potential of informal sport programs for evangelism and began incorporating them into their church social programs, youth camps, and interchurch relations. In 1924, Southwestern Baptist Theological Seminary in Texas offered a course in "church recreation" to train leaders in the new venture, and in 1954 the Southern Baptist Convention established a Church Recreation Department. For many evangelical congregations, sport competition represented a rare break from the tedious isolationism in their ranks, something noted in the mid-seventies analysis of evangelicalism by Richard Quebedeaux, who identified church league sports as the only official, universally approved form of interaction evangelical churches have with liberal Protestant or Catholic churches.[29]

The trend of inserting sport into church programs and supporting those programs with the church's general budget has vastly accelerated in recent years, and enthusiasm runs high. The jacket of a recently published book enthuses: "As an open-group, open-door strategy, recreation and sport ministries may represent *the most effective way to reach the postmodern culture of today*" (italics added). Beyond vague references to "evangelistic outreach" or "fellowship," specific goals for these programs are rarely spelled out; even less prominent are descriptions of specific policies and procedures that would put a distinctive evangelical stamp on the competition. Convenience, social comfort, the chance to mingle with like-minded friends, and perhaps a prayer before the game seem to exhaust the possibilities.[30]

Affixing sport to the church's social mission has not come cheaply. Budget allocations for athletic facilities and support staff, especially in megachurches, have been truly enormous. Congregational tithes are sometimes used to support associate ministers for sports and recreation and their staffs. The Southern Baptists have been avid supporters of church sports backed by leadership training through their LifeWay Christian Resources in Nashville. But they are far from alone. Church sport ministry has become a Christian college, Bible school, and seminary concentration. Malone College, for example, offers Sports Ministry majors in at least three areas along with a graduate concentration. Bible schools offer certification programs in sport evangelism, and support for training leaders is available through such organizations as Church Sports International and the Association of Church Sport and Recreation Ministers.

Churches aren't the only sponsors of this small-bore, behind-the-grandstand sport evangelism. A surprising number of parachurch organizations cluster their programs around sport. One of many examples,

Ultimate Goal Ministries, seeks to make "the soccer field our mission field" and use it as "a platform for sharing Him" by sending teenagers and young adults on short-term foreign mission trips. After-school and camp sport programs of Sport Ministries, Inc., have similar goals. Another sport ministry called Upward was founded in 1986 as a local project to promote "Christlikeness and good sportsmanship" through basketball for elementary-age children; the program has since expanded into a range of sports, serving upwards of 400,000 participants from 40 or more denominations. While the aims of these programs may be admirable, none have established a reputation as sponsors of a truly radical approach to sports that a conscientious application of Christianity would seem to require.

One exception is 360° Sports, an organization that attempts not only to educate athletes and coaches using a "Kingdom of God Perspective," but to influence the ethos of sport itself. "Sport," says its advocates, "is not merely an add-on tool for evangelism"; it has value in and of itself, "simply because God created people of sport who are wired to live, move and be."[31] By developing coaches whose approach to sports differs sharply from the degraded examples too often seen in high-level sport competition, the organization seeks to surround athletes with a "biblically transformed sport community committed to developing the whole person. By and large, the potential of such programs to change the face of modern sports remains in doubt. Although incremental changes in the way the Christian community approaches informal sports may well be seen in the near future, evangelical impact on spectacle sport is much less likely. This is due, in large part, to the fact that major sport evangelism organizations whose missions are inextricably tied to the specatacles of big-time sports continue to eschew suggestions that sports are in need of radical, spiritual transformation.

The evangelical co-option of sports has been a phenomenon largely unexamined by evangelical scholars, its dynamics and rationales left to be worked out by those most committed to using it. That sports open doors to a vast audience of the unwashed is clear; far from clear is whether a sufficient amount of thought has been given to the implications of this strategy. Mostly the evangelical-sport machine has chugged along on a set of unexamined assumptions about the Christian approach to competition, sport's influence on the character of athletes, the place of prayer in sports, Christian athletes' spiritual obligations to their bodies, and the role of sport in evangelism. The next five chapters will examine these topics in some detail.

6

CHRISTIANS AND THE KILLER INSTINCT

Competition is an indispensable element of sport. Rid sport of competitors' mutual striving for a prize available only to one of them and you change it into something entirely different. But competition also is the element in sport most difficult to align with the Christian faith. A fair reading of the history of the relationship between sport and the church suggests that it was the fruits of competition, more than anything else, that sparked moral outrage. Conscious of this dissonance—at least at a subliminal level—the Christian athletic community has crafted a rhetoric aimed at rounding off the rough edges between the competition and Christian ethics, though not always in honest ways. Nevertheless, for those who are willing to see, the dissonance between competition and Christianity remains. Striving to be recognized for having proven oneself better in a certain category of athletic exploits is part of what makes sport fun. It also is what makes sport dangerous, especially to Christians.

In her book *Misery and Company*, Candace Clark tells of anthropologist Colin Turnbull, who lived with and studied the Ik, a mountain people of central Africa. The Ik were a gentle and kindhearted people until the Ugandan government forced them to move from fertile, low-lying lands into a hilly country where droughts and hunting restrictions caused a famine. Under these dire circumstances, the Ik developed an approach to life based exclusively on self-interest; the "one-sided giving of food, water, assistance or even sentiment to anyone, family members or foe, was [regarded as] a waste." Turnbull was astonished at how other people's misery became a source of humor to the Ik. They laughed as their feeble and frail neighbors tripped and fell in the streets. He describes an incident in which men sitting around a fire rather nonchalantly watched a curious child crawl toward a fire, and "burst into gay and happy laughter as [the child] plunged a skinny hand into the coals." Bizarre though it seemed, Turnbull found himself inching toward the same disposition after living with the Ik for a few months. He returned from his field experiences profoundly impressed with the power of social contexts to shape how we think, feel, and act toward one another.[1]

No social ethic runs at sharper angles to the gospel claimed by evangelicals than "ikishness"—pursuing one's own interests without sympathy for anyone else. Scripture is unequivocal in its loathing of self-absorption, which, claims Christian ethicist R. E. O. White, "lies behind all wrong social relationships described in the Bible." The Christian is exhorted to "love others as you love yourself," but far greater emphasis is placed on self-denial in order to ensure the welfare of others. The Christian's duty is to bestow honor on others, seek their advancement, recognize their superiority, and show esteem for their gifts, something that occurs, said Carl Henry, "only where the natural tendency to self-honor and self-exaltation, ambition and the desire for pre-eminence are renounced by the Christian." The [Christian] soul's enduring satisfaction in the life of meekness," wrote Henry, "is quite contrary to the spirit of Greek philosophy that found it in self assertion."[2]

Scripture sets an extraordinarily high standard of personal conduct, especially in a society where the urge to compete is moving American society in the direction of the Ik. There is a marked tendency for us "to be harder on others if we think the results will benefit us," says social critic Nicolaus Mills.[3] Many of the ills of the business, legal, governmental, and educational worlds can be traced in one way or another to the urge to better ourselves at the expense of others. Self-centeredness has even found its way into the comic pages; Dilbert works in a competitive "cube-farm world" where intimidation and humiliation are regarded as smart ways of advancing one's career. *Seinfeld*, a TV sitcom featuring self-absorbed characters connected by shallow parasitic relationships, owed its enormous popularity in part to a growing recognition that there is more than a little of Jerry, Elaine, George, and Kramer in all of us.

For the Christian, the fact that sport plays to this urge to put our-selves at the front of the line may be its most troublesome aspect. What-ever other positive features sport might have (and there are many), its nature contains the seeds of ikishness by demanding that players place certain limits on their regard for those against whom they compete. Most of the time we manage to play without being overwhelmed by the ikish impulses that are integral to sport, but it cannot be denied that they still nudge us in that direction. I simply cannot engage you in an enjoyable game of tennis unless I ignore the trouble you are having returning my blistering serve, just as you must squelch sympathy for me as I struggle to return your down-the-line backhand. If either of us allows sympathy to overwhelm self-interest and begins placing our shots where the other can easily return them, we will have lost the spirit of the game. Sports are zero-sum in nature: I can only win if you lose. In committing myself to winning, I am at the same time committing to making you lose. If victory comes my way, it does so at your expense.

How evangelicals, mindful of scriptural exhortations to "unity of spirit, sympathy, love of brethren, a tender heart, and a humble mind," can momentarily claim release from this obligation is not easily explained (1 Peter 3:8). Viewed from a strictly objective standpoint, the picture of Christians deliberately suspending concern for one another (even in this limited sense) and engaging in deception, cunning, and physical domi-nation in an effort to further their own interests is a very troubling one indeed. True, players only suspend mutual sympathy in an illusory sense as part of play, but even in pretending to be motivated by self-interest, they are pretending not to be the Christians that they claim to be.

The inability to contain this urge toward ikishness destroys rela-tionships, in and out of sport. Richard Mouw, president of Fuller Theological Seminary, writes: "to seek to manipulate others and to bend their wills to one's own selfish goals is also to engage in 'shame-less acts.'"[4] Using one's God-given rational faculties to plot self-enhancement, says Mouw, reflects the workings of a "base mind." Pro-fessor Mouw was talking about politics, but his remarks seem equally applicable to sports. Dressing up this uncomfortable reality in educa-tional jargon about "learning through defeat," bubbly philosophical cant about "a shared mutual quest for challenge," or patriotic pap about how competition "strengthens the national character" shouldn't blind us to the fundamental similarities in the psychological and spiritual character of competitive sport and those Mouw associates with "the workings of a base mind."

Of course players don't suspend feelings for their opponents in an absolute sense: it is a limited, illusory suspension, necessary for playing the game. If a player is injured, for example, the game is stopped while the player receives medical attention. The problem, unresolved through centuries of trying, is how to limit the antagonistic spirit central to game playing to this illusory world. What we discover time and again is that the boundaries between the play world and the actual world are extraordinarily fragile. Team spirit and the urge to win easily morph into animosity; a desire to win becomes greed, a quest for excellence becomes an urge to dominate, and a victory celebration becomes a ritual of self-approbation. We struggle to "control" sports, to buffer their appeal to our ikish instincts, but so often our best efforts and intentions fail. If the impulses of games take us to the edge of impropriety, the weakness of our souls takes us over the edge. This worried C. S. Lewis. He was hardly a prig, but he was keenly aware of the way competitive sports could "lead to ambition, jealousy, and embittered partisan feelings, quite as often as to anything else." He was right. If one were to design a social exercise that tempts Christians toward such sins, they couldn't do much better than competitive sports.[5]

Evangelicals implicitly recognize their spiritual obligation to shun sinful temptations, but under the guise of sports they seem more often to organize them, sponsor them, and celebrate them. There isn't much honest talk about competition in evangelical athletic quarters, where airy rhetoric about "excellence," "achievement," "honoring God by doing one's best," and even "demonstrating our God-given talents" are the prime distracters. Those unconstrained by evangelical sentimentality, however, can be more realistic. "Basketball without deception, football without aggression, baseball without cunning and trickery can't be played," said theologian and social commentator Michael Novak in his famous defense of sports. "Our sports are lively with the sense of evil," Novak noted; they "provide an almost deliberate exercise in pushing the psyche to cheat and take advantage, to be ruthless, cruel, deceitful, vengeful, and aggressive." If the call to Christian witness is also a call to a new set of social relationships, the realm of competitive sports seems an unlikely place to find it.[6]

THE KILLER INSTINCT

Clyde Hodges said he feels like [former Chicago linebacker] Dick Butkus. "I want to hit. I don't see the opponent as a person but as a target, an object to be crushed." Catherine Freeman confesses that when she plays sports, she "metamorphizes [sic] into a different person," into "somebody fairly unpleasant" that wants to "mangle her opponent." Neither are big-time athletes. Freeman is an amateur bowler. Hodges is a diminutive computer salesman who plays bridge. Yet both confess to becoming a bit "ikish" when they compete. In the heat of competition, they, like many athletes, develop "the killer instinct," a disposition one psychiatrist has defined as the capacity to "relentlessly and without inner prohibition or a sense of guilt keep the pressure on opponents while achieving victory." Sport psychologist Bruce Ogilvie reported that almost every truly great athlete he had interviewed "consistently emphasized that in order to be a winner you must retain the killer instinct." Sports commentators prefer to describe it in softer tones such as "mental toughness," "grit," or "competitive fire," but by any name, it means ridding yourself of sympathies for your opponent that might inhibit you in applying your full resources to furthering your own cause. When the whistle blows, says Jon Gruden, former coach of the NFL's Tampa Bay Buccaneers, "we're not going to worry about anybody else's feelings—all we care about is ourselves."[7]

As the anecdotes above show, the killer instinct rears its head in some of the most unexpected places. One might consider sailing to be a fairly docile and gentlemanly sport, but seasoned sailor Stuart Walker says that good competitors should "feel no concern for the opinion and feelings of others . . . If you don't care what the other fellow thinks, you can tack on him wherever you wish." After all, says Walker, "competition is not Christmas." Novak puts it in blunter, though more eloquent terms: "So long as an athlete is a rival, so long as we are in a contest, I am entitled to hate him, to envy him, to defeat him and pull him down a peg in any way I can; and he is out to deflate me. One should not underestimate the murderous sort of hatred contests draw upon . . . One hates one's opponents justly . . . These are not defects in sports. They help us burst the bubbles of hypocrisy."[8]

Novak is not an athlete, but he has keen insight into sport. His sentiments are echoed by scores of elite athletes who routinely accept social distancing as a fundamental requirement for competitive success. Players often mention "turning on a switch" that alters their personality when they enter the arena. Buffalo Bills football star Terrell Owens told a reporter that he becomes a different person when he runs onto the field: "I take a step and—bang!—I turn into this completely different person." New York Giants guard Rich Seubert says, "On game day you've got to change. You've got to be mean and nasty, you've got to be physical. You can't go out there being a nice guy. The whole game is dirty—it's a dirty business."9 But changes in personality aren't engineered only by those who play violent games. Olympic gold medal sprint cyclist Marty Nothstein, one of the best U.S. cyclists to race in international competition, uses violent images on the track to motivate him as well. "I put myself in a mental state where all I want to do is win no matter what the cost. Just go into the race ready for battle. Destroy the guy. End it quick. Boom. One knockout punch." According to her youth coach, U.S. Olympic swimmer Amy Van Dyken had a dual personality. Out of the water, he said, she was a giggling thirteen-year-old who loved to race. But in competition the other Amy appeared, described as "a steely-eyed assassin" who "learned to intimidate opponents by staring at them, spitting into their lanes, grunting, and clapping her hands." Says Van Dyken, "if they are weak enough to let that get to them, that's their problem." Such strategies helped her win three gold medals in the 1996 Olympics.10

Because sympathetic instincts can be a liability in the athletic subculture, it is essential to root them out. Feelings of sympathy toward opponents are not encouraged and are often not tolerated by those in control of sports at the highest levels, something vividly demonstrated during a 1989 NFL game when Freeman McNeil, a running back for the New York Jets, unintentionally shattered an opponent's knee in carrying out a routine blocking assignment. While the ikish culture of football dictated that McNeil ignore the man writhing in pain before him, McNeil apologized to the victim, took himself out of the game, and knelt tearfully on the sidelines as the injured player was carried from the field. His act of contrition wasn't appreciated by his coach: "I understand his feeling, but that's the way the game goes. Obviously, what happened out there [McNeil allowing grief to affect his play] wasn't good, and he realizes it." Ultimately McNeil was pressured to apologize to his team for "not staying focused" and "not being a leader." Just as the arid climate and struggle for survival sucked feelings of sympathy out of the Ik, the struggle for survival in the arenas and stadia of our country can suck them out of our best coaches and athletes.11

It is surprising how many athletes talk about hate in describing the psychological transformation that is required for them to become aggressive competitors. "I don't switch modes until right before we go out there for pre-game," says a veteran NFL linebacker. "I start to build a hatred for the other team. You put things in your head that make you really want to go out there and play this game in a violent nature."[12] Obviously, not all athletes conjure up hate for their opponents, and sport psychologists might suggest other, more profitable mental states; nevertheless, hate is widely used by athletes to help sustain the killer instinct. "To play this game," said legendary football coach Vince Lombardi, "you must have that fire in you and nothing stokes that fire like hate." Larry Cain, Olympic canoeing gold medalist, says, "I try to develop a little bit of anger in order to have more explosiveness on the starting line," and claims that "at times there's intense hate." Former international German swimmer Monika Schloder said she experienced a remarkable psychological transformation when she entered the water: "I'd psyche myself up to treat the other swimmers as opposition forces, like it was good against evil, a fairytale thing. My eyes actually changed color; they took on a dark hue. I think it was hormonal. It was a positive anger and I felt myself become totally invincible. You couldn't beat me. If I didn't achieve this frame of mind, I didn't succeed."[13]

Hatemongering has long figured in the bag of tricks some coaches use to get their teams in a competitive frame of mind. Locker room speeches such as the famous plea by the late great Notre Dame coach Knute Rockne to his team to "win one for the Gipper" are tame fare for youngsters weaned on Rambo, rap videos, and PlayStation 2's "God of War." They need something cruder, more inflammatory, even more barbaric, like Washington Redskins interim coach Terry Robiskie's locker room speech in December of 2000: "I'm ready to go to war. You know me—I'm going to Dallas [the Redskin's next opponent] and if you ain't gonna bring your balls with you, I'm gonna cut 'em off and send you back where you came from." Perhaps Robiskie had learned from the antics of Mississippi State Coach Jackie Sherill who, before his team's season opener with the University of Texas Longhorns, had a longhorn castrated on the practice field in front of the players. Sherrill claimed it was intended as an educational experience. If an award were to be given for this lunacy, surely it would go to the high school coach in Florida who, before his team's game against its archrivals,

"The Golden Eagles," painted a chicken gold, told players to think of it as an eagle, and stood by as they chased it around the field and stomped it to death. "From the psychological need to win," says historian Allen Guttmann, "a thousand distempers grow."[14]

Thankfully, most pregame rituals are less sensational. Pep rallies, inflammatory news clippings, and banners posted in locker rooms and the like are relatively mild methods of priming the killer instinct, yet all are at aimed at creating social distance and dulling sympathetic feelings between competitors. And, like coaches' theatrics, they can warp in tone and taste when the pressure to win builds. Parents were shocked when the aphorism "defeat is worse than death because you have to live with defeat" found its way into high school locker rooms some years ago, but it seems fairly innocuous by comparison to the sign found in the locker room of football power Permian High School in Odessa, Texas. Before its big game against Odessa High during the 1988 season, someone posted a quotation by H. L. Mencken: "Every normal man must be tempted, at times, to spit on his hands, hoist the black flag, and begin slitting throats."[15]

Coaches and players who have become acculturated to this worldview can easily mistake sport competition for war. In the days leading up to the final game in the 2004 NBA quarterfinals, Minnesota Timberwolf Kevin Garnett was asked about his team's chances in a game reporters expected to be one of hard fouls and trash talking. Garnett said: "This is it. It's for all the marbles. I'm sitting in the house loading up the pump. I'm loading up the Uzis, I've got a couple of M-16s, couple of nines, couple of joints with some silencers on them, couple of grenades, got a missile launcher. I'm ready for war." Garnett later apologized, but in light of the atmosphere surrounding the game, his comments seemed strangely appropriate. In fact, by declaring sport a war, he had put himself in good company. "The true mission of American sports," said former president Dwight D. Eisenhower, "is to prepare young people for war."[16]

Another way of quelling sympathetic feelings between competing sides is to prevent fraternization in the hours before a contest. It may seem a sensible enough educational practice to have both teams share a pregame meal and learn something about each other, but in sports there is always the fear that it will dull the competitive edge. When the bowl committee at the 1973 Fiesta Bowl planned a pregame steak fry for both the Pitt and Arizona State players, ASU coach Frank Kush publicly worried that it would cause his team to soften their resolve against their Pitt opponents: "You can't tell kids that they're going up against a bunch of ogres, then have them sit across the table from the opponents at a banquet and find out they're really pretty nice guys." Sometimes arrangements are made for limited pregame interaction between competing players, but it doesn't always produce its intended consequences. As part of the festivities for a 1986 bowl game, Penn State and Miami players had assembled for a pregame dinner when Miami's all-American defensive tackle stood, ripped off his clothes to display army fatigues, and shouted at his teammates: "Did the Japanese sit down and eat dinner with Pearl Harbor before they bombed it?" *No!* yelled his teammates, and together they stormed out. Misguided, bizarre, even psychopathic perhaps, but the young man was only carrying a popular athletic sentiment to its logical conclusion.[17]

Friendship is the enemy of the killer instinct. "Friendlies" is a term used in European football to denote games usually played as warm-ups to official World Cup competition. Although the games usually aren't any more "friendly" than their official counterparts, the term is instructive, implying that when fame, fortune, and competitive survival don't hang in the balance, players of opposing sides can risk being friendly. But when a championship is at stake, coaches and teammates get nervous when friendships cross partisan boundaries. Several years ago, professional basketball players Patrick Ewing and Alonzo Mourning, both of whom had played for Georgetown in college but were now on different teams, were criticized by teammates for having dinner together before taking to the court. One told Mourning, "I know Pat loves you and you love Pat, but save it for the summer." It is not an accident that sport played at the highest levels is largely between strangers. Without the tender embrace of friendships to buffer the egocentric impulses of the game, players can be unrestrained in their pursuit of victory.[18]

Athletes who have competed against each other often form deep and lasting friendships, but that doesn't happen as much as it should. In most high-profile sports, the expectation is that competition inevitably will affect and be affected by friendly relationships. When then University of Miami coach Butch Davis was asked about his relationship with Steve Spurier, coach of Miami's upcoming opponents in the 2000 Sugar Bowl, Davis described the relationship as "good," and then added, "because we've never played [against each other]." A former high-level official on the women's tennis tour was quoted as having said, "If it comes down to choosing between winning and maintaining a friendship . . . successful players sacrifice the friendship . . . There's no place for sentiment. It's a matter of survival."[19] Cultivating human understanding on the street corner, in the office, or in the home is fine, but on the football field or baseball diamond it can lead to a string of losses. To paraphrase poet Henri Machaux: "The wolf who understands the sheep will starve."[20]

It shouldn't be surprising then that when friends must compete against each other it can be a conflicted and awkward experience. Boris Becker acknowledged before the 1991 Wimbledon Championships final match that he wasn't looking forward to playing against fellow German Michael Stich. He said it was much easier to play somebody you hate, yet, gritting his teeth, he said, the "killer instinct comes with this hallowed turf." Tennis pro Magdalena Maleeva said she found competing against her sisters particularly difficult: "To play tennis you need the killer instinct [and] it's hard to have the killer instinct with your sister." Friendships between coaches can also make games uncomfortable. Before a 2001 NCAA playoff game, Duke coach Mike Krzyzewski fumed about having to play the University of Missouri, then coached by his former player and assistant coach Quin Snyder. "Given a choice in the matter," said Krzyzewski, "I would choose not to play Quin's team at any time because it's Quin's team. He's like a member of my family, and I'm a member of his." Competing, we are left to presume, comes easiest if the parties don't like each other.[21]

Not surprisingly, competitive victories won against friends can be lackluster affairs, spoiled by the thought that they have come at the friend's expense. The storied rivalry between tennis great Martina Navratilova and Chris Everett was played out against a backdrop of a long friendship which, for Navratilova at least, siphoned off some of the joy she might have felt from consistently beating an opponent. When Venus Williams defeated her sister Serena in the semifinals of the Wimbledon Championship in 2000, both were visibly in pain on the winners' podium, so much so that observers said it was difficult to tell the loser from the winner. Tim Heinman played the then reigning king of men's tennis, Roger Federer, at the 2006 Wimbledon Championship, losing in three straight sets. Afterwards Federer told reporters that his friendship with Heinman had taken some of the gloss off the win: "It's not a lot of fun beating a friend like this, that's for sure," said Federer. A year later a newspaper headline over a story about Andy Roddick's upcoming match in the 2007 Australian Open against his close friend Mardy Fish blared, "Roddick Puts Friendship Aside, Heads for Semis."[22]

It logically follows that athletes who are by nature compassionate and friendly compete at a distinct disadvantage in the Darwinian world of athletics. Few things are more damning in an evaluation of an athlete's prospects than an accusation that they are "too nice." In 2004, upon the return of NBA star Jermaine O'Neal to the Indiana Pacers after a suspension for fighting, a sportswriter said, "The January return of Jermaine O'Neal could be pivotal [for playoff hopes]. O'Neal has never had a killer instinct to match his colossal talent. If he comes back with a chip on his shoulder, the struggling Pacers will make up ground fast." When former University of Texas basketball player Kevin Durant was being evaluated for the NBA draft, a popular online scouting report recommended that he "become more aggressive, develop more nastiness.[23] Even heavyweight boxing champion Floyd Patterson, who beat forty men unconscious during his professional career, was accused of lacking the killer instinct; "too introspective to enjoy the brutal requirements of his sport" was the rap. Critics simply were unable to forget Patterson's unforgivable faux pas of helping a battered Pete Rademacher to his feet in a 1957 championship match. There is more than a kernel of truth to the sign posted in the Duke basketball team's locker room after they had defeated Temple in the quarterfinals to move on to the Final Four at Kansas City the following week; the sign read: "The Meek Shall Inherit the Earth, but they're not going to Kansas City."[24]

Obviously, these vignettes don't represent all athletes or all types of competitive sports, but they are a few of many examples that could be cited to make a point: to deny that a unique psychological transformation is necessary to engage in competitive sports is to deny the reality of competition itself. Sport philosophers like to describe sport competition as "a mutual quest for excellence in the intelligent and directed use of athletic skills in the face of a challenge"; such descriptions may rest more gently on our consciences, but such thoughts don't seem uppermost in the minds of high-level coaches and athletes. Under any rubric, mutually striving for excellence necessarily involves creating social distance between competing parties; when this happens, says philosopher Drew Hyland, there is always the risk that players will be less friendly at the end than at the beginning. The quandary is not lessened for evangelicals simply because they, along with their opponents, willingly accept this risk in exchange for the fun of the game. Acts of dubious morality are hardly cleansed of their obliquity when perpetrated as part of a mutual agreement entered into for purposes of entertainment.[25]

EVANGELICALS AND THE KILLER INSTINCT

The inherent friction between the ethos of competitive sport and Christianity, so vehemently denied by evangelicals in the sports world, is accepted as a matter of course by those outside it. Some shaving off the corners of the Christian ethic, some tweaking of Paul's vision of the fruits of the Spirit as love, joy, peace, and gentleness is required to compete. We don't go to sporting events to see the Sermon on the Mount in action; pregame sermons for players aren't crafted around Paul's instructions to the faithful to shun vainglory and to avoid provoking one another. Do we honestly expect athletes performing in front of 90,000 partisan fans to embody humility, what Carl Henry called "the hallmark of Christian ethics?"[26] Do we really expect the basketball court to be a place where players put the concerns of others ahead of their own? Probably not, especially if your coach is Pat Riley, who once imposed fines on players who had the audacity to help opponents from the floor.

Realists in the sports community at large appreciate the dissonance between Christian and competitive ethics, and this is one reason they have so much difficulty understanding the evangelical invasion of sports. "To even hint that the 'Christian ethic' is to be maintained in sport is to contradict the very existence of sport as we know it," said philosopher-cum-sports agent Howard Slusher. Non-Christians expect that a Christian disposition naturally will dispossess an athlete of competitive ferocity. "If a Christian pitcher wins 20 [games], his faith is never mentioned. But if he loses 20 the reason given is that he loses because he is a weak, noncompetitive believer in Jesus," complained Eric Show, a former San Diego Padres pitcher. When baseball star Darryl Strawberry struggled to reconcile his conversion to Christianity with the need for a competitive spirit on the field, a teammate fretted that he had "lost the anger from his swing." Said a Christian teammate, "Darryl is having problems realizing that you can be a Christian and a ruthless person on the field too." Another, said Strawberry, "told me I had to start getting mean."[27]

In candid moments, some evangelical athletes will admit to struggling with the conflict between the demands of their faith and the disposition stoked by competition, although, thanks to the tutelage of chaplains and sport evangelists, they usually can be brought around to see that competition can be a "praise performance" that "glorifies God." Players in recreational leagues also struggle with the conflict between competition and their faith. Sociologists Robert Dunn and Chris Stevenson, in their interviews with church league hockey players, were told by one player, "at the recreational level sport shouldn't take the place of your Christian morals . . . [But] it's not easy . . . I get caught up [in it]." Another player told them: "Competitiveness and aggressiveness [tax] your Christianity."[28]

Cheating, doping, violence, and crowd disorder all have their genesis in the distortion of human relationships integral to competition. Although faltering athletes may interpret their failings as attacks by the devil, they are more accurately viewed as sins of the social sort, traceable to the social relationships invited, even required, by competition. As sport sociologists have pointed out, most of the egregious blemishes on the face of sport come not from *violating* established rules and traditions but from *over-conforming* to the norms and expectations of the competitive ethos. "Positive deviance" is the term used to describe behavior that, while it is in accord with the spirit of the game, ultimately reaches some ill-defined point where it is labeled excessive and wrong. Where that point lies is anybody's guess. Where winning is the supreme outcome of contests, positive deviance makes a great deal of sense. All of the things we hate most about sport, says Alfie Kohn, are only the logical outcomes of a social activity in which one person's success hinges on his or her ability to deny that same success to another.[29]

On the whole, evangelicals have not managed to reconcile the competitive element of sports with their faith much better than Samuel Johnson's dog managed to walk on its hind legs. "It is not done well," said Johnson, "but you are surprised to find it done at all." My experience is that many evangelicals would agree with Bill Bright, who believed that "competition is a gift from God," part of God's created design. Presumably, the urge to compare our talents, prove ourselves superior to others, and plot our victory and their defeat is divinely enmeshed in our DNA. The argument is that our biological dispositions insist that this urge be given expression and that sport is a divinely ordained institution to allow it to be expressed in socially harmless ways. To accept this hypothesis, one must presume that God intended his creatures periodically to dedicate themselves to their own interests in the pursuit of fun, ignore the interests of others, and seek opportunities to compare and display their achievements before throngs of onlookers.[30]

Fans from the Reformed tradition tend to view competitive sports, like most of culture, as "a created good" that, while it has come to be perverted under the curse of the fall and is in need of redemption, is inherently part of "created givenness."[31] It is not the Christian's calling to eradicate and supplant it but to redeem it and restore it to its God-intended form. "Structure," says Reformed theologian Albert Wolters, "denotes the 'essence' of a creaturely thing, the kind of creature it is by virtue of God's created law." "Direction," on the other hand, refers to "a sinful deviation from that structural ordinance and renewed conformity to it in Christ." Discerning the difference, however, between structure and direction is anything but an exact science. One might easily agree, for example, that human sexuality is a "created essence" (structure) and pornography its perversion (direction), but the distinction isn't quite as simple when it comes to competition. Is competition really an unavoidable part of being human, a created given, or might it be the perversion (direction) of some other, more general created essence?[32]

I don't believe it is, and here is the reason why. If competition is part of humanity's created essence, then we might expect all humans to share the urge to compare and test themselves against each other, and by extension, all societies would incorporate competition as a way of organizing their social relationships. But the urge to compete may be better traced to social conditioning than biology. Much of the training and child-rearing practice common in American society, for example, centers on competition. We arrange our educational systems and youth sport systems as one way to teach our children to compete. Yet, sociologist David Reisman asked, why should our society "have to contrive such a thorough program of socialization if competition were part of human nature?" Having trained our children to compete, we see it in practice everywhere, and then we point to its ubiquity as evidence of its being part of our natures.[33] Moreover, we are left to explain why there is wide variation in individual attraction to it: some enjoy testing and comparing their efforts against others while others shun it at every opportunity. We should also expect to find competition to be a universal feature of societies, yet societies also vary in the importance they attach to competition. Competitive reward structures, for example, are not part of the societies of the Kalhari Bushmen, Australian Aborigines, the Iroquoi, or the Inuit of Canada. Some societies place more stress on competition, others on cooperation. In fact, children from noncompetitive societies are often found to cooperate more effectively than children raised in competitive societies.

Competition might more fittingly be seen as a distortion of the created essence of "human relationship" or "community." Unlike competition, the universal urge for community is self-evident. A library of theological opinion can be mustered to support the contention that God created humans as relational beings, designed to relate not only to each other but also to him. However, the form that relationship takes is left up to his children. Could it be that competition is a perversion of this created essence of relationship?

There is a notion implicit in many defenses of sport that the human relationships formed and reinforced in competitive sports are, like sports themselves, mere pretense and shouldn't be evaluated by the same standards used to judge human conduct in our ordinary lives. According to this argument, games are bracketed in ethical parentheses; seeking one's own advantage at the expense of another in sport is somehow different from doing the same thing at the office. To a certain extent this is true. As was shown earlier, sport is possible only when competing parties suspend sympathy for each other, at least in the context of achieving the designated goals of the game. Competitive sports may set player against player and athlete against athlete, but when games go as they should, antagonisms are contained and used to further the enjoyment of everyone. At the same time, whether the dispositions and feelings of the heart stirred by competition can be dismissed entirely merely because they arise in the context of a game is doubtful. The old Harrow school song that speaks of "loving the ally with the heart of a brother, and hating the foe with a playing at hate" and former President Reagan's suggestion to a college football team that they can legitimately harbor a "clean hatred" for their opponents "because it's only symbolic in a jersey" both envision a dual morality that cannot easily be shoehorned into a Christian conception of ethics. The difference between quelling one's sympathy for an opponent during a volleyball game and quelling sympathy toward the poor, the sick, and the disenfranchised when the game is over is difficult to grasp.[34]

Some evangelical defenses of competition are actually defenses of something entirely different, often of human qualities more easily reconciled with the faith than competition itself: "struggle," "hard work," "commitment," and "respect for excellence." Surely sports require self-determination, self-struggle, and self-commitment, but none of these are competition. "Is it unspiritual to want to rise to the top, to excel?" asked Bright. "Competition teaches us to thrive in demanding situations.

We develop spiritually, physically, and mentally when we engage in competition with a proper, biblical perspective."[35] Such tricks of argument
divert attention from competition's singularly *relational essence*; they
don't help us to understand this peculiar aspect of sport or to reconcile it
with Christian ethics.

Definitional misdirection also occurs when competition is described
not as a struggle against another person but as a "struggle with oneself." Typical is an evangelical sport psychologist's suggestion that
competitiveness "should not be so much against another person or team
as much as it should be against one's potential." Struggling with oneself
is thought to be a way of reaching higher and higher levels of excellence;
it helps the athlete attain his or her maximum potential and seemingly
circumvents the thorny problem posed by competition to the Christian
athlete. The problem with such suggestions is that they try to convert
competition into an individual, isolated experience that it can never
be; *they deny the relational essence of competition*. Philosopher Robert
Simon's elegant definition of competition as "a *mutual* quest for excellence" may not give full credence to the antagonistic element inherent in
competition, but it quite correctly describes it as a *social* rather than an
individual endeavor (emphasis added). The killer instinct may rest easier
on the evangelical conscience when it is thought of as a self-contained,
internal experience of the individual, but competition gutted of its interpersonal dimension isn't competition at all.[36]

Another problem arises when the interpersonal element of competition is downplayed in favor of competition's value in personal development. "Christ came to restore life to its fullness (John 10:10)," says a
Christian educator. "We can celebrate this fullness through our engagement in competitive sport that displays God-given human potential and
encourages growth toward that potential." At first blush this seems like a
healthy way to look at competition, but upon closer inspection, I'm not
sure that it is any less selfish in its ramifications than all-out, dog-eat-
dog competition. When sports rely on an internal dynamic in which athletes' primary spiritual obligation is to maximize their own performance,
sports can easily become a means of diminishing the personhood of
those against whom one competes. The temptation is to approach sports
thinking that the only relationship in the competitive setting that has any
ethical or spiritual significance at all is that between the athlete and his
or her God. But contests are inherently social; if Christian athletes are to

seek enlargement of potential in competition, one would think it would be enlargement of both their own and their opponents' potential.[37]

In this talk of self-actualization lurks the "triumph of the therapeutic," a subjectivism and urge for psychological self-fulfillment that is preached from many evangelical pulpits. Nearly a quarter of a century ago, religion scholar James Davison Hunter warned that such self-help theology was sucking the vitality out of modern evangelism. Evangelical rhetoric seemed fixated on maximizing "the potentiality of the human being," albeit "under the Lordship of Christ," and Hunter thought this fixation uncharacteristically narcissistic, even hedonistic, for a religious group with its roots in a constructive, spiritually centered asceticism. The past two decades have expanded this brand of evangelicalism. Alan Wolfe, looking at evangelicalism from the outside, was astonished at the doctrine of self-betterment taught in evangelical churches, noting that at times he found it difficult to tell where "the immensely popular language of self-help therapy begins and the language of salvation through Jesus ends."[38]

This shift in theological current has been especially fortuitous for the evangelical sports community, where commitment to excellence, self-improvement, and self-fulfillment not only meets a presumed spiritual obligation but paves the way to winning performances on the athletic field. It surfaces in countless testimonies of athletes, like that of a five-time Olympic gold medalist who said: "I've been given a gift to swim fast, and I think God expects me to use that gift to the best of my ability to reach my potential."[39] Maximizing one's potential is fine, of course, but when "being all that one can be" is elevated to a Christian virtue, the reality of the opponent on the other side of the net or field or in the adjacent lane can get lost in the process. It denies the real possibility that there may be occasions when faith puts a heavy constraint on athletes, compelling them at times to "be less than what they could be."

This does not mean that competitive sports cannot enlighten us in ways other human experiences cannot. Learning about one's own personal strengths and weaknesses, the limits of one's physical capacities, and techniques of self-control and interpersonal negotiation, for example, all seem possible through competition. Moreover, in some circumstances, sports can be important "crucibles of sanctification," tests of Christian humility and "other-seeking" that present the Christian with costly tests of Christian character. But passing such spiritual tests has virtually nothing to do with the score; in fact, it may require a willingness to lose, and one doesn't hear much about losing in evangelical rhetoric. While I agree with colleagues Nick Watson and John White, who believe that competitions, "including those of a physical and aggressive nature," can be "potential places of learning virtuous character development in which athletes can learn about different forms of love, patience, compassion, and self-sacrifice," the operative word is "potential."[40] To believe that sports as played in modern society actually teach such virtues, one must overlook not only an extensive body of literature on character development in sports (chapter 8) but the fundamentally egocentric impulses inherent in competition itself.

JESUS AS THE MODEL COMPETITOR

Religious movements propelled by unchecked orthodoxy tend to conjure up their own images of Christ. Given the harsh realities of the sports world, a meek and gentle Jesus whose mission exemplified servanthood, peace, and reconciliation is an unlikely model for stoking the killer instinct. A more severe, no-nonsense, bare-knuckled Jesus is needed, a Jesus who can fight it out in the trenches, a Christ who needs a deodorant. "Christ ran the money changers out of the temple," said Tom Landry, citing a favorite passage of the evangelical sports community. "He showed strength in adversity, as well as gentleness." The Christ of the evangelical sports world is a caricature drawn by the ethos of sport that has infinite possibilities for priming the athletes' competitive pumps. "If He were sliding into second base he would knock the second baseman into left field to break up the double play," said a representative of Baseball Chapel, Inc. "Christ might not throw a spitball but he would play hard within the rules." These visions of Christ as brawny jock, impelled by self-interest and team spirit, capable of shutting down feelings for others when the whistle blows, loving it when he comes out ahead of others, are perfect illustrations of what Niebuhr called "personifications of abstractions." Cherry-picking the gospels to find a Christ that "always . . . seems to agree with their interests or the needs of the time," said Niebuhr, so qualifies one's loyalty to Christ that "He is abandoned in favor of an idol called by his name."[41]

Writer Kay Lindskoog, looking in from outside the world of sports, cuts to the heart of the matter: "I don't know. I'm a positive thinker. But if Christ were an overgrown Miami Dolphins defensive tackle instead of the Morning Star, I don't think I'd have a chance in life. I have no doubt he could play in the National Football League. I have no doubt he could be the world's toughest jet fighter pilot. I have no doubt he could make billions in big business. I have no doubt he could be the greatest tap dancer the world has ever seen. More significantly, I have no doubt he could turn stones into bread. It all seems a bit beside the point."[42]

If competition really is a "mutual striving for excellence" as modern sport philosophers claim, then the Christian athlete ought, as sociologist Dennis Hiebert has suggested, "to be able to visualize Jesus as being his opponent just as easily as being his teammate, and have confidence that in either case Christ would smile at him regardless of the score." Here is a concept that all evangelicals should be able to embrace. It stands in sharp contrast to the "Jesus my coach" or "Jesus my teammate" or "Jesus my fan" images that are the stock and trade of the evangelical sports community. Such images may help some athletes anchor their faith, but on the other hand, they play to predictable partisan instincts. Jesus is always on *my* side, rooting for *my* interests. But when Jesus is envisioned on the other side of the net or wearing a jersey of a different color, such partisan instincts seem strangely out of place. All of the traditional notions about the purpose of the contest and how it should be played, how I should think and act, and even how we should keep score are turned on their head.[43]

Sometimes the evangelical conscience seems impenetrable to suggestions that the convictions of the Christian athlete's faith might make it difficult, perhaps impossible, to buy into the manufactured partisanship that frames our games, or to summon up the killer instinct. But every once in a while an athlete boldly raises the question and, on even rarer occasions, decides that they cannot in good Christian conscience continue to compete. One such athlete was Andrea Jaeger, who in the mid-1980s was the second-ranked female professional tennis player in the world. Even before a shoulder injury cast a cloud over her career at age 19, she had been pondering the disconnect between her faith and the spirit required to win on the tennis tour. Eventually she realized that her faith could no longer allow her to play her hardest when doing so brought so much disappointment and suffering to those who were victims of her talent. "It was traumatic for me to beat a player and go into the locker room and see her crying or all upset," Jaeger says. After a particularly big win, she sat in her hotel room thinking: "Well, everybody thinks I'm great because I won, but what about the person I beat? How's she feeling? I was tormented." The longer she played on tour, the more her competitive zeal flagged. "There were times that I could not give my best because it caused a disharmony in me to do so. I gave my best but not at the cost of hardening my heart, or grieving my soul or wounding my spirit."

The night before her match against the legendary Martina Navratilova for the 1983 Wimbledon Championships, Jaeger got into a heated argument with her father and coach, Roland, and stormed out of her flat. She knocked on the door of a neighboring flat that had been rented by Navratilova. Although Navratilova did not talk to Jaeger, someone in the champion's inner circle consoled her and helped her arrange transportation to other lodging. Jaeger had beaten Navratilova previously, but this time she lost the match in 53 minutes. In light of such exceptional kindness, said Jaeger, "I never could have looked in the mirror if I went out and tried my heart out and won. The win would have been invalid to me." Today Jaeger is an Episcopal nun. "I did my best according to my values and morals," she says. "I did my best according to what I believe to this day that God does approve of: 'Be true to who you are in the person I have molded you to be.'" The evangelical athletic community has not rushed to Jaeger's defense or to hold her up as a model of the intersection of sport and faith. But I think her story has this to offer evangelical athletes and fans: she is an example of the radical stance on sports that can come when one takes their faith seriously and chooses to examine sports competition unrestricted by the mind-numbing constraints of modern sports theology.[44]

These serious reservations about competition notwithstanding, I don't hoist my flag with those who believe competition is irredeemable. Converting sports into entirely cooperative ventures or opting for the George Leonard school of "winning-isn't-everything-it-is-nothing" are not paths to redemption as much as they are paths to extinction. Sport that does not involve opposition and is not framed in the possibility of winning is not sport. At the same time, evangelicals earnest about aligning competitive sports with their theology will appreciate how their public witness can be undermined when they elevate competition to anything other than the simple organizing principle for playing games. Competitive sports, competitive politics, competitive business—*anything* competitive is always treacherous ground for Christians to tread, for it threatens to realign human relationships and sever bonds of fellowship that their faith enjoins them to protect and nurture. Sensitive Christians will approach this dangerous territory, not inflamed with religiously inspired zeal to prove themselves vastly superior to those against whom they compete, but as a way of underscoring their common humanity; not by giving in to the passions of institutional or community pride but by erecting safeguards to ensure that competition does not become the *raison d'etre* of the game itself.

As it now stands, sports competition is seriously in need of redemption, and that will require more than hackneyed allusions to it as "a gift from God" or as a vague exercise in "spiritual self-fulfillment." At the very least, it will require courageous athletes willing to subordinate athletic excellence to their commitment to character formation and who, in some cases and in some circumstances, choose to stay in the shadows of the stadium rather than run onto the field. Redeeming the competitive element in sports will require athletes who realize that the call of God isn't always to the end zone. Competition will have taken on some flavoring of the Christian message when Christian athletes envision Christ on the opponent's team, when they rid themselves of images of God as a fan, coach, or teammate and stop thinking of him as a cosmic anabolic steroid for improving their chances of success.

Redeeming the competitive element in sports will require the Christian athletic community to take a bold look at competition, not as a wired-in biological trait, but as something we have learned; not as something we are impelled to do by force of nature, but as a humanly designed way of relating to each other that, even under the best of circumstances, mixes awkwardly with the faith. It will require athletes and coaches willing to consider how sin can manifest itself, not only in individual behaviors but in social institutions as well. Redeeming sport will require more than a subtle nod to the theological concept of grace that too often is used to bless everything Christians choose to do. It will not kidnap Scripture verses to inspire positive deviance, and it will make itself known in the actions—more than the words—of athletes and coaches. It will nudge them less in the direction of the Ik and more in the direction of the Master.

7

Building and Sacking the Temple

Until you hear the music, it looks like any other exercise video. An attractive, healthy-looking exercise leader in the foreground, backed up by a handful of willing novices, takes viewers through a series of light weight exercises, stretching, and low-impact aerobics in a large, comfortable room. But the music isn't the typical blend of rock and bebop that blares in commercial exercise parlors; it's "Just as I Am," made famous as an invitational hymn sung at Billy Graham crusades. Leslie Sansone and her *Walk the Walk* exercise video leads the assembled through what the tape jacket calls "a Christian inspired workout," assuring that the experience will "keep the focus on God's blessings, so you're not just challenging your body . . . you're nurturing your soul." A competitor in the faith-fitness business offers more rigorous fare. In her best-selling tape, *Sweating in the Spirit*, former NBC *Weekend Today* fitness expert Donna Richardson takes her charges through a tough workout punctuated by gospel rock, words of encouragement, a smattering of "amens," and cameo appearances by gospel singers Kirk Franklin and Yolanda Adams. The session culminates in quiet prayer.

Welcome to the new face of Christian asceticism. The body, once regarded by ancients as a vessel of unruly passions and therefore something to be mortified in anticipation of the final escape, is getting renewed attention within evangelical circles. But there is a big difference. For the ancient ascetics—"athletes of God" whose lives were "wrestling rings"—who struggled not to produce slim and toned frames, but to keep their bodies and their urges in check, often fleeing to the desert to live lives of solitude, unimaginable discomfort, and deprivation was a way of better contemplating God. In Hilarion's meager subsistence on bread and water, or in Simon Stylites' life lived for thirty-seven years atop a sixty-foot pole, we see not simply indifference to the body, but the logical playing out of a conviction that the soul is at war with the body. But for modern "exercites," the body is the soul's friend; pain and sacrifice are routes to a more beautiful body, not an emasculated one. Self-flagellation and mortification are out; muscle burns, groaning on diabolical exercise machines, and sweating to the cadence marked off by bouncy aerobics experts are in. High-protein drinks and low-carb diets have replaced bread and water; spandex is the new hair shirt. The new liturgies of body mass indexing, cardio-treadmill tests for vascular integrity, skin fold tests for percent body fat, and cholesterol screening have replaced chants, all-night vigils, and earnest contemplation. Eventually the cult of the desert died an inglorious death; *cultus aerobicus* is now in full bloom.

THE MODERN EXERCITE

The body has always been a bit of a problem for the Christian community. Surely, stereotypical characterizations of early Christian ascetics as filthy, body-punishing hermits don't describe all those who sought refuge in the desert. Monastic conceptions of the body, at least from the fourth century on, were ambiguous at best. John Climacus' writings in the seventh century, for example, depict the body as a repository of sin and temptation, yet at the same time he spoke of the Christian's bodily life as "an essential and enduring element in his personhood." However, when, in the mid-nineteenth century, two founders of the Disciples of Christ church repudiated the human form, one calling it a "degraded" and "vile abode," and the other calling it a victim to "all the evils of mortality," it wasn't clear that the church had advanced all that much from its understanding of the body since Stylites took his seat atop the 60-foot pole in fifth-century Antioch.[1]

Body suspicion received no warrant from Scripture. The Old Testament made no distinction between body and soul; the human person was not body *and* soul but an undivided unity. The ancient Israelite would have pointed out: "I do not *have* a body, I *am* my body." By and large, the same holistic view of the body prevails in the New Testament. Commentators who portray the Apostle Paul as a body hater and metaphysical dualist for whom the body ("flesh") was constantly at war against "the spirit" have it wrong. As used by the apostle, "flesh" refers not to the body but to the entire human entity separated from God and in rebellion against him. "Spirit" refers not to one's soul, but to "human personhood in its entirety, body and soul together living in obedience to God and in communion with Him." The Bible speaks of the body as one of God's highest creative acts that, in some inexplicable way, reflects the Creator's image; the Bible also condemns harmful gluttony as one of the seven deadly sins (Proverbs 23:1-3), describes the body as a temple of the Holy Spirit, and urges believers to glorify God in their bodies (1 Corinthians 6:19-20).

The fact that Paul denounces self-abasement and severe treatment of the body as being of no value against fleshly indulgence (Colossians 2:23) seems a direct repudiation of ascetics who glory in denigration of the body. And no higher stamp of importance could be placed on the body than the Christian doctrine of the incarnation, the belief that God, in the form of Jesus Christ, became fully human without surrendering his divinity. In the scriptural view, the body deserves respect as the *imago Dei*, a living expression of faith, a gift and gesture of love and divine creativity.[2]

Evangelicals have more or less accepted this, in theory if not in practice. For many, perhaps most, it has been honored in the negative—avoiding overconsumption of alcohol, smoking, and use of recreational drugs—more than in the positive, which might require rigorous adherence to exercise regimens. Years of viewing the teachings of Scripture about the body merely as warnings *against* rather than calls *to* action has resulted in the inglorious fact, says sociologist Dennis Hiebert, "that the Spirit too often resides in not vandalized but dilapidated quarters."[3] If the laity haven't been moved to renovate, it hasn't been through lack of urging on the part of their leaders. Evangelical ethicists more or less consistently underscore Christians' obligations to their bodies, pointing to God's "holistic intention" for each person. But none have pushed the doctrine quite like those in the evangelical diet and exercise movement. God wants, even demands, that his followers have fit bodies, and it is the Christian's obligation to keep the temple of the Holy Spirit in good repair.[4] Kenneth Cooper, director of the highly respected Cooper

Aerobics Institute in Dallas, talks of his "fitness conversion" in which he understood "perhaps for the first time that my body was truly a temple of God." It dawned on Cooper that "it was clearly up to me to keep that temple in shape if I hoped to live a complete life and fulfill the plans God had for my life."[5]

Whether this newfound interest in the stewardship of the body represents a well-defined trend or is simply the church's search for relevance in a society enamored with health, longevity, and a trim frame is anybody's guess. In her book *Born Again Bodies*, religion scholar Marie Griffith suggests that this preoccupation with a fit body projects a new face of evangelicalism. According to Griffith, the devotional emphasis given to the body among Christian exercise devotees, especially the emphasis put on bodily appearance, has supplanted traditional "spiritual indicators of Christian character such as love, joy, peace, goodness and temperance." Even in espousing the explicitly pious goal of reflecting God's glory, says Griffin, the worldly benefits of a thin body are given the greatest emphasis.[6]

The connection these "exercetics" envision between body and soul tends to be more instrumental than intrinsic; references to holism and holiness often seem like add-ons intended to help sell a message: the soul can help get the body in shape. The goal of the ancients was spiritual health abetted by strict management of the body, but the exercetics invert the formula: bodily health is abetted by the spirit. Cooper tells readers they can "strengthen and use [their] beliefs to maximize [their] energy levels, stave off illness, and live as long as God has designed [them] to live." In diet guru Gwen Shamblin's book *Rise Above*, readers are encouraged to find in their spiritual lives the will to manage bodily cravings and thereby control their weight. And for Billy Blank, faith not only saves one's soul; it also helps believers complete his strenuous workout. For the ancients, self-denial and sacrifice were processes for focusing and energizing the soul. For the exercetic, suffering and self-denial are practical means toward a very material end: a healthy, toned, and slim body that, by mirroring society's corporeal aesthetic, is thought to glorify the Creator.[7]

It is difficult to fault Christians for wanting to get in tune with their bodies, yet it is hard to ignore the way much of the movement seems aimed merely at producing bodies that will put a more attractive face on Christianity. "When we first got married," Millie Cooper (wife of Kenneth Cooper) tells audiences, "my husband told me one day: 'look

Millie, I'm giving my whole life to the cause of fitness and I can't afford to drag a fat wife around the country, so start losing or start looking.'" In a society that fawns on the female form that boasts "washboard abs," a devotional plan guaranteeing health and sex appeal encased in a glitzy somaticism ("fat-is-sin-and-the-righteous-are-thin-amen") can be very beguiling. And for devout men it elevates another ideal, a brawny, muscular Christ, fittingly captured in the logo of "Lord's Gym," a national network of fitness centers: a pumped-up Christ doing push-ups with an enormous cross on his back.[8]

The body-spirit movement has spawned an enormous market for evangelically skewed diet and exercise books, instructional tapes, and diet and exercise programs. Writer Lauren Winner has estimated the economic impact of the Christian diet industry to be $1.5 billion annually. Shamblin's bestselling "Weigh Down Workshops" are now offered at a reported 30,000 locations internationally. Her book *Weigh Down Diet* is said to have sold over 1 million copies. Ben Lerner says his bestseller *Body by God*, which contains tips on exercise, diet, and reducing stress, was written "as a supplement to the Bible." La Vita Weaver's program *Fit for God* has been especially popular in African American churches. For exercetics who find their zeal flagging, there is *Faith and Fitness Magazine* "for building physical and spiritual strength," while Christian fitness trainers can update their body theology and exercise routines by joining the nondenominational Christian Wellness Association or the International Christian Health and Fitness Alliance. Whether all of this enthusiasm has translated into a vibrant, robust, and especially healthy laity is open to question. Sociologist Ken Ferraro doesn't think it has. His research found that although religious-minded people are less likely to smoke or overindulge in alcohol, they are more likely to be overweight. Apparently many "firm believers," said Ferraro, do not always have "firm bodies."[9]

If evangelicals are exercising less and eating more, it isn't because their churches have let them down. Gymnasia and fitness centers, some more spacious and better equipped than YMCAs and commercial gyms, grace the grounds of many mid-size to large evangelical churches. Perhaps the most ambitious of such programs is at Dunwoody Baptist Church in Atlanta, Georgia, whose Cecil B. Day Sports and Fitness Center is overseen by a staff of seven and headed up by a minister of sports and fitness.[10] Whether it's the "Word Walkers" who walk laps while reciting Scripture at Union Avenue Baptist Church in Memphis, the aerobics classes offered in the fellowship hall of Mt. Sinai Baptist Church in Omaha, or the "PraiseXercise classes" held each Saturday at Shiloh Missionary Baptist Church in Plano, Texas, churches of all sizes seem to have jumped on the fitness bandwagon. The online *Gospel Aerobics Directory* of church-based exercise programs compiled by Victoria Johnson Fitness Ministries identifies programs offered in 23 states. As a condition of being included in the directory, classes must use "clean" contemporary Christian music with no inappropriate language and must offer prayer before, during, or after the presentation. For years, evangelicals have overloaded their plates at church pot luck suppers; now they have an opportunity to cleanse both their moral and coronary arteries, all without leaving the church complex.[11]

Those in the movement haven't been any more clear in explaining how faith is appreciably affected by fitness than were the "body-as-temple men" of an earlier era, which may be why the focus tends to be more on the body than the soul. Beneath the layers of rhetoric about physical-spiritual harmony lays an undeniable dualism that sets the body apart as something to be admired on its own worldly merits. Griffith notes that Protestants who have argued that "slimness should be an explicitly pious goal because it reflects God's glory" have at the same time "vigorously advocated its benefits, including health, beauty, love, and prestige."[12] The "temple-of-the-spirit" characterizations of the body don't threaten to elevate the spirit at the expense of the body; we see precisely the opposite tendency. There is a curious parallel here to the race to build bigger and more elaborate houses of worship. Where size, splendor, square footage, and amenities are regarded as symbols of success, the spiritual life of the church can easily become subservient to its architecture. So too, when evangelicals are enamored of the biological architecture of their "temples," the soul can become subservient to the body. Faith becomes less important as an all-encompassing worldview than as a handy instrument for pushing believers through strenuous workouts and helping them avoid unhealthy food.

The faith-based fitness movement played out in elaborate church facilities and programs stands in bold relief against a world plagued by unprecedented poverty. A family struggling to scrape by may well wonder if funds diverted to slimming the contours of overeating believers might be better spent on enlarging those of their malnourished neighbors. Furthermore, one may well question the need for church-based fitness programs, at least those housed in lavish facilities. The muscle tone gained

from exercising on shiny equipment in a $5 million church campus facil-
ity isn't likely to be much different from that gained at the neighborhood
Y. Women high stepping to aerobics on the linoleum floors in the fellowship hall of Mt. Sinai Church have every reason to expect the same health
returns on their investment as do participants of aerobics classes offered
in the more plush surrounds of Champion Forest Baptist Church Family
Life Center in Houston.

If theology actually was the stimulus for such programs, one might
suppose that churches would be exploring ways of integrating their pursuit of the healthy life with their sense of mission and outreach. For all
of its practical benefits, exercise can be a singularly indulgent and selfish
experience. Perhaps redirecting the physical energy invested in tread-
mills or stationary bicycles to vigorous acts of public and private service
would be a more profitable and justifiable way to glorify members' bodies. While there is little question that Scripture teaches Christians to care
for their bodies, there are many ways of fulfilling this spiritual obligation;
it hardly requires replication of commercial gymnasia or programs that
divert time, energy, and money from missions and other spiritual matters traditionally vouchsafed to the church.

There is no biblical basis for imagining that God is glorified more by
a beautiful body than a less endowed one. Christians with sculpted pecs
and six-pack abs may be better billboards for the faith than those with jig-
gly frames, but not on the basis of any spiritual claims. Indeed, promoting
fit bodies as living illustrations of faith would seem to violate some basic
principles of truth in advertising. Perhaps more to the point, the ethic
of self-concentration and cosmetic beauty so evident in the evangelical
fitness movement threatens to cloud evangelicals' view of the body's real
cosmic beauty. As medical researcher Thomas Elkins so splendidly put it,
the body's beauty "is most apparent in the simplest acts of meaningful-
ness, acts in which the body serves as a vessel of servanthood, a trans-
porter of joy, a bridge to fellowship—and thus becomes a truer image
of the Creator himself."[13] The saints should rejoice in physically active,
robust bodies, not because a fit body projects a culturally attractive image
of the faith, but because good health can be the basis for a richer life, even
for spiritual renewal—less "buns of steel" and more hearts of gold.

SPORTS AND THE BODY

The Christian community has long advocated sports on the same basis
that it has advocated exercise—as a way of satisfying the scriptural

mandate to care for the body, enabling its use for worship, devotion, and service. Sport-for-body development was a recurring theme in treatises by medieval theologians long before the Southern Baptist Theological Seminary dedicated its new gym to the production of "broad-shouldered ministers" in 1897. Sport continues to be cited in evangelical circles as a path toward spiritual as well as physical fitness. "Regular and intense participation in sports," says Calvin College physical education professor Marv Zuidema, "is . . . one way of maintaining optimal health fitness," which is important because "the care of the body is a moral responsibility and part of our reasonable service to God." "Through sports," says an evangelical professor, "man's body, a temple of the Holy Spirit, is maintained and developed in an enjoyable manner." Some years ago, the dean of a Christian college told readers of an evangelical publication, "Athletics are intrinsically good as they develop and preserve the body . . . because the body is part of man's oneness before his Creator."[14]

Claiming sport as a health-inducing experience, however, runs into a number of difficulties. First, like most people, evangelicals most often experience sports not on the court or athletic field, but on their backsides watching them being played. For a nation addicted to and suffering the health consequences of a sedentary lifestyle, watching sports can hardly be recommended for its healthful effects.

Secondly, the prospect of improved health doesn't explain why most people, especially elite athletes, play sports. The attraction of play, said Johan Huizinga, is not its prospective benefits, but its "intensity, absorption, [and] power of maddening." "People start playing even before they ask themselves why they are playing," say philosophers Scott Kretchmar and Bill Harper, "and they play while continually ignoring the question." The sacrifices of the Olympic runner are not made for the benefit of an improved cardiovascular system; baseball, football, and basketball players don't play as a way of strengthening their bodies. By the same token, it is not the prospect of a reduced waistline that causes the deaconess to take her turn in the batter's box at the church's weekly softball game. If there is a theological justification for sport, it will be found in its appeal to players' spirits, not as a health-inducing experience.[15]

Third, playing sports isn't always a particularly efficient way to improve health. Systematic exercise brings about enormous physical benefits, but the health benefits conferred by a season of competitive basketball, a program of weekend tennis, or seasonal softball are far sketchier. Some sports require a fairly high level of fitness as a precondition for participation (e.g., wrestling or marathon running), while others (e.g., archery or bowling) require very little. Sports playing may produce very high levels of specialized "performance fitness" but not necessarily "health fitness." Cyclist Lance Armstrong, marathon runner Paula Radcliffe, and Olympic swimmer Michael Phelps have attained amazing levels of highly specialized performance fitness, but viewed from the perspective of a lifespan, the effects are short term, destined to diminish when their grueling training schedules cease.[16]

Finally, for every imaginable health benefit that might come from participating in sports, similar benefits are available through other less expensive, less self-indulgent, less ethically challenging activities that may be more in line with evangelicals' professed theology. Physically challenging, health-reinforcing acts of Christian kindness—mowing sickly neighbors' lawns, delivering meals to shut-ins (while jogging of course), or helping build homes for Habitat for Humanity—may be ethically superior choices for a religious group that recognizes sin is as often committed in omission as in commission. For all of these reasons, attempting to rationalize sport as a "temple builder" runs into difficulties, but none demolish it quite like the body of evidence suggesting that playing sports is just as likely to raze the temple as build it up. It is an important and controversial claim which deserves a more complete explanation.

SACKING THE TEMPLE

Steve Brown, a fourteen-year old suburban Pittsburgh Little League pitcher whose team trailed by two runs, found himself at a critical juncture of the game. His team was on the verge of making a comeback. The only obstacle was the opposing team's best batter, against whom he was currently struggling. His mother later told reporters that she had urged Steve to "give the game everything you've got." He did precisely that, uncorking what may have been the fastest pitch he had ever thrown. Then there was a loud crack; people who were one hundred yards away claim to have heard it. But it wasn't the sound of the bat hitting the ball; it was the sound of Steve's arm breaking in two places as his biceps muscle was torn from his upper arm bone.[17]

Brown's injury may have been unusual, but it wasn't an isolated case. Orthopedic surgeons at Cleveland Clinic Hospital have witnessed a four-fold increase in elbow reconstruction surgery for teenage pitchers in recent years. In the professional leagues, tearing of the rotator cuff muscles—a particularly debilitating injury—is the bane of a pitcher's professional career. Dr. Paul Jacobs, a sports medicine specialist involved in the rehabilitation of Cy Young Award winner Pete Vuckovich, told a reporter: "I think every pitcher is liable to get a [rotator cuff] tear. *God did not mean you to throw a baseball 90 miles an hour.*"[18]

The risk of injury confronts athletes every time they step on the field or court, a fact buried in health statistics rarely seen by athletes, coaches, and parents. Between July 2000 and June 2001, approximately 4.3 million sports- and recreation-related injuries were treated in U.S. hospitals, accounting for 16 percent of all unintentional injury-related emergency room visits. For males aged 10–19, football, basketball, and cycling were the most dangerous; for females in the same age bracket, playing basketball led to the most injuries. Approximately 12 percent of the 10,000 cases of spinal cord injury that occur each year in the United States and an estimated 30 percent of the million or so cases of traumatic brain injury occurring each year are sports related. The alarming injury rate has inspired the Centers for Disease Control to label sports injuries "an important public health concern for both children and adults"; the CDC has further urged that high-risk activities, places of occurrence, and risk behaviors be identified in efforts to control the alarming trend.[19]

Obviously many life activities, such as driving or performing many kinds of work, also entail the risk of bodily harm. Even orchestral musicians are plagued by tendonitis, muscle cramps, pinched nerves, and anxiety, problems which have driven some to resort to "beta blockers," the same antianxiety drugs that have been banned in sports by the Medical Commission of the International Olympic Committee as a form of doping. But to reduce the ethical issue of body defacement to probabilities and risk-ratios overlooks the point that under any circumstances, Christians would seem obligated by their theology to use common sense in avoiding activities in which serious injuries are common occurrences. There has been no more consistent theme in the theological literature related to sports over the past 600 years than the teaching that Christians should avoid sports that are dangerous to themselves and to others. In *Mortal Engines: The Science of Performance and the Dehumanization of Sport*, social critic John Hoberman writes, "It is now widely accepted that high-performance sport is a medically hazardous activity." But as the statistics above suggest, victims of sport injuries aren't just elite athletes. Formerly arcane medical terms such as "rotator cuff injury" have become part of the weekend tennis or softball player's nomenclature. Sports medicine has become a booming medical specialization, and university programs for preparing athletic trainers—the first responders who minister to injured athletes—are experiencing a surge in enrollment.[20]

Evangelicals who erect gymnasia so that their congregations can "build up the temple" need to explain how, at the same time, they can lend so much support to activities that virtually assure that those same bodies will be at least temporarily incapacitated. Obviously, the benefits of sport, like anything else, must be weighed against its limitations, but the calculus often underestimates the frequency and severity of injuries that can occur. Athletic injuries are usually described as "accidents," and some of them truly are unintentional, unforeseen happenstances. But for those competing in elite sports, injuries are a given. They can hardly be called "accidents." Concussions are expected in boxing, for example, where fighters are awarded victories for inflicting them on opponents; some laws require a physician or other medical personnel to be in attendance at high school football games, and an ambulance usually waits in the shadow of the stadium to transport players to the hospital. Behind such policies is the widely accepted assumption that people who play sports will get hurt, sometimes seriously.

Neither do athletic injuries become accidents simply because players do not intend to injure themselves or their opponents. The person who jumps from a two-story building or rafts on an inner tube down Class IV rapids may not *intend* to be injured, but a logical person would conclude that injury is the probable result. Likewise, when humans of massive proportions collide at breakneck speeds, when runners subject their bodies to multiple marathons, when the knees and hips of gymnasts endure tens of thousands of crushing dismounts, their bodies surely will pay the price.

Sports, of course, aren't all equally dangerous. Competitive bowling, swimming, softball, and basketball, for example, result in injuries, but substantially fewer than collision sports like boxing, American football, hockey, and soccer. The American Medical Association (AMA) and the American Academy of Neurology (AAN) have taken strong positions against boxing: the archives of the *Journal of the American Medical Association* contain hundreds of articles warning of its threats to the brain and other organs of the body. A punch from a professional boxer impacts the opponent's head with a force equivalent to that generated by a thirteen-pound weight being swung at twenty miles per hour; a boxer typically absorbs dozens and perhaps hundreds of such blows to the head during a ten-round fight.[21] Chilling replays of his 2005 fatal match revealed that Leavander Johnson had received over four hundred blows to the head. The number of deaths annually suffered in the ring is surprisingly small, but the cumulative, insidious damage from receiving repeated blows to the body is not. Chief among these medical horrors is *pugilistica dementia*, chronic brain injury resulting from repeated trauma causing the brain to bang against the interior walls of the skull. It is silent, only revealing itself over time as the fighter experiences problems with memory, speech, and coordination.[22]

In many ways football is a greater threat to health than boxing, not simply because there are more participants, but because the sport is so integral to American culture. The mythic allure of football has a way of sanitizing its violence. Although deaths in football are rare, at less than one death per 100,000 participants, it has been implicated in the largest number of catastrophic injuries reported to the National Center for Catastrophic Sports Injury Research. It is estimated that over a seven-year period, a professional football player will be involved in as many as 130,000 collisions. Spectators, of course, are fascinated by these collisions. Television commentators relish them and producer-directors replay them, often serving up slow motion videos of athletes in the process of being crippled. For fans in the stadium or on their sofas, these are cartoon people suffering cartoon injuries, the violence and its results as unreal as a soap opera. They are spared the thunderclap of colliding pads and helmets, the grunts and groans, the screams and sobs of players writhing on the field. "Fans? They don't have a clue," says All-Pro linebacker Ray Lewis. "They sit at home and watch and go Ooooo, owwww, woooo. But then do they ask themselves, I wonder does his head hurt now? How many hours did he sleep comfortably last night?"[23]

Psychiatrist Arnold Mandell spent a season as a staff member for the NFL's San Diego Chargers, and he eventually resigned his position after witnessing the incredible carnage up close and personal from the sidelines. At the last game he attended, a drunken spectator had fallen thirty feet from an upper tier seat; as the man lay jerking on the ground, Mandell thought:

> [But] the players, they are doing that to each other *all the time*
> . . . broken necks and broken legs and broken ribs and fractured
> this and fractured that and concussions and unconsciousness.

But they are in uniform and psychologically segmented off . . . They are not *humans* . . . and [then] suddenly it's a human being that hits the ground and jerks around. And all the while the band played and the loudspeakers gave out their announcements and the teams went on about their business, and suddenly it was too naked. Suddenly that was the essence of everything, and I couldn't go back.[24]

It is impossible to overstate football's assault on the dignity of the human body. Of the 62,000 injuries suffered in high school sports each year, 68 percent come from playing or practicing football. Estimates are that 5.5 million youths play football annually; 28 percent of those aged 9–14 are injured, resulting in 187,000 hospital visits each year. Brain injuries in college and especially professional football are becoming a national calamity; they have been featured in front-page stories in the country's leading newspapers and are a serious concern for the *Journal of the American Medical Association*. The real seriousness of these injuries is muted by athletic jargon. One doesn't bruise one's brain, one "gets one's bell rung"; an athlete's cerebral cortex isn't traumatized, he or she "gets dinged."[25]

In many cases football players suffer concussions without knowing it, but the cumulative effects eventually reveal themselves, often in tragic ways. Repeated "dings" can lead to post-concussive syndrome, accompanied by memory loss, lethargy, neck pain, persistent fogginess, and constant migraines. In the NFL, concussions are known as "career enders" because they have done precisely that for scores of players. New York Jets wide receiver Al Toon announced his retirement in 1994 due to post-concussive symptoms. All-Pro San Francisco quarterback Steve Young retired three games into the 1999 season after a blow to the head left him with his fourth concussion in three games. All-Pro Dallas quarterback Troy Aikman, who had suffered six concussions and serious back surgery in the course of his career, told a reporter he had hoped to play in the NFL for ten years, but then asked: "How in the world could anybody endure *this* for 10 years?"[26]

Many players don't realize the price they have paid until they have retired. Pittsburgh Steelers Hall of Fame center Mike Webster always prided himself on the gouges and dents in his helmet, but after seventeen years of repeated concussions, he retired to the life of a disoriented vagrant, glassy-eyed, punch-drunk, addicted to narcotics he used to numb the searing pain of a litany of orthopedic injuries. He

"Tased" himself repeatedly, saying it was the only way he could get to sleep. When he died in 2002 at the age of 50, teammates gave him the dubious epitaph of one of the greatest to have played the game. Another former Steeler, 45-year-old lineman Terry Long, died from *pugilistica dementia* in 2005. Andre Waters battled depression after he left football, and in 2006, over ten years after his retirement, he took his own life. Neuropathologists described his brain as characteristic of an 85-year-old man with Alzheimer's disease; they concluded that the successive concussions sustained playing football had either caused the condition or expedited its advance.[27]

High school football players haven't escaped the scourge of head injuries. As a rule, catastrophic injuries are much more common at college than high school levels, but catastrophic *head* injuries are three times more prevalent in high school, perhaps because the brain of the high school athlete is still developing or because of inferior medical care and equipment for high school athletes. The problem is exacerbated by young players' naïveté. Unappreciative of the severity of their injuries, they are more likely not to report them to their coach and to return to games before their brains have healed. According to research by the Center of Injury Research and Policy at Nationwide's Children's Hospital in Columbus, Ohio, over 40 percent of high schoolers who incur a concussion go back to compete prematurely. In 2008 in North Carolina, two high school football players died as a result of returning to action shortly after having suffered concussions. *New York Times* reporter Alan Schwarz interviewed a high school player in Springfield, Illinois, who had suffered three concussions. Asked if he would tell his coach if he suffered a fourth, the boy replied: "No chance. It's not dangerous to play with a concussion. You've got to sacrifice for the sake of the team. The only way I come out is on a stretcher."[28]

Head injuries in football are explained by basic principles of physics. All things being equal, the greater the momentum (mass times velocity) developed by players, the greater the potential for injury when they collide. In the NFL, both mass and velocity have been increasing for years. For example, the starting interior offensive line for the Pittsburgh Steelers averaged 241 pounds in 1964, 260 pounds by 1984, and 309 pounds in 2004. Players have also become faster too, often by reducing or shunning protective padding. Now most of the receivers and even some linebackers in the NFL wear no pads on their legs except for thin thigh pads. A hypothetical collision between a 240-pound lineman and a 240-pound runner has been estimated to release enough kinetic energy to move a 33-ton locomotive one inch. To get a real idea of the forces involved in football collisions, says North Carolina State physics professor David Haase, dive off a thirteen-foot ladder and land on your head and shoulders or try to catch a bowling ball dropped from a height of thirteen feet. Carolina Panthers coach John Fox wasn't merely speaking figuratively when he told a reporter: "We've got a violent game and these guys are human projectiles."[29]

Football's toll on the body extends far beyond concussions. Players suffering injuries to weight-bearing joints are five to seven times more likely to develop degenerative arthritis later in life than nonplayers. Joint and back deterioration are so common in retired NFL players that an executive for the NFL Players Association called the trauma inflicted on players' joints "an orthopedic surgeon's dream." Like concussions, the extent of damage often is not known until long after a player has retired. A full 38 percent of retired NFL players report that they currently suffer degenerative arthritis, a significantly higher incidence than among the population in general. The late Hall of Fame quarterback Johnny Unitas had two knee replacements and during his playing days suffered a smashed elbow in the magical arm that threw hundreds of touchdowns. By the time he turned sixty, his arm was nonfunctional: "I can't use a hammer or saw around the house. I can't button buttons. I can't use zippers. Very difficult to tie shoes . . . You give me a full cup of coffee, and I can't hold it." When former All-Pro Oakland Raider Jim Otto retired from his long career, he had suffered more than a dozen fractures to his nose, two hundred stitches to his face, four operations on his left knee, five on his right, operations on both elbows, fractures to all of his fingers, and broken ribs. He suffered a chronic bad back and bad shoulders and was classified as permanently disabled. In retirement, he petitioned the IRS to allow him to depreciate his body as a declining asset like one might depreciate a piece of factory equipment.[30]

None of this is lost on current players, for whom avoiding injury is a number one priority. Asked what he hoped to get out of an upcoming game with the New Orleans Saints, the New York Jets' Chester McGlockton replied, "Get out of the game healthy." Lito Sheppard, star cornerback for the Philadelphia Eagles, adds, "I don't want to hurt anybody seriously, and I don't want to get hurt seriously. What we've got to do is find a way to play this game without killing each other."[31]

Football and boxing can't be blamed for all of the injuries incurred in sports. Approximately 715,000 sports and recreation injuries occur each year in school settings. Baseball provides for little contact between players, but it too can be dangerous, not only to pitchers but to catchers as well. Former All-Star catcher Bob Brenly matter-of-factly ticked off his injuries for a reporter:

> Foul tips have broken my shoulder, knuckles, fingers, torn nails off my toes. By the end of the season I feel like a used car . . . both fingers become numb for six months from catching 90-per hour fast balls . . . My hands get so sore I can't grip the bat properly. At the end of last season I had calcium deposits, bone chips, and a cartilage problem that required arthroscopic surgery in both knees. But to be a major league catcher, you must play even when you're hurt. You can take your body into the shop for repair at the end of the season when there's plenty of time for doctors, operation, healing.[32]

Soccer injuries are now receiving a great deal of attention from the medical community. In one study, 264 soccer players, competing at a variety of levels, were followed over a one-year period. A total of 568 different injuries were recorded, 59 percent of which were classified as moderate to severe. Only 18 percent of all players had no injuries at all. Head injuries have become almost as serious a medical problem in soccer as in football. An investigation by an orthopedic surgeon discovered that nearly half of the injuries experienced by a group of soccer players between eleven and fourteen years old involved symptoms of concussions, most of them the result of heading the soccer ball. Dutch researchers who compared brain function in adult amateur soccer players with runners and middle-distance swimmers discovered that those playing amateur soccer scored lower on tests of memory and planning; the degree of impairment correlated quite closely with the number of incidents of traumatic brain injury the players had incurred. Other researchers have documented brain atrophy, electro-encephalographic changes, and deficits in memory, concentration, and alertness in veteran professional soccer players, most of which are believed to have come from heading the ball.[33]

Among athletes competing in a variety of sports and at all levels of competition, there is an epidemic of torn anterior cruciate ligaments (ACL), a tough fibrous band that is required to stabilize the knee.

Approximately 80,000 torn ACLs occur each year; the highest incidence is among fifteen- to twenty-five-year-olds who play sports, especially female soccer and basketball players. Other noncontact knee injuries resulting from rapid shifting of body weight, rapid change in body direction, and simply asking the body to do more than it was designed to do are also plaguing sports.[34]

Injury from chronic overuse in what might seem to be harmless activities—throwing baseballs, hitting tennis balls, performing gymnastic routines, swimming, or running marathons and triathlons—can lead to a lifetime of joint, skeletal, and muscular problems. The long-term damage done to the arms of tennis players and baseball pitchers; the hips, feet, and ankles of gymnasts; and the backs and legs of runners is well known by those in the sports medicine community. A debilitating disorder called "swimmer's shoulder" is caused by repetitive motion of the arms. (Estimates are that elite class swimmers cycle through 600,000 strokes in a season.) Young athletes, many of whom are pressured by their parents and coaches into unrealistic training and competitive practices, are being injured at an unprecedented rate. In a 1997 tennis tournament for youth players in Florida, one-fourth of the players had to withdraw due to injuries. An informal survey of the players participating showed that 69 percent of the participants had experienced injuries that required a visit to a doctor or sidelined them for at least three days. The director of the tournament told reporters she believes that kids are training and playing too much.[35]

CULTURE OF RISK

What is it that encourages athletes to submit to the body-wrecking trauma of a sport, even to the point where they continue to play while injured? For one thing, athletes know that injuries can lead to a permanent place on the bench. High school players sitting on the bench aren't given scholarships; professional athletes who ride the bench may lose their livelihoods. Yet dealing with the realities of injury day in and day out requires something more than this: at the very least, an acceptance of an alternate reality manufactured by coaches, fans, publicists, reporters, television broadcasters, and fellow athletes, a world in which risking life and limb makes sense. Sociologists call it "a culture of risk," a culture that normalizes the giving and receiving of pain and injury. When injuries are normalized, they aren't seen as moral issues or even personal tragedies; they simply are dismissed as "all part of the game."

How we frame the world can affect our perception of pain. Theologian Arthur Glucklich, for example, shows how pain suffered when accompanied by a setback can be excruciating, but pain from an injury incurred while scoring a touchdown can "almost feel good." In the culture of risk, sprains, broken and dislocated limbs, and other disfigurements of the *imago Dei* become emblems of moral conviction and strength rather than an unnecessary maiming of a sacred vessel; the "varsity limp" becomes a badge of courage rather than evidence of a sacked temple.[36]

Spectators are not insignificant parties to this alternate reality. By applauding the injured as they are carted from the field or giving heroic welcomes to the permanently disabled when they return to the stadium—often in wheelchairs or on crutches after physical therapists have done what they can do to restore some semblance of normal functioning—spectators add to the delusion that risking the vitality of one's body for the sake of public entertainment is not only a reasonable thing for young men and women to do but a morally admirable act. Even the sports medicine profession can assist in fostering the culture of risk. A particularly provocative study of the inner workings of an athletic training room, for example, discovered a "conspiratorial alliance of coaches, athletic administrators, sport medicine personnel, and others whose activities perpetuate the acceptance of athletes of risk, pain and injury in sport."[37]

In a culture of risk, bodies that fail can be treated with a coldness that borders on contempt. The most familiar form of this contempt is injecting illegal steroids as a way of purchasing short-term gains at the expense of early heart disease, bad cholesterol profiles, increased incidence of tendon injuries, liver tumors, and emotional disturbances. Willful submission to the violence in sports like boxing, football, and hockey may be possible only when athletes disassociate from their bodies, relating to them as though they were athletic equipment, or imagining that they occupy a separate space from the rest of their being. Psychiatrist Stephen Ward observed the strange way athletes relate to injured body parts, especially following contests in which their team has lost: "[The athlete] is unable to accept the fact that his body has failed in its requirements, but he will choose one small area of his body and single it out for attention and disapproval."[38] Canadian researchers interviewing injury-crippled athletes found the same phenomenon. Athletes resented their injured bodies for having betrayed them, even to the point that they refused to acknowledge that the injured body part was their own. "It's like it's not a part of you," said one athlete, "like it's a totally different portion or something."[39]

This attitude of detachment is often fostered by what researchers call "risk rhetoric." Risk rhetoric denies the existence of pain or injury and, when this isn't possible, seeks to diminish its significance. It raises the threshold for pain tolerance and justifies playing when hurt, even when doing so may compound the seriousness of the injury. Risk rhetoric might even wax poetically about the pain and injuries suffered in sports. In his twilight years, Don Meredith, long-time quarterback of the Dallas Cowboys, once reflected romantically on the sensuous pleasure of having his nose broken and "feeling the warmth of the blood running out"; one can't help wondering if the incident was viewed in substantially less aesthetic terms the day of its occurrence.[40]

All things being equal, it is much better to be on the giving rather than receiving end of violence, although in collision sports violence is a shared experience and neither the instigator nor receiver of collisions can predict the results. In spite of the severe toll football had taken on his body, former New York Giant Michael Strahan still found it exhilarating to clobber opponents. In fact, for Strahan, sacking a quarterback could be a near ecstatic experience:

> Explode and drive to the quarterback. Don't slow up, because if you slow up, you'll get there right when he throws it, or the tackle will cut you from behind . . . When you hit, you feel him go *uufffff*. It's the best feeling in the world. Oh, man, it feels great. The only thing you hear is complete silence during the play, then after the sack, it's like somebody has the radio turned up on max volume. Instant adrenaline rush. And then you jump up like you just won the lottery.[41]

Strahan's fondness for incapacitating a quarterback is hardly an anomaly in the ranks of defensive football players. The gold standard of defensive ends, the legendary Lawrence Taylor, often referred to as "the most feared man in football," had this to say about rushing the quarterback:

> I don't like to just wrap the quarterback. I really try to make him see seven fingers when they hold up three. I'll drive my helmet into him, or, if I can, I'll bring my arm up over my head and try to axe the sonuvabitch in two. So long as the guy is holding the ball, I intend to hurt him . . . If I ever hit the guy right, I'll hit a nerve

and he'll feel electrocuted, he'll forget for a few seconds that he's on a football field.[42]

Coaches for whom "sacrificing your body" on the athletic field is analogous to doing the same on the battlefield help sustain this culture of risk. When the adrenaline begins flowing, common sense becomes cowardice. Author Pat Conroy surely exaggerates, but perhaps not very much, when he has the coach in *The Prince of Tides* tell his team: "A real hitter loves pain, loves the screaming and the sweating and the brawling and the hatred of life down in the trenches. He likes to be at the spot where the blood flows and the teeth get kicked out. That's what this sport's about men. It's war, pure and simple." Legendary football coach Vince Lombardi would reportedly walk into training rooms where athletes were receiving medical attention and yell, "Nobody's hurt, get out of here!" When Green Bay Packer Bob Long lay writhing on the ground after destroying the cartilage in his knee, Lombardi "came running out there screaming and hollering: 'Long, get up, run on that leg, there's no pain in that leg.'" Says Long, "two days later they operate, and the doctor says its one of the worst torn cartilages he's ever seen."[43]

In the culture of risk, athletes come to appreciate that success in collision sports depends upon playing with abandon and not flinching. "As a ballplayer," said a former Big Ten football player, "I am expected to do as I'm told, lay my body on the line or else get out of the way for somebody who will. Everybody in the room knows and understands this and, when asked, will put himself in harm's way with the dim, deluded hope that he will come out the other end a star."[44] Young athletes can end up being unwitting partners in spectacles of brutish and malignant dimensions. One of the most poignant and pathetic vignettes recorded in *Friday Night Lights*, H. G. Bissinger's award-winning book about Texas football, shows how young athletes can be conditioned to disregard their own and others' bodies. In its drive to win a state championship, Permian High School faces crosstown rival Odessa High in a must-win game:

> Odessa High got the ball back on the kickoff with less than a minute left in the half. Patrick Brown, the Broncos' best player, went around the left end on a pitch and was hit. He went airborne and Wilkins, coming full speed from his cornerback position, lowered his helmet and hit him in the side with a savage crack like the sound of a shot from a revolver. Wilkins came off the field a hero among his teammates. "Way to go Stan!" "Good

stick." . . . Brown lay crumpled on the field . . . the initial prog-
nosis was that he had broken some ribs, but he got up after
several minutes. The half ended. The Permian players ran to the
locker room with whoops and hollers . . . Brown meanwhile,
with a person on either side of him, slowly made his way up the
steps to the dressing room before being swallowed up in the
darkness.[45]

There was no sense of regret for having leveled the opponent, no concern
about his physical condition, and, surprisingly, no sense of indignation
or injustice from the player crumpled on the field.

BODY MACHINES

In the culture of risk, athletes are often defined by their bodies. They are
much more likely to be characterized by coaches, reporters, or broadcasters as "a six-four, 325-pound defensive end" or "a six-ten power forward" than as, say, "a fun-loving biology major from Oshkosh who likes
country music." Bodies have little intrinsic worth in the world of sports;
their value is in the uses to which they can be put for the team. Recognizing that bodies frequently fail, the sports culture inculcates a casu-
alness toward arms, legs, backs, fingers, and skulls. They are regarded
not only as separate from souls, but as expendable appendages of athletic production. Injuries are the cost of doing business. After a game in
which Detroit Piston Ben Wallace went down with a sprained medial
collateral ligament in his left knee, his coach's entirely predictable first
remark to reporters was to emphasize the loss to the team: "It looks like
we will lose him for some number of games. We're not sure how many.
That's a blow." No indication here that the coach thought of Ben Wallace's body as an inextricable component of his being, indivisible from
his soul. Rather his knee was at best an attachment to his soul, expendable if not repairable.[46]

Sportscasters are archperpetrators of such mechanical distortions
of the body, but athletes perpetuate the view as well. While defending
her decision to pose nude for an Australian art magazine, WNBA basketball star Lauren Jackson seemed to relate to her body much like one
relates to a new car. "I've worked so hard to develop my athletic body
that it felt good to show off what I've accomplished. It's my temple." But
nothing quite so depressingly signals the desacralization of the body in
sport than a listing on eBay that offered to sell bone chips that had been

surgically removed from Seattle Mariners pitcher Jeff Nelson's pitching arm for $23,000.[47]

Many of the advancements in athletic achievement owe to the work of performance scientists whose research guides the training and conditioning of athletes. But performance science, with its emphasis on the mechanical efficiency of the body, also can help fashion an antisacral view of the body. In scholar John Hoberman's opinion, the ascendancy of technology and technique in sports training, and particularly the trend toward psychological engineering, aims to reduce the athlete "to a one-dimensional being," a robot who is "possessed of an inhuman force of will." When athletes are reduced to scientific specimens to be manipulated in a relentless assault on human limits, it becomes easy to think of them as soulless packages of muscle, bone, and nerve rather than human beings with feelings, emotions, and an eternal destiny. Perhaps, says Hoberman, the specter of the "human thoroughbred" that had so worried Olympic visionary Pierre de Coubertin is now upon us.[48]

Nearly a quarter of a century ago, evangelical medical ethicist Kenneth Vaux warned of the rise of a cult that seeks biomechanical perfectibility by exploiting science and technology in a way that ignores the body's theological significance. When the body is reduced to a workable instrument, said Vaux, "the body magnificent becomes the body tremulous, the body vulnerable, the body fixable, with interchangeable parts from the body shop of modern medicine." Vaux was concerned primarily with medical ethics, but he could have just as easily been referring to sport science, where the exchange of body parts may loom in the not too distant future. This seemed to be what a pitching coach was thinking when, after watching Texas Rangers pitcher Jeff Zimmerman suffer through four elbow operations in three years, wondered "why you can't just donate some of your body parts after you're finished playing." It is a cold, robotic view of the body that fades almost imperceptibly into the Playboy philosophy in which, writer Jim Sire has pointed out, "people are sex machines; oil them, grease them, set them in motion, feel the thrill." The dominant view of the body in sport isn't that far removed: people are sport machines; train them, psychologically manipulate them, set them on collision courses, feel the impact.[49]

In the end, it may be no more possible for modern sports aficionados to appreciate the bodily abuse that occurs in competition than it was for ancient Romans to view the death battles in the arena as bloodthirsty cruelty. The sheer ubiquity of athletic injuries has worn calluses on the Christian conscience. Some years ago a traveling act featured a man who, for purposes of amusing sold-out crowds at nightclubs and rock concerts, would staple paper to his forehead, grind out cigarettes on his tongue, shove a long nail up his nostril, lie face down on broken glass, and have darts thrown at his back. Most of us would likely see a thousand shades of difference between this geek show and some of our most violent sports, yet it is only a slight of our imagination that enables such a distinction. Debauching the body in a boxing match isn't all that different from debauching it with darts. Dishonoring the body in a football stadium in front of thousands isn't all that different from dishonoring it in an inner-city "shooting gallery," save for the fact that society applauds the former and outlaws the latter. In both instances, the masterpiece of creation is offered in cheap trade for the promise of a few moments of excitement.[50]

EVANGELICAL REACTION

If one dominant theme has emerged from centuries of Christian commentary on sports, it is an utter intolerance for sports that are harmful to the body. Somewhere in the devolution of evangelical ideas about sport, however, the theme was scuttled. When sports were taken under the wing of the church around the turn of the century, sport violence became rationalized in evangelical circles. Today, on the rare occasions when evangelicals raise questions about the harm sports do to the body, they do so in an almost backhanded, apologetic way, as though the critic fears being drummed out of the manly club of sportsmen. For example, in an excellent delineation of a Christian philosophy of leisure, Wheaton College professor Leland Ryken pointedly suggested that leisure choices for the Christian should always factor in the moral implications of the activity for physical and emotional health. He singled out boxing, professional wrestling, football, and skiing as having bad track records, noting that "the relative likelihood of injury in such sports is a moral issue." But he seemed to offer his criticism with trepidation, observing that "devotees of such sports will not like my negative comments." In his very worthwhile essay on the Christian play ethic, evangelical philosopher Arthur Holmes urged application of Aquinas' injunction not to engage in indecent and injurious play, registering strong objection to the sport of boxing but only "moral reservations about football." Tony Campolo, an evangelical who came to the public's attention when he served as spiritual adviser to President Clinton, included a chapter about sports in his book *20 Hot Potatoes Christians Are Afraid to Touch*. Campolo, a former athlete, was harshly critical of evangelicals' unquestioning acceptance of big-time sports but failed to bring his theology to bear on the injury problem.[51]

In the evangelical sporting mind, God desires sexually pure, unstained, and undrugged bodies but apparently isn't all that concerned that they remain physically intact. To give one example, at the American Heritage Academy—a Christian school in Carrollton, Texas, which has won state championships in football, basketball, and baseball—players are required to sign an honor code in which they state, "I realize my body is the temple of the Holy Spirit" and pledge to "yield to the transforming power of the Holy Spirit" by avoiding drugs, alcohol, tobacco, and gangs. In light of the epidemiological evidence on sports injuries in football, requiring athletes to acknowledge their bodies as holy vessels before participating in a sport that virtually assures that those vessels will be profaned makes for an odd honor code indeed.[52]

Although the moral implications of injury in sport aren't given space in the evangelical press, hundreds of pages are allotted to accounts of how the Lord helped to rehabilitate injured athletes, enabling them to return to the very action that injured them in the first place. Former Los Angeles Dodgers pitcher Orel Hershiser endured a long and painful rehabilitation of a serious shoulder injury and attributed his recovery to the Lord's intervention. His surgery and the public attention showered on it gave him a rare opportunity to highlight his personal faith (and a chance to sing the Doxology on the Johnny Carson Show). But the evangelical press was not interested in addressing whether Hershiser's faith might have militated against a return to a sport involving the unnatural act of propelling a sphere at speeds approaching one hundred miles per hour or whether it might have been at least indelicate to invoke Divine Providence's assistance to help him recover so that he could resume the activity that had led to his injury in the first place.[53]

There may be no more heartwarming and inspiring biography in sports, nor one more publicized in the evangelical press, than that of pitcher Dave Dravecky, whose courageous struggle with cancer was detailed in his book *Comeback*. After extensive surgery on his tumor-laden pitching arm, Dravecky returned to baseball, only to have his career end when the stadium was rocked by the sound of his arm bone snapping in two places as he threw a pitch. Dravecky's pluck and courage through the rehabilitation process were admirable, but one is left perplexed by the cosmological scheme that allowed him to resubmit his body to the incredible stress of pitching, especially after surgeons had warned that cancer had made his arm vulnerable to injury.[54]

It is hardly coincidental that evangelicals who can't imagine a life without sports entertainment find it difficult to imagine that sports injuries have moral and theological implications. Injury becomes a moral question, they would say, only when it is inflicted intentionally. When he was asked about the violence and injuries of football, evangelist and former Cleveland Browns defensive end Bill Glass told an interviewer: "I never intentionally tried to hurt anyone. I seldom knew of players whose objective it was to injure an opponent. It is ridiculous to call professional sports immoral because of the violence involved."[55]

Being a party to this kind of violence is only possible if athletes are able to override God-given instincts for self-preservation. A football player told sportswriter Michael Silver, "You've got to force your body to perform actions that your mind is dead-set against . . . For a player to accept that bargain on a consistent basis, he'd better have a sense of something greater than individual gain, be it faith in a god or coach, a bond with his teammates, or a profound fear of failure." Evangelical athletes often find this sense of something greater in their faith, relying on it to help them live with the inherent risks of sport. One might think, for example, that former All-Star baseball player Kevin Seitzer, after being hit in the head three times by blistering fastballs, would have interpreted the injuries as a sign from God to spend more time in the dugout. Yet amazingly, Seitzer's faith urged him to do the opposite: "God gave me the strength to overcome my fear and get back in the batter's box," he said. Recounting his first trip to the plate after having been beaned, Seitzer said, "I had done a lot of praying, and a lot of my friends and family prayed for me too. Once I got in the batter's box, an incredible peace came over me. It was God's power, I believe. I was fearless." Thus a religious belief system that affirms the body and soul as sacred and inseparable is marshaled once again in support of a decision by an athlete to put himself at serious risk. It is a measure of how skewed theology can get when it is brought onto the baseball diamond.[56]

It will not be easy to penetrate the consciences of Christians on the matter, especially hardcore sports enthusiasts. When the editor of *Christianity Today*, who has made many otherwise important contributions to the discourse on sports, softens the unspeakable violence of boxing by hinting that it may "ennoble the humanity of the participants" and worries that if we apply "knee-jerk ethics" in rejecting boxing we will have to do the same about "many sports that bring us joy and meaning," one gets a sense of the uphill battle facing those who seek to elevate the Christian conscience on the issue.[57]

Reconciling the license for bodily harm and disfigurement granted athletes under the rules of many of our games with the Christian truth that the body is "not only *a* manifestation of the Spirit, it could well be *the* manifestation," seems well nigh impossible. Would it not seem that evangelicals who oppose abortion because "life is sacred" would, at the same time, apply that standard to the world of sports? The incarnation—a "full and complete union of matter and spirit, God and man, in the historical person of Jesus of Nazareth"—grants the human body a special sacramental respect and gives Christians a responsibility reflected in the sacrificial care Christians and their institutions have always shown the body through hospitals, medical missionary efforts, and other ministries. If "healing was central to Christ's ministry as a sign of God's inbreaking kingdom," willingly risking the integrity of the body in sports would seem to mock his mission.[58]

Evangelical sports enthusiasts' obliviousness to this theological point isn't all that unusual in an evangelicalism that Alan Wolfe has shown to be largely uninterested in doctrine. Evangelical enthusiasm for exercise shouldn't be mistaken for an internalized, meaningful theology of the body. The same brand of evangelicalism that has given rise to the Christian Tattoo Association with its adornment of bodies with crosses, and to body piercers who view their piercings and punctures as a way of identifying with Christ's sufferings on the cross, has also spawned an athletic theology that spurs a fearful, previously injured basketball player to get back into the thick of things by "mental[ly] prepar[ing] himself for each practice and game by picturing himself going after rebounds as an expression of his love for God." I believe that any reasonable person of any theological persuasion would conclude that in *some* sports, the risk of injury is simply too substantial to justify participation. For Christians, the impact of such a conclusion is magnified a hundredfold by the fact of Christ's incarnation, which conferred on humans a startling personal and spiritual dignity.[59]

8

Sport and the Sub-Christian Values

"I see that more NFL players are in trouble with the law," Jay Leno told his late night audience. "Imagine how bad it would be if football didn't develop character." Pushed to explain why sports are vital to society or to their personal lives, sooner or later most people will point to the way they strengthen moral fiber and instruct players and coaches in the right ways to live their lives. Cynics such as Leno aside, most of us like to think that sport builds character, even to the point of making claims for it that it can never reasonably be expected to deliver. When a Swedish legislator, apparently forgetting the riots that habitually plague European soccer stadia, nominated soccer for the 2001 Nobel Peace Prize, citing its capacity for cultivating "understanding between people," or when the provocative French philosopher Albert Camus claimed that all he knew about ethics he learned in soccer, there is little doubt that enthusiasm can run in front of reasoned judgment.[1]

The notion that sports develop good character has a long history. Plato and Aristotle were not ardent sports fans, but both valued the strenuous training and sacrifices endured by athletes and regarded them as experiences that could teach lessons of sacrifice and endurance in the larger scheme of life. In the thirteenth century, the suggestion that sport could play a role in shaping character found its way into theologians' carefully measured endorsements on the same grounds and continued to make periodic appearances in various theological writings over the next three centuries. The idea found full expression in mid-nineteenth-century British boarding schools, where muscular Christians heralded sports as "the wheel around which moral values turned," capable of impressing on players "virtues which no books can give them."[2]

The idea was imported into the United States in the late nineteenth and early twentieth centuries and eventually was embedded in the hopeful theories of play that swept across the land during the progressive era. Educational theorists, anxious to introduce sports into the calisthenics-centered physical education programs of the day, seized on their character-building potential as a central plank in their arguments. Among other things, being a member of an athletic team was credited with "cultivat[ing] the youth's empathic facility and help[ing] him to understand 'reality' from the other person's point of view." As we saw in chapter 4, religious activists, proponents of the social gospel, and the "body-as-temple" theologians followed suit, at times romanticizing the presumed moral derivatives of sport. All of these groups hailed the gymnasium as "a fundamental and intrinsic part in the salvation of man," and competition was seen as rivaling the Ten Commandments as a teacher of fair play. Some even thought it was "easier for a boy to be a Christian in the gymnasium than when back of a hymn book." That the on-field conduct of players didn't always support such hopeful hypotheses did little to dampen enthusiasm. After all, it was the golden age of sports, and excitement ran high; lovers of sports accepted such pufferies as revealed and convenient truths needing little or no validation.[3]

The belief that sports shape character has continued more or less unabated to this day, having been given periodic assists by presidential avidity. Theodore Roosevelt, Dwight Eisenhower, John F. Kennedy, and Richard Nixon were particularly enthusiastic, but perhaps none was quite as euphoric as Gerald Ford, a former football player at University of Michigan. Ford linked participation in sport not only with personal development but also with national and civic well-being: "Broadly speaking," said Ford, "outside of a national character and an educated society, there are few things more important to a country's growth and well-being than competitive athletics. If it is a cliché to say athletics builds character as well as muscle, then I subscribe to the cliché." Even today, the President's Council on Physical Fitness and Sports confidently proclaims that "sport activities help individuals develop character, discipline, confidence, self-esteem, and a sense of well-being."[4]

Confidence in sport's power to calibrate an athlete's moral compass reaches across political, social, and religious divides, although those at the conservative end of the spectrum tend to be the most effusive. In 1976, conservative intellectual and former football player William J. Bennett reacted to a flurry of books critical of sports (written, as he pointed out, "mostly by non-athletes") by outlining a "defense of sports" in the neoconservative magazine *Commentary*. Bennett argued that far from being an exploitative, morally corrosive, and fascist enterprise, as Marxist critics claimed, sports were "an arena in which children can grow in light of ambiguous, tangible universal standards and measures." He also claimed that sport had been "relatively unaffected by the general erosion of standards in the culture at large." That same year, conservative Catholic commentator Michael Novak penned his best-selling *Joy of Sports*, in which he called sports "the highest products of civilization and the most accessible, lived, experiential sources of the civilizing spirit."[5]

Few have been as effusive in their praise of the character-building effects of sports as leaders in the religious community. There may have been no firmer believer in the morally redemptive powers of sport than Pope John Paul II, a former athlete, who told followers that sports help one to "perceive the value of simple and immediate things, the call to goodness, the dissatisfaction with one's insufficiency, and to meditate on the authentic values that are the basis of human life." This was no idle talk by the pontiff, who in 2004 created an Office of Church and Sport within the Vatican to promote a vision of sports as a means of personal growth and "as an instrument in the service of peace and brotherhood among peoples." Similar rhetoric also can be heard in Protestant quarters. Renowned Protestant church historian Martin Marty, for example, has said that "part of the charm of sports is that they offer a compelling image of virtue—the spectacle of human talents channeled toward a goal."[6] While there can be little question that the ambitious and expensive intercollegiate sports program at Liberty University was intended primarily to publicize the school, the late Jerry Falwell nevertheless allowed that it also had an educational function, telling a reporter that the program "develop[ed] character and discipline among students and help[ed] a school build an identity around which students and alumni [could] join hands." Similarly, the athletic mission at Oral Roberts University has set the lofty goal of developing "group loyalty, self-esteem, and pride of accomplishment that will assist the student athlete to be successful upon graduation."[7]

Defending sports on grounds that they promote civility, pluck, doggedness, fair-mindedness, social harmony, and other traits thought to reflect character is one thing; crediting them with teaching spiritual lessons moves the discussion onto a considerably higher plane. Yet the belief that sports can be an adjunct to the Christian life is fairly widespread. In his foreword to a book on baseball, controversial theological ethicist Stanley Hauerwas envisions parallels between learning to be a baseball fan and learning to be a Christian: "To be and survive Christianity requires the willingness to live by the ever new surprises of God. So it is not surprising that we will learn much about ourselves as Christians—what it means for us to survive as well as flourish as God's people—by attending to the relationship among our faith, baseball, and God."[8] Such talk is especially common in evangelical circles. The late NFL football star Reggie White, nicknamed "the minister of defense" for his rugged style of play and his bold theologizing, once told readers of an evangelical sports magazine that "playing football is helping me in my spiritual life because it's helping to build my character, and it has allowed me to see a lot of things that a lot of other people won't be able to see." Former FCA staffer Gary Warner, who didn't flinch in pointing out problems in the evangelical sports world, nevertheless believed that competitive sports develop self-discipline and self-control, the latter "an important prerequisite to the growing process of the believer" as well as a fruit of the spirit mentioned in Galatians 5:22-23.[9]

Websites of Christian colleges often point to the spiritual nurturing that takes place through their intercollegiate athletic programs. One top-tier school claims that its athletic program helps athletes "grow deeper in [their] relationship with God and our understanding of how to honor him." Another features comments from athletic alumni who tell how "soccer taught us about love, passion, and the pursuit of excellence" and how their coach taught them "what it means to work together for a goal greater than oneself, about using our resources for the Kingdom, and how to be men."[10] Conservative Dallas Theological Seminary thought the issue sufficiently important to organize a website featuring responses to the question, "How have sports influenced your life?" Athletes from a variety of backgrounds explained how what they had learned in sports carried over to their spiritual journeys.[11]

The notion implicit in these claims is that sports develop what C. S. Lewis called "the sub-Christian values."[12] Lewis coined the term "sub-Christian values" while arguing a case for the importance of culture. (By "culture" Lewis was especially interested in literature but was open to the possibility that other aspects of life may possess the same qualities.) Reading literature, he said, builds up a kind of "storehouse" of the "highest level of merely natural value lying immediately below the lowest level of spiritual value" (hence "sub-Christian"). Such values, he said, "are of the soul, not the spirit," yet because God created the soul, they "may be expected to contain some reflections or 'antepast' of the spiritual values." Literature will not lead one to conversion, but it may get an unbeliever moving in that direction. "Though like is not the same," said Lewis, "it is better than unlike. Imitation may pass into initiation. For some it is a good beginning."

Since Lewis rejected "any of the moral and almost mystical virtues which schoolmasters claim for [sports]," it is possible that he would have balked at a suggestion that sport, like literature, could also serve as a storehouse of the sub-Christian values.[13] But Lewis faced essentially the same problem with literature, some types of which celebrated values (pantheism, material prosperity, liberation of impulses) that he acknowledged were far from Christian. Yet he continued to maintain that, on balance, reading literature could move one closer to the regenerate life. To complicate matters further, Lewis' harsh views of sports didn't cause him to reject them outright; on at least one occasion he regretted that he hadn't been given "the impulse" to play.[14] Consequently it is neither foolhardy nor entirely novel to suggest that sports might serve as schoolmasters in the Christian graces, much like Lewis had envisioned for literature. Certainly it is a claim worthy of examination.

WHAT IS CHARACTER?

Whether or not sport develops character and instills the sub-Christian values is hardly a trivial issue for Christians. Sports sap enormous amounts of time, energy, and money from their personal budgets and agendas and from the students, staff, and resources of their institutions. At the same time, sports produce nothing in and of themselves. In light of the biblical mandate to "redeem the time" and be good stewards of God-given resources, evangelicals—like their Puritan forebears—would seem especially obligated to demonstrate that their digressions into the play world have some ultimate payoff. Playing sports for mere enjoyment is fine, and evangelicals can defend them on this count up to a point. As evangelical theologian Lewis Smedes, himself an advocate of the playful life, reminded readers some years ago, "Our inner sense of obligation keeps telling us that we ought to do more than we have done. Every child of God is expected to repeat every night: 'forgive us the good we have left undone.'"[15]

Whether or not sports reap benefits proportional to the time and money we devote to them is an open question. One thing is for certain: there are lessons to be learned in sports. No one who has engaged in athletics at a serious level can doubt that they teach us something about the value of concentrated effort, how to handle disappointments, and how to keep calm under stressful situations, or that they provide us with valuable experience in testing our psychological and physical limits. Some people could point to lifelong friendships forged through sport experiences; others could tell how playing sports prepared them for difficult challenges and trained them for success in a competitive world. Many parents of youthful athletes have witnessed firsthand sport's power to develop discipline, self-confidence, and appreciation of hard work in their children.

There is good reason to believe that sports, in some circumstances, may help nurture some "life skills" useful in academic work, career advancement, and other aspects of daily living. Data from two large longitudinal studies suggest that students who participate in sports in high school are more likely to attend college, be successful in math and science courses, have higher academic self-concepts, have better school attendance records, and spend more time on homework. High school students who participate in sports tend to be more attached to their school and often have a richer network of friends. While the results of these studies cannot claim participation in sport to be the cause of the good effects, the data are encouraging nonetheless.[16]

Yet it is important to keep in mind that such benefits can come from participating in a broad range of human pursuits; certainly one needn't play sports to learn these lessons. Iris Murdoch, for example, makes an excellent case for learning a foreign language that sounds remarkably similar to some claims made for sport: that it helps the student understand his or her abilities in light of an authoritative structure, gain insight into reality, and become more humble and honest in the process. Clearly, playing sports can produce some good effects, but given the ticklish questions that so often surround our games, it is legitimate to ask whether Christians might better seek these effects in other, less ethically complicated human activities.[17]

There are widely varying notions as to what is meant by "character." Although sociologists and ethicists point to an "inner and distinctive core of a person from which moral discernment, decisions and actions spring," they hardly agree as to what this distinctive core might be. When an educational sociologist enthuses on the basis of his research that "sport *does* build character," it's important to keep in mind that "character" in his study was measured in math and English scores along with self-esteem, locus of control, and homework completion—not the types of values or virtues that Christians might associate with spirituality. The term "character" is given rather explicit meanings in the trenches of organized athletics, its definition revolving around traits bearing a close relationship to competitive and military success and athletic excellence. Usually, "character" in athletic parlance means self-sacrifice, loyalty, mental toughness, learning from adversity (a poor season), and enduring hardship without complaint. When a teammate complimented former New England Patriots quarterback Drew Bledsoe for "showing a lot of character," it wasn't for honesty or fairness or generosity, but for continuing to play despite having fractured his finger in two places. Self-reliance also is part of athletic character. When the New England Patriots pulled out a last-minute victory against Denver, the Patriots cornerback told reporters: "I think we proved today that this team has character. We know we can't depend on anybody except the guys in the locker room, the guys who are out there fighting."[18]

In the sports culture, demonstrations of character almost always affirm the ethos of athletics. An athlete with "a lot of character" is by definition a successful one. Had the high school athletic director who described character as "a willingness to try no matter what the situation . . . an attempt to continually improve . . . a willingness to give all up for the cause" been asked instead to name the most important personal characteristics for success in sports, he probably would have listed precisely these same qualities. Ground through the filter of the reigning orthodoxy of big-time sports, "character" means heeling to the status quo, rarely if ever questioning or acting in ways that would diminish your team's chances of success.[19]

Athletic character, with its emphasis on qualities such as courage, toughness, endurance, and self-sacrifice, is central to the military model of sports featured on sports fields at any level. The Duke of Wellington famously, though perhaps erroneously, is remembered for having said that "it was here [on the athletic fields at Eton] that the battle of Waterloo was won."[20] At West Point, where the athletic program is committed to "the development of character and leadership by emphasizing spirited competition, ethical conduct and sportsmanship," visitors to Michie Stadium pass under gates inscribed with a quotation from General Douglas Macarthur: "On these fields of friendly strife are sown the seeds that on other fields and other days will bear the fruits of victory."

These practical and heroic qualities are important not only in war or athletics but in ordinary life as well, but they are not intrinsically virtuous. Heroic virtues easily can morph into militant enthusiasm that, as Conrad Lorenz pointed out, can reverse our value orientations, "making them appear not only untenable but base and dishonorable." Practical character can be made to serve many masters. Surely diligence, tenacity, mental toughness, and courage learned through sports can help people cope with family stresses, gain distinguished civic achievements, pursue successful careers that benefit society, and even endure spiritual struggles. On the other hand, these same character traits are equally serviceable to successful pornographers, gang leaders, or illegal drug traffickers who may rely as much on their diligence, tenacity, and mental toughness as the soldier or the athlete. This category of "character," then, becomes "virtuous" only when exercised in the service of virtuous living. In and of itself, heroic character seems an improbable foundation upon which to structure the sub-Christian values.[21]

A second version of character talked about in connection with sports bears more directly on virtues that are thought to reflect the inner moral core of the individual. Consistent displays of justice, unrestricted mercy, pursuit of peace, generosity, humility, fairness, honesty, caring, compassion, magnanimity, and respect for others, for example, are widely thought to reflect an intact moral interior, just as consistent acts of bias, stinginess, deviousness, callousness, and disregard of others might reflect a dilapidated moral interior. These passive virtues, unlike the heroic virtues so often talked about in athletics, bear the closest resemblance to those singled out in the New Testament and to those Lewis suggested might serve as imperfect "reflections" of spiritual values. If playing sports nurtures this type of character, one would logically expect it to be most immediately manifested in the way athletes and coaches conduct themselves during games, a cluster of actions commonly called "sportsmanship." Sportsmanship isn't easy to define, but most of us know it when we see it displayed. Usually it is expressed in attitudes and behaviors which reveal an allegiance to an ethical standard over and above concern for self-advantage or winning. Justice, fairness, kindness, and humility are some of the traits we associate with good sportsmanship. Many of these are consistent with New Testament teachings about Christian conduct. Obviously, the good sport may not always act on the basis of Christian belief, but one could argue that Christian belief should always inspire good sportsmanship.

Poor sportsmanship occurs when athletes, coaches, or fans act only in their own self-interest, not merely by cheating but by being unkind, insensitive, duplicitous, and arrogant. To say one is a "poor sport" sanitizes what, in the Christian view, are indefensible acts wrought by indefensible motives. When the businessperson cheats, we call it tax evasion; when the professor harbors grudges and grades papers unfairly, we call it tyranny; when the church member lies to her neighbor, we call it sin; but in the arena or the stadium, all of these acts are "poor sportsmanship," which somehow seems less morally consequential than sin. Poor sportsmanship requires no apology, no confession, and no forgiveness and is supposedly easy to correct simply by reminding athletes to mind their manners and be nicer.

Sportsmanship can be an important barometer of sport's power to mold character in desirable ways. Quite simply, if such traits aren't displayed in the context of games—the experience thought to develop them—it is difficult to imagine how game playing could lead to grand transformations in character in athletes' lives off the field. Furthermore, if character bears a "dose response" relationship with athletic experience, those with the longest and deepest immersion in athletics should be the most sportsmanlike in their athletic behaviors, and by extension should display the sub-Christian values in their everyday lives.

Lowered Expectations

In 1987 the Bulldogs of Rockdale County High School in Georgia, led by coach Cleveland Stroud, had a season most teams can only dream of: twenty-one wins and five losses and a come-from-behind victory in the Georgia boys' state basketball championship game. After the game, when it was discovered that one player who had participated in the first of the team's post-season games had been academically ineligible, there were some murmurings about keeping the matter quiet; after all, the player had played in a single game, having only entered during the last forty-five seconds when his team was ahead by twenty-three points. Yet Stroud reported the problem and forfeited the championship. "You've got to do what's honest and right," said Stroud. "People forget the scores of basketball games; they don't ever forget what you're made of." This simple, decent act propelled Stroud to national fame in the days following his decision.[22] Stroud's act was decent and honest, but the same gesture displayed in the course of daily living would have drawn little attention; certainly it wouldn't have earned front-page coverage in the *New York Times*. What made Stroud's act distinctive was that it was done in connection with sports. Quite simply, we don't expect coaches to act in ways that are detrimental to their and their teams' self-interest even if it is the right thing to do.

We are more used to coaches like the NBA's Pat Riley, who, following a last-second win made possible by an obviously mistaken call by an official, insisted that his team won the game. It was unabashed thievery.

Taking something not rightfully yours can get you in a lot of trouble in real life, but doing the same thing in sports can earn you a championship. This twisted ethical scheme has worked its way into the texture of sports so seamlessly that self-professed evangelicals are just as likely to personify it as anyone else. No professional team has garnered more attention for its Christian policies, leadership, and sheer number of born-again players than the Colorado Rockies, who, after eking out a win in a tie-breaker game in the 2007 season against the San Diego Padres, went on to appear in the World Series. But the tie-breaker was marred by an umpire's blown call at home plate. Rockies player Matt Holliday had charged home, apparently scoring the winning run, but close inspection of postgame replays showed that his foot, blocked by the catcher, had never touched home plate. After the game, Holliday, one of a throng of evangelicals on the Rockies team, thanked God for the victory and the blessings of the season, deftly sidestepping reporters' questions about the incident at home plate. If implicating God in an undeserved victory seemed a bit audacious, it wasn't nearly so audacious as the Rockies' unabashed evangelical management, who refused to correct the injustice in spite of the CEO's comments made to *USA Today* several months before: "I think character-wise we're stronger than anyone in baseball." Strong perhaps, but not strong enough to rectify a wrong that would have sent San Diego rather than the Rockies to the playoffs.[23]

This case reflects a chink in the armor of many who have distinguished themselves in sports. Coach Stroud's modest gesture makes him seem a pillar of righteousness compared to legendary University of Nebraska coach and outspoken evangelical Tom Osborne, who refused to forfeit his team's undeserved win over the University of Missouri in 1997. Nebraska had managed to tie the score in the final second of regulation play on an illegal maneuver unnoticed by the referee. Wingback Shevin Wiggins, falling short of the goal, kicked the ball back into the air, where a teammate caught it with a spectacular dive into the end zone. The catch enabled Nebraska to go on and win the game in overtime. Intentionally kicking the ball in such situations is strictly prohibited by the rules of football, but it wasn't clear to officials that the intended receiver had purposely kicked the ball. All doubt was removed after the game, however, when Wiggins publicly admitted that was precisely what he had in mind. Despite Wiggins' confession, Osborne and Nebraska refused to give up their victory, and the player who caught the ball attributed his catch to the Lord.[24]

A similar and more publicized situation arose in a game between the University of Colorado and the University of Missouri. Colorado, then coached by Bill McCartney, pulled out a last-second victory on their march to the national championship. The victory was achieved only by virtue of game officials' oversight that mistakenly awarded Colorado an extra (5th) down with 30 seconds left in the game. The mistake was soon discovered, but not until after the final whistle had blown. The league considered the mistake sufficiently serious that it suspended all eight game officials, but since the rules did not provide for altering the final score, the undeserved victory by Colorado was allowed to stand. McCartney, a fiercely religious man, felt no compunction to rectify the injustice; in fact, he suggested that his team had deserved to win because of the poor condition of the field. The undeserved victory enabled Colorado to become Division I-A national champions. McCartney was named United Press International Coach of the Year and was later inducted into the Colorado Sports Hall of Fame and the Orange Bowl Hall of Fame for his outstanding record of victories. Aside from his fifteen minutes of fame and a handful of acclamations, Coach Stroud's gesture earned him few rewards and not always positive comments from his coworkers.[25]

Honesty, especially when it is costly, is dispensable in sports. There are examples of honesty in sports, but one has to look far and wide. When golfing great Bobby Jones lost the US Open by one stroke after he had penalized himself for unobtrusively and inadvertently moving his ball, he was incredulous that some people praised him for his sportsmanship. What he had done, noted Jones, was simply be honest. "You might as well praise a man for not robbing a bank," he said. Former coach of Cedarville College's women's volleyball team, Teresa Clarke, has amazed referees, fellow coaches, and fans simply by insisting that her players be honest by informing the referee when they touch the ball before it careens out of bounds.

Far from developing traits of honesty, generosity, and fairness, the sport culture seems to suppress it. Deceit, on the other hand, is a staple of organized sports. Ken Burns, the maker of the brilliant PBS documentary on baseball, told an Associated Press reporter, "I have never seen an instance when a player's had a call go his way when he knew it was wrong and he's fessed up." The deceitful athlete is much more likely to be lauded for his or her brilliant gamesmanship than singled out for criticism. In his book *Integrity*, Stephen Carter describes watching a televised football game in which a receiver fumbled the ball before he hit the ground. The player rolled over and jumped up, celebrating as though he had caught the ball, causing the referees to mistakenly award the catch. Commenting on the replay, which clearly showed the player had not made the catch, one of the broadcasters raved: "What a heads-up play!" It was the equivalent, says Carter, of saying: "Wow! What a great liar this kid is. Well done!"[26]

Such behavior may get little more than a shrug even from the most scrupulous of sports fans. We have become accustomed to treating sports as unique moral enclaves, partly because games, like all forms of play, often proceed according to customs forbidden in real life. When the game is over, the umpire's whistle breaks the spell and sets "real life" going again. In the finite, imaginary, set-apart world of baseball, for example, the baseball player who "steals" second base really isn't stealing. Sacking the quarterback may earn a linebacker kudos; sacking his professor will probably get him kicked out of school. Identical acts, different only in context and intent, can be cleansed of their sin when committed in games and executed "according to the rules." The problem is that this dual ethic—so vital to the playing of games—can easily be generalized to an entire ethical scheme so that sports become answerable only to their own internal moral code.

This moral code is shaped by a host of factors: changes in public taste, commercial influences, and the whimsy of sports organizations. What is impermissible in one decade may become permissible in the next. Perceptions of rightness and wrongness in sports can also be shaped by the outrageous conduct of athletes and coaches. Each episode of bad behavior stretches the parameters of what we are willing to accept as normal conduct in sports. The real danger posed by the antics of Roberto Alomar, Bobby Knight, or Latrell Sprewell is not that impressionable youngsters will emulate them. Thankfully, most thirteen-year-olds still recognize that the act of spitting on an umpire or choking a player or your coach is sociopathic. The real danger is that such antics define moral conduct downwards. By demonstrating the depths to which humans can descend into mean-spiritedness and self-interest, these public acts lower our expectations not only for the behavior of others but for our own behavior as well.

As a result, coaches who simply keep their programs free from scandal come to be regarded as saints worthy of emulation by their colleagues, and Christian colleges are left feeling pretty good about themselves when contests against cross-state rivals come off without ugly incidents. Simple acts of kindness that pass without notice in real life—a handshake, showing concern for an injured person, or congratulating another on a fine performance—become charities worthy of a Nobel Peace Prize when displayed on the football field or basketball court. We need to be reminded that the bad behaviors of our public icons, in sport as much as in everyday life, don't pass harmlessly from our collective moral memories. Subtly, they cause us to reposition the fulcrum on our moral scales so that, in time, we come to accept as normative behaviors that in the not-too-distant past wouldn't have been tolerated.

The NCAA annually bestows sportsmanship awards for acts that demonstrate one or more of the following: fairness, civility, honesty, unselfishness, respect, and responsibility. In some cases, the awards have recognized truly remarkable demonstrations of generosity and civility. For example, after being awarded the MVP for his play in the Big South Basketball Tournament, High Point University's Danny Gathings opted to give the trophy to Larry Blair from Liberty University, who Gathings thought was more deserving. George Audu, Penn State's triple jumper, won the 1999 Big Ten title but gave the trophy to a Purdue player who would have been his strongest opponent if he hadn't been injured a few weeks earlier. The Mesa State football team set itself apart by refusing to accept a forfeit victory in its Division II playoff game against Central Oklahoma when the Oklahoma players came to the game with cleats longer than the rules allowed. The Mesa State team intervened and waited until their opponents changed their shoes so that the game could be played, a game that they eventually lost.

Other awards have been based on far less exemplary conduct. Surely the Framingham State College women's soccer coach deserves to be complimented for instructing his players to allow their opponents to score a goal after his team was mistakenly awarded a goal earlier in the game, as does high jumper Carrie Long of Purdue University for informing the official that she had been incorrectly given credit for clearing a height that she had not. Surely we would like to see more players like Hap Hines on the football field, a kicker who earned the sportsmanship award because he consoled his opponents following his team's victories, and more track athletes like javelin thrower Jarrett Erwin, who corrected an official's mistake made in his favor. But if these acts of common decency are the most vivid examples of sportsmanship to have occurred over an eight-year span of time in the vast network of the NCAA's sports programs, one might well wonder how committed the organization is to developing sportsmanship in its players. More to the point, by singling out these acts of elemental decency for awards, the NCAA implicitly acknowledges that most of its coaches and athletes, faced with the same set of circumstances, probably would not have acted in the same honorable way. Where money drives sports and winning is paramount, as it is in the NCAA, sportsmanship is little more than an afterthought. How else is one to explain the fact that virtually all of the sportsmanship awards given by the NCAA over the past eight years have gone to athletes or coaches engaged in the less visible, non-revenue-producing sports or to athletes associated with lower-tier competitive programs?[27] Ironically, the truly ethical act is not always honored with sportsmanship awards in the value-challenged world of big-time sports. As some athletes have discovered, putting honor and decency ahead of victory can incur the wrath of one's teammates, fans, and organization. In a legendary case famously known as the "Immaculate Concession," a young Jack Nicklaus playing in the 1969 Ryder Cup match had sunk his birdie putt on the last hole, leaving his opponent Tony Jacklin with a four-footer to tie for the Cup. As Jacklin was readying the crucial putt, Nicklaus walked over and shook his hand, thereby conceding the putt and ensuring a tie between the Europeans and the Americans. This decent act of sportsmanship was said to have sparked livid criticism from Coach Sam Snead and from others on the American team who resented Nicklaus for failing to put the pressure on Jacklin to make the putt.

With this kind of thinking engrained in the public mind, even modest recommendations for elevating the tenor of games can seem absurdly idealistic. Suggesting that the ethical life valued beyond the gymnasium walls be equally valued within them—that McCartney and Osborne, for example, should have volunteered to forfeit their teams' victories, or that, as a gesture of fairness and justice, Holliday should have called the umpire's attention to the fact that he hadn't touched home plate—hardly seems radical, especially for Christian athletes and coaches. Yet in the dog-eat-dog world of athletics, such suggestions will get you labeled a dreamer. Modestly proposing that Christian college athletic programs enumerate in their mission statements such fundamental objectives as "cultivating a sense of justice, caring, and compassion toward opponents" or "being exemplars of Christian charity," and further suggesting that they implement policies to ensure these statements' realization, is likely to get you laughed out of the schools' board rooms just as quickly as it gets you laughed out of their locker rooms.

MORE BAD NEWS FROM RESEARCHERS

If these anecdotes leave you a bit dubious about the effects of competitive experience on sportsmanship, research findings on the topic stretching back nearly a half century might well strip you of faith in sports altogether. Before we begin, however, we must acknowledge the caveat that design problems in most of the research on character and sports make it impossible to determine whether the character traits observed in athletes come from their participation in sports or whether subjects have become athletes because they already possessed these traits (the "self-selection process"). My suspicion is that it is probably a combination of both; those temperamentally suited for sports are attracted to them and retained and their temperament is further shaped by the competitive atmosphere and interactions with coaches and fellow athletes. It is noteworthy that, despite these limitations, almost all of the studies on character and sports tend to point in the same unfortunate direction.

The power of the athletic milieu to shape character was recognized nearly half a century ago in a research project involving 335 high school boys who differed in the amounts of experience they had in sporting environments (one-third were athletes, one-third spectators, and one-third were neither spectators nor athletes). It was discovered that those with the greatest amounts of athletic experience distinguished themselves, not by demonstrating superior sportsmanship, but by displaying a much lower level of sportsmanship than those with little or no competitive experience. At about the same time, sociologist Harry Webb asked youngsters in grades 3 through 12 what they thought to be most important in playing a game. They ranked three factors: play the game as well as you are able, beat your opponent, or play the game fairly. Webb found that as children moved through the elementary grades, they tended to rearrange these priorities in line with what he called "a professionalized attitude toward play" in which playing a game well was valued more than playing it fairly. A follow-up study found that students in grades 8 through 12 who participated in organized athletics had a much more professionalized attitude toward play than those who had not. To the extent that one's definition of sportsmanship places a priority on playing fairly, findings from these studies suggest that sport may not be the best place to develop it.[28]

Other studies conducted over several decades have painted an even dimmer portrait of the relationship between the experience of playing sports and attitudes toward sportsmanship. A study that examined athletes' values at the United States Military Academy found that intercollegiate athletes scored lower on an ethical value choice survey than intramural athletes. A widely cited investigation of 233 athletes at fifteen colleges and universities found that non–letter winners earned higher sportsmanship scores on an "Action-choice Test for Competitive Situations" questionnaire than did letter winners; athletes who were not receiving athletic grants scored higher than those receiving grants. Football players distinguished themselves by scoring lower than all other athletes. Although athletes at private and church-affiliated institutions scored higher than students from state institutions, the degree of the athletes' religious activity seemed to have little effect on their responses. Another investigator who had athletes and non-athletes examine photographs of sporting figures who were committing various acts of violence (hitting hard and fighting) found that experienced athletes—those the investigator called "survivors of the sport socialization process"—were more likely than non-athletes to rate violent acts as legitimate.[29]

Studies of European soccer have also found that as players move up the ranks of competition, their tolerance for violent actions and violation of the rules increases as well. A study examining the ethical perspectives of young soccer players in England and Finland found striking differ-ences between amateurs and players who had some affiliation with pro-fessional clubs. A majority of the professionals (55 percent) thought it acceptable to stop a fast opponent "by any means, lawful or otherwise," while only 37 percent of amateurs thought it acceptable; 56 percent of professionals thought it acceptable for a coach "to urge a player to knock out of the game a dangerous player of the opposing team," something thought proper by only 35 percent of amateurs. A strong majority of both categories—82 percent of the professionals and 59 percent of the amateurs—thought it appropriate for a player to earn a penalty kick by pretending he had been badly fouled; 70 percent of professional players and 42 percent of amateurs agreed that "a player may attempt anything provided he is not caught." In every category of these and other ques-tions the pattern was similar: those playing sport at the highest levels, and presumably with the most athletic experience, displayed the lowest standards of sportsmanship.[30]

Findings from a recent survey of over 4,200 high school athletes con-ducted by the Josephson Institute of Ethics in Los Angeles hardly brighten the picture. Describing their results as painting "a chilling picture of a confused moral relativism and self-serving rationalizations," investiga-tors at the institute found that 58 percent of male athletes (24 percent of females) think it proper to inflict pain in football in order to intimidate an opponent; 47 percent of males (19 percent of females) think trash-talking to a defender is proper; and over half of the male athletes (45 per-cent of female athletes) believe that in the real world "successful people do what they have to do to win even if others consider it cheating."[31]

In a world in which 75–80 percent of high school students admit to engaging in "serious" academic cheating, more than half admit to having plagiarized papers, and more than half see nothing wrong with cheat-ing, it's tempting to shrug off poor sportsmanship as simply more of the same. But there is reason to believe that, as off-course as students' moral compasses can be in their daily lives, their moral reasoning and conduct in sports is even worse. Brenda Bredemeier and David Shields, two inves-tigators at the forefront of the study of moral development in sports, have identified a "divergence in moral reasoning" about sport and daily life that occurs as early as the 6th or 7th grade and extends into the college years. Generally, they have found that the level of reasoning employed to solve moral dilemmas in sport operates at a lower level than that used to solve similar problems in real-life contexts. For example, one football player, asked to determine whether a player ("Tom") should follow his coach's orders to injure an opponent, said: "If Tom looks at it as a game, it's OK to hurt the guy—to try to take him out of the game. But if he looks at it as a person, and tries to hurt him, it's not OK." And then he added this chilling explanation: "When you're on the field then the game is football. Before and after, you deal with people morally." Bredemeier and Shields made this glum assessment: "Despite the diverse instruments— from psychometers to content analysis of written stories, from a 'study of values test' to a 'critical incidents' inventory—a surprisingly uniform picture emerges. When compared to non-athletes, athletes tend to have less 'sportsmanlike' attitudes or values, and more elite athletes have less 'sportsmanlike' attitudes than other athletes."[32]

The proverbial nail in the coffin comes from the work of Sharon Stoll and her associates at the University of Idaho's Center for Ethical Theory and Honor in Competition and Sport. Over the past quarter of a century they have evaluated the moral reasoning abilities of over 70,000 athletes. Using a questionnaire that presents athletes with standard sport-problem scenarios that require moral reasoning for their solution, they have found that athletes consistently evaluate the problems using significantly less mature moral reasoning skills than the general student population. Stoll has also noticed a sharp drop in scores in recent years, especially among athletes who participate in contact sport athletes such as football, lacrosse, and hockey. (Athletes in tennis and golf use higher levels of moral reasoning but still score lower than their non-athletic classmates.) For example, in a study of more than one-hundred and fifty college athletes, Stoll and her colleagues discovered only 10 percent who thought an athlete should be courteous to opposing players, although most felt an obligation to be fair and courteous to their own team. Asked if they should be fair to their opponents, a group of football players cynically responded: "You do what you gotta do to win"; "You do to them before they do to you; fair has got nothing to do with it"; and "You ain't trying if you ain't cheating." A universal conception of good sportsmanship includes learning to "gracefully accept the results of a match or game," but some of the players Stoll interviewed had a much different view. Asked if they would gracefully accept the results of a game, the players said the following: "Sure, if we win"; "If we lost, no way am I being gracious"; "If you lose, you're nothing. You never accept losing."[33]

Stoll's interviews with coaches showed some to be as confused as their players about moral decisions in sport. During one interview, some grew uncomfortable with being forced to face the ethical quandaries presented in the questionnaire. One told Stoll, "These questions are very ideal and real sport is not like that," and "It depends on what level of sport as to what is acceptable practice." This, it should be noted, is the same moral relativism that inspired Victor Conte, founder of the Bay Area Laboratory Co-Operative (BALCO), which specialized in peddling performance-enhancing drugs to some of our most famous athletes, to say, "It's not cheating if everybody is doing it."[34]

SEARCHING FOR THE CAUSE

One often hears it said that sports are "morally neutral"—they are neither good nor bad in themselves. As the esteemed philosopher Aldous Huxley once put it, "used well . . . [sports] can teach endurance and courage, a sense of fair play and a respect for the rules . . . used badly [they] can encourage personal vanity and group vanity, greedy desire for victory and hatred for rivals." If athletes' moral bearings get a bit skewed at times, unscrupulous coaches, overbearing parents, or some other nefarious outside force is to be blamed. Such claims usually are intended to underscore the importance of putting sport in the right hands or, as early twentieth-century social gospellers liked to put it, to ensure that sports are surrounded "with proper safeguards." To a large extent Huxley was right: the scruples of the coach, the influence of social support systems, and the social contexts in which competitions take place exert substantial influences on a player's sense of ethical proportion. We might imagine Coach Stroud's players to have learned an important lesson from their coach about fairness, honesty, and justice, just as we might expect bad results from the youth sports league in Florida that presented members of the 5th grade losing team in the state championships plaques inscribed with the Lombardian quote, "There is a second place bowl game but it is a game for losers played by losers." Evangelical sport enthusiasts consistently preach the moral neutrality of sport, blaming its problems not on the inherent processes in sport but on the corruption of the human heart. "Don't blame sports. Look within yourself for the moral mess of sports," they would say, thus echoing the title of evangelist Bill Glass' defense of professional football, *Don't Blame the Game*.[35]

But laying all of the blame for the skewed morality of sports at the feet of corner-cutting coaches or on imperfect souls gives an undeserved pass to the egocentric pulls of competitive sport itself. Earlier generations of evangelicals appreciated the power of social institutions and

environments to shape individual moral perspectives and heaped condemnations on popular sports more than on those who snuck off to
play them. Often they overreached, but they were on the right track.
To assume that players can inhabit a culture in which self-worth and
achievement hinge on a single-minded, unyielding determination to further their own cause at the expense of others without that culture shaping their worldviews and their perceptions of right and wrong is just as
fatuous as assuming that they won't learn some positive qualities like
self-discipline, sacrifice, and mental toughness through the same experience. Columnist David Brooks' observation about Washington politicians, that none "can withstand the onslaught of egotism and come out
unscathed," is just as true for athletes competing at the highest levels.[36]
Sadly, as we currently honor and revere and organize them, sports more
often play to our moral weaknesses than to our strengths. That athletes
who spend major parts of their lives in a competitive microcosm often
develop moral calluses shouldn't surprise us. In fact, to imagine that a
sense of fairness and sensitivity toward others will bloom from an experience that is by nature self-concentrated and self-absorbed is to expect
that oranges will grow where one has planted apple seeds.

Sport philosophers and ethicists endlessly debate the finer points
of morality in sport, but their elegant prose seems never to penetrate
the sports world, where almost all ethical issues are resolved in favor of
enhanced performance. It may grate on our ears to hear swimmer Mark
Spitz, who won seven gold medals in the 1972 Olympics, say that athletics didn't prepare him to live in society "because athletics is selfish," or to
read the late legendary basketball coach Al McGuire quoted as saying that
"what it takes to be a great player, beyond raw talent, is self-centeredness
and a certain numbness to the crowd," or to read that legendary Red Sox
slugger Jim Rice told a luncheon crowd of four hundred that greed and
cheating were essential to success in professional baseball, or to hear the
Christian first baseman for the Colorado Rockies say, "We're dirt bags, like
99 percent of the world. Maybe worse, because we are baseball players,"
but given the social environment inhabited by athletes, should we really
be surprised? Obviously, the ethical coach and enlightened institution
can help buffer a degree of the self-assertiveness central to sports, but as
the long history of relations between sport and the church has shown, the
intrinsic urge for self-promotion in sports will always trump the efforts of
well-intended persons, however spiritually minded they might be, and
ultimately impress its stamp on the character of players.[37]

Sportsmanship on a Broader Front

One might argue that the true test of sport as a developer of character is whether it produces changes in the lives of players and coaches in the broader reaches of life beyond the sports arena. It seems highly unlikely that the prized moral values associated with sportsmanship would be carried over into the daily lives of athletes when they so rarely make an appearance in the world of sports themselves. It is possible, I suppose, that in spite of being buried in a body-denying, socially dispassionate, self-solicitous subculture, athletes still might pass into the real world embodying the important Christian virtues of compassion, caring, sympathy, and humility, but this would be possible only if they somehow managed to swim upstream against the current set in motion by all-out competition. Even if this were the case, one would have to conclude that athletes developed the traits in spite of, rather than because of, their participation in sports.

Research suggests that faith in the power of sport as a character-builder is largely misplaced. While a study involving 1,600 high school students found encouraging links between participation in sport and increased self-esteem and higher valuation of academic achievement, it also found links between participation and increased aggression, irritability, and a lower valuation of honesty. Another study compared the value orientations of football players on winning and losing teams from universities, state colleges, and private schools. Winning teams, presumably populated by the best athletes, scored lowest on a social variable that loaded heavily on personality motives consistent with love of people, kindness, sympathy, and unselfishness, values that the researchers noted "could well represent the outcomes of a sportsmanlike attitude toward life." The same pattern was observed by other investigators who compared university teams to players in colleges and private schools where athletes were presumably less accomplished and perhaps less experienced. The investigators also found that university football players also scored higher on an economic variable, which exemplified "the person who prefers luxury over beauty, the accumulation of wealth, and who may be said to make his religion the worship of Mammon."[38]

These studies, along with others that could be cited, are backed up by a running account in our sports pages of the moral lapses of famous athletes. The tales of Michael Vick, Mike Tyson, Barry Bonds, Marion Jones, Bobby Knight, and O. J. Simpson can hardly be dismissed as isolated examples of the idiosyncratic styles of a few misguided souls. There simply are too many such stories out there. If sports help produce model citizens, how does one explain the out-of-control gambling and drinking among college athletes? True, sport itself may not be the culprit, but something seems amiss in the values intrinsic to the sports subculture when college athletes report having more sex partners, contract a greater number of sexually transmitted diseases, are inordinately involved in sexual violence, and show significantly greater approval than non-athletes of statements supportive of rape (e.g., "many women secretly desire to be raped" or "drunk women at a party are fair game for everyone"). Not only are athletes more likely than other students to be involved in campus violence, they appear to play significant roles in initiating it.[39]

The problem has become sufficiently serious to prompt many big-time athletic departments to introduce ethics workshops for athletes and coaches, their decisions guided by the faulty belief that attitudes and moral discretion can be altered without altering the environments that help form and perpetuate them. The National Association of Intercollegiate Athletics' "Champions of Character" program under the spirited direction of Rob Miller, the Josephson Institute's "Character Counts" program, and Sharon Stoll's "Winning with Character" four-year curriculum all aim in the right direction, yet I believe they ultimately will prove to be weak antidotes to the inherent impulses of sport itself. As long as performance and technical achievement remain the yardstick by which excellence is measured, and as long as newspaper headlines and financial jackpots go to those blessed with technical but not necessarily moral skills, moral uplift will be at best an accidental outcome of sports. You can have public, formalized, glamorized competition and you can have morally inspiring sport, but I don't think you can have both. In the oft-iterated words of two sport psychologists, "If you want to build character try something else."[40]

EVANGELICALS AND CHARACTER

By and large, evangelical institutions seem far more intent on distinguishing themselves by their competitive achievements than through the far more courageous task of attaining ethical distinction. Sportsmanship is given much greater emphasis, for example, on the website of the secular National Association of Intercollegiate Athletics (where it is backed up with an ambitious program for character education) than on the website of the evangelical National Christian College Athletic Association, where sportsmanship is given a back seat to athletic accomplishments. The website is crammed with fawning tributes to athletic achievements of athletes and coaches, yet no explicit mention is made of sportsmanship in any of the 24 awards it bestows on athletic personnel. The NCCAA is quick to tell about its athletes' involvement in community work, mission fields, or evangelization efforts, but admirable though they may be, these efforts are entirely tangential to the attitudes and character that athletes display in their direct connection with sports. As Rob Miller, director of the Champions of Character initiative at the NAIA, told me, "You can be very involved in community service, but still display some pretty crummy behaviors on the athletic field."[41]

Regrettably, the flood of evangelicals into big-time sports has not been accompanied by a flood of examples of Christian sportsmanship. Andrea Jaeger's faith-inspired decision to drop out of big-time tennis has no counterpart in the evangelical traditions of sport, save perhaps Eric Liddell's refusal to run an Olympic race on a Sunday in 1924 and the brave stance White Sox pitcher Al Worthington took against cheating in the 1960s. Committed to carrying his Christian faith onto the field, Worthington balked when he discovered that his team was using a binocular-equipped staff member to steal signals from the opponents' catcher. Worthington confronted his manager, telling him, "I get paid to win, but I've got to win honestly." Unable to change the manager's mind, Worthington quit.[42]

These acts became worthy of the label "character" because they entailed costs. "Before we are ready to impute to a person the quality of character," noted writer Marvin Scott, "he must be seen as voluntarily putting something on the line."[43] Coach Stroud's action, for example, cost his team the state championship. Evangelically inspired sportsmanship, on the other hand, seems to require very little in the way of sacrifice, perhaps something that should be expected from the no-cost, drive-thru sort of evangelicalism popular in much of the evangelical sports community. Keep your temper in check, shake your opponent's hand, maintain a semblance of civility, don't rock the sports establishment boat, and give 110 percent as a way of honoring God, and you are well within the bounds of expected behavior in the evangelical sports world. It remains a startling coincidence that actualizing evangelical sportsmanship almost always improves rather than limits the chances of competitive success.

Of course, evangelicals place great importance on playing by the rules, often to a fault, granting them near-sacred status. Former NFL player and evangelist Bill Glass, who glamorized the senseless violence of football perhaps more than any other popular figure in the evangelical community, hedged his enthusiastic endorsement with this single caveat: "Christians shouldn't break the rules or play dirty."[44] The exalted place rules assume in the moral scheme of evangelical athletes surfaced repeatedly in sociologist Chris Stevenson's enlightening interviews with members of a sport-evangelism team. Stevenson found that while many of the athletes claimed to want to follow the rules and play with respect for authority, "they also continued to accept the dominance of the values, beliefs, meanings, and expectations of the competitive sport culture and allowed these to control their motivations and their actions—they were, after all, simply 'doing their job' as athletes."[45]

But rules of games carry no moral force in themselves; they are mere conventions, subject to the dictates of those who shape a sport's traditions. They cannot be the arbiter of a Christian standard for sport conduct because they themselves are subject to a higher moral authority. Indeed, there may be instances where following the rules puts an athlete on morally slippery ground. When Christians invest rules with moral authority, they too conveniently relieve themselves from the difficult task of making moral choices. "The referee was there, and she did not call anything, so it was not cheating," is the athlete's way of looking at it, claimed the director of officials for the United States Soccer Federation.[46] If the rules permit violence, deception, and dishonesty, then these things are also permitted for the Christian. Of course, evangelicals will agree that there is a limit to the Christian exercise of violence and deception for pleasure's sake, but usually it will be spelled out, not in the still small voice of the Christian conscience, but in the rule book.

In *Losing Our Virtue*, David Wells points out that laws are intended to enforce right conduct by checking the urge for self-gratification and expressive individualism. Thus they can be seen as occupying one side of the moral landscape, with freedom and license (simply doing what is in one's own interest) occupying the other. Between the two lies a vast territory Wells calls "character." On this middle ground, behavior is not driven by laws or license but by private virtues such as honesty, decency, and other kinds of moral obligations. One operates on a moral plane above the law, guided by the "dictates of the unenforceable." But this middle territory, says Wells, has been largely deserted, replaced with moral relativism and individualism. As a result, "law must now do what church, family, character, belief and even cultural expectations once did by way of instructing and restraining human nature." What Wells sees as occurring in ordinary life is magnified a hundredfold in the world of sports, where the insatiable thirst for winning seems controllable not by moral conviction or "obedience to the unenforceable," but only by rules. Those who doubt this need only consult the ever-expanding NCAA rule book, now nearly five hundred pages in length, accompanied by thousands of pages of rule interpretations enforced by sizable cadres of university-funded compliance officers and an NCAA enforcement division whose job it is to keep athletes and coaches in check.[47]

If the vast middle ground between law and license is truly where character resides, then the distinctive mark of Christian sportsmanship, the sub-Christian values, will reside there also. A distinctive Christian sportsmanship won't show itself merely in the doing of what is required by the law but by standards that are *self-imposed*. Far from deferring ethical decisions to the rule book, a Christian sportsmanship will test the morality of the rules themselves. Evangelical athletes who routinely volunteer their fouls and missteps to officials step onto this middle ground, as do college teams that drop out of athletic conferences where winning has become the ultimate standard of performance. When evangelicals modify their sports to align with a New Testament ethic based more on caring than on athletic tradition, they will be headed for this middle ground. And when they have allowed their religious beliefs to penetrate the rigid meritocracy of big-time sports with a competitive ethic grounded in grace, they will have arrived.

Few things touch me more deeply than those rare occasions when athletes resist the urge for self-promotion and do the costly, civilized, thoughtful, sympathetic, "Christian" thing. The most dramatic example I have encountered occurred on November 2, 1969, in the enormous Bernabeau Stadium in Madrid, where the Real Madrid team was pitted against Sabadell in a Spanish football league championship match before 80,000 rabid spectators. At the 50-minute mark and with the score tied, Sabadell right wing Pedro Zaballa received a pass, and just as he was about to shoot, the Madrid defensive back and goalkeeper collided, both falling to the ground unconscious. It was later learned that one had broken his jaw. Zaballa, now facing a defenseless goal, had only to nudge the ball into the net and, in all possibility, secure the championship for his team. Yet in that instant, when the roar of the crowd, the egocentric pull of the game, and the expectations of his teammates and supporters all conspired to urge him to blast the ball into the net, Zamballa did the unexpected. Without hesitating, he kicked the ball *away* from the net and over the touch line, opting not to score what might well have been the winning goal. In fact, his team eventually lost by a score of 1–0. As you might expect, he was roundly criticized, although ultimately he was given the Fair Play Award by the International Fair Play Association for "reflecting all that is finest and purest in sport."[48]

Zamballa never explained what caused him to do what he did, merely noting that he had "followed a natural impulse not to score under the circumstances." I think the church can learn a lot by reflecting on his behavior that afternoon. With a mere flick of his foot, he showed us that the real value of sport lies not in its celebration of character traits that assure victory but in the opportunities it affords for marginalizing success. He thumbed his nose at the raw instincts of competitive sports, not ostentatiously and certainly not to depreciate competition, but as if to make this fundamental point: the human experience of sport achieves its divine purpose *not* when athletes respond reflexively to its ikish enticements to self-aggrandizement, but when they seize it as an opportunity to demonstrate those human qualities that mark us as God's highest and most noble creations. Despite what the traditions of sport may tell us, what is truly highest and finest about God's people is not their capacity to sacrifice and work hard in order to bask in the rewards of long-coveted goals but their capacity, when the right moment comes, to give up those rewards willingly in order to do the right thing.

9

TOUCHDOWNS AND SLAM DUNKS FOR JESUS

On the evening of February 4, 2007, two men embraced at midfield in Miami's Dolphin Stadium, unaffected by the falling rain. Tony Dungy and Lovie Smith, long-time friends and brothers in the faith, had just experienced the ultimate of athletic encounters: their teams had met in the Super Bowl. Dungy's Indianapolis Colts had beaten Smith's Chicago Bears 29–17. In the postgame media frenzy, Dungy heaped praises on Smith and his team and publicly celebrated a historical first: two African American NFL coaches had faced off for football's crown jewel. He told sportscaster Jim Nantz: "It means an awful lot to our country, but again, more than anything, I said it before, Lovie Smith and I are not only the first two African Americans, but Christian coaches showing you can win doing it the Lord's way. We're more proud of that."

Precisely what Dungy meant by "doing it the Lord's way," a phrase he has used on more than one occasion, has never been explained. Perhaps he was referring to the fact that he and Smith eschew cursing, smoking, and drinking, that they read their Bibles, that they customarily give God credit for victories, or that they live humble lives and refuse to humiliate players as a way of extracting one last ounce of performance. Perhaps he was pointing to the importance he attaches to prayer in his coaching strategy. In the locker room after the game, he set aside the Lombardi Trophy, joined hands with his team, and led them in a group prayer, focusing "on what was really important." Whatever "God's way" was, Dungy seemed to intimate that he and Smith were the first two NFL coaches to have followed it, an intimation not overlooked by some critics. If "doing it the Lord's way" means following the teachings of Christ, one can assume from Dungy's comments that it is indeed a rarity in the coaching world of the NFL.

Dungy's testimony to the more than 92 million fans watching the game represented the zenith of a flourishing sport evangelism enterprise that has evolved from mostly ad hoc, freelance postgame tributes cobbled together by spiritually minded athletes into a grand, organized effort to spread the gospel through sports. Never before has a Christian athlete or coach enjoyed such a moment with such a large public. A few weeks later Dungy would receive top billing in a star-studded list of celebrities participating in Luis Palau's two-day evangelistic festival in Tampa. Backed by the efforts of over 500 churches in the area, the festival featured not only a testimonial by Dungy, but spine-tingling performances by Christian daredevil motorcyclists and a concert by Christian rockers P.O.D., Mandisa from American Idol, and country superstar Wynonna, all to be enjoyed with Philly cheesesteaks, funnel cakes, frankfurters, and other goodies sold by street corner peddlers. Dungy's book *Quiet Strength* would soon make the hardcover religion bestseller list.

The moment also was of considerable consequence for the burgeoning sport evangelism industry, especially for Athletes in Action, whose guiding hand was behind Dungy's and Smith's public proclamations. "That's a pretty far-reaching pulpit, which is exactly what Dungy and Smith had in mind," said Bill Pugh, its executive director. "That was one of the ways that both Tony and Lovie agreed that *we* would be able to use this unique platform, not only two African-American coaches, but two men of faith," he added, noting that both men have been involved with AIA since their playing days.[1] AIA also paid for a full-page ad in *USA Today* featuring the two coaches. The evangelical *Sports Spectrum* magazine, basking in reflected glory, told its readers that Dungy "deflected the glory to Someone bigger than himself—a truly humble act by a man of integrity and honor." On its website, the Baptist Press pointed out that both coaches had given God credit in their victories in conference championships a few weeks earlier, and the article went on to publicly vet the religious credentials of Lovie Smith, noting that he has gone on record saying that "he believes in Christ" and "listens to Christian music when driving his car." Despite rumors that after "winning it all" Dungy would retire, he decided to continue in his role as coach (eventually retiring in 2009). He said, "It does give you a platform and that is one of the reasons."[2]

Here was a vivid reminder, not only of evangelicalism's taste for drawing attention to itself through secular achievements, but of the extent to which sport has been insinuated into the evangelical subculture as a way of capturing the attention of the sports-starved masses. Among the smorgasbord of cultural expressions tapped by evangelicals to spread the word, sport is arguably the most influential and far-reaching, drawing the attention of millions each year. Evangelicals rarely ask whether or not exploiting sports for evangelism is a good thing, largely because sport evangelism represents, hands down, the most important connection evangelicals have been able to imagine between their faith and big-time sports. Thus, to suggest (as I am about to) that evangelicals may not be well served by the current enthusiasm for sport evangelism threatens the very foundation upon which many evangelicals have constructed their defense of sports.

Evangelicals and Evangelism

In the diverse and often ambiguous creeds of modern evangelicalism, a core defining doctrine continues to hold sway: Whether through traditional preaching and teaching or through "lifestyle evangelism," Christians are obliged by the demands of their faith to reach out to lost souls with the good news of Christ's redeeming work. To do this, modern evangelism seeks to engage with the world rather than challenge it, edging toward H. Richard Niebuhr's model of Christ of culture and away from the fundamentalist's Christ against culture. The idea, said the late evangelical theologian Stanley Grentz, is to bring "the Christian gospel into conversation with the generation God has called us to serve" and to express "the gospel through the 'language' of the culture—through the cognitive tools, concepts, images and thought-forms, by means of which people today speak about the world they inhabit." This strategy for bridging the cultural divide has spawned a lively Christian pop culture featuring Christian movies, music, and consumer goods in which the Christian message is eased, as it were, in the back door. It has given birth to "seeker churches" intent on reducing rather than accentuating the differences between the cultures of believers and nonbelievers. Religion scholar Mark Shibley, no doubt with tongue in cheek, has called it "the Californication of conservative Protestantism."[3]

Augustine may have started the church down this path in the fifth century by arguing that "the church should not reject a good thing because it is pagan." Adopting pagan customs wasn't "borrowing" from them as much as it was "taking from them what is not theirs and giving it to the real owner." Such things, Augustine said, "may be consecrated for His worship." But in engaging culture by adapting God-given practices to Christian ends, evangelicals have ended up being shaped by the culture far more than they have impacted it. This homogenization of the gospel message with culture, says religion scholar Alan Wolfe, has entailed big costs:

> It's very important to places like Wheaton College in Illinois and Calvin College in Michigan to attract high-quality students, to attract a distinguished faculty. But when you do that, you inevitably become part of the whole admissions game and, in some places, of the sports culture. I'm fascinated, for example, by Baylor University, which retains a very strong Christian commitment, yet somehow that Christian identity in no way got involved with becoming as aggressively basketball-oriented as a school can be, and then having all the same forms of corruption and sin that go along in any big-time athletic conference. It's a fascinating study in contradictions.[4]

For musicians like Dale Thompson, leader of the Christian heavy metal band Bride, evangelism means fitting Christian sentiment to pulsating beats and flashing strobe lights. "How will [young people] understand if I do not speak their dialect?" he asks. Sport may be even a more appealing dialect. The Southern Baptist Convention bases its ambitious sport evangelism program on the dubious assumption that "96 percent of the population is linked to sports in some way." But as philosopher-theologian Jacques Ellul has pointed out, Christianity absorbs culture like a sponge, and precisely how much of culture it can absorb without changing itself is a question rarely asked by those at the heart of the sport evangelism movement. Speaking a dialect the modern world understands always entails the danger that the dialect will morph into an entirely different language. Any time the church latches on to a popular phenomenon, says theologian Bryan Stone, "the antennae of Christians ought to go up."[5]

Thus the challenge facing evangelicals is how to communicate their faith in a largely unsympathetic culture without contorting the core of the message itself. The overwhelming choice has been to treat the message as a product to be advertised. Sport evangelists, like evangelists on the broader front, have joined sport to the gospel in what Virginia Stem Owens likened to "a giant advertising campaign for salvation." When the Birmingham Steeldogs, an arena football team in Alabama, replaced players' names on the back of jerseys with Scripture references, they employed the same Madison Avenue stratagem that brought us "Air Jesus" T-shirts portraying Christ as an about-to-dunk Michael Jordan, candy sold as "Testamints," pantyhose with rhinestone crosses, Holy Smoke fire-starter sticks, and "Resurrection Eggs." The flash and dazzle of big-time sports is a perfect way to spread a flash-and-dazzle gospel. "If athletes can sell razor blades and soft drinks," asked John Dodderidge of the FCA, "why can't they sell the gospel?"[6]

Heeding textbook advertising strategy, sport evangelism has become focused on "parachurch" groups that, freed of churchly or denominational entanglements, are able to tweak the gospel to the latest tastes, images, and jargon of their target audiences. The gospel according to the Christian Anglers Association may not differ in its basic thrust from the gospel according to the Christian Motorcyclists Association, the National Christian Barrel Racers Association, the Fellowship of Christian Magicians, the Fellowship of Christian Cheerleaders, the Fellowship of Christian Puppeteers, the Fellowship of Christian Poets, the Christian Tattoo Association, or the Fellowship of Christian Athletes, but each group gives it a unique twist that makes it more palatable to unbelievers. Religion sociologist Robert Wuthnow has estimated that there are as many as 800 such "special purpose groups" nationwide; of these, Tony Ladd and James Mathisen have speculated that anywhere from 50 to 150 shape their ministries around sports.[7]

SPORTS AS EVANGELISM

As sport has become more popular, so has sport evangelism. To evangelists it is a matter of mathematics: "Why golf outreach?" asks the In His Grip Golf Association on its website. "Thirty million-plus golfers in the US, sixty-plus million golfers worldwide . . . Golf is not just a game; it is a passion for millions." A workshop included in a three-day conference sponsored by the North American Mission Board of the Southern Baptist Convention and the Second Baptist Church of Houston was titled "Evangelism Bridges to a Sports-Crazy World."[8] But the public's unrelenting appetite for sports seems a pitifully shaky plank upon which to build a ministry, certainly no more sound than using the public's fascination with American Idol, Britney Spears, or Texas Hold'em poker as justification for the same purpose. Public taste is never a good barometer of morality. John Gardner's lament about modern art would seem to be just as applicable to modern sport: "Art has never been more admired, more adulated, than it is now," said Gardner; "it draws larger crowds and attracts more money than ever before, and yet the art itself is impoverished."[9]

There is another reason to believe that sports might be constitutionally ill-suited for evangelism. Methods of evangelism, one might imagine, should bear some intrinsic connection to the experience of conversion. In "old-style evangelism," for example, there was always some discernible connection between method and purpose. An invitation followed a carefully reasoned sermon, a hymn, a personal testimony, or a modeling of Christian witness. All these experiences converged together to elevate soul and religious conscience. Sport lacks this soul-elevating power. It may evoke a geyser of emotions, but none are likely to be confused with the whisperings of the Spirit. The efforts of missionary doctors treating HIV/AIDS–stricken African children are a concrete expression of their witness. Healing the sick and satisfying the hungry in the name of God, after all, is inherently "evangelistic." Drama, literature, and music co-opted for evangelism at least have the potential for penetrating the conscience, exposing the futility of a life without God, and pointing to the truth. But how does slugging home runs, knocking down opponents, or slam-dunking basketballs in front of braying crowds point to God?

In fact, rather than prompting feelings of spiritual inadequacy in the unconverted, a sense of God's majesty, and a hope for redemption, sports seem more likely to anesthetize them. Philosopher Peter Heinegg was at least partially correct when he called sports "a flight from the pain of existence," and so was Pascal, who located the powers of attraction of games and sports in their capacity to divert attention from the "natural poverty of our feeble and mortal condition." If angst and feelings of spiritual inadequacy are emotional paths toward conversion, sports are unlikely forums for their realization.[10]

In fact, judging from the way they talk about sports, even evangelicals wouldn't hold out much hope for them in this regard. Rather than valuing sport as an art-path that heightens athletes' and spectators' spiritual sensibilities, evangelicals seem more often to value it for its opposite effect as an outlet for hostility that can tame "aggressive instincts."

Thanks to the spread of naturalist Conrad Lorenz's (largely debunked) thesis that sports can play an important role in the cathartic discharge of "aggressive urge," many evangelicals believe that playing and watching sport offers a healthy way to release a dangerous form of aggression Lorenz termed "militant enthusiasm." The editors of *Christianity Today* relied upon this theory in several editorials in the 1970s, in one case recommending sport as a palliative for civil unrest: "These are days when Christians need to contribute an extra dose of effort in holding down social hostility," said the editors; "baseball helps." A book by a professor at evangelical Biola University seems to go down the same path: "Having played football and experienced the grime, the grit, and the gore of the field, I would rather see my son head to the gridiron than the battlefield on any given Sunday. Despite Jesus' blessing of the peacemakers, football, violence, and war are still very much with us."[11]

Precisely why Christians, of all people, might harbor pent-up hostility in sufficient amounts to require its hydraulic purging through combative sports isn't given much explanation. Judging from the commentators of some of the leading evangelical thinkers, it is because aggression (like competition) is thought to be instinctive, part of our created natures. Mark Noll, for example, once suggested that "a surfeit of human emotion that, thanks to the Fall refuses to focus on God . . . is better spent on football than on ideological or personal strife." The late British theologian Daniel Jenkins speculated that aggressive instincts were a "hangover of evolution." Controlled play, said Jenkins, channels and releases these energies in a harmless, enjoyable, and sometimes socially constructive way. Reformed theologian Albert Wolters points to Lorenz in arguing that aggressiveness is part of the created order; "the need," he said, "is to sanctify aggression, not suppress it," and argued for its channeling through "socially acceptable outlets." Obviously, how one responds to such arguments hinges a great deal on one's definition of aggressiveness, but in retrospect, it is a novel theological notion that a human activity (sport) can avert sin by simulating the very actions it is thought to prevent.[12]

A stream of studies has shown aggression to be a learned rather than an instinctive behavior. We know, for example, that societies that play aggressive sports are more likely to wage war than those that do not, which is precisely the opposite of what the cathartic hypothesis would predict. If playing combative sports discharges pent-up aggression, non–contact sport athletes should have higher levels of measured aggression than contact athletes, whose aggression would be dissipated, but research has shown the opposite trend. Rather than hostility levels of football players and wrestlers being dissipated over the course of a season, they have been found to increase. On balance, it would seem that a much more convincing case could be argued that sports, far from harmlessly venting hostilities, manufacture their own. "What organized football did to me," said philosopher and former professional football player John McMurtry, "was to make me suppress my *natural* urges and re-express them in an alienating, vicious form." Playing combative sports may confer many benefits, but dissipation of pent-up hostilities and aggression does not appear to be one of them.[13]

Watching sports tends to be credited with having the same purging effect. "Sports relieve the weight of life," writes *First Things* writer James Nuechterlein. "[Playing sports] satisfies, in an innocent way, our competitive urges." Well, perhaps, but a number of studies have shown otherwise. Spectators, for example, have been found to have higher levels of hostility after watching basketball or football, but not after watching the less violent sports of gymnastics or swimming. Researchers have found that fans psychologically connected to their teams show a remarkable willingness to commit acts of violence against opposing coaches and players, especially following their teams' defeat. Interestingly, rugby fans are more likely to show aggressive behaviors when their teams win than when they lose. For many fans, hostility, violence, and displays of aggression are what attract them to sport in the first place. Spectator enjoyment of hockey, for example, has been found to run roughly proportional to the viciousness of the game, something detected in significant correlations between penalty minutes and ratings of enjoyment.[14]

To recap, the point here is that many of the dispositional effects of playing and watching combative sports appear to be inimical with the types of spiritual affectivities that one might suppose would lead to conversion. Even if sports could be shown to be cathartic, athletic performances sufficiently hostile, pugnacious, and militant to bring about this alleged release hardly frame a social occasion for inspiring unbelievers to reflect on their spiritual state. In this narrow sense, then, "sport evangelism" is a misnomer. As human experiences, our sport spectacles seem unlikely places to find God "softly and tenderly calling"; the calls of the stadium are from another land and another god.

Performance as Evangelism

Many athletes and coaches, proponents of lifestyle evangelism, will tell you that sports become evangelistic not so much through testimonies like Dungy's but rather in how they are played. Christian college athletic departments often claim that their programs aren't really as much about winning and losing as about evangelism. The Asbury College Athletics Department website, for example, describes its mission as "provid[ing] student-athletes with the opportunity to be a witness of faith through intercollegiate competition." When coaches at the thirteen member institutions of the Christian College Consortium (CCC) were asked to identify the objectives of their athletic programs, "evangelism and ministry" headed the list. Athletes also uniformly identified the athletic venue as "a public forum from which to demonstrate Christian virtues, with the evangelism of non-Christians as an ultimate goal."[15]

Yet, as coaches at these schools well know, it is much easier to theorize about intercollegiate athletics as instruments of Christian witness than it is to translate that theory into practice. The CCC survey, for example, found strong support across campuses for the notion that athletics on Christian colleges should somehow be "different" (70 percent), yet there was an alarming paucity of ideas and even less consensus as to what these differences should be. Coaches, burdened by the often unrealistic expectations of fans, alumni, and administrations, aware that career advancement requires winning records, and finding their options constrained by regulations of athletic conferences not always sympathetic with their spiritual aspirations, have to settle for fitting in tinges of Christian witness around the edges, being careful in the process not to challenge the reigning orthodoxy of intercollegiate athletics. Consequently, winning—whether acknowledged or not—remains the chief objective of Christian college athletic programs. Thus we see a West Coast Christian college firing its baseball coach who had a remarkable record of ministry to his athletes, but retaining the women's soccer coach who produced winning teams but was the target of complaints about verbal abuse he inflicted on players. "Exemplification rather than accommodation" should be the church's primary evangelistic strategy, says theologian Bryan Stone; but in athletic programs at Christian colleges, exemplification takes a backseat to winning.[16]

"Christian witness" can be a dodgy term in sports. Sometimes it looks more like a production of the front office than the Bible, more likely to win games for the team than souls for Christ. Outspoken evangelical NBA All-Star Dwight Howard says he plays only "to preach the word of God in the NBA"—not by "standing on a podium before a game telling everybody to follow Christ," but by preaching with his actions. Surely the qualities Howard enumerates as reflecting his witness—"being an aggressive defender, putting the needs of the team first, and humbly doing the dirty work"—help his team, but they bear at best an oblique witness to the unique motivations, values, and orientation of the Christian life. When the men's soccer coach of a western Christian college tells an interviewer: "if an athlete claims that their motivation is to play for the glory or the honor of God, that ought to show itself in the effort category," he is parroting the doctrine of "total release performance," which, according to the architect of the doctrine, means that the athlete "would give the same great intensity in each athletic performance as He [Christ] demonstrated going through the scourge and crucifixion." Giving one's all for the team and giving all for one's Savior may be fundamentally different motivations in the outside world but, happily for the sports industry, not in the arena. Why the evangelical athletic community has chosen to organize its conception of "witness" around a minor ethical concept, the Christian's responsibility to work diligently, rather than around theological constructs such as grace or servanthood is explainable only by appreciating the forceful imprint made on evangelicalism by the competitive ethos of organized sports.[17]

Somewhere along the way the institution of sport hijacked traditional understandings of witness and made it a servant of competitive zeal. When the conventional ideal of living a life formed by love, hope, faith, presence, patience, humility, courage, and the costly embodiment of Christian virtue gets filtered through the reigning mythology of modern sports, what emerges often bears faint resemblance to witness as commonly understood in the broader Christian community. Christian football players who believe that the cause of the gospel is advanced by their manliness and ability to withstand pain, or baseball players who remind impressionable youngsters that "just because you are a Christian, doesn't mean you have to be a wimp," project a twisted and tortured image of the faith. Sport evangelism that serves at the pleasure of the sports establishment seems hauntingly reminiscent of theologian James Gustafson's characterization of a religion propagated for its utilitarian value, wherein "individual pieties and social pieties . . . [are] instrumental not as gratitude to God, the honor of God, or service of God, but to sustaining purposes to which the Deity is incidental, if not something of an encumbrance."[18]

"Nothing is more hurtful to the Christian," reminded John Stott, "than the words, 'But you are no different from anybody else.'"[19] Christian colleges whose teams *could* present sport "in a distinctive way such that the alluring and 'useless' beauty of holiness can be touched, tasted, and tried" have opted instead to project the typical triumphal image of sports, fielding teams that operate on the same assumptions, heed the same ethos, celebrate the same myths, follow the same scripts, evoke the same images, and often become snared in the same ethical traps as those they claim to be evangelizing. The not terribly surprising result is that sport played "as a witness" tends not to look all that much different than sport played for fame, glory, revenge, or money. After the crowds have left the gymnasium, the bleachers have been rolled in, and the press releases distributed, how the accrual of this worldly recognition has advanced the public understanding of what it means to be a Christian remains unclear.

The Medium and the Message

A phrase coined in the 1960s by media critic Marshall McLuhan—"the medium is the message"—has had enormous influence on our understanding of how information is conveyed in the media and in public rituals. McLuhan's theory was far more complex than many have taken it to be, but the core point was that nuances in the way messages are conveyed can have a profound influence on the way the messages are received. The way a production team at ESPN chooses to televise a sporting event, for example, sends a powerful message in its own right, affecting the way viewers interpret the event. The images, language, camera positions, and commentary by the sportscasters can carry their own messages. Producers know, for example, that games that are described by sportscasters as involving rough play or as being between hated foes are perceived differently (and more enjoyably) than if described as being between friends. Over time, said McLuhan, distinguishing the effects of the medium from the effects of the content of the message becomes extraordinarily difficult.[20]

Sports are not, as evangelists seem to believe, a blank slate upon which one can write a Christian message. The Christian message is always competing against the message conveyed by the medium. When NASCAR driver Jeff Gordon uses his celebrity as "a platform to show other people what God has done for me in my life," he isn't simply endorsing his faith; he is also endorsing the not-so-Christian business of NASCAR. Joe Nemecheck's prominently displayed cross on his racing car, Morgan Shepherd's "Jesus #89" logo on his car, and Brett Rowe's "John 3:16" decal on his racing truck strike a rather impotent witness for the faith compared to the witness of their personalities to the spectacle of auto racing.[21] Patriots tight end Ben Watson's testimony ("There are people who would listen to me because I play the game of football. It gives me an incredible platform to influence people good or bad") is at the same time a testimony to the glory of the NFL. When local churches organize their services around a Super Bowl theme or participate in "Faith Nights" at the local ballpark, they become unwitting sales reps for big-time sport. When *Sport Spectrum* magazine peddles its "Power to Win 2008 Halftime Home Pack" with an evangelistic video to play for your neighbors at Super Bowl parties, it becomes at the same time an evangelist for what an NFL vice president called "the ultimate collision of sports and entertainment and music and marketing."[22]

But big-time sport doesn't really need evangelists; it evangelizes on its own terms. It "doesn't care at all for religion's moral strictures . . . or endless promises or consequences," said Bart Giamatti, "it only "cares for itself, in [a] uniquely free, ceremonial and subversive way."[23] Sports evangelize through their symbols, rituals, and time-honored traditions. The message sneaks into the soul and psyche when the audience's moral defenses are down. The message isn't simply about the game; sports evangelize for a worldview. "Noticed or not," says religion scholar Bonnie Miller-McLemore, "football expresses a complex system of coherent affirmations about ultimate reality through its myths and rituals—through its creation of sacred time and sacred space."[24] The subtle way this can happen was captured by Pulitzer Prize–winning author James Michener in his book *Sports in America*. Michener had been a sports fan all of his life, but it wasn't until late in life that he began to notice the confluence of symbols radiated by our major sport spectacles. One evening while watching a Monday night NFL halftime show, it dawned on him that "football games had become a heady mix of patriotism, sex, violence and religion . . . It was difficult, at times, to tell whether I was in a strip-tease show, an armory, a cathedral, or a ball park."[25]

Refreshing though the public witnesses of sincere men like Tony Dungy may be, they are mere whispers in a cacophony of the more beguiling voices of big-time sport spectacles that herald muddled views of goodness, truth, beauty, and the glories of self-determinacy, self-assertion, and self-absorption. The gospel of Christianity is revolutionary, life-changing, other-directed, and subversive—all of which are anathema to the ethos of sports. The theology of sport evangelism doesn't challenge assumptions; it plays to our natural dispositions and to our preferred views of the world. Those who "have ears to hear," I suppose, will still find ways of hearing the evangelists (and perhaps respond), but not without hearing a competing gospel embedded in the medium.

Sport requires its own platform for evangelizing its worldview. It needs television and cheerleaders and hype and bloviating sportscasters, but it also needs a certain model of sport, one that sport sociologist Jay Coakley calls "the power and performance model [PPM] of sports." The PPM is characterized by antagonistic relationships, aggressive domination of opponents, excellence achieved through dedication and hard work, the setting of records, pushing bodies to human limits, rigid selection systems based on ability, and hierarchical authority structures. It thrives on a full-throated drive to win. Over and against the PPM, Coakley describes a model that reflects a fundamentally different worldview. "The pleasure and participation model" values active participation over watching, enjoyment through personal expression, health and well-being, empowerment through physical experiences, inclusive participation, democratic decision making, and interpersonal support rather than hardnosed competition. Power and performance sport is heavily financed, highly publicized, highly marketable, and played by the few for the entertainment of many. Pleasure and participation sports are played behind the bleachers, so to speak, watched by few, uninteresting to the media, and chained to no agenda other than the intent of experiencing a good game. Power and performance is mainstream sport; pleasure and participation sports are counterculture.[26]

Only someone with a severely skewed view of the gospel taught by Jesus and the apostles would conclude that the worldview of the PPM better exemplifies the gospel's fundamental core than the pleasure and participation model. Yet it has been the PPM, not the pleasure and participation model, that evangelists have chosen to help bridge cultural barriers and usher souls into the kingdom. The reason seems clear enough, but it is hardly defensible. The PPM, far more than a countercultural model, fits snugly within a theological zeitgeist attuned to the audience's lived and perceived values. Like counterculture sport, counterculture Christianity doesn't have a very large consumer base.[27]

CELEBRITY SPORT EVANGELISM

Nothing sells athletic shoes or the gospel quite like celebrities. In 2006, Nike spent over $476 million to have sport celebrities endorse its products ($20 million to Tiger Woods alone) in the hope that the aura would rub off on its products. Three principles are used to fit celebrities to products: attractiveness, credibility, and meaning transfer. The overall attractiveness of the celebrity—physical appearance, intellect, athletic competence, and lifestyle—enhances consumers' memory of the brand that they endorse. As prodigal stars like Marion Jones, Michael Vick, and Kobe Bryant discovered, bad publicity can rapidly damage an athlete's attractiveness in the public square and quickly extinguish the flow of endorsements. By the same token, winning, coupled with a squeaky clean image, can bring advertisers pleading for endorsements. After previously unheralded New York Giant Eli Manning led his team to victory in Super Bowl XLII, his endorsement became one of the most sought after in sports. As one advertising executive put it, "all of a sudden, he's got a new air of legitimacy he didn't have before."[28]

The second principle, the *credibility* of the celebrity—his or her trustworthiness—influences consumers' *acceptance* of the product. Buick commercials stopped featuring Tiger Woods driving Buick sedans because, according to a market consultant, "there is just no believability that Tiger is dying to drive a Buick and without believability a celebrity endorsement is worthless." The third principle is *meaning transfer* between the celebrity and the brand; consumers must see some logical connection between the product and the sport star's identity, personality, and lifestyle. Greater meaning, for example, is likely to be transferred between LeBron James and Nike shoes than between him and the Microsoft Vista operating system he once endorsed. Wearing his shoes might make you a better basketball player, but using Microsoft software probably will not.[29]

Using much the same model, evangelicals have used celebrity to sell the gospel. "When a Reggie White or a Jim Harbaugh profess their faith, people take notice," explained the chief operating officer of FCA. The dynamics of selling Christ are not much different than the dynamics of selling basketball shoes. The celebrity pitching the gospel, like the celebrity pitching athletic shoes, must embody an attractive image, and in the athletic world this means that he or she must be a winner. Physically attractive, successful, wealthy, nationally acclaimed athletes are in demand by evangelism groups; stumbling, error-prone, marginal players are not, even though they may be far superior models of the Christian life. This is because in the broad reaches of society, winners project a more appealing image than losers, and at root level, sport evangelism is fundamentally about image. "Bit by bit, object by object," said Virginia Stem Owens, "the picture of Christian, no longer with Bunyan's backpack and staff, but in a basketball uniform or a three-piece executive suit, is put before us. The point is to make the picture so appealing that the customer wants to see himself within the frame." Unbelievers exposed to the image, said Owens, "would not have an inkling that the original pattern these people profess to imitate was a vagrant celibate whose own seminar on happiness elevated the mourning meek rather than the smiling success."[30]

In sport evangelism, just as in any Madison Avenue campaign, the usefulness of sport celebrities to the cause hinges on the attractiveness of their images, and this can quickly plummet when they stub a spiritual toe, something that has been a continuing problem for the sport evangelism movement. Atlanta NFL player and evangelical Eugene Robinson's embarrassment at having been arrested on a charge of soliciting an undercover police officer for sex also embarrassed Athletes in Action, which had given Robinson its Bart Starr Award for "outstanding character and leadership" on the same day. Jeff Gordon's evangelistic currency took a tumble after he went through a messy divorce and began to express interest in examining other religions. When it was learned that Dwight Howard had fathered a child out of wedlock, the sport-evangelism groups riding his coattails found themselves blindsided. (An evangelical magazine abruptly canceled a scheduled article about him.) These and other similar cases underscore the harsh truth that a pitch for the gospel constructed on the backs of celebrities—whether musicians, television preachers, or athletes—will always be as vulnerable as those whose image is used to proclaim it.[31]

Just as credibility issues cropped up when Buick featured Tiger Woods driving a medium-priced Buick sedan, similar credibility questions crop up when athletes immersed in hardcore competitive sports endorse a gospel that in so many ways conflicts with the images of their sporting lives. We don't expect Tiger to drive a Buick, and we don't really expect athletes to emulate the teachings of Christ or exude a gospel of love and humility when locked in desperate struggles on the court or field. "Do we really expect him [the athlete] to practice the Ten Commandments in front of 60,000 people?" asked philosopher Howard Slusher. "I think not. We might *like* him to. But we don't *expect* him to."

It may well be the case, as the director of a sport evangelism group says, that images of NFL players and other professional athletes "as fierce, rugged warriors" often belie "the tender, loving, submissive and dependent side" that Christian athletes model in their families and Bible studies. While this is probably true, it ignores the more important fact that it is precisely the *public competitive image*, not the private image, that sport evangelism aims to exploit.[32]

Finally, just as consumers must see some logical connection between an athlete's claim to fame and the product they are pitching, so, one would think, unbelievers must see some connection between an athlete's accomplishments and their own need for salvation. Why should a factory worker in Erie, Pennsylvania, decide to become a Christian because Evander Holyfield or David Robinson or Randall Cunningham is a Christian? It is, noted Owens, a logical non sequitur. The fact is that the disjunction is made necessary because the true Jesus doesn't sell all that well. Christ is, says Owens, "motivationally equivalent to Geritol," and any ad man knows "there is no point in putting out a picture of Geritol. Instead he shows a picture of a youthful, happily married couple who attribute their health and success to Geritol." Intentionally or not, sport celebrities end up selling the faith not on the merits of Christ's image or message but on the strength of their own. The connection is left to the audience's imagination.[33]

CHAPLAINS IN THE TRENCHES FOR THE LORD

Less visible but no less important in the efforts to evangelize through sports are the chaplains who give inspirational talks, lead prayers and Bible studies, and counsel injured and discouraged athletes. Chaplains serve a broad spectrum of the sports industry; there is no question that they help athletes in their personal lives, and to this extent their work is to be lauded. Most of the more than one hundred teams in the sports of football, basketball, and baseball are served by at least one chaplain. Some are full-time pastors moonlighting as spiritual advisors, while others are full-time employees of sport evangelism groups. While chaplains may not seek publicity, all necessarily bask in the reflected glory of big-time sports. The job may not come with a large salary, but there often are season tickets and a considerable amount of cachet that comes from being associated with a local professional sports franchise. It is no secret in the industry that on occasion, competition among sports-minded ministers and assorted hangers-on for the honor of giving the pregame prayer or sermon can be as ferocious as what occurs in the arena.

From one standpoint, it is not entirely clear why the Christian community needs to invest in the work of chaplains who serve big-time sports. Chaplain ministries in hospitals, retirement centers, the military, and even on college campuses are easily understood, but the rush to minister to the needs of an outrageously paid and catered-to group of elite entertainers who choose to participate in an enterprise that exacts heavy tolls on life, limb, and Christian witness is not. Usual justifications point to the peculiar pressures that face the athletic star: vulnerabilities brought on by instant riches, the demands of the press, the threat of injury, the dangers posed by sycophants, and the lure of inviting women. But unlike patients in hospitals and nursing homes who struggle with difficult circumstances beyond their control, athletes struggle with pressures, anxieties, injuries, and emotional ups and downs brought on by circumstances of their own choosing. These are all part of the bargain struck when they sign a contract or accept a scholarship. Another reason given is that, as a former president of Athletes in Action put it, "athletes get prostituted. People pay for their services with little regard for their needs." When they make it to the pinnacle of their profession, he went on, "they begin to realize there's something significant missing." This might be true for athletes, but it also can be the case for successful teachers, executives, and professionals laboring outside the stadium walls who experience the same feelings and get by without a chaplain.[34] The fact that special chaplains are needed to serve athletes is, in itself, condemnatory of big-time sports, an indictment of what we have allowed sports to become. Carl Zylstra, the late president of Dordt College, was sympathetic to the work of chaplains in hospitals and family counseling, but wondered, "why would we want to put sports in the same category as death, divorce and cancer—something you have to endure in order to survive?"[35]

There is no reason to believe that team chaplains are anything but earnest and honest in their efforts to counsel athletes in spiritual matters or help them adjust to the realities of the sports world. At the same time, sports chaplains find themselves in a delicate and compromised position, with their evangelistic mission necessarily domesticated by the conditions of their office. Working hand in glove with the sports organization and recognizing that continued access to players requires that they remain silent about the seamy underbelly of sports, chaplains to professional sports teams or big-time college teams cannot be part of any effort to redeem the soul of sports. They can no more challenge the presumptions of the coaching fraternity or the ethos of the stadium than a military chaplain can challenge the justness of a war. When a sport evangelism organization *approvingly* quotes a coach's instructions to one of its chaplains—"Just help me build winners. Do whatever you do, but that's the philosophy"—it is clear exactly for whom chaplains are working. Chaplains who are provided with offices in team headquarters, given team jerseys and tickets to games, solicited for help in recruiting players, and described by coaches as "central to our mission" waive all rights to speak truth to power. If they counsel the truth, it must be a carefully hedged truth. In this respect, the sport chaplaincy bears more than a faint resemblance to the role the church played in the post-Constantinian world, where its faithful served, not the cause of the gospel, but the interests of the empire. As the Christian community should have learned from that bracketed piece of history, once the church becomes absorbed into any dominant social or political structure, it soon loses its power to bear faithful witness or to exercise anything like an evangelical nonconformity in the world.[36]

How this can play out in the world of big-time sports was evident in a case involving former Cincinnati Bengal Anthony Muñoz, a committed Christian and one of the best ever to have played in the NFL. Shortly after joining the Bengals in 1980, Muñoz lost his motivation to play; he was calculating the toll the game would take on his body and wondering if he might serve the Lord in some other capacity. He sought counsel from a representative of a major sport evangelism organization on the night before the team's big game with Seattle. The evangelist, far from imploring Munoz to consider prayerfully whether or not he should continue to play the game, told him: "For you football can be a way to worship the Lord . . . The more aggressively you play, the more intensity you play with—the louder you're saying 'Thank You' to God . . . ask yourself out on that field tomorrow: 'How loud am I saying "Thank You" to God through my performance?'"[37] Muñoz responded with a remarkably aggressive game. The episode, given proud coverage in *Heroes of the NFL*, a book published by the organization, has the coach telling the author, "I want you to know that in all my years of involvement in football on every level, I have never seen one man dominate everybody put over him the way Anthony did yesterday."[38]

Because many chaplains are themselves products of the sporting culture, they can find it extraordinarily difficult to entertain the possibility that big-time sports may be in need of a moral cleansing. In the most extreme cases they have become ambassadors for the same Darwinian, competitive mentality that their message should be helping to modulate. This was startlingly pointed out a few years ago when a team chaplain for the Kansas City Royals, trying to defend evangelical baseball player Mike Sweeney's vicious assault on an opposing pitcher who he believed was throwing at him, caught the attention of sportswriters everywhere with his defense of Sweeney's actions: "Christ did not say turn the other cheek every time," said the chaplain. "Mike felt like he had turned the other cheek too many times. He needed to make his point. It seems to me he was thinking less about baseball and more about his faith." Is it impossible for sport team chaplains to bear faithful, unfettered witness while at the same time accepting discipline from the logic of competitive sports and the traditions of the industry? That, I suspect, depends entirely on one's view of "faithful witness."[39] Most chaplains would dismiss any suggestion that they *should* be evangelizing the institution of sport. Their aim, they would say, is the redemption of souls, not the redemption of sports. Unlike the social gospellers of the late nineteenth and early twentieth centuries, who were consumed not only with using sport to shape individual lives but with bringing sport under the empire of Christian ideas and forces, the ministries of chaplains rely on sport staying pretty much as it is.

In the end, the sport evangelists try to do too much by applying to their evangelistic efforts the same strategic calculation, grit, and muscularity that promise success in athletic competition. Lost in the blaze of glory, the flash of spectacle, and the Nike-perpetrated "just do it" mantra is an appreciation of the sheer evangelistic power of simple Christian obedience lived out in daily practices and habits, both on and off the sports field. The Apostle Paul's acknowledgment that he prefers to find his joy and pride in the very things that were his weaknesses (2 Corinthians 12:7, 9) and that he is "content, for Christ's sake, to live with weakness, contempt, persecution, hardship and frustration" (12:10) couldn't be further from the dominant evangelical athletic focus on strength, power, domination, and celebrity.[40] Not much is heard in evangelical circles today about martyrdom. It is a particularly foreign notion in big-time sports, where serious evangelism may require precisely this: the martyrdom of choosing not to help further the aims and purposes of an institution that lacks a moral compass.

This realization came late to Reggie White. No athlete had so blatantly affirmed sports as a platform for sounding the gospel as Reggie; no Christian athlete had responded so willingly to the solicitations of sports-faith organizations; none had been so prominently featured on the pages of sport evangelism literature. Yet shortly before his untimely death, White changed his views: "In many respects," he noted, "I've been prostituted. Most people that asked me to speak at their churches only did so because I played football, not because I was the great religious guru or theologian . . . I came to the realization that what God needed from me was a way of living instead of the things that I was saying." White seemed to say that only when sport becomes the embodiment of the message will sport evangelism have found its footing. Until then, the path of the truly obedient Christian life may circle around the stadium rather than to the center of the field.[41]

10

PRAYERS OUT OF BOUNDS

Homer's *Iliad* contains what modern sportscasters would call "a color commentary" of a footrace held as part of the funeral games honoring the slain warrior Patroclus. Ajax breaks out in the lead at the start, followed so closely by Odysseus that Ajax can feel him breathing down his neck as he runs "lightly and relentlessly on." It doesn't look like Odysseus has a chance. Then, coming down the home stretch, Odysseus does what many contemporary athletes would do in this situation: he prays. And his prayer is answered. The goddess Athena not only gives him a super-natural boost of adrenaline, but she also causes Ajax to slip and fall in a pile of cow dung, assuring Odysseus' victory. After the race Ajax accepted the second prize of an ox, but not graciously. As he spits out cow dung he complains: "Curse it, that goddess tripped me up. She always stands by Odysseus like a mother and helps him."

That the gods of ancient Greece would intervene in something as mundane as a footrace doesn't seem all that unusual in a society in which the gods were undependable and frivolous. But praying to the omnipotent, omniscient, omnipresent Christian God for victory has also been an accepted practice, at least since the church began its flirtations with sport. As we saw in chapter 2, when chariot racing, once despised and reviled by the early church, was "Christianized" in third-century Rome, some charioteers began visiting chapels to say prayers before the start of the races. Prayers were also a part of Siena's sixteenth-century palio where both jockeys and their horses received the priest's blessing on the day of the race, a practice continued to this day. And in England and France, vengeful, bloodthirsty knights resorted to prayer, kneeling with their "chaplains" before taking part in bone-jarring, often fatal contests in the lists.

But in no age has prayer become so woven into the fabric of sports as in the modern era. In Joseph Marbeto's 1967 survey of college and university athletes and coaches, 55 percent acknowledged praying in connection with athletic events, usually at the beginning of the game and usually to ask God to bless their performance and help them win. At church-related colleges Marbeto found the incidence of prayer even higher: 82 percent of coaches said they prayed before games, 51 percent of whom believed that their prayers affected the outcome of the contest. Today, prayer is a celebrated part of the pre- and postgame rituals of professional and college teams, as well as high school, youth-league, and church league teams. The ritual of NFL players and their opponents gathering at the center of the field to pray after the game has become so common it no longer is regarded as a curiosity by sportswriters or television cameras.[1]

Prayers in sports take many forms. Team prayers, offered in locker rooms before and after games, often are supplemented by private petitions. Pregame invocations are no longer offered over the public address system in public institutions, but they continue to be part of pregame ceremonies at many Christian schools. Some athletes regard their performances as forms of prayer in themselves; others insert gestures into the game intended to recognize God's presence. Making the sign of the cross before foul shots, pointing to heaven after hitting a home run, or kneeling in the end zone have become as familiar in big-time sports as the "high five." This trend of praying in sports has been on the rise for at least thirty years. By 1995, so many football players were praying in the end zone after scoring touchdowns that the NCAA sought to ban it under the provisions of a rule banning "showboating," defined as "any delayed, excessive or prolonged act by which a player attempts to focus attention upon himself." An enraged Jerry Falwell saw a world of difference between a player praying in the end zone and the strutting, taunting, and gloating that the rule seemed designed to target, and he brought suit against the NCAA under the provisions of the 1964 Civil Rights Act.[2]

In fairly short order the NCAA caved in, agreeing to allow end zone prayers provided the players do not kneel in such a way that it "is delayed" and "excessive," that the act "doesn't focus attention on the player," and that, in the opinion of the referees, the prayer is "spontaneous and not in the nature of a pose." Both the original and revised rulings set off a firestorm of controversy. Critics and sportswriters wanted to know, Why must these players pray *in the stadium*? What is *"excessive* prayer?" and How can such prayers *not* be focused on the player? Little did Philadelphia Eagle Herb Lusk know when he first knelt and prayed in the end zone more than thirty years ago that he was at the vanguard of a movement that would make prayer the legally and religiously preferred alternative to "boogaloos," cartwheels, and backflips.3

There is something about sports, and particularly football, that whets the appetite for prayer. The urge to pray seems to rub off on everybody. Band members and referees sometimes pray before games; so do cheerleaders and dancers who provide the entertainment. The North Carolina Top Cats dance team, for example, gather in a circle to say a pregame prayer for "health, good memories, and boundless energy" before taking the field to gyrate to hard-edged music in seldom pious routines. Fans feel the need to pray too. Soon after Ohio State University hired outspoken Christian Jim Tressel to coach its football team, a local Columbus church posted a message on the church marquee asking the public to "Pray for the OSU football program and Jim Tressel." A market for sport prayer fetishes has emerged: internet access and a credit card will get you Christmas ornaments decorated with "The Coach's Prayer," "The Athlete's Prayer," "The Golfer's Prayer," "The Fisherman's Prayer," the "Coach's Prayer Plaque" (with laminated front and fancy frame for $26.95), and a T-shirt emblazoned with "A Baseball Coach's Prayer."4

Precisely how engrained prayer is in the sports culture surfaced a few years ago after the Supreme Court handed down its decision banning invocations at public high school football games, a venerable tradition at southern high schools. The reaction of fans was organized, swift, and bitter. Nationwide protests erupted. Ad hoc groups such as "No Pray, No Play" mobilized. The families who had sued the Santa Fe, Texas, school district to stop pregame prayers reportedly became the object of death threats. In Hattiesburg, Mississippi, 4,500 fans stood at a high school football game and recited the Lord's Prayer in unison; 25,000 attended a similar rally in a football stadium in Asheville, North Carolina. A popular New Jersey high school football coach, forbidden by his principal to lead

pregame prayers for his team, quit his job in protest and became a *cause
célèbre*. The president of FCA blasted the court's ruling, declaring it hostile "to all things religious in public life," and promised that athletes and
fans everywhere would continue to pray.[5]

In truth, most of these invocations had been marginally sectarian at
best, severely hedged by sensitivities to religiously pluralistic audiences.
Precisely how generic they could be came to light when officials at the
University of Oklahoma, after consulting with their lawyers, decided to
permit the local Presbyterian minister to continue to offer an invocation before football games because, in their opinion, his prayers weren't
"identifiable with any religious faith." Similarly, when the Santa Fe school
district pled its case before the court to allow prayer to continue to be
offered at its football games, it did so not by arguing that its pregame
prayers were fitting tributes to a Christian God or meaningful expressions
of athletes' faith, but on grounds that they were "civic and non-sectarian"
rituals intended to "solemnize the event," "promote good citizenship,"
and "establish the appropriate environment for competition."[6]

PRAGMATIC PRAYERS

A coarse pragmatism flavors much of the prayer in the world of big-
time sports. Some pregame prayers by coaches and athletes do not seem
intended to express, awaken, and sustain piety as much as to ready the
team for competition. Former Washington Redskins coach George Allen,
a man touted by sport-faith organizations yet uniformly described by
those who knew him as pathologically obsessed with winning, insisted
on a locker room prayer on game days because "it does more to produce togetherness and mutual respect than anything else I've found in
21 years of coaching." Grant Teaff, former Baylor head football coach and
executive director of the American Football Coaches Association, suggested that the reason "well over 50 percent of the coaches have prayers
before a game" is to strengthen team bonds. "To take that knee," he said,
"is such a feeling of unity."[7]

Advocating prayer as a way of solidifying team unity—even
if it works—seems to miss the purpose of prayer: it is only a shade
removed from recommending it as a means for lowering blood pressure or improving flexibility in the knees. Praying for unity in the spiritual life, of course, is an entirely different matter. Unity was the focus
of Jesus' longest prayer and of the Apostle Paul's repeated urgings in
his letters to young churches. But there is a vast difference between

praying to instill unity of team spirit and praying for the kind of spiritual unity that Paul had in mind. When Paul exhorted the Ephesians to unity, he was not trying to psych them up for a weekend track meet against the church at Corinth.

In recent years, sport psychologists have become interested in using prayer "as a type of pre-competition awareness training that helps center the performer and alleviate[s] performance-related anxieties." Athletic prayers have also been pushed as a way of checking the profligate lifestyles of players that hamper the team's performance and reflect badly on the reputation of the team. "Why not see prayers on the fifty-yard line [in NFL games] as evidence of an antidote to the social irresponsibility that professional athletes too often display?" asked a writer in the Catholic journal *Commonweal*. But prayer organized around ulterior motives seems too easily exploited, something apparent when the Labrador Tigers, an Australian rules football club, signed a prayer contract with the Christian Community Church on the Gold Coast. After being repeatedly embarrassed by reports of the sexual misconduct of several of its stars, the team signed a contract with the church: the team would require team members to attend at least one church service each season. In return, the church would provide a pastor who would agree to pray for the team's success.[8]

Prayers offered in the foxhole-like atmosphere of the locker room can fade seamlessly into the coach's pep talk. In his ethnography of Texas high school football, H. G. Bissinger describes the Permian High School football coach's pregame prayer, which came just after a private session with defensive ends in which the coach told them to "knock the hell out of" the opposing team and to "put some helmets on" the opponents' star player. Gathering his players around him in the locker room, he told them that "a supreme, fanatical, wild-eyed effort" would be required to win the game, and then, abruptly, he knelt on the floor: "Help them, dear God, to play to the very best of their ability. Help them to play with some quality that they've never played with before, give them that something extra that they've never had to call up before."[9]

Such artful and dramatic uses of prayers in the locker room, clearly designed to elevate competitive intensity, are difficult to take seriously. They are too reminiscent of the sport-crazed chaplain in Peter Gent's novel *North Dallas Forty*. Gent, a former Dallas Cowboy, apparently wrote from experience in sketching an especially satirical vignette of the sport minister's locker room prayer, whose "amen" is quickly followed by a player's vulgar exhortation to violence. "It's Ok," says the chaplain, "I know how you feel." Pat Conroy includes a similar vignette in *The Great Santini*. Conroy, a former collegiate athlete, describes the transformation that came over Coach Spinks ("a generalissimo in the land of the jock") just before a big game. "I want you to feast on some medium rare West Charleston High School *****. I want us to win. Win. Win." Then his face suddenly mellowed, "his eyes glistened, his gaze became beatific. 'Let us pray,' he said and all the heads on the team dropped floorward as though they were puppets strung on the same wire."[10] Some athletic prayers seem inauthentic because they are so crassly opportunistic. God may not be worth centering one's life around, but it's good to know that he's there in a pinch when needed. "I don't pray daily," NASCAR star Dale Earnhardt Jr. told a reporter, "but I ask God for strength in certain situations . . . *Most of the time right before qualifying*" (emphasis added). The disconnect between the way many coaches wax religious in the locker room and the short shrift given to religion in their private lives led curmudgeonly former Michigan State University football coach Duffy Daugherty to suggest that "all those coaches who require pre-game prayers by their players ought to be made to go to church once each week."[11]

Against the backdrop of money-grubbing, scandal-ridden, big-time sports, any sort of prayer, any acknowledgment of a higher power, can seem like a breath of fresh air. Even a coarse blend of God, guts, glory, and profanity, some might say, is better than no prayer at all. Some evangelicals might even see in these prayers, however facetious and hypocritical, the specter of common grace. But it is hard not to view entreaties inflamed with zealotry and war rhetoric as downright spiritual fraud. When Jesus taught his disciples the Lord's Prayer—by far the most popular prayer in locker rooms—he didn't intend it to mesh with the athletic jingoism invoked by testosterone-fueled gladiators as a way of psyching themselves up for the mock wars that pass for some of our most popular forms of sporting entertainment.

Such prayers stand in sharp contrast to the "heart attitude" that Lutheran theologian Olle Hallesby said God accepts as prayer: "faith" and "helplessness." "Only he who is helpless," said Hallesby, "can truly pray." At prayer, he said, "God crushes our self-conceit and self-sufficiency." Encounters with "the wholly other," said renowned theologian Rudolf Otto, leave one awestruck by majesty, overcome with a diminished sense of self, a feeling of littleness, weakness, and dependence. But while such a disposition may be fine for a quiet morning's meditation, it isn't likely to serve the pragmatic ends of athletes who have put on their "game faces." Conjuring up a diminished sense of self in the dressing rooms of sport palaces built as testaments to the glories of human power, strength, and self-sufficiency is all too likely to lead to a diminished score.[12]

Sometimes the pragmatic perceptions of prayer in the athletic world are so elementally twisted that one must laugh if only to keep from crying. Former New York Yankee Reggie Jackson, known for his overbearing persona and his knack at elevating his game in playoff and World Series competition, waxed theological to reporters on the benefits of prayer after belting three home runs in game 6 of the 1977 World Series: "Man is not big enough to handle these intense pressure situations by himself," said Jackson. "In a no-deposit, no-return game like this, you have to find some sort of way to key down, to find an inner peace so that you can let your native talent express itself . . . I ask the Big Man Upstairs for a good pitch to hit, and then whatever happens happens." Like many athletes and coaches who pray, Jackson was not a particularly religious man, but after hitting an especially important home run on the way to winning the World Series, he admitted to having sent up a prayer in the on-deck circle. "I told Him," said Jackson, "that if He let me hit a home run, I'd tell everyone He did it."[13]

But Jackson was not any further off base than Jerry Falwell, whose sport fanaticism prompted some bizarre comments, not only about prayer but about the entire relationship between sports and faith. He once told a *Sports Illustrated* reporter that one method he used to recruit pitchers for the school baseball team was to invite coach and former Yankees great Bobby Richardson to be a guest on his television show and ask him, "Bobby, if God could grant you one wish, wouldn't He send you a 6'4" left handed pitcher who can throw the ball 100 miles per hour and know where it's going?" The reporter asked, "But what if Richardson said he would ask God for world peace instead?" "Well, that would be all right too," said Falwell. "Either that or the pitcher."[14]

THE TRIVIALITY OF ATHLETIC PRAYER

Committed Christian athletes and coaches seek the proper role for prayer in sports against this backdrop of concocted piety. For most evangelical athletes, prayer is part and parcel of their holistic spiritual lives. Since more than two-thirds of evangelicals pray daily, it is hardly surprising that athletes of their number also pray before, during, and after athletic contests.[15] But the athletic setting isn't quite like most other settings in which evangelicals pray. One difference is that sport, a derivative of play, is what some philosophers call "an activity of maintaining an illusion." "Play," says philosopher Kenneth Schmitz, "reveals itself as a trans-natural, fragile, limited perfection." Its rules, traditions, and customs are human devices fabricated for the sake of our amusement. Former Commissioner of Major League Baseball and Renaissance scholar Bart Giammati once described sport as being based on "a practical joke," "a conscious agreement to enjoy, a pleasurable self-delusion." Sport spectacles manipulate images and create drama much like that served up in novels and movies; it is not the drama of real life. We play sports as if they had ultimate importance, in a world some have described as being "outside and beyond the world of nature," in a state of mind that philosopher Eugene Fink called "non-pathological schizophrenia."[16] To suggest that pretending is essential to the playing of games does not mean that athletes don't or shouldn't play seriously. Philosopher William Morgan says this "set-apartness" of the sports world enables players "to telescope all their attention, effort, and concentration and to summon as much strength and energy as they can muster to meet the competitive challenges presented to them."[17]

Can prayers offered in the context of this set-apart, illusory world be taken seriously? One answer posed by religion scholar Joseph Price is that prayer and play may not be fundamentally different phenomena. Price points out that both are set off from real life, both are voluntary, both are bound by spatial and temporal limitations, and "both seek to contact the Wholly Other in order to refresh, sustain, and nurture the spirit." But viewed another way, the aim of prayer in sport is to puncture the bubble of the illusion of the game: it represents an umbilical cord to the serious world of the athlete's faith. The more important question, it seems to me, is whether or not prayer, when interjected into the world of play, can ever escape the illusory, make-believe nature of sports themselves. Richard Wood, former dean of Yale Divinity School, touched on this point when he said, "To suggest that God has a direct involvement in athletic contests trivializes the whole notion of God's involvement with the world." "It doesn't seem odd that God would know in detail what happens in football games," said Wood; "What seems to me odd is that God would care."[18]

Most evangelicals—especially athletes and coaches—would be less willing than Wood to say that God doesn't "care" about our games; in fact, many would even argue that he takes a direct hand in determining the winner. According to popular evangelical author Philip Yancey, nothing is too trivial to bring to God in prayer: "Everything about me—my thoughts, my motives, my choices, my moods—attracts God's interest." But the critical question is not whether God cares or is present at big-time athletic contests but whether or not the unfolding of events in a sports contest are matters sufficiently important in the divine scheme of things to be prayed over. Asking whether or not God *could* intervene in an athletic contest is not the same as asking whether it is appropriate to ask him to intervene.[19]

Answering the question is difficult for evangelicals whose notions about the purpose and appropriateness of prayer are largely conditioned by their own perceptions and love of entertainment sport. Passionate and prayerful sport fans, for example, find it nearly impossible to imagine that God is any less interested in popular sports than they are. Surely the outcome of the World Series weighs heavier on the mind of God than the outcome of a church league volleyball game or a backyard game of badminton—because most of *us* are more interested in the former than the latter. If NBC is willing to pay $600 million through 2012 to telecast the Super Bowl, surely God must take a $600 million interest as well. Less culturally conditioned competitive events, by contrast, are deemed to be played without God giving much notice. Evangelicals may feel a proud glow when, in the intermissions of violence of a football game, players kneel in the end zone, but had Joey Chestnut, winner of the 2009 annual Nathan's Famous Fourth of July International Hot Dog Eating Contest, prayed before polishing off sixty-eight hot dogs in twelve minutes or, after ingesting the final bun, knelt to thank God for helping him find that additional niche in his stomach, it would have given most of them indigestion.

The point is not that sports can't be appropriate places for prayer; it is that the settings and circumstances that surround most popular sports do not seem well suited for prayer. Perhaps that is what guided the Fifth Circuit Court of Appeals in its 1999 decision to allow prayers at high school graduation ceremonies but not sports events, because, unlike sports, graduation ceremonies were considered "singularly serious." Athletic prayers would seem more fittingly placed in the context of what Josef Pieper has described as a feast. In his book *In Tune With the World: A Theory of Festivity*, Pieper shows how even secular festivals—properly celebrated, and springing from "the praise of God in ritual worship"—can be important occasions for deepening spiritual lives and focusing participants' visions on eternity. But the festival succeeds, says Pieper, only when we accept the divine gift lying behind the busyness of the festival.[20] Over forty years ago, Pieper saw evidence that the festival was in steep decline, gradually being replaced with what he called "pseudo-festivals." As Pieper described them, pseudofestivals sound a great deal like our sports spectacles: "virtually purchasable surrogates which convey a counterfeit of the things that can be had only with true festivals." Instead of rapture, oblivion of ills, and a sense of harmony with the world, our sport spectacles give us cheap thrills, noisy pomp, and titillation. Almost without thinking, participants become enamored with the tinsel on the package rather than the festive gift itself. In place of unity with and assent to the Creator, our games thrive on combat and partisanship, borrowing, as Kurt Eisner has put it, "the means from war and the mood from festivals."[21]

Prayer at a festival as Pieper described it would be a natural thing; prayers at the pseudofestivals of our sports spectacles can come off like the proverbial brown shoes mistakenly worn with a black tuxedo, fundamentally out of sync with the partisan, militant spirit of the stadium. I once heard a Christian athlete argue that prayers offered in conjunction with sports spectacles can be a good check on sport's excess, materialism, and violence. It reminded me of a tack taken recently by the owner of Bucharest's professional soccer team, who played hymns over the stadium loudspeakers before games in a futile attempt to reduce hooliganism and on-field violence. Neither praying nor adding a few hymns is likely to convert a pseudofestival into the real thing.[22]

In fact, experience enables us to predict with a fair degree of accuracy that precisely the opposite will happen. Pseudofestivals have a way of rubbing off on religion in the most remarkable ways. Sportswriters' humorous but sacrilegious characterizations of the mural of Christ with upraised arms that looms over the Notre Dame football stadium as "Touchdown Jesus" is but one example. A theologian at the school ventured that if God did intervene in human affairs it probably would be in something more important than a football game, adding that he thought praying for one's team was okay "as long as these things aren't taken too seriously. Once it's taken seriously, then you are on dangerous ground."[23]

But discerning the line between the serious and the nonserious isn't always easy. The hype of a big game can push even the most sober-minded cleric over the edge. Some years ago, a popular evangelical minister from

Pittsburgh delivered the pregame sermonette and prayer for the Houston Oilers before their upset of the heavily favored Steelers. Later in the year, when the Oilers returned to the city for a critical playoff game against the Steelers, the team again asked him to give the locker room prayer. He declined, telling them, "This time my heart is with the Steelers. The Oilers aren't losers anymore. They've proven themselves and *don't need me*" (emphasis added). The Steelers won the playoff game, thus extending the minister's streak to 2–0. When a well-regarded evangelical minister becomes the object of a tug of war between two professional football teams, we get an idea of how frivolous religion and prayers in sport can be. Even Yancey seems prepared to accept certain limits on God's patience with our praying: "Surely, some prayers go unanswered," he says, "because they are frivolous." Among the frivolous prayers he mentions are those offered by athletes.[24]

Sport's erosion of the serious foundations of prayer reached something of a crescendo when silly invocations became the rage in the 1970s. In a particularly noteworthy case, Reverend Richard Bailar, minister of a United Church of Christ in Miami, offered this prayer over the stadium loudspeakers in a televised game between the Miami Dolphins and the Cincinnati Bengals in 1974:

> Creator God: Father and Mother of us all, we give You thanks for the joy and excitement occasioned by this game. We pray for the physical well-being of all the gladiators who run the gamut of gridiron battle tonight . . . but, knowing that the tigers are voracious beasts of prey, we ask You to be especially watchful over our gentle dolphins. Limit, if You will, the obfuscations of [sportscaster Howard] Cosell's acidulous tongue, so that he may describe this night truly and grammatically as it is . . . A great game, in a great city, played before Your grateful children, on whom we ask peace and shalom. Amen.[25]

Bailar's prayer brought scathing criticism from evangelicals across the country; some described it as unadulterated blasphemy. Not all fans, however, thought the prayer inappropriate. It was, after all, interrupted by a total of twenty-six seconds of applause, and Bailar was showered with letters and phone calls, most of them supportive. His photo was displayed in sports bars; he was stopped on the street for autographs and flooded with requests for copies of the prayer, "all of which," said Bailar, "says something about the sterility of religion and idolatry of sports in

America." A writer to the Miami Herald called it a mockery of prayer, betting that "the invocation didn't make a dent in the mind of God." There was a time when I would have agreed with the writer, but now I wonder if rather than a mockery of prayer, it pointed to the mockery of most prayers offered at bombastic athletic spectacles. Silly, irreverent, and banal, the prayer now seems to me to have been the perfect supplication for the spiritually vacuous events transpiring in the stadium that night, and perhaps that is what Bailar's prayer was pointing to all along.

GESTURES, PRAYER CIRCLES, AND END ZONE PRAYERS

The ebbing of public invocations at sports events has brought with it a perceptible rise in on-field prayer gestures by athletes. These individually crafted gestures (chest thumps followed by index fingers pointed skyward, bowing the head or kneeling in the end zone, etc.) are tailor-made for sport spectacles. Performed in other contexts the same gestures would lead to a great deal of head-scratching. We wouldn't quite know what to make, for example, of an evangelical professor who knelt in front of his class or pointed skyward when students performed well on his or her exam. These gestures are almost always enacted when the events of the game have turned in the athlete's favor. Rarely does the baseball player who has committed an error, the football player who has dropped a pass, or the basketball player who has fouled an opponent exhibit them. These gestures are not supplications, confessions, or pleadings; mostly they are reflexive gestures of joy.

Some Christians view these gestures as "witness," but others regard them as an inelegant mixture of teeth-gritting competition, violence, self-promotion, and a religion that trifles with the deeper messages of the gospel. "Somehow that post-game [prayer] huddle leaves me feeling uncomfortable," said former Cincinnati Bengal and sports broadcaster Cris Collinsworth. For every Christian who believes such demonstrations advance the faith, scores of others regard them as inappropriate intrusions of a player's religious preferences into a secular event. "In my faith as a Christian," said Hall of Fame quarterback Terry Bradshaw in 2004, "I am not called to put on a display and call attention to myself . . . I don't look at [an on-field gesture] as religion, I look at it as selfish." Even Tom Landry had reservations about on-field prayers: "I'm afraid these little 'God helped me score a touchdown' and 'God helps me be a winner' testimonials mislead people and belittle God."[26]

If the intent of these demonstrative gestures is to give witness to the players' faith, some rethinking might be in order. Such gestures seem just as likely to alienate as convert. Even sportswriters and narrators sympathetic to evangelical athletes have grown weary of what they see as two-bit theologizing and staged piety. One television reporter quipped: "There's a rule with me. You get one 'I thank the Lord Jesus Christ.' The next one we're going back to the booth. I'm not waiting for the director to cut away." This poor reception by the media shouldn't necessarily be interpreted as the price the Christian bears for costly witness. Theologian Bryan Stone's assessment of those who regard trendy T-shirts or witty bumper stickers as "witness" is just as aptly applied to public sport prayers: "If those around us take offense at our witness," said Stone, "it is not because they have taken seriously the import of our beliefs; they just find us annoying."[27]

On-field or on-court religious gestures also can come off as seeming too theatrical, too showy, reflecting what theologian Carl Henry called "the righteousness of ostentation" exhibited in the prayer of the Pharisee that Christ condemned. There is no reason to believe that Christ's words—"When thou prayest, enter into thy room and when thou has shut thy door, pray to thy Father in secret" (Matthew 6:5)—are any less incumbent on modern athletes than on his ancient followers. Regardless of the athlete's sincerity or intent, prayers and gestures offered in full view of the crowd and television audiences are inherently demonstrative, intended to "be seen by men." "When a person kneels in the end zone," said an NCAA attorney, "nobody but that person and God knows whether he is praying or not. But *everyone* is looking at him and that is the point."[28]

Defenders of public athletic prayers see Jesus' admonition to his followers to "let your light shine before men" (Matthew 5:16) as softening his injunction to avoid showy prayers. Yet the verses appear to point to two different sins, cowardice and vanity. To pray as a way of seeking attention is vanity, yet not to bear witness for fear of harm or punishment is cowardice. A few years ago, when NFL players who met at the center of the field to pray after games were coming under criticism, an evangelical seminarian tried to make the case for praying by suggesting that the players were modern-day counterparts to first-century martyrs "who were forced to participate in the Roman Coliseum games. Picture that while crowds roared, the believers bowed and prayed as a witness to their faith.

Do I think such an action would have been approved by the apostles and leaders of the early church? I suspect it would." But professional athletes are hardly martyrs; they play because they want to play, and by praying they don't risk a serious threat of persecution. Thus choosing to pray can hardly be labeled martyrdom, and choosing not to pray isn't cowardice. Under the circumstances, the athlete seems lured far more by the temptation to vanity than the temptation to cowardice.[29]

Whether athletes intend it to be so or not, their public prayers lend Christian sanction to the spectacle. Their prayers may aim at glorifying God, but as writer Jason Kelly so aptly pointed out, they seem just as likely to "[glorify] the game itself by invoking the name of the Lord in an otherwise insignificant instance." In a gem-filled little book titled *Praying at Burger King*, Richard Mouw describes his well-established custom of asking the blessing for his food, whether at home or in the public environment of a fast food restaurant. Part of the reason he does it, says Mouw, is to acknowledge God's presence; even in a noisy Burger King "there is indeed a God whose mercy reaches out to me." Mouw's prayers differ in an important way from those offered up in the arena. They are private prayers, offered in a public but largely inattentive environment. Mouw's prayers aren't part of the show; they don't even indirectly glorify French fries or hamburgers. But the prayers of athletes aren't private; offered at critical points of the game with television cameras rolling, they become inseparable from the spectacle itself.[30] Dietrich Bonhoeffer knew that prayer, even *private* prayer, carries the risk that the supplicant will become "the one who at the same time prays and looks on." To his way of thinking, prayer should be "the supreme instance of the hidden Christian life," and for this reason "it is never given to self-display, whether before God, ourselves, or other people." What Bonhoeffer would have thought of prayer offered up by devout athletes in the heat of battle before teeming crowds and television audiences is anybody's guess, but it seems likely that he would have suggested that they save it for the locker room.[31]

PRAYING FOR SAFETY

In interviews with evangelical athletes, Daniel Czech and his associates found that prayers for safety were among the most common pregame petitions, and for good reason. The dangers facing athletes can be very real. Race car drivers, for example, are specialists in foxhole praying. Says veteran NASCAR driver Mark Martin, "One of the reasons there are so many Christians involved in motor sports versus some other sports is that we deal with risk. The risk factor is a little bit higher in our sport than some sports. We understand that. And I personally want to be prepared."[32] Athletes know that fear can distract, inhibit, and even paralyze their responses, increasing the possibility that they will be injured or killed, and prayer plays a role in suppressing that reality. The cliff divers of Acapulco know how dangerously irrational it is to dive into a narrow channel of water one hundred and fifty feet below; that is why they kneel at the shrine of the Virgin of Guadalupe before their plunge. The same fear drives football players, boxers, hockey players, bullfighters, and rodeo bull riders to their knees before they enter arenas where they will push their bodies beyond reasonable limits or expose themselves to sometimes unimaginable risks.

Surely God, if he chooses to, can protect athletes, just as he can protect the person who elects to wrestle alligators or walk a tightrope stretched over a deep gorge. But the issue is whether or not it is appropriate for athletes to ask God to save them from the predictable results stemming from their own willful, dangerous actions. Asking God to keep you safe before running onto a football field where injuries are virtually assured borders on an unbiblical testing of God, like asking him to prevent the playing out of the natural chain of cause and effect. Prayer is always morally conditioned, says ethicist R. E. O. Smith. Prayers for forgiveness, for example, are unlikely to be answered unless the supplicants are themselves forgiving. So too, answers to the athlete's prayers for protection may be morally conditioned by their having done all they can do to avoid that which they fear. In some situations, this may mean refusing to play those sports that pose the greatest physical risks. If the old adage is true that "God helps those who help themselves," does it not follow that God will refuse to help those who don't help themselves?[33]

My point here is not to overlook the many injuries that occur in sports that can be truly defined as "accidents," nor am I diminishing the physical and psychological suffering athletes endure as a result of those injuries. But I do wonder if, in some sense, those who take unreasonable risks in order to meet the demands of brutal games waive their right to ask God to protect them, or to come to their aid after being injured. Only Sportianity can try to make theological sense out of players joined in a circle asking God to save the life of Curtis Williams as he lay comatose on the football field at the University of Washington after a helmet-to-helmet collision left him paralyzed and destined for an early death eighteenth months later.[34] Such scenes are so breathtaking in their drama and so moving in the sympathy shown by players and coaches that the fundamental ethical point can be easily overlooked. Prayers looked upon as insurance policies are dubious at best, but even an insurance company won't offer loss protection unless the insured does his or her part by following safe practices. And if it seems presumptuous for athletes to ask God to protect them before they engage in sports known to be injurious, it seems doubly presumptuous for them to ask God to heal the injured party. And it seems triply presumptuous for them to return immediately to the same activity which led to the injury.

Praying to Win

When then unheralded golfer Zach Johnson was interviewed following his surprising victory at the 2007 Masters, he touchingly gave Jesus "all the credit," tearfully mentioning that "Jesus was with me every step," a comment that gave rise to a few irreverent jokes on the Internet about the strict "no robes and sandals" policy at Augusta National. A few months later, after the glow of winning had dimmed, Johnson thought better of his remarks, declaring, "I don't know if [God] has anything to do with golf."[35] The proper way for evangelical athletes to position winning in their theological zeitgeist has long been a source of debate. Does God control events of a game like he controls other events in the universe? Does he really determine who will win a game? Is it appropriate to pray for victory? For the Christian athlete, such questions are important because they arise with the advent of every game.

Many of those immersed in the subculture of sport find it unthinkable that God does not dictate each turn of events in a game, including picking the winner. If veteran St. Louis Rams All-Pro receiver Isaac Bruce is to be believed, his team's victory in the 2000 Super Bowl was secured days before the game was played, "down on our knees praying for it." After catching the game-winning pass, he told the media, "That wasn't me. That was all God . . . I had to make an adjustment on the ball, and God did the rest." (And "the rest" seemed to have included blinding referees to the fact that the Rams illegally had an extra man on the field during the play.) Television audiences watching Boston's defeat of the Yankees in Game 6 of the 2004 American League playoffs were witnesses to the heroics of pitcher Curt Schilling, who continued to pitch despite blood soaking his sock as it oozed from stitches related to a recent ankle surgery. Afterwards Schilling told the assembled media: "I've got to say, I became a Christian seven years ago, and I've never in my life been touched by God as I was tonight. Tonight was God's work on the mound."[36] And who can forget the confident prediction of former champion Evander Holyfield before his celebrated fight with Mike Tyson in 1997? "There is no way I cannot win. I believe in God, so I will surely beat Tyson." As it turned out, Holyfield won because Tyson, not in a prayerful mood, bit a large chunk out of Holyfield's ear and was disqualified.[37]

Over and against such sentiment are the opinions of an increasing number of Christian athletes, though probably still a minority, who are aware that glib references to God's involvement in games can come off as theologically naïve. They go out of their way to set reporters straight on the issue. Former New York Yankee Chad Curtis, for example, told reporters that devotional meetings among team members are not to try to get favor from God on the field: "I mean God doesn't care how many wins I have. That's not a concern of his. What matters is that I'm being a good servant to him, and I'm helping other people." Even some sport evangelists see it this way. "I think God could care less who wins or loses," remarked James Mitchell, former Tennessee Titans chaplain and national director of outreach for Pro Athletes Outreach. "God may intervene at times when it truly matters—when Hitler threatens to conquer the world—but He doesn't concern Himself with boys' games."[38]

A few years ago, a *Sports Illustrated* article asked several theologians if "God cares who wins the Super Bowl." Richard Mouw said that he doesn't believe that God is aloof from it all and that he cares about how people play the game, but he cautioned against "identifying God with any partisan cause." "God isn't a Michigan or Notre Dame fan," said Mouw.[39] But Joseph C. Hough, president of the faculty at Union Theological Seminary, called prayers for victory "religiously offensive" and "anti-Christian at [their] core." Such prayers "make God look immoral and arbitrary," he says. A more stringent judgment was rendered by Christopher Evans and William Herzog, authors of *The Faith of Fifty Million*. "To believe that God grants divine favor to a specific individual or team," they wrote, "is not only nonsensical, but a form of the worst marriage between pseudo-faith and self-centeredness."[40]

Theological opinions notwithstanding, it is extraordinarily difficult for athletes, whose training, sacrifice, planning, and practice are all directed at winning, to imagine that God doesn't share their concern about the outcome. Despite familiar evangelical platitudes that the "most important thing is to play to the best of my ability" or to "glorify God with

my effort," winning remains the object of every athlete's training, practice, and sacrifice. Being a perennial loser won't get you a scholarship, a
trophy, or an invitation to the church supper to give a talk. It won't get
you on the cover of *Sports Illustrated*; it won't even get you on the covers
of *Sports Spectrum* or *Sharing the Victory*, evangelical magazines whose
writers adamantly, though ironically, emphasize that Christian athletes
don't place a premium on winning. Suggesting to the dedicated athlete
that God isn't interested in the outcome of a sport contest is tantamount
to saying that he isn't interested in the full fruition of the athlete's sacrifice, training, and practice. If so, we might wonder if he is equally uninterested in the fruition of the teacher's, the businessman's, the plumber's,
and the author's labors. And if sports are "boy's games," in which God has
little interest as Chaplain Mitchell suggested, how is it possible for evangelical athletes to glorify him with their talents through participation in
something in which he has no interest?

Sorting out answers to these questions requires theological competence well beyond that of the author, but a few observations here may
help frame the issue. Sports, as already described, are derivatives of play
and as such are part of an illusory experience. Athletes deal with manufactured obstacles, manufactured goals, manufactured struggles, and
manufactured hardships. Praying for victory in games is tantamount to
asking that the illusion unfold in a predetermined way—all in all, not
much different from praying that the heroine will be saved in the last
pages of a novel. Uncertainty and adventure are central elements in the
illusion; not knowing how a game will turn out, for example, is central
to the sport experience itself. Arguably, the spirit of uncertainty is part of
the divine gift of play. Praying for victory belies an unhealthy impatience
with this gift; like reading the end of the novel before reading the beginning, victory prayers aim at shortcutting the adventure and robbing the
game of the play spirit. Of course uncertainty remains because victory
prayers are not always answered, but it is the spirit behind the prayers
that counts, and praying for victory reflects a dubious spirit, an unwill-
ingness to trust in God for a good game simply by taking the best of what
the game offers. Also, praying for victory disregards the possibility that it
is in the adventure of the game that God speaks, not in its conclusion.

Religion professor Joseph Price has suggested that connecting athletic success and divine favor may represent a reintegration of athletic and
religious rituals, a "restoration of metaphysical and mystical impulses
that generated or characterized early forms of play and expressions of

piety." I would be the first to applaud the revitalization of genuine religion in sport, but I am not convinced that connecting athletic success to divine favor will do this, nor am I convinced that the type of sports that fill our arenas and stadia nurture the play spirit that Price's vision rests upon. Over seventy years ago, Huizinga lamented the demise of the play spirit, a development he labeled "puerilism"—a blend of "adolescence and barbarity" that (among other things) manifests itself in "the insatiable thirst for trivial recreation and crude sensationalism." Authentic play is a perfect place for authentic prayer; play can inspire and nurture prayer. As Price notes, play can be a kind of prayer in its own right. But as history has shown, puerilistic play has a way of evoking puerilistic prayer.[41]

Prayers for victory inevitably come to be interpreted within the agonistic context of the sport. Prayers offered by one team invariably come off as partisan appeals to a partisan God, set off against competing prayers by its opponents. This begs the adolescent image of God as a fan with loyalties to both teams, caught in the middle and agonizing over which set of prayers he will honor. Even uneducated Beau Jack, lightweight boxing champion of the 1940s, understood the futility of this. Asked if he ever prayed to win, he answered: "I pray nobody get hurt." "Don't you ever pray to win?" asked the interviewer. "No," he said, "I would never do that. Suppose I pray to win. The other boy, he pray to win, too. Then what God gonna do?"[42] Such an elementary conception of a God torn between team loyalties reduces him to a "superfan" whose interest in the event, like that of spectators, is wrapped up only in its conclusions. It overlooks the possibility that God may not buy into the antagonisms that frame our play, that his interests might center on the experience of playing rather than on its conclusion, that he is more interested in sport as a way of *being* than a way of *doing*, or that his entire conception of sport and play may be foreign to that prescribed by the NCAA rule book or ESPN. God surely is present at our games, but how they end may not even be a blip on his celestial radar screen.

The uncomfortable reality of victory prayers is that they are backdoor requests for your opponents' defeat. Sport competition is zero-sum in nature; it is impossible to pray for your own victory without implicitly petitioning for your opponent's defeat, a request that is difficult to imagine being honored in the reality of war, and much less in the illusory, leisure-time world of sports. Even where stakes to the winners are low, winning brings with it an elevated reputation, a boost to self-esteem, and a sense of having proved oneself. Asking God to bless you with these socially derived fruits of victory while he inflicts discouragement and disappointment on others makes sense only in the minds of those whose worldviews have been contorted by incessant competition. This hasn't stopped some athletes and coaches from directly petitioning God to hinder their opponents' efforts. One of several notable cases occurred during the 1991 Super Bowl when a group of New York Giants knelt on the sidelines while their opponents prepared to kick what turned out to be the game-winning field goal. They later admitted that they had been praying for kicker Scott Norwood to miss. Regardless of their efficacy, prayers for victory or prayers for the defeat of one's opponents are dubious from an ethical standpoint, something driven home a few years ago in a thought-provoking article titled "Prayers for Assistance as Unsporting Behavior."[43]

Viewed from this angle, praying to win seems an insufferably selfish act, only a shade removed from praying, like Janis Joplin, for a new Mercedes Benz. If such prayers aren't answered, it is because they are unanswerable. The idea that God would grant the wishes of athletes with an aching need to be recognized won't sit well with evangelicals mindful of the cross believers are called to bear. But victory prayers make a great deal of sense to proponents of the prosperity gospel, which thrives in the world of sports. One of these is former San Francisco 49er Darnell Walker, who believes that "it's never His will for us to lose. He wants us all to prosper."[44]

Without doubting God's Old Testament promises or New Testament verses promising believers that what they pray for in faith they shall receive, one can question whether God is likely to align himself with such sublimated selfishness. Every deathbed, every war, every famine and plague, and especially Christ's unanswered pleas in Gethsemane are reminders that prayer isn't the infallible gimmick so often celebrated by "name it and claim it" prosperity gospel proponents. Evangelical theologian Carl Henry called prayer "the great school of selflessness" that "militates against selfish motives," and few things seem quite as selfish as praying for victory to assuage a thirst for recognition. Evans and Herzog view such prayers in even harsher terms: "The very fact that so many contemporary athletes see God's hand as the primary reason why they hit a home run, or make an impossible catch, goes to show that Augustine and other theologians were right to suggest that the essence of our 'fallen nature' is personal selfishness: perhaps the pattern of athletes invoking the Deity every time they win is just another illustration of original sin."[45]

The Lord's Prayer—the most popular prayer of the locker room—has been called "relentlessly plural." By reinforcing community and solidarity of life through such plural phrases such as "*our* daily bread," "*our* debts," and "*our* debtors," it "vivifies the social spirit and militates against selfish motives." Given that it was Christ's model for prayer, we might safely say that Christians should not be part of any human social invention that makes it impossible to pray for the benefit and welfare of others. For the athlete, the social spirit of the prayer should extend to everyone, not simply one's teammates but to opponents as well. But intercessory prayer—asking God to act on behalf of one's opponents as well as oneself—has not figured prominently in locker room piety because such prayers are necessarily hedged by the agonistic structure of sports. Christian athletes may truly want the best for their opponents and may pray, as many do, that their competitors will come out of the game uninjured or even that they may play well. But it is extraordinarily difficult—perhaps impossible—for them to ask the Lord to allow their opponents to win. Sport may be the one situation besides war where this is the case.[46]

The reason is plain enough. It would be hopelessly cynical for athletes to pray that their opponents be granted the victory while working their hardest to prevent that from occurring. At the same time, not to try to win ruins the game and violates the player's near sacred oath to try their best so that the opponent will enjoy a good and honest game. (Athletes who don't try to win are spoilsports and universally detested, which is why "throwing a game" is such a difficult sin for one's teammates to forgive.) Christian athletes who feel compelled to pray for outcomes in sports contests, then, are caught in this trap: they must either ask God, in a most un-Christian-like way, to limit his blessings by granting them the victory; ask God to allow the opponents to win and work to achieve that end, thus undermining the spirit of the game; or ask God to grant victory to their opponents but work hard to prevent that from happening, thus making a mockery of their prayers. It seems to me that the only way this puzzle can be solved is for athletes to refrain from praying altogether about the *results* of contests other than that they will result in profound joy being brought to the players' lives.

PRAYER AS MAGIC AND SUPERSTITION

Although athletes, coaches, and fans might dismiss them as quaint and even silly, magic and superstition infest big-time sports. When Clemson alumnus "Pitchfork" Ben Tillman was governor of South Carolina in

1893, he was said to have placed a curse on the University of South Carolina that has been blamed for its long list of athletic disappointments. In 1992, some USC fans took matters into their own hands by hiring a witch doctor to perform rituals designed to remove the curse. The New Orleans Saints had long labored under a curse thought to have been placed on the Superdome because it was erected on an ancient burial ground. Before a critical 2000 playoff game against St. Louis, the team hired a Yoruba priestess to "rid the dome of all curses." The Saints won their first playoff game in thirty-four years. And sportswriters still puzzle over golfer Sergio Garcia's thinly veiled reference to sinister forces conspiring against him when he lost the playoff in the 2007 British Open: "I'm playing against a lot of guys out there," he said, "more than the field" (meaning his fellow competitors).[47]

Tales of players' superstitions are legion, and baseball players may be the most superstitious of all. Most, for example, refuse to step on the first and third base foul lines when taking the field. Mentioning that a pitcher has a no-hitter going is strictly taboo. Hall of Fame third baseman Wade Boggs always traced the Hebrew letter *chai* in the dirt at the plate before he batted, just as he religiously ate chicken before every game. Basketball players often try to be the last to shoot the ball during the warm-up, making sure that their last shot before leaving the court goes in the basket. Some hockey players believe that crossing their stick with a teammate's during the pregame warm-up or looking at the red goal light when referees test it is bad luck. Famed race car driver Mario Andretti would never sign an autograph in green ink.[48]

According to British anthropologist Sir James George Frazier, who quite literally wrote the book on the subject, magical practices are based in a mechanical conception of the universe in which human acts dictate the course of events, a line of thinking that is miles apart from the evangelical conception of a supernatural, conscious, personal God who controls the order of nature. Magic may or may not include a belief in a supernatural power. Anthropologist Bronislaw Malinowski described magic as a practical art that aims at well-defined ends; it is simple, trite, and predictable, while religion is complex, serious, and more uncertain. Unlike magic, which is always a means to an end, prayer may be an end in itself. Practitioners of magic manipulate forces entirely for self-serving ends; in contrast, prayers may consist of praise and thanksgiving that spring from adoration and godly fear. Malinowski and Frazier might have shortchanged the reach of Christian prayer a bit, but they did capture one important difference. Prayers that are crassly manipulative and self-serving, performed mechanically in a routine fashion and for a specific end, risk crossing the barrier from religion into magic.[49]

Although evangelicals as a group shun magic, paranormal beliefs, UFOs, astrology, communication with the dead, and other forms of psychic activity, evangelical athletes flirt, often unwittingly, with the boundaries of magic and superstition. Painting crosses on their shoes, carving Scripture references into their equipment, or performing pregame rituals are very magic-like acts. When evangelical quarterback Kurt Warner brought his St. Louis Rams back to the Superdome following the Saints' voodoo priestess' incantations, he was reported to have stopped in the tunnel to read Scripture his pastor had given him and to pray with his teammates as a way of counteracting the spell she was thought to have cast. Straight-laced former UCLA coach John Wooden would seem to be the least likely person to practice superstitious rituals, yet during his legendary career he was said to have made it a practice to walk around campus looking for hairpins, which he always stuck in a special tree. Some athletes seem to believe that incorporating prayers or religious references into such rituals rids them of their magical undertones, but it is more likely that prayers themselves will become magical. On balance, there is little difference between the United States Olympic softball team throwing their bats and equipment in the shower to rid them of an alleged "voodoo curse" and the Major League Baseball player who, unable to make the pregame chapel, sent his bats along nevertheless.[50]

When prayer is woven into superstitious pregame routines, it verges on the kind of "vain repetition" and mechanical prayer that evangelical theologian John Stott labeled hypocrisy and a sin and that ethicist R. E. O. Smith labeled "unanswerable." One of Joseph Marbeto's interviewees told him: "I never play my best if I haven't recited the Lord's Prayer first," a difference in kind perhaps from the athlete who must always lace his shoes the same way before each game, but not so different in intent. The evangelical NFL player whose game-day routine consists of first having prayer with his wife, then driving to the stadium, drinking one cup of coffee, eating three pieces of French toast, then some pasta with sauce, and then Bible study—in that order—blurs the line between prayer and superstition, in spite of claims that "it's more routine than superstition." When an athlete prays because she fears what might happen if she doesn't, her prayers become manipulative, done not so much to express her interior relation to God but to coerce the future turn of events. If they aren't magic, prayers said only for the prospect of personal reward certainly seem to move in that direction, becoming nearly indistinguishable from those of Odysseus or the Yoruba priestess.[51]

Ultimately, the opinion one holds regarding prayers offered in the locker rooms and arenas across the land will hinge largely on his or her impression of how big-time sports fit into the larger Christian worldview. However, I would venture one unqualified role for prayer in sports, although it is not likely to figure prominently in the locker rooms and arenas of our day. Evangelical athletes and coaches who insist on praying should include in every pregame or postgame or on-field prayer a petition for the redemption and restoration of sport to its created design. But having uttered such prayers, many might find it difficult to walk out into the arena.

11

Notes Toward a Well-Played Game

Reimagining sport in the Christian life will require readjusting old views and taking steps to bring the way sports are organized and played into harmony with the new vision. This will be difficult, not simply because the entrenched sports establishment brooks no attempts to change the way it does business, but because a religion of sorts is already woven into sports. Scholars have characterized sport in various ways: a "cultural religion," a "natural religion," a "civil religion," and a "folk religion." Sociologist James Mathisen observes that all of these terms refer not only to the way sport "encapsulates, magnifies, and reflects back to us the primary beliefs and norms of American culture," but the way sport itself "raises up particular values and myths of its own and projects them onto culture with a normative certitude."[1] This religion of sport embraces a host of ideologies such as an unquestioned belief in the character-enhancing properties of sport, belief in the inherent goodness of mass consumerism, and faith in competitiveness and confrontation as keys to personal growth. Its "cultic acts" are evident in the tribalism of tailgating, the nods to patriotism inserted into the pageantry of Saturday afternoon football games, the utterance of non-sectarian prayers to a civil god who presumably helps both teams win simultaneously, and militarism transported to the field in the name of school spirit.

Synthesized with the cultural religion of sport is yet another religious impulse, the evangelical-like religion of Sportianity. Having rounded off the sharp, offending edges of the Christian gospel and watered down its vital doctrines so as not to threaten the presumptions undergirding big-time sports, Sportianity has been allowed to serve as public chaplain to the sports establishment. With religion ubiquitous in athletic quarters, professing Christian athletes in such abundance, and sport so obviously harnessed to evangelistic missions, why, one might wonder, do we need another religious interpretation to add to the mix?

The answer can be found in all that is wrong with sport in American society, in wrongs that have gone unchastened, unnoticed, and even abetted by a Christian community unable or unwilling to draw firm lines between the ethos that has a stranglehold on sports and that which lies at the core of some of its most cherished teachings. Sportianity advocates on behalf of violence and razor-sharp, take-no-prisoners competition, while shielding its eyes from the broken bodies our sports produce. It kidnaps Scripture, making it the handmaiden of hypercompetitiveness, and refuses to acknowledge competition's corrosive effects on human relationships. Sportianity sanctions self-aggrandizement, self-interest, and retribution in the name of a gospel that minces no words in excoriating them. It elevates the ideology of success, even something as ephemeral as winning a game, in the name of a gospel "that gave the kingdom to the poor, not the rich; the feeble, not the mighty, to little children humble enough to accept it, not to [athletes] who boast that they can attain it by their own powers."[2] It celebrates self-reliance and teaches the meritocratic rewards of hard work to propagate a theology dominated by the radicalism of grace. It lauds winners more than losers, forgetting that all are unworthy and undeserving. Unlike an earlier day when the pagan deities decorating the Roman coliseum, the circus, and the athletic stadia were sufficient reason for Christians to shun them, modern Sportians rush to our sports arenas to worship the god of commercialism.

Because these ways of conceptualizing sports and their relationship to the faith have become so hardened in the collective Christian imagination, thinking in bold new ways will be especially difficult. For athletes whose training has encouraged unquestioned acceptance of the dominant model of sports; for coaches, administrators, and athletic trainers whose livelihoods are inextricably linked to the status quo; and for institutions who have invested heavily in programs that depend upon the perpetuation of the dominant myths of sport, imagining new approaches may well nigh be impossible. But the path taken by this book has led inevitably to this destination. Reimagining sport within the Christian worldview will involve more than generating a list of recommendations for how sport could be better organized and played, although that certainly is central to the task. Addressing the *how* questions (e.g., "*How* can sports be made a spiritually affirming rather than spiritually challenging experience?") before addressing the *what* and *why* questions (e.g., "*What* is the purpose of sports in the Christian life?" and "*Why* should Christians play sports?") is unlikely to be productive, if only because the way we play sports is largely a reflection of the purposes that we envision for them.

The Christian community is in serious need of a book that addresses the *what* and *why* questions, but this is not that book. The task of welding together theology, ethics, and sports should be left to those more skilled and better prepared than I. Nevertheless, the pages that follow sketch out some modest parameters that such a philosophy/theology might incorporate and follow with some implications for Christian practice, tentative answers to the *how* question. These are intended to be the initial rather than the final words on the subject. Their contribution should be judged not by their influence in bringing about the change called for here but in jump-starting a badly needed dialogue on the subject. If they do so, they will have achieved their purpose.

NONESSENTIAL SPORT

Sports are unique because they are not essential. They are elective, discretionary, and voluntary. They are entirely dispensable, not needed for the smooth functioning of society or the healthy existence of individuals, and not instrumental to our survival. They are the icing on the cake of existence; they can make rewarding lives even more rewarding, but they don't rescue them or sustain them or add to their moral value. In terms of tangible rewards, they produce little except perspiration and fleeting moments of pleasure. We do them, as it were, on the margins of our existence, at intervals carved out from the unrelenting obligations of life. Because sports are not essential, we decide whether or not to play or watch them, including where, when, with whom, and for how long we will play. Although this element of freedom often is tempered by the demands of organized athletics, even the college or professional athlete remains free to choose whether or not he or she wants to continue to submit to the rigors of conditioning and practice. Another way of saying this is to say that sports are played in leisure where, released from immediate claims and obligations, players are free to pursue their hearts' desires. In a very real sense, then, leisure is the mind, body, and spirit sensing and expressing the deepest desires of the heart. That is why philosopher-theologian Josef Pieper identified worship as "the deepest springs by which leisure is fed."[3]

As an expression of leisure, sports are both identity forming and identity revealing. What you play and how you play it reveals more than your taste in sports. Barlett Giamatti put it this way: "We will watch or play games or sports that reflect how we think of ourselves or that promote how we wish to be perceived." At leisure, released from the crushing demands of daily life, the Christian has a few moments of freedom to shed the camouflage of natural man, to polish up the *imago Dei*, to regain spiritual balance, and to recover a sense of who he or she really is. For Christians ineluctably wedded to the world, leisure is the opportune time for enlarging, not their own ambitions or an already outsized appetite for entertainment, but their spiritual visions. If it indeed is true that inside every furrow-browed, culture-constrained, work-manipulated Christian, there is a more ethical, sensitive, radiant, vibrant, joyous, worshipful Christian trying to get out, one would logically expect this latent side to appear in its most splendid form when the Christian is most free to choose. "Leisure," reminded the late campus pastor and writer Gordon Dahl, "offers Christians the greatest opportunity they have this side of eternity, to be and become the new man after Christ's own splendid example."[4]

We have become so used to thinking of sports in the work rather than the leisure sphere of life that a sweeping transformation in the way Christians conceive of sport will be required. Sports played within the spiritual framework of leisure can hardly be approached as cathartic experiences for venting emotions that, if allowed to accumulate, might morph into "serious sin." Nor can they be played as a way of proving yourself to anybody. The spirit of leisure flows from the fount of contentment. A leisure view also rejects the notion that sports and ordinary life are lived out in separate ethical spheres and that sports require some adaptations, however modest, of Christian ethics. It debunks the idea that sports should be hard tests of the Christian faith or that games naturally should tempt Christians to sacrifice their witness for the Darwinian impulses of the game. In fact, a leisure view moves players, coaches, and spectators in precisely the opposite direction; games are played not with the expectations that they will challenge the athlete's faith, but with the expectation that they will be an opportunity for helping the athlete, coach, and fan recover their spiritual centers of gravity.

AUTOTELIC SPORT

Sports may be among the most impractical things that we do. We construct artificial obstacles that make achieving our goals more difficult (fixing the basketball goal ten feet above the court, limiting the size of the hole in golf, etc.) and then make it even more difficult by imposing artificial rules (soccer players can't touch the ball with their hands, basketball players can't run with the ball, etc.). And when athletes have mastered a skill, they and those of us who watch them receive no intrinsic reward other than the unique human experiences derived from playing and watching. Sports are what philosophers call autotelic activities, which is to say they are their own end. Eminent philosopher George Santayana thought this so obvious that only "a barbarian" would fail to recognize it: "[Sport's] possible uses are incidental," he said, "like those of the fine arts, religion, or friendship."[5]

The Christian community has harbored an excruciatingly utilitarian view of sport since at least the thirteenth century. Sports played for no productive reasons were suspect, so they were made less suspicious by imagining that they produced tangible, profitable results. By conjuring up what Thorstein Veblen once called "colorful pretenses,"[6] church leaders managed to convince themselves and their followers that sport conforms to "the generically human canon of efficiency for some serviceable end." The problem isn't simply that many of the instrumental goals typically envisioned for sport are unlikely to be attained, that they have little to do with what attracts people to sport in the first place, or that focusing on sport's practical benefits deflects attention from the uniqueness of sport as a human experience. When Christians value sport only as it serves extraneous ends, the experience is diminished in the Christian imagination.

Reimagining sport as an autotelic, leisure-based experience means shunning flaccid rhetoric about the sports field as a training ground for character, or as a way of building strong bones and muscles, or as a fertile field for evangelism, or realizing any other practical benefit. Trying to justify sports on instrumental grounds is as misguided as trying to justify symphony orchestras on grounds that they develop endurance in the muscles of violin players, or justifying meals at three-star restaurants because of the superior nourishment found there. Playing the violin may indeed improve muscular endurance, just as eating at restaurants can nourish, but these hardly get at the reasons why violinists play and why people visit fancy restaurants. Orchestras enrich our lives through the sense of listening and gourmet meals enrich through taste, just as sport enriches our lives through moving and watching. In the end, it is the experience that counts, and this alone is sufficient reason for the Christian's involvement.

Symbolic Sport

Although the history of sport and Christianity is largely one of the church imagining ways to use sport to further its own ends or as a practical aid to earthly living, there was a brief moment in the life of the medieval church when ball games were valued as religious experiences. Like dance, they were incorporated into the liturgy and other ceremonies perhaps as ways of focusing congregants' attention on certain spiritual realities. Actually, the medieval churches were latecomers to the game. Sport made its first appearance in culture as religious ritual, as we saw in chapter 1. Games continued to be played as religious ceremonies well into the nineteenth century, when some American Indian tribes were still offering them "to the gods, with the object of securing fertility, causing rain, giving and prolonging life, expelling demons, or curing sickness."[7] From the long view of history, says historian Richard Mandell, "we may be making artificial separations if we remove sport very far from ritual, the dance, and the theater."[8]

Warped by the modern secularizing forces of specialization, rationalization, bureaucratization, and quantification, sports have long since lost their religious overtones, dislocated from their indigenous role in society: "The bond between the secular and the sacred has been broken, the attachment to the realm of the transcendent has been severed," says historian Allen Guttmann. When the religious rationale for sport disappeared, our attention shifted to human achievement and the setting of records: "We can no longer run to appease [the gods] or to save our souls, but we can set a new record. It is a uniquely modern form of immortality."[9] The dislocation can't be blamed only on forces external to religion. Christianity's insistence on denying sport's appeal to the human spirit, subverting it with external objectives, may have played a greater part in achieving distance between sport and religion than have the forces of secularization.

Obviously pagan sport-religions have little in the way of symbolic content to offer to a Christian apology of sport, but it may be enough to reflect on the fact that sport first appeared in society as an intrinsic element of religious expression. For Christians who believe that creation conveys, though in a veiled way, God's design for the universe and that the Christian's responsibility is to restore sport to its created essence, the fact of sport's religious roots may have some significance. As mentioned earlier, determining exactly what has been given in creation and what has been tainted by the perverse hand of humanity is far from an exact science. However, if sport (or more likely play) is part of the created design, it is reasonable to inquire not only into the ways it has been corrupted but also into the ends to which its restoration should be directed. Catholic theologian Hugo Rahner believed that the Creator had endowed his creatures with "a different and more finely attuned relation between body and soul than that which we now possess" and urged the church to get about the business of rediscovering it. If corrupting influences have diverted sport from realizing its divinely ordained purpose as religious expression, then surely any efforts at restoration must take this into account. Let me be clear here. I am not recommending that sport be converted into liturgy—that churches hang basketball hoops from choir lofts, roll bowling balls down the aisles of their sanctuaries, or hold swimming races in their baptismal pools. I'm simply suggesting that Christians have much to gain from organizing and playing their sports in ways that enable the cultivation and expression of religious meaning.[10]

Convincing the Christian community that the human experience of sport has religious significance may be an uphill battle. After registering a complaint about the politicization, moralization, and criticism of sports by modern sportswriters, *First Things* senior editor James Nuechterlein went on to implore those who write about sports to "resist with self-denying intensity the temptation to treat sports as metaphor, allegory, or anything beyond itself." In this view, sports have no symbolic value, no deeper meanings; what you see is pretty much what you get. They are, he said, little more than harmless momentary respites from "the burdens that life visits upon us." Driving the point home even more deeply, he paraphrased Freud's famous line that "a cigar is sometimes just a cigar." "Just so," said Nuechterlein, "the Super Bowl is always just a football game."[11]

Nuechterlein was dead wrong. Sports are always invested with symbolic meaning; they are always fundamentally expressive of something. Religion scholars, sociologists, and historians have filled volumes with writing about the religious-like overtones of sports. "To say 'It was only a game' is the psyche's best defense against the cosmic symbolic meaning of sports events," says Catholic social commentator Michael Novak. "If you give your heart to the ritual, its effects on your inner life can be far-reaching."[12] Some, like religion scholar Charles Prebish, have gone so far as to proclaim sport a new emerging religion, not unlike Christianity or Judaism. Modern athletes also sense something in sport that borders on the religious and that, in some inexplicable way, makes contact with their religious zones. None have been as perceptive and as eloquent as was the late physician-philosopher-runner George Sheehan, who in his book *Running and Being* talked of running as "purging and rinsing the inner man" and showing "the good and true and beautiful." It was during a run, he said, that he came upon proof of the existence of God.[13]

Images of sweaty huffing and puffing athletes don't always blend easily with traditional notions about religious states of mind. Sports religion scholar Jack Higgs, for example, draws sharp lines between sport and the holy and intimates that solitude and stillness are essential conditions for spiritual experience; he frets about the "glorification of bodily movement." But there is no reason to believe that religious affectivities are necessarily blunted by physical activity or the busyness of games. English evangelical David Watson has convincingly argued that experiences of moving the body can be important forms of praise, especially in a world that has become increasingly word-resistant. Dance, for example, has a long history as a natural expression of praise and worship in the Judeo-Christian tradition. Miriam led women in praising God with timbrel and dance after the Israelites crossed the Red Sea, and the people danced when the prodigal son returned home. Jeremiah described the restoration of Jerusalem as a time for dancing, and David danced before the ark of the covenant as it was brought into Jerusalem. Without taking time to debate the finer points, there is reason to suppose that were it not for cultural forces at work, David might have just as naturally shot baskets before the ark to express his thanksgiving and praise.[14]

GOD-GLORIFYING SPORT

In this regard, athletes in the evangelical community who refer to their athletic experiences as "praise performances" or "worship experiences" and express a desire to "glorify God" through their athletic performances seem to be headed down the right path by sensing sport's intrinsic appeal to the spirit. Unfortunately, such expressions often are grounded in the cultural ethos of sports and linked to athletic production rather than being grounded in the more expressive framework of their faith. Contrary to the reigning orthodoxy of Sportianity, we glorify God not by the sweat of our brow, by giving 100 percent, by winning, or even by losing. As the late theologian Lewis Smedes reminded us, glorifying God simply means applauding God, and that, he noted, is never very productive.[15]

Clear lines must be drawn between worldly fame and glorifying God. Somewhere along the line the evangelical sports community confused glory with fame, even though the desire to be better known than other people, as C. S. Lewis once observed, is a competitive passion that seems "more of hell than of heaven."[16] Winning trophies brings publicity to athletes, extends the coach's contract, and helps advertise the religious convictions of those involved. A league championship showers accolades on a Christian school and helps it recruit new students. One might question, however, whether these acts glorify God. Surely glorifying God isn't a hydraulic process in which humans first earn glory for themselves and then, in a demonstration of piety, heartfelt gratitude, and Christian charity pump it all up to God. In fact, imagining that God needs our fame is to head down a treacherous theological path. When athletes are intent on earning God some fame through their athletic productions, they fail to see that one purpose of the game might be simply to receive a divine gift.

Neither does playing with an all-out effort glorify God. Clearly playing hard is important to be successful in athletics, but it is best not to confuse it with glorifying God. Many unchristian behaviors appear in sports in the name of excellence: performance-enhancing drugs, shrugging off family responsibilities, and questionable training tactics. Appreciating athletic excellence as a manifestation of common grace and as a marvel of divinely created motor control and cardiovascular systems is one thing; easy characterizations of this excellence as bringing glory to God is quite another. The point is not to defend inept performance in the name of religion; rather, when God-glorifying gets mixed up with technical competence and the material rewards it brings, it is too easy to get the idea that God wants you to be a champion when all he wants is you.

Just like art, dance, and music, athletic experiences can be spontaneous outpourings of inward spiritual feelings that reach their highest religious potential as offerings rather than agents of something else. Athletic offerings don't produce anything; in fact, like offering the first fruits, they can be costly. H. M. Best's characterization of Christian music is just as applicable to Christian sport: "An offering is not a means, because it cannot earn anything. It is not an end, because it cannot be worshipped. The essence of a sacrifice, and its only glory, is that it can be surrendered."[7] Surrender isn't a metaphor likely to be appreciated by athletes whose coaches have psyched them up to go to war. But for an aging, rag-tag group of basketball players in the church gymnasium who don't keep score, don't attract spectators, and who long ago stopped worrying about giving the game an all-out effort, surrender comes easily. God is glorified when athletes, coaches, and spectators respond to his presence and greatness, something just as possible in defeat as in victory and, I believe, more likely to happen on the sandlot than on Astroturf.

"UNSAFE" SPORT

I once listened to a history professor and football coach at a Christian college tell students that "games are things of the body and thus of a lower order than things of the spirit."[8] The professor expressed an opinion that is fairly widespread in the Christian community. By attempting to divorce sport from the soul, Christians hope to make it "safe." Conceived as a feature "of the body" and not "of the soul," it can be presumed to be morally neutral and religiously irrelevant. It is similar to philosopher Nancy Pearcey's description of how some evangelical academics approach the subject matter they teach, dividing it into top tiers occupied by such subjects such as philosophy and literature (presumed to be religiously relevant) and bottom tiers occupied by "religiously irrelevant" subjects such as business, engineering, and professional studies. Top tier subjects are considered inherently "dangerous" because they are subject to interpretation from a variety of worldviews; hence great care must be taken to approach them in a distinctly Christian way. Not so for the bottom tier subjects, which are presumed to be technical and utilitarian and hence on "safely neutral" grounds because they don't appear to raise any serious religious questions. According to this way of thinking, engineering can be approached in basically the same way whether at a Christian or secular college.[9]

In the evangelical mindset, relegating sport to the "body compartment" moves it to the lowest of the lower, the most technical of the technical, the most useful of the utilitarian, the safest of the safely neutral tier. Sport hasn't been taken seriously as an experience of religious expression because evangelicals find it difficult to imagine that it can speak to participants with a religious voice or that it can help shape a cosmological vision. It is, we are left to presume, a religiously blank slate. Pearcey offered a sharp corrective to this kind of thinking: no matter what people do or study, she said, "[they] are interpreting [their] experience in the light either of divine revelation or of some competing system of thought."[20]

The way sport can shape a worldview tends to be grossly underestimated by most sports enthusiasts. Yet sports, like art or drama, can act "expansively and powerfully [as] part of our artistic or imaginative impulse," says Bart Giamatti. Sports are a lot like books in this respect, which critic John Leonard has said can "sneak into unsuspecting heads and rearrange the neurons, the hierarchies, the values."[21] Sports are inherently evangelical; they compete for our religious sensibilities. They "can open the door either to genius or madness," says religion scholar Lonnie Kliever, which is why the church has tried throughout history to control them.[22] Mark Galli, editor of *Christianity Today*, put it perfectly: "The sports god is an enticing deity; he offers splendid moments of transcendence while never demanding that we take up our cross, forgive our enemies, or serve the poor."[23] This quality of sports makes them deserving of the Christian's watchful eye, but it also makes them worthy of consideration as human experiences that can be integrated with Christian thought and practice. "Unsafe" sports, like "unsafe" philosophy, can be fitted to many different worldviews; whether they become threat or promise depends upon the purposes envisioned for them.

THE SPIRITUAL FOOTING: SPORT AS PLAY

One need not be a sports aficionado to appreciate how the experiences of playing and watching sports differ from most other things that we do. Sport affects us in ways that the perfunctory activities of balancing our checkbooks, driving our cars, or mowing our yards cannot. There are worlds of difference between the experiences of playing and watching golf, tennis, softball, and skiing and the mundane experience, say, of repairing a broken water pipe. Surely plumbing is an important activity (especially when one is knee-deep in water), and it can be performed to the glory of God, but the ordinary experiences of cutting, fitting, and soldering pipes aren't likely to quicken the imagination or transport a person to an imaginary world quite like playing and watching sports. We care about sports in a way that we don't care about plumbing, and it is that caring, says philosopher William Morgan, that enables us to become emotionally invested in them.[24]

Sport is not the only human activity that touches us in this way. It is characteristic of all human activities in the family of play, whether golfing, hiking, playing chess, or participating in the community theater. All have a way of riveting our being, transporting us to a different time and space, and affirming a different order of existence. Play, says theologian Robert Johnston, takes place against the distant horizon of our everyday world, deepening and widening our field of vision, quickening our sense of possibility, and stimulating our imagination.[25] The evangelical sports enthusiast who desires to understand how sport fits into the Christian experience must first recognize it and nurture it as play.

Thus all forms of play are expressions of the same characteristic human response to the world, a response so universal—evident in animals as well as humans—that it is difficult not to believe that it is part of God's design. It is not unduly stretching the evidence to suggest that play is a divine gift, presumably granted with the expectation that Christians will not simply enjoy it but nurture and protect it as well. The hockey player is responding to the same impulse, albeit in a much different way, as the mountaineer or the concert pianist. The inveterate gambler is moved by the same impulse as the hang glider, the dancer, or the quarterback. It is right to construe this impulse to play as a divine gift, but probably wrong to think that God has ordained any particular form of play, including sports. I cannot think that God is the author of either Major League or Little League Baseball. Nor do I believe that organizing play around the principle of competition was his doing. Competition is merely one way we organize play, a spice to make it more fun and interesting, just as poetry adds to language, and music to sound.

Culture is an undeniably powerful shaper of the play impulse, something evident in international preferences for sport: the popularity of baseball in America and Japan, the love of the Irish for Gaelic football, and the Australian devotion to cricket. Cultural forces have led to games in our society being structured to ensure fairness and to give players equal chances for success. Culture has also been at play in determining that games are pointless unless they are quantified, that sport should be made a public relations arm of educational institutions, that championships are needed to sort out the very best from the very worst, and that sport realizes its highest potential when played in front of packed stadia and made a product of mass consumption. Consequently, no form of play, however deeply engrained in culture, is granted immunity from the penetrating gaze of the reflective Christian.

PLAY—A CLOSER LOOK

French sociologist Roger Callois' four-part taxonomy of play, first published in 1958, continues to be a reliable guide to the ways in which the play impulse is expressed. *Alea* includes games of chance; *mimicry* involves make-believe such as acting or mime; *illinx* is the term assigned to activities that stimulate sensations of vertigo, exhilaration, and disorientation; and *agon* is play in which symbolic adversarial relationships are acted out and which requires qualities of speed, endurance, skill, and ingenuity, "exercised in such a way that the winner appears to be better than the loser in a certain category of exploits." Callois further placed each of these types of play along a continuum; *agon* play, for example, can range from from *paidia*, informal and spontaneous competition (children playing cowboys and Indians), to *ludus*, play that is regulated by rigid rules and which requires application of technical skills and strategies (World Cup competition). Organized competitive sport falls near the ludus end of the *agon* continuum, but "what must be understood," says physical education theorist Daryl Siedentop, "is that the primary power of improvisation and joy—which is *paidia*—is in no way to be considered as having more value [or being "more playful"] than the taste for imposed difficulty—which is *ludus*. They are both play; they are both ways of playing; and, indeed, if there is to be a judgment, it must be that *ludus* contributes increasing meaning to play."[26]

We have already seen that sport (ludus) is dispensable, is directed toward no external ends, and aims at nothing more than the experience of playing. To this can be added five additional attributes: 1) it is experienced as nonserious seriousness; 2) it takes place in an imaginary world set apart from the ordinary; 3) it offers players an uncommon sense of freedom; 4) it envelops players in a sense of adventure and possibility; and 5) it is fundamentally expressive and impressive. All of these can be important in nurturing players' apprehension of religious sensitivities.

Nonserious seriousness. Play is not a characterization that the Christian athletic community normally ascribes to competitive sports; in the athletic culture, "play" means frivolity and as such mocks the hard work and dedication of the athlete. "Come on you guys, stop playing around," says the coach to the team that seems not to understand the serious challenge confronting them. It somehow seems more appropriate, says philosopher Scott Kretchmar, to say that "one works sport, not plays sport."[27] Viewed in its larger context, however, play has little to do with effort or relaxation, earnestness or silliness, competition or cooperation. Stern young men and women wearing themselves out on the soccer field can be at play every bit as much as free spirits tossing a frisbee on the dormitory lawn, and frisbee players can be every bit as serious as soccer players. Seriousness, in fact, is essential to play; the game can't exist unless players convince themselves that the game is serious and that the outcome is vital. At the same time, though, they realize that the game isn't ultimately serious; it is serious only in a limited, illusory sense. Thus they maintain what theologian Lewis Smedes called "the dialectic of playful seriousness—being seriously involved in something we do not interpret as serious business." Often efforts to play are ruined by players' inability to navigate this precarious boundary between the serious and nonserious. The excitement of the game can cause one to attribute to it an ultimate seriousness that it does not deserve. Play also can be corrupted by spoilsports who ruin games because they don't take them seriously enough. The key, as philosopher Randolph Feezell put it, is to "play ironically" in a detached yet enthusiastic way, "as if [the game] really matters, while at the same time [being] able to recognize its relative triviality in the larger scheme of things." To put a theological twist on it, when the game is on, the player is "in the world but not of the world."[28]

Suspension of the ordinary world. In the secluded world of play, bracketed off from ordinary life, players experience what often is called "sacred time" and "sacred space." The start of a game transforms the game space, setting it apart from "paramount," or ordinary space that lies only a few inches outside of it. Playing field hockey, for example, is possible only when special symbolic significance is attached to the space outlined by the boundary lines, to the time frame of the event, and to the rules that govern behavior there. "Entering a baseball game," said the esteemed philosopher Paul Weiss, "is more than an act of going on a field. A bat is a piece of wood, a baseball diamond is a flat surface, a player is just a man—until they become part of a game."[29] Play also takes players into "sacred time," a unique temporal existence set apart from the clocks that govern normal life, offering what one philosopher has called "an asylum of time." Games are played in the timeless present; they carry "a spark of eternity." This characteristic of play moved Peter Berger to think that it had special religious significance, a "prototypical human gesture" pointing beyond itself to a supernatural reality. By flooding players with a spirit of joy and allowing them to step out of one chronology into another, said

Berger, play "becomes eternity," its "intrinsic intention" pointing beyond itself to "a supernatural justification."[30]

Freedom from and freedom to. At play, said theologian Hugo Rahner, "the mind is prepared to accept the unimagined and incredible, to enter a world where different laws apply, to be relieved of all the weights that bear us down, to be freed, kingly, unfettered, and divine."[31] Rahner was underlining the air of freedom that is indispensable to play. Freedom may be the last thing one would expect to experience in a world in which players are bound by rules. "Strange paradox," says philosopher Drew Hyland, "that subjecting oneself to constraints more limiting than those of everyday life should be experienced as freedom, the freedom of exhilarating play. Yet that is what happens."[32] Play knows nothing of "shoulds" and "musts." We can't play when we are forced to do so. The tennis partner who would prefer to be studying for an exam but, at her partner's urging, reluctantly agrees to play another set will find it difficult to fully "play"; so will the father who, more from paternal duty than free choice, invites his son to a game of catch. In this sense, the freedom of play operates conterminously with the spirit of leisure, disclosing the Christian's deepest desires and offering a haven for spiritual recovery.

Adventure and possibility. "Without full acceptance of the unexpected," says religion scholar Robert Neale, "all stories and games are perverted."[33] Neale thus put his finger on another critical component of play: its capacity for involving us in adventure. The unadventurous find it difficult to play because surprises and risks are central to the sporting experience. Batters risk missing pitched balls, divers risk landing on their bellies, golfers risk slicing their drives into the woods. Each possibility is a micro-adventure within the context of the game, each game a macro-adventure within the context of life. Each shot at the hoop, each backhand, each kick at the goal, and each stride toward the finish line offers what a philosopher has called "a confrontation with possibility, genuine, yet benign, possibilities outside the context of daily life."[34] "Responsive openness" is the term philosopher Drew Hyland coined to describe the way athletes must remain open to the unexpected yet at the same time be ready to respond. Responsive openness might also be an apt description of the spiritual substrate of sports. The Christian athlete, like the festival-goer described in Catholic theologian Josef Pieper's marvelous essay on festivity, must remain "expectantly alert" to the unexpected gifts of the festival, "being able to look through, and, as it were, beyond the immediate matter of the festival . . . engag[ing] in a listening, and therefore necessarily silent, meditation upon the fundament of existence."[35] This is possible for athletes only as they remain open to the game's spiritual possibilities and, like Pieper's festival goers, divest themselves of economizing, calculating mentalities, affirm the goodness of the world as a whole, and prepare to receive the hoped-for gift of joyous festivity.[36] The Christian view sees play as a celebration and affirmation of that which they could never have earned. Play for the Christian is anchored in grace.

EXPRESSIVE AND IMPRESSIVE PLAY

Sports, like all play, are intrinsically expressive; emotions and spirit are captured in the kinetic activity of muscles, bones, and nervous systems and harnessed to the aims and objectives of the game. But the way we play expresses more than our mundane reaction to events of the game; play has a way of baring our souls, of telling the world about us in ways words cannot. The expressiveness of play can be distorted by pretense when Christian athletes, on orders from their coach, work to project a "Christian witness." This is theater, players acting out the expressiveness of the coach. When athletes must be instructed to express something other than the impulses stirred by the game, it is a pretty sure sign that something is wrong with the game. Play is also impressive, leaving its imprint on the character and spirit of players. Drew Hyland identified an intriguing dynamic in sport involving both its impressive and expressive side. All of us experience a sense of incompleteness, said Hyland, or a need for fulfillment; games can help complete us in some ways that other aspects of our lives cannot (Christians would draw some well-marked theological lines around this). This is the impressive side of sport. The other element of the paradox, said Hyland, is that while striving for completeness we also experience a kind of "overflowing" such that "we pour out something of ourselves, almost as a gift, to someone or to the world." It is "a gift of the abundance of what we are."[37] This is the expressive side of sports. Hyland stopped short of exploring the theological significance of his model, but for the Christian player who remains "responsively open," the possibilities of play abound: a renewed sense of dependence upon God (incompleteness) coupled with a fresh perspective on God's grace (praise). The game is a gift; the athlete's response is an offering.

If sport deserves a place in the Christian life, then, it is as an opportunity for stepping into the free, detached, adventurous, autotelic world of play to express and be impressed by what theologian-ethicist James Gustafson called "religious affectivities." By this Gustafson meant senses, attitudes, dispositions, and affections which, when interpreted by persons of religious conscience within the context of a particular religious framework, can confirm and give assent "to the Ultimate Power on which all of life depends."[38] The experiences of sport do not have to be made "religious"—converted into evangelism and overlaid with prayer and other cosmetic pieties—to be construed in this way. In fact, the affectivities themselves (love, wonder, gratitude, perseverance, etc.) may not be uniquely religious at all, but they can be *construed* as being religiously significant within the context of the Christian narrative—the language, stories, preaching, and other aspects of religious life that shape the Christian's worldview. This does not happen automatically, simply by participating or watching; it places demands on players' aesthetic and creative senses, themselves reflective of God's image. Some sentiments stimulated by sports—arrogance, self-promotion, a thirst for violence, and revenge, for example—wouldn't be candidates for this, and to the extent that sporting experiences evoke such sentiments, they deserve to be questioned. But others—a sense of community, hope, hunger for perfection, appreciation of ritual, courage, harmony of body and soul, a sense of bodily potential and finitude—could well be given such interpretations. This interplay of impression and expression may occur in real time as athletes, coaches, and spectators immerse themselves in the game, but also through postgame reflection and discussions among team members, coaches, and spectators.

Since sports generate the experiences, the trick is to bring sport in line with the desired affectivities. At the very least this will oblige Christians to give their formal and informal sports a distinct "slant" that is likely to be as radical as the Christian ethic itself. Games designed for the specific purpose of complementing rather than challenging the Christian's better instincts are not likely to look like sports played in most places today. Realistically, this will be possible only where the Christian community controls the shape and purpose of sports and all participants and sponsors agree that games should serve such a purpose. Sports played informally in churches, at youth camps, and in Christian institutions offer the best promise. But even under the most sympathetic circumstances, the burden of moral discernment will continue to rest upon the shoulders of players, coaches, and spectators. Games will always be "unsafe"; like all life experiences, they will continue to exact their toll on Christian witness. But surely, there is much to commend in renewal efforts aimed at ensuring their status as leisure activities that not only permit but encourage Christians to express the brightness of their faith. Idealistic as it might seem, I do not believe this is merely an option for the Christian community; it is more of a moral imperative. Unless sport is approached as a derivative of the God-given play impulse, invested with religious motivations and meaning, and structured in a way to facilitate this religious function, an honest positioning of sport in the context of the Christian life will be difficult, perhaps impossible.

TWO MYTHS

Beyond approaching sport as a human experience for impressing and expressing spiritual realities, there need to be some overarching myths, some particular aspects of the Christian narrative that give life to sport and offer a center for thinking about it in a Christian context. By myth, of course, I don't mean fables or manufactured stories, but narratives that help frame sports within the Christian worldview. Two such myths are the myth of eternity—the Christian hope that the end of the present life is but the beginning of an eternal life in heaven spent with God and fellow believers with incorruptible bodies and everlasting joy—and the myth of God at play in creating the world. Earlier pages took note of Berger's characterization of play as a "signal of transcendence," intimating or foreshadowing eternity. The theme has been echoed by theologians like Hugo Rahner, who believed play helped orient Christians to "the state of the blessed in the world to come" and, while not belittling play in the least, called it but a "feeble imitation" of the true playing that will begin "only when this world has been left behind." "There is," he said, "a sacral secret at the root and in the flowering of all play: it is man's hope for another life taking visible form in gesture."[39] Along the same lines, Wheaton College philosophy professor Arthur Holmes pointed to Zechariah 8:5, in which the streets of heaven are full of boys and girls playing, as reason for Christians to believe that play "finds meaning and purpose in a place reserved for them in God's Kingdom."[40] Tennis is not eternity and baseball is not heaven, but they may bear a symbolic relationship to the real thing lying outside of our immediate experience. Play may serve the purpose in the Christian life that C. S. Lewis once ascribed to good books or music; sports are "only the scent of the flower we have not found, the echo of a tune we have not heard, news from a country we have not yet visited." "Though like is not the same," said Lewis, "it is better than unlike."[41]

The second myth giving life to play is the myth of God at play in creation. Calling play "one of the phenomenological clues to the spiritual dimension of human existence," Dominican philosopher Ruth Caspar described it as the believer's fleeting imitation of God, described in Proverbs 8:27-31 as Divine Wisdom, playing during the creation of the universe and delighting to be with the children of men. "At play," said Caspar, "*homo ludens* is most profoundly *imago Dei*."[42] Catholic theologians aren't alone in seeing the parabolic significance of play. In his splendid little book *The Christian at Play*, evangelical theologian Robert Johnston described play as mirroring the adventure (and play) of God himself; as such, play can be "a parable of the surprising reality of grace."[43]

Humans are quite capable of perverting the myth of eternity by imagining that sports really are heaven, a mistake that Lewis believed would turn things into "dumb idols." The myth of creation is perverted when players imagine that they aren't merely shadowing a playful God, but that they are gods themselves. Kept in proper perspective, however, these two myths can powerfully influence revitalization efforts in the Christian sports community. The first offers a vision for sports: the games we play, the forms they take, and the sentiments they evoke ought to bear some resemblance to our understanding of our existence in eternity. The second myth also carries a prescriptive message, nicely articulated by evangelical philosopher David Naugle: "If human play is indeed rooted in divine play, then humans ought to develop our abilities at play and cultivate a spirit of playfulness." And when our sports go as they could and should, they can become a means of spiritual formation that, as Johnston says, can lead to an "experience of the reality of God through his special revelation in the Exodus and in Jesus Christ." It also can be an experience in which "God can, and often does, meet with us and commune with us."[44]

NOTES TOWARD THE WELL-PLAYED GAME

In light of how deeply the Christian community has embedded itself in culture, and especially in the culture of popular sports, the prospects for fundamentally changing the way it thinks about sport are far from rosy. Yet without instituting such commitment, the forms and meanings of sport in the Christian life will continue to be shaped by the decidedly unchristian ethos modeled in the thriving sports industry. As long as leaders in Sportianity continue to tell coaches and athletes that they are bound by Scripture "to remain in that same condition as he was in when he became a Christian" (1 Corinthians 7:24), massive defections from the usual way of thinking about and doing sport aren't likely.[45] Even for ardent fans sitting in the pews, suggesting that sport be recalibrated to bring it more in line with the gospel message preached from the pulpit would be more likely to stir indignation than a suggestion that the structure of the worship service be changed. This is especially likely if spiritually recalibrating sport saps it of that which they find most entertaining.

The tragedy is not the colossal failure of Christianity to have any impact on the way sports are played; the tragedy is not to have seriously tried at all. The reasons are clear enough; taking one's faith to the sport fields, especially at the highest levels of competition, is likely to entail costs. Whatever the contorted doctrines of Sportianity might claim to the contrary, serious applications of the Christian ethic do not lend themselves to winning championships. Consequently, we might expect reform to be resisted most forcefully where winning or losing games has serious economic or public relations implications. Yet resistance also is likely at lower levels of competition where, despite the absence of high stakes, games continue to be modeled after those played in the media spotlight. The first step toward a well-played game will come when Christians appreciate the death-grip that big-time sports have on sports played at any level and when they recognize how this can snuff out the spiritual potential of sports.

At a minimum, evangelicals should stop pandering to big-time sports as a way of adding to their church rolls, polishing up their social images, and making the gospel "more relevant." Objective, biblically guided thinking about sports is well nigh impossible when churches, caught up in a sport frenzy, reschedule services to accommodate the Super Bowl, participate in "faith nights" at their local ballparks, feature Christian sport celebrities in their programs and publications, use professional athletes as exemplars of the Christian life, incorporate athletic lingo into sermons and appeals, and continue to use sport as a tool for evangelizing the sports-starved masses. Thinking clearly about sports requires some degree of distance that sports fandom doesn't offer. Considerable credibility is to be gained in the religious marketplace if evangelical churches would dare to speak out about the egregious abuses in big-time sports. The epidemic of injuries and the devastating effects of long-term participation in athletics deserve a reaction from the religious community, as long as it claims a sacred status for the body. Other targets include violent sports like boxing and Ultimate Fighting, corruption in collegiate athletic departments, steroid scandals, spectator atrocities, outrageous salaries, and criminal exploits of star athletes.

Sport evangelism organizations laboring in the trenches of big-time sports face a particularly difficult choice: whether to allow the core message of the gospel to be disciplined by the logic of the industry in exchange for the opportunity to serve as its chaplain or to stand against its ills in a larger, more sweeping commitment to restore and redeem the sports industry. No doubt Christian athletes have had and will continue to have a positive influence on the private lives of those with whom they associate, but the notion that a Christian athlete can help bring about the redemption of sports while perpetuating its ethic seems fanciful at the very least.

Athletes and coaches face even harder choices. It is extraordinarily difficult, though not impossible, for a professional athlete to serve God and their sports franchise at the same time. If, as I have suggested, sports deserve a place in the Christian life only as they incorporate the dynamics of play and offer experiences that can be construed within the context of the Christian narrative, then big-time sports, chained as they are to the work and entertainment ethics, offer little in the way of potential. There will continue to be those in the Christian community who cling to what Stark called "the miracle motif," the belief that if only more athletes would become believers, the ills of sport would disappear.[46] The morally derailed schemes in the athletic precincts of Christian institutions that have been outlined in earlier chapters in this book, and the seeming inability of Christian coaches and athletes to find that middle ground where they can play "ironically" should disabuse us of this notion. The uncomfortable reality is that a strong Christian presence has not had an appreciable effect on the character of big-time sports. Remedying the corruptions in sport will require, as Mark Galli has noted, "more than a few heroic religious individuals to make a difference. Probably something on the order of a company of people, a people called out, set apart—a fellowship grounded in such a way that not even the gates of Hades will overcome it."[47]

Evangelicals may have a chance at influencing big-time sports when they cease using Scripture and theological clap-trap to paper over the realities of hard-nosed competitive sports. Reform will start when Christian college faculty and administrations show a willingness to wrest control of their sport programs from alumni and sports-dazzled constituencies and get serious about integrating their spiritual missions with their intercollegiate athletic programs; when Christian coaches at all levels eschew the "code of silence" of their profession and call into question the unethical coaching practices of colleagues; and when professional athletes courageously speak out against the ethic of competitive excess, violence, objectification of opponents, and riotous spectators. The costs of uttering prophetic voices could well be high. Christian athletes who disavow the killer instinct, refuse to spout the militant rhetoric of the locker room, engage in authentic demonstrations of kindness and sympathy for opponents, and stand against the ethic of competitive and material excess may find that they have a very short shelf life in high-profile sports. The courageous ones will find a way.

Ultimately, how evangelical athletes, coaches, and sports promoters deal with the thorny ethical issues of sport will be between them and their Christian consciences. But conscience serves as a better guide when it is informed, and in this regard I recommend that they spend at least as much time studying the social and ethical dynamics of sports as they spend studying playbooks and game films. I am convinced that some evangelical athletes and coaches, if sufficiently informed, would choose to take a stand, especially as the moral climate of sport continues its downward spiral. If so, that stand may come first with respect to the type of sports evangelicals play and watch. The indiscriminate acceptance of sport by Christians today is just as dangerous as was centuries of the church's indiscriminate rejection of sports. Some sports offer more possibilities than others. Games centered on side-by-side competition, such as golf, swimming, or cycling, seem the most compatible with the Christian ethic. Side-by-side sports are safer and less likely to create social distance between competitors than either face-to-face noncontact sports (tennis, baseball, or volleyball) or face-to-face contact sports, in which strategic thwarting of opponents' efforts is central to the game. High-risk collision sports such as football, hockey, and boxing would be last on my list of sports to be encouraged in the Christian community. Violence and the mental states required to submit to and administer violence do not model either the Christian vision of heaven or the Divine Wisdom at play with the father at creation. As the brutality of football continues to show itself in ever more striking terms, Christian schools that sponsor football programs will be faced with the uncomfortable choice either of modifying their menu of athletic offerings or revising their understanding of the theological significance of the body.

Another stand might be taken with respect to the environments in which sports are played and watched. For centuries, the Christian brief against sports had as much to do with the unwholesome atmosphere at venues where games were played as with the games themselves. Watching athletic contests from a seat in the stadium can be a riveting but far from edifying experience. The roar of the crowd adds a dimension that escapes those who watch on television. Crowds inflamed with equal parts partisanship, bad manners, and beer can render stadia decidedly unholy venues. To some, such as Mark Galli, this needn't drive Christians away:

> The mind reels at the image of Jesus trafficking with violent, self-centered, greedy athletes, immersed in an institution infamous for steroids, multi-million dollar contracts, trash talk, and indecent end zone celebrations. It's a scandal. It's also the gospel. Indeed, if the grace and presence of God cannot be discerned in modern sports, then it will not be found in the modern world.[48]

While it is true that God may choose to reveal himself in the most unlikely places, the images of him cheering on the Duke Blue Devils from an under-the-basket seat or joining with Philadelphia fans to boo Santa Claus and singers of the national anthem are cartoonish, to say the least. Mindful of what happened to Augustine's young friend Alypius, I doubt that Christian spectators can either resist or serve as an antidote to the boorishness seen in the modern stadium. The crowds are drawn, of course, by the drama of the game and the actions of the athletes. Consequently, Christian athletes cannot shrug off responsibility for the increasingly debauched moral climate of the stadium. How refreshing it would be to hear of at least one evangelical athlete who, instead of negotiating for a beefier contract, lobbied for tighter controls over spectator behavior, censored their teammates, coaches, or team mascot when they incited crowd hostilities, or perhaps even suggested that alcohol be banned from their stadium.

Evangelical athletes and coaches also would do well to consider whether their cause is best served by displays of on-field prayers, religious gestures, postgame testimonies, and media profiles featuring their faith. Cheap advertisements of the faith embedded in the cheap milieu of big-time sports smack of cheap grace. Let evangelical athletes' prayers before games reflect the seriousness of their faith commitment, not their obsessions with winning or performance excellence. Those tempted to plead for God's intervention in the game should avoid reference to the outcome. Ask instead that the experience will give full vent to expressions of Christian sentiments and will impress participants' spiritual lives or that the contest will be the means by which both sides will be drawn closer together in bonds of Christian friendship.

How to keep competition, an indispensable organizing principle of games, from becoming an exercise in self-interest remains the most pressing problem for evangelicals in the sports world. Clearly some creative thought and experimentation on the part of those closest to the athletic scene will be needed. The best (and perhaps the only) chances for this to happen will be in precincts over which Christians exert direct control: churches, church camps, community outreach programs, and Christian schools and colleges. Here are a few suggestions:

1. Christian institutions desperately need to achieve some clarity of purpose for their athletic programs and to formulate plans for periodically assessing progress toward that purpose. A first step for Christian colleges might be to gather the college community on the soccer or football field and, after setting a roaring bonfire, ceremoniously burn their cliché-ridden athletic mission statements, especially the fuzzy claims enumerating outcomes that defy measurement or have almost no chance of being realized. A week-long symposium on sports could follow, aimed at drafting fresh missions for their athletic programs that bear plausible and verifiable connections to their faith statements. Evangelical churches that are about to invest precious funds in gymnasia, athletic fields, and sports programs are advised to pause, even before architectural plans are drawn, so their pastors and boards and congregations can take time to educate themselves about sport and iron out a set of objectives. Having specified how sports should be played, let those same churches emblazon the objectives on large banners, hang them from the rafters in the church gymnasium, and oversee sports to ensure that the objectives are met.

Evaluating progress toward such goals need not be complicated. It may be as simple as making provision for players, coaches, and spectators to reflect on their experiences, asking and answering such questions as:

Did the experience of competing draw you closer to those against whom you competed or did it drive you further apart?

Were there occasions in the course of the game when you applauded the efforts of your opponents or shared in their joy or in their disappointments?

Give an example of how grace and mercy were demonstrated in the game. Were you humble in victory, gracious in defeat?

Did the experience of playing mostly deepen your faith or did it challenge it? Explain.

How might you construe the experiences of your just-concluded game within the context of your faith narrative? How did they, for example, deepen your understanding of joy, love, and peace, God's goodness, or your own sense of dependence upon him?

If the game transported you to "another reality," was it a reality that in some sense reflected a vision of your eternal destiny? Did the events of the game and the dispositions of the players help sharpen your understanding of the play of God in creation?

Did you play with "expectant alertness," keeping an open heart for the beauty and joys of the game, yet at the same time maintaining a sense of detachment that allowed you to be reflective?

Were you consumed by the game and the urge to win?

Such exercises alone won't solve the recurring problems in Christian sport, but they will help focus the attention of players and spectators on the quality of the sport experience, which would, in and of itself, be a welcome change.

2. Gleaning the spiritual fruits sports have to offer is only possible if they are approached with an aesthetic disposition, with a keen eye focused on the broad array of emotions and attitudes they evoke. Coaches who deny such experiences to their athletes are like art teachers who deny young painters an opportunity to reflect on their impressions of color, texture, and light or music teachers who, in a flutter to prepare for the big concert, forget the importance of tempo, timbre, melody, and rhythm to the musician. If the first demand art makes on the viewer is to "look" and the first demand made by music is to "listen," the first demand sports make on the athlete is to "feel." Taking time to reflect on those feelings in light of athletic goals and the athlete's spiritual journey seems to me a fundamental requisite for an athletic program that bills itself as "Christian."

3. Anyone who follows sports realizes that simple warnings "not to overemphasize winning" or to "keep the game in its proper perspective" have been colossally ineffective in correcting anomalous conduct in sport. The need for "dialectic playful seriousness" is apparent; how to ensure that it graces games is the problem. This won't be easy for athletes who have been socialized into sport from an exclusively internal (subjective) perspective rather than from an internal as well as an external (detached) perspective, a duality that philosopher Randolph Feezell calls "ironic play." The "athletic ironist," says Feezell, "is a playful competitor whose playfulness reinforces his humility and moderates his competitiveness," "whose engagement is modified by his objective detachment and whose detachment is mediated by immediate engagement."[49] Developing ironic players will require some fierce reeducation of athletes and coaches. The coach for whom winning remains the primary reason for playing sports will not favor athletes who approach sports from the duality of a reflective-yet-invested mindset, although it needn't be assumed that the athletic ironist will be any less committed to excellence than those whose consciences are imprisoned by subjectivity. Feezell points out that the "stance" of the ironic athlete "will make a difference in how she comports herself—how she competes within the constraints of rules, how she relates to others in the sports world, how she reacts to victory and defeat, how she handles her life in sports in relation to the rest of her life." Feezell's notion that humility is the key should be especially encouraging to evangelicals. Just as a humble disposition derives from an objective, detached perspective on life itself and works "against our tendency to inflate the significance of our personal projects and success," so it also works against the "athlete's natural reaction to our culture's glorification of athletic success."[50]

4. Any substantial changes in the way evangelical institutions implement their athletic programs will require the cooperation of institutions against whom they compete. After all, sport is a relational enterprise; Christian sport will go best when all involved share not only the implicit agreements that undergird all sports but an agreement on a general worldview, and a shared belief that the Christian faith radicalizes all walks of life, including sports. It is wildly unreasonable to expect secular institutions to agree to a competitive format framed by the Christian ethic, which will be an obstacle to reform among Christian colleges that align with secular institutions in athletic conferences.

5. For a radically Christian model of sport to emerge from *representational* sport would be difficult, but not impossible. Representational sport is any contest played in the name of a larger cause—school pride, hometown glory, nationalism, fans, even parental pride—and in which players and coaches are portrayed as "representing" some institution or other constituency. It is in no small measure grounded in a militaristic perception of sports; armies represent countries, and teams represent alumni. Representational sport draws spectators; it also plays to our worst instincts. "If fair play is on the ropes," notes historian Allen Guttmann, "it is representational sport, not money, which landed the hardest punch . . . The impulse to give someone the elbow, to take drugs, to get in one more punch after the bell has rung, becomes harder and harder to resist as the psychological drama of representational sport becomes more and more intense."[51]

Representational sport is part and parcel of a commercialized sporting ethic. Dividing teams so that they represent different interest groups is central to its economic and public relations function and fundamental to the way spectators view sports. The best chance for moving to nonrepresentational sport will be sports played in informal settings. What would happen, one wonders, if First Baptist's softball game wasn't played *against* First Methodist but *with* them? (Perhaps special jerseys could be handed out); one team could be "Grace," the other "Humility." Games wouldn't be played to "defend the honor of the church" or with an eye to showing which congregation's theology had been right all along. Players would play ironically and humbly. The objection, of course, is that spectators wouldn't have a vested interest in either team's fortune and therefore would be denied the opportunity to root for one team over the other. And that is precisely the point.

As the ethos of our games are ceded more and more to the selfish and petulant demands of spectators, many of whom seem to think their high-priced tickets entitle them to distasteful behavior, I find myself siding with philosopher Kenneth Schmitz, who regarded the mere presence of spectators as a major threat to the cultivation of the play spirit. If Schmitz is correct in his assessment, and if, as I have argued, the spirit of play is foundational to any expression of Christian affectivities, evangelical institutions might well ask themselves if fostering rivalries and fanning the flames of partisanship in the name of school spirit impede the realization of the spiritual potential of sports.[52]

6. Simple, inexpensive, yet dramatic rituals might help leaven the anomalous and egocentric forces of sports contests played at Christian institutions. As we saw in chapter 6, friendship between opponents is, hands down, the best buffer of hot sporting blood. It seems logical, therefore, that Christian institutions would ensure that intercollegiate sports competitions under their aegis never take place without the safety net of mutual acquaintances, if not deep friendships, between competitors. Beyond the perfunctory pregame handshake and the occasional shared pregame meal, institutions should insist that athletic departments provide opportunities for athletes to form healthy perceptions of their competitors as creatures made and loved by God—and this *before* they meet on the athletic field or in the arena. Some thought also should be given to seating fans from opposing teams together rather than on opposite sides of the court or field. While such an arrangement threatens to undermine the tribalism that attracts many to games, it might increase the possibility of friendships forming between partisan spectators and encourage fans to honor and applaud excellent athletic performances irrespective of the color of jerseys worn by the athletes. If, as evangelical athletes and coaches and their institutional websites are quick to claim, winning and material gain truly are secondary to the greater desire to please God, let Christian colleges demonstrate this by having their athletes, like the ancient Greeks, recite a sacred vow before entering the arena, pledging to play hard, to preserve at all costs the spirit of play, to ensure that the game reflects a foretaste of eternal glory, and to put forth efforts that mirror their conception of the divine play of their Creator.

7. In either secular or Christian precincts, evangelical athletes and coaches should distinguish themselves by vigorously rejecting any glory that society attempts to shower on them for their accomplishments. Recognizing that one of sport's greatest temptations is the temptation to pride, fiercely resist the urge to celebrate when you score a home run. Shun any effort to put yourself in the spotlight; refuse awards, restrain yourself from postgame celebrations, console the losing team. Refuse opportunities to grant postgame interviews or to talk about your achievements, even when such occasions might be opportunities for advertising your faith. Reject any efforts to inflate the importance of a victory; don't be a party to any effort to invest the game with extraneous and artificial meanings that accentuate the importance of winning.

Perhaps the first signs of sports reform will be fragmentary episodes in which athletes, moved by something more powerful than an urge to win, point us to sport's possibilities. Pedro Zamballa, who refused to score against an injured goal keeper, and Andrea Jaeger, whose Christian commitment led her to forsake fame and fortune on the professional tennis circuit, are good examples. So is the singularly Christian act of two softball players on Central Washington's women's softball team during a game in 2008. When Western Oregon player Sara Tucholsky hit a home run, she seriously injured her knee rounding first base; the injury was so severe that she couldn't continue her run around the bases. Without touching the remaining three bases, her hit would have been ruled a single. Rules prevented her teammates from helping her. In a remarkable gesture of mercy, two players from Central Washington, with the umpire's permission, picked her up and carried her around the bases.[53] I don't remember which team won, but I remember this simple act which, in its generosity and in its defiance of the Darwinian impulse of athletic competition, pointed the way to a Christian vision of sport.

If God chooses to reveal himself in our popular sports, I believe it will be through these modest gestures, not in desperate attempts to win for God's glory. Evangelicals have much to learn about merging their faith and their approach to sports. Let them take some of their cues from a soccer game memorialized in Johan Kramer's award-winning documentary, *The Other Final.* On the same day that Brazil and Germany competed for the coveted World Cup title in 2002 before hundreds of millions of onlookers, a team from the mostly Christian Caribbean island of Montserrat traveled to the Buddhist kingdom of Bhutan in the Himalayas to play in the first and only FIFA-authorized match staged between the *bottom-ranked* teams in the world ranking. The game was without sponsors, commercial interests, or advertising. Admission was free. Twenty-five thousand people watched Bhutan win the game 4–0. Following the game, the teams shared a trophy that had been sawed in half. In the film, a Montserrat player rips off his jersey and reveals a white T-shirt with the handwritten words: "We love Bhutan. Thank You." Again, it was a simple gesture that made all that had come before relative, a gracious act to which all those awaiting a Christian transformation of sports might respond with a loud "Hallelujah."

I remain convinced that sport will reach its highest purpose in the lives of Christians when sports are organized and played in ways that help players maintain a stance of responsive openness and allow them to know what the early church fathers knew so clearly: that play is an expression of both body and soul, a vision, however clouded, of the Christian's eternal promise, and an opportunity on earth to become imitators of "the Heavenly Wisdom who plays upon the earth, co-fashioner with God."[54] This will only happen when Christians approach sports, not as "junk experiences" that, like junk food, make us feel better in the short term but threaten our vitality in the long term, but as times and places for recovering our spiritual centers of gravity and for rehearsing spiritual truths, keeping in mind that our games are but dim images of the real game that will begin when this world has been left behind.

NOTES

INTRODUCTION

1   W. St. John (2004), *Rammer jammer yellow hammer: A journey into the heart of fan mania* (New York: Crown), 15; M. Roberts (1976), *Fans: How we go crazy over sports* (Washington, D.C.: New Republic), xi.

2   CBC News (2007, July 31), TV revenue up, but big money is in cable, satellite, *CBCNews.ca*, http://www.cbc.ca/arts/tv/story/2007/07/31/broadcast-numbers .html; NBA Media (2007, April 19), NBA sets all time attendance records, *NBA .com*, http://www.nba.com/news/attendance_070419.html; S. Rushin (2000), SI View, Air and Space, *Sports Illustrated*, *93*(23), 21.

3   U.S. Census Bureau (2008), *Statistical Abstract of the US: 2008* (Washington, D.C.: U.S. Department of Commerce), table 1206, table 1223.

4   This week's sign that the Apocalypse is upon us (1998), *Sports Illustrated*, *89*(5), 35.

5   Making church a guy thing (2006, October 14), *Greensboro News & Record*, B4.

6   D. Dishneau (2003, January 26), This church encourages cheering from the pews, *Greensboro News & Record*, C7.

7   T. Ladd & J. A. Mathisen (1999), *Muscular Christianity: Evangelical Protestants and the development of sport* (Grand Rapids: Baker Books), 183. The ad appeared in various evangelical publications in 1990–1991.

8   D. Pulliam, Religion uncovered on the gridiron, *Get Religion.org* (2007, January 23), http://www.getreligion.org/?p=2173; A. Stricklin & J. B. Hannigan, Steelers' Polamalu: "Faith is foundation," *Baptist Press* (2009, January 28), http://baptistpress.org/bpnews.asp?id=29748.

9   J. D. Davidson (1987), *Evangelicalism: The coming generation* (Chicago: University of Chicago Press), 62.

10 R. Balmer (2001, January/February), Is God a Rams fan? *Sojourners*, 20–24.

11 R. J. Higgs (1995), *God in the stadium* (Lexington: University of Kentucky Press).

12 G. Vecsey (2008, July 3), A race with a cleaner, if anonymous image, *New York Times*, C14; P. Allen, Tour de France becomes drug-fuelled disgrace, *Telegraph .co.uk* (2007, July 26), http://www.telegraph.co.uk/news/worldnews/1558602 /Tour-de-France-becomes-drug-fuelled-disgrace.html; A. Shipley (2000, June 12), Under their own flag, star athletes spring to notoriety, *International Herald Tribune*, 2; K. T. Greenfield (2005), The good life? *Sports Illustrated*, *102*(1), 52.

13 S. J. Hoffman (2007, January 17), Colleges betray their mission as they chase after football glory, *Greensboro News & Record*, A6.

14 R. Borghesi (2008), Widespread corruption in sports gambling: Fact or fiction? *Southern Economic Journal*, *74*(4), 1063; O. Guinness (1994), *Fit bodies, fat minds: Why evangelicals don't think and what to do about it* (Grand Rapids: Baker), 84.

15 M. Sperber (2000), *Beer and circus* (New York: Henry Holt).

16 M. Lopresti (2007, August 24), Need a team update? Check the police blotter, *USA Today*, 10C; ESPN (2008, July 26), Penn State football off the field problems (includes an interview with Joe Paterno), *Outside the Lines*, http://espn .go.com/video/clip?id=3506616.

17 Too much noise, too much funk (1998), Scorecard, *Sports Illustrated*, *88*(19), 27.

18 A. Murphy (2000), Duck soup, *Sports Illustrated*, *93*(22), 44; D. Picker (2007, December 11), Measures considered to curtail fan behavior, *New York Times*, C14; R. Reilly (2002), Comeback kid, *Sports Illustrated*, *103*(9), 74.

19 J. Sire (1997), *The universe next door* (Downers Grove, Ill.: InterVarsity); N. Pearcey (2004), *Total truth* (Wheaton, Ill.: Crossway), 2004. A worldview is described by Christian apologists variously as a "mental map, a "conceptual universe," or "a set of presuppositions about how reality functions."

20 R. Lipsyte (1975), *SportsWorld* (New York: Quadrangle), xiv.

21 Survey data from C. Smith (2002), *Christian America: What evangelicals really want* (Berkeley: University of California Press), 204, table 3; 200, table 1.

22 Editorial (2004, June), Clean air for ears, *Christianity Today*, 25; J. W. Kennedy (2000, May 22), Redeemed bad boys of the WWF, *Christianity Today*, 70.

23 Higgs (1995), *God in the stadium*, 69.

24 F. Deford (1976), Religion in sport, *Sports Illustrated*, *44*(16), 88–100.

25 M. Noll (1994), *The scandal of the evangelical mind* (Grand Rapids: Eerdmans), 7.

26 T. Turnau (2002), Reflecting theologically on popular culture as meaningful: The role of sin, grace, and general revelation, *Calvin Theological Journal*, *37*, 283, quoted in K. J. Vanhoozer (2007), What is everyday theology? How and why Christians should read culture, in K. J. Vanhoozer, C. A. Anderson, & M. J. Sleasman (Eds.), *Everyday theology* (Grand Rapids: Baker Academic), 45.

27 C. L. Albanese (1981), *America: Religions and religion* (Belmont, Calif.: Wadsworth), 322.

28 Deford (1976), Religion in sport; Analyses of Sportianity can also be found in S. J. Hoffman (1985), Evangelicalism and the revitalization of religious ritual in sport, *Arete: The Journal of Sport Literature*, 2(2), 63–87; and S. J. Hoffman (1976), The athlete Dei: Missing the meaning of sport, *Journal of Philosophy of Sport*, 3, 42–51.

29 Ladd & Mathisen (1999), *Muscular Christianity*, 218–19.

30 Hoffman (1985), Evangelicalism, 82.

31 Sport can transmit religious values, may distort them (1992, August 1), *Harrisburg* (Penn.) *Patriot News*, 1.

32 G. Warner (1979), *Competition* (Elgin, Ill.: David C. Cook), 75.

33 H. Rahner (1972), *Man at play* (New York: Herder & Herder), 33.

34 A year after "The Series" (1977, April), *Christian Athlete*, 24.

35 The school is Brentwood Academy: http://www.brentwoodacademy.com; Recruiters at the gates (1998), *Sports Illustrated*, 89(6), 29; R. O'Brien (1997), Serving America's youth, *Sports Illustrated*, 87(6), 24.

36 K. Anderson (1998), Rebel uprising, *Sports Illustrated*, 88(1), 88; J. Pakin (2001, January 21), Fame's toll: Does it include loss of fun, humiliating foes? *Greensboro News & Record*.

37 The Beat (2006), Sign of the Apocalypse, *Sports Illustrated*, 104(15), 24.

38 K. Keller (1994), Competition in church sport leagues, in P. Heintzman, G. A. Van Andel, & T. L. Visker (Eds.), *Christianity and leisure: Issues in a pluralistic society* (Sioux City, Iowa: Dordt College Press), 206–12. Inverness First Baptist women and men reign (1999, November 30), *St. Petersburg Times*, 4.

39 J. Huizinga (1950), *Homo ludens: A study of the play element in culture* (Boston: Beacon), 1–4.

40 A. Holmes (1981), Towards a Christian play ethic, *Christian Scholars Review*, 11(1), 41–48.

41 Rahner (1972), Man at play, 65.

CHAPTER 1

1 H. I. Marrou (1956), *A history of education in antiquity* (New York: Sheed & Ward), 11. For insight into the relationship between sports and culture in the Greco-Roman world, see: S. Miller (2004), *Ancient Greek athletics* (New Haven, Conn.: Yale University Press); M. Poliakoff (1987), *Combat sports of the ancient world* (New Haven, Conn.: Yale University Press); and E. Köhne & C. Ewigleben (Eds.) (2000), *Gladiators and Caesars: The power of spectacle in ancient Rome* (Berkeley: University of California Press).

2 Tacitus, Dialogue 29, quoted in D. Williams (1999), *Paul's metaphors: Their context and character* (Peabody, Mass.: Hendrickson), 284 n. 69; H. A. Atkinson (1915), *The church and the people's play* (New York: Pilgrim), 27; R. L. Fox (1956), *Pagans and Christians* (New York: Alfred Knopf).

3 See Miller (2004), *Ancient Greek athletics*, 170–75, on ball playing by ancient Greeks; also Poliakoff (1987), *Combat sports*, 107.

4 J. G. Davies (1965), The early Christian church (New York: Holt, Rinehart & Winston), 67.

5   Marrou (1956), *History of education*, 67.

6   The description of the Olympics is from the authoritative "reconstruction of a festival" in Miller (2004), *Ancient Greek athletics*, 113–28.

7   T. Perrottet (2000, June/July), Sacred frenzy, *Civilization*, 82.

8   Poliakoff (1987), *Combat sports*, 90.

9   Quoted in Perrottet (2000), Sacred frenzy, 82.

10 E. N. Gardiner (1910), Greek athletic sports and festivals (New York: Macmillan), 219; Poliakoff (1987), *Combat sports*, 19.

11 Miller (2004), *Ancient Greek athletics*, 213–14.

12 Perrottet (2000), Sacred frenzy, 78, 82–83.

13 Poliakoff (1987), *Combat sports*, 105.

14 A. Cameron (1976), *Circus factions: Blues and greens at Rome and Byzantium* (Oxford: Clarendon), 217.

15 A. Futrell (1997), *Blood in the arena* (Austin: University of Texas Press), 79.

16 See historian Fik Meijer's excellent account of the animal fights and gladiatorial contests: F. Meijer (2004), *The gladiators* (New York: St. Martin's).

17 C. Brinton (1959), *A history of Western morals* (New York: Harcourt Brace), 34; W. Umminger (1963), *Supermen, heroes and gods* (New York: McGraw-Hill), 185.

18 Köhne & Ewigleben (Eds.) (2000), *Gladiators and Caesars*; A. Guttmann (1986), *Sports spectators* (New York: Columbia University Press), 13–34.

19 A. Barton (1993), *The sorrows of the ancient Romans* (Princeton, N.J.: Princeton University Press).

20 Barton (1993), Sorrows; and Futrell (1997), Blood in the arena, offer excellent discussions of the role of violence in Roman society. Nero's brutality is described in: H. A. Harris (1966), *Greek athletes and Greek athletics* (Bloomington: Indiana University Press), 215. Brinton (1959), *History of Western morals*, 82.

21 Commentator is Ammianus Marcellinus, quoted in Guttmann (1986), *Sports spectators*, 28; Cameron (1976), *Circus factions*, 217; Estimates of size of racecourse from: M. Junkelmann (2000), On the starting line with Ben Hur: Chariot racing in the Circus Maximus, in Köhne & Ewigleben (Eds.) (2000), *Gladiators and Caesars*, 86.

22 Junkelmann estimates the combined weight of driver and chariot together at no more than 240 pounds. Gordon quote from PaddockTalk (2005, October 9), Kansas: Jeff Gordon NASCAR Nextel Cup race quotes, http://www.paddocktalk.com (accessed October 10, 2005).

23 Junkelmann (2000), On the starting line, 87, 101–2.

24 From a fourth-century mandate suppressing circus contests on Sunday in Constantinople. See P. R. Coleman-Norton (1966), *Roman state and Christian church: A collection of legal documents to A.D. 435*, vol. 2 (London: SPCK), 442.

25 Junkelmann (2000), On the starting line, 102; A. Cameron (1973), *Porphyrius the charioteer* (Oxford: Clarendon), 255.

26 Harris (1966), *Greek athletes*, 235.

27 Brinton (1959), *History of Western morals*, 34; Umminger (1963), *Supermen, heroes and gods*, 185.

28 See, e.g., D. Van Dalen & B. Bennet (1971), *World history of physical education*, 2nd ed. (Englewood Cliffs, N.J.: Prentice-Hall), 82.

29 Fox (1956), *Pagans and Christians*, 294, 537.

30 St. Augustine of Hippo (1991), *Confessions*, trans. Henry Chadwick (Oxford: Oxford University Press), 100–101. Some Jewish converts' former separatist tradition had already forbidden attendance at spectacles, not simply on grounds of the pagan rites and nudity of the athletes (which violated Mosaic Law), but also because sports were blatantly Hellenistic, a dangerous threat to Jewish ethical codes and customs. However, there is reason to think that this belief did not hold for all or even most of the Jewish population. Some Palestinian Jews as well as those scattered throughout the region had been attending and even participating in athletic contests as early as two centuries before Christ. The eminent Jewish theologian Philo of Alexandria is known to have frequented the athletic contests of his day, often offering critical and informed commentary on them. He also was known to have attended the chariot races. If the Maccabean story of an unscrupulous high priest of the second century BC is true, even the priesthood had difficulty resisting the addictive pull of sports. Jason was the leader of a pro-Hellenist faction in Jerusalem who, in an effort to facilitate the integration of the Greek and Jewish cultures, did an unthinkable thing: he erected a gymnasium in Jerusalem, "enrolled the most influential young men and 'brought them under the Greek hat.'" It was an immediate success, attracting Jewish priests who "no longer showed any zeal for the offices of the sacrifices, and were anxious to share the unlawful facilities of the palestra in their keenness to challenge one another in throwing the discus." H. A. Harris (1976), *Greek athletics and the Jews* (Cardiff: University of Wales Press), 95; Harris (1966), *Greek athletes*, 133; Harris (1976), *Greek athletics and the Jews*; 2 Maccabees 4:7-20.

31 M. M. Felix, *Octavius*, quoted in Davies (1965), *The early Christian church*, 111, 116.

32 J. A. Kleist (Trans.) (1948), *The epistle to Diognetus* (New York: Paulist Press); Tertullian (1931), *Apology: De spectaculis*, trans. T. R. Glover (London: W. Heinemann).

33 Coleman-Norton (1966), *Roman state and Christian church*, vol. 3, 1114.

34 Theodore of Mopsuestia's address to baptismal candidates, quoted in M. L. W. Laistner (1951), *Christianity and pagan culture in the later Roman Empire* (Ithaca, N.Y.: Cornell University Press), 6–7.

35 E. Renan (1866), *The apostles*, trans. M. Levy (New York: Carleton); R. N. Swanson (2002), Augustine and the art of gardening, in R. N. Swanson (Ed.), *The use and abuse of time* in Christian history (Rochester, N.Y.: Boyden), 3; Poliakoff (1987), *Combat sports*, 129.

36 B. J. Kidd (1976), *A history of the church* (New York: AMS Press), 540; *The Apostolic Constitutions* 2:61; also see Davies (1965), *The early Christian church*, 158.

37 Novatian (1972), The spectacles, in R. J. DeSimone (Trans.), *Novatian: The Trinity, the spectacles, Jewish foods* (Washington, D.C.: Catholic University of America Press), 116–17.

38 Fox (1956), *Pagans and Christians*, 15; Poliakoff (1987), *Combat sports*, 123.

39 Cassiodorus, *Variae*, III, 51, quoted in H. A. Harris (1972), *Sport in Greece and Rome* (Ithaca, N.Y.: Cornell University Press), 231–32.

40 Tertullian (1931), *Apology*.

41 M. Gaddis (2005), *There is no crime for those who have Christ: Religious violence in the Roman Empire* (Berkeley: University of California Press), 203. Accounts of Telemachus can be found in various historical sources. For an especially moving rendition, see L. C. Vass (1884), *Amusements and the Christian life in the primitive church and in our day* (Philadelphia: Presbyterian Board of Publication); and Davies (1965), *The early Christian church*, 278–79.

42 R. A. Markus (1990), *The end of ancient Christianity* (Cambridge: Cambridge University Press), 32, 216; Fox (1956), *Pagans and Christians*, 295.

43 Quoted in Fox (1956), *Pagans and Christians*, 19.

44 Miller (2004), *Ancient Greek athletics*, 6; Cameron (1976), *Circus factions*, 218–21; E. Kohne (2000), Bread and circuses, in Köhne & Ewigleben (Eds.) (2000), *Gladiators and Caesars*, 8–30; Meijer, *The gladiators*, 202.

45 Scripture-emblazoned T-shirts, e.g., are available through the ironically labeled Website "ShopZeus" (http://www.shopzeus.com/product.php?sku=zeusd1-AWGR-549016).

46 Novatian, quoted in Poliakoff (1987), *Combat sports*, 146; Novatian (1972), The spectacles, 116.

47 I am indebted to two exhaustive treatments of the athletic metaphors: V. Pfitzner (1967), *Paul and the agon motif* (Leiden, Neth.: Brill); and D. Williams (1999), *Paul's metaphors* (Peabody, Mass.: Hendrickson), 257–92.

48 Williams interprets the verb "labor" in Philippians 2:16 in the context of training for athletic competition, but others view it in a military context. See, e.g., E. Krentz (2003), Paul, games, and the military, in J. P. Sampley (Ed.), *Paul in the Greco-Roman world* (Harrisburg, Pa.: Trinity), 103. See E. Sauer (1966), *In the arena of faith: A call to the consecrated life* (Grand Rapids: Eerdmans), 54, for a discussion of the technical term Paul used in 1 Corinthians 9:27.

49 Williams (1999), *Paul's metaphors*, 257–92.

50 Williams (1999), *Paul's metaphors*, 264–66.

51 Pfitzner (1967), *Paul*, 31, 188.

52 R. F. DeVoe (2003), *Christianity and the Roman games* (Philadelphia: Xlibris), 108–9.

CHAPTER 2

1 C. Harrison (2002), Augustine and the art of gardening, in R. N. Swanson (Ed.), *The use and abuse of time in Christian history* (Rochester, N.Y.: Boydell), 22.

2 R. J. Higgs & M. C. Braswell (2004), *An unholy alliance: The sacred and modern sports* (Macon, Ga: Mercer University Press), 140.

3 A. Arcangeli (2003), *Recreation in the Renaissance: Attitudes towards leisure and pastimes in European culture: 1425–1675* (New York: Palgrave Macmillan), 72. Arcangeli's brief but information-packed volume on recreation in the Renaissance is a treasure chest of source material on this under-studied topic. I have relied heavily on his work in this section.

4 Theodoric, quoted in H. A. Harris (1972), *Sport in Greece and Rome* (Ithaca, N.Y.: Cornell University Press), 232–33.

5 A. Cameron (1976), *Circus factions* (Oxford: Clarendon), 152, 231; R. D. Mandell (1984), *Sport: A cultural history* (New York: Columbia University Press), 108.

6 This section on the tournament draws heavily on the authoritative work by J. R. V. Barker (1989), *The tournament in England: 1100–1400* (Suffolk, England: St. Edmundsbury); and R. Barber & J. R. V. Barker (1989), *Tournaments: Jousts, chivalry, and pageants in the Middle Ages* (New York: Weidenfeld & Nicholson); A. Guttmann (2004), *Sports: The first five millennia* (Amherst: University of Massachusetts Press), 52.

7 B. Daniels (1995), *Puritans at play* (New York: St. Martin's), 164.

8 T. Hendricks (1991), *Disputed pleasures* (New York: Greenwood Press), 53; N. J. Moolennijzer (1973), Our legacy from the Middle Ages, in E. F. Zeigler (Ed.), *A history of sport and physical education to 1900* (Champaign, Ill.: Stipes), 242; J. Huizinga (1956), *The waning of the Middle Ages* (Garden City, N.Y.: Doubleday). On the erotic elements of tournaments, see also: A. Guttmann (2004), *Sports*, 55–57; Hendricks (1991), Disputed pleasures, 53, 74. On the parade, see A. Guttmann (1986), Sport spectators (New York: Columbia University Press), 42.

9 Hendricks (1991), *Disputed pleasures*, 26.

10 Hefele & H. Leclercq (1912), *Historie des conciles* (Paris), quoted in Barber & Barker (1989), *Tournaments*, 17. Details of Bromyard's diatribes are presented in Barber & Barker (1989), *Tournaments*, 144.

11 J. de Vitry (1890), *Exempla*, quoted in Barber & Barker (1989), *Tournaments*, 143; Barber & Barker (1989), *Tournaments*, 141.

12 Barber & Barker (1989), *Tournaments*, 140–42.

13 Barber & Barker (1989), *Tournaments*, 141; Pierre du Bois, quoted in Barber & Barker, 145.

14 C. Dawson (1958), *Religion and the rise of Western culture* (New York: Doubleday), 143, 151.

15 On trial by ordeal, see J. Huizinga (1950), *Homo ludens: A study of the play element in culture* (Boston: Beacon), 81–82; and Mandell (1984), *Sport*, 114–15.

16 R. Hutton (1994), *The rise and fall of merry England: The ritual year 1400–1700* (Oxford: Oxford University Press), 28.

17 R. C. Davis (1994), *The war of the fists: Popular culture and public violence in late Renaissance Venice* (New York: Oxford University Press), 13, 167.

18 G. Hanlon (2004), Glorifying war in a peaceful city: Festive representation of combat in baroque Siena, *War in History*, 11(3), 249–77.

19 D. Brailsford (1969), *Sport and society: Elizabeth to Anne* (London: Routledge & Kegan Paul), 53. Frenchman's comment quoted in F. P. Magoun (1931), Shrove Tuesday Football, *Harvard Studies and Notes in Philology and Literature*, 23, 27.

20 A. Dundes & A. Falassi (1975), *La terra in piazza* (Berkeley: University of California Press), 33.

21 R. MacMullen (1984), *Christianizing the Roman Empire* (New Haven, Conn.: Yale University Press), 79.

22 Hutton (1994), *Rise and fall*, 72.

23 John Chrysostom, quoted in R. A. Markus (1990), *The end of ancient Christianity* (Cambridge: Cambridge University Press), 227.

24 Markus (1990), *End of ancient Christianity*, 121.

25 Augustine, quoted in Markus (1990), *End of ancient Christianity*, 114.

26 Markus (1990), *End of ancient Christianity*, 216.

27 Severus, quoted in Markus (1990), *End of ancient Christianity*, 120; Caesarius, quoted in Markus (1990), *End of ancient Christianity*, 207.

28 *Salvian* (1930), *On the government of God*, trans. E. M. Sanford (New York: Columbia University Press), 6.7, 6.11.

29 Markus (1990), *End of ancient Christianity*, 210, 217; H. Rahner (1972), *Man at play* (New York: Herder & Herder), 83. The Cistercians, in fact, complained about the flabby Benedictines and advocated a vigorous program of athletics and exercise. See J. M. Carter (1992), *Medieval games: Sports and recreations in feudal society* (New York: Greenwood Press); and P. McIntosh (1979), *Fair play: Ethics in sport and education* (London: Heinemann), 40.

30 Henderson (2001), *Ball, bat and bishop: The origin of ball games* (Urbana: University of Illinois Press), 42; Arcangeli (2003), *Recreation in the Renaissance*, 62. As Arcangeli points out, Covarrubias did not condemn bullfighting on grounds of cruelty to animals but because of the psychological attraction of its dangers to spectators (66).

31 D. B. Van Dalen & B. L. Bennett (1971), *A world history of physical education*, 2nd ed. (Englewood Cliffs, N.J.: Prentice-Hall), 116.

32 R. Henderson (2001), *Ball, bat and bishop: The origin of ball games* (Urbana: University of Illinois Press), 53.

33 Henderson (2001), *Ball, bat and bishop*, 38.

34 R. Wendover (1923), *A wrestling match in the city of London*, in Morgan (Ed.), *Readings in English history*, vol. 2 (Cambridge: Cambridge University Press), 88–89.

35 Hutton (1994), *Rise and fall*, 28.

36 Henderson (2001), *Ball, bat and bishop*, 54.

37 Arcangeli (2003), *Recreation in the Renaissance*, 52–55.

38 J. Chrysostom, *Commentary on Matthew, Homily 6.6*, quoted in Rahner (1972), *Man at play*, 98; Rahner (1972), *Man at play*, 71; Arcangeli (2003), *Recreation in the Renaissance*, 66–67; Moolinijzer (1973), *Our legacy*.

39 Rahner (1972), *Man at play*, 65–90 includes an informative discussion on the role of dance in the early church. J. Chrysostum, In illud, vidi Dom, *Homily 1*. quoted in M. Daniels (1981), *The dance in Christianity* (New York: Paulist Press), 19.

40 Saturus, quoted in E. R. Hardy (1960), *Faithful witness: Records of early Christian Martyrs* (London: World Christian Books), 31.

41 Prynne, quoted in H. Wagner (1992), *Puritan attitudes toward recreation in early seventeenth-century New England* (Frankfort: Lang), 62; R. Baxter (1673), *A Christian directory: or, A Summ of practical theologie, and cases of conscience* (London: R. White and N. Simmons), 274.

42 Arcangeli (2003), *Recreation in the Renaissance*, 68–70; Moolinizjer (1973), *Our legacy*, 245.

43 Piccolomini, quoted in J. McClelland (2003), Montaigne and the sports of Italy, *Renaissance and Reformation*, 27(2), 41–51.

44　Francis de Sales, quoted in Arcangeli (2003), *Recreation in the Renaissance*, 46, 53.

45　J. B. Thiers (1686), *Traite des jeux et des divertissments* (Paris: A. Dezallier), quoted in Arcangeli (2003), *Recreation in the Renaissance*, 10.

46　Arcangeli (2003), *Recreation in the Renaissance*, 53.

47　T. Aquinas, *Summa theologica* (Question 168: Modesty as consisting in the outward movements of the body), accessible at Summa Theologica, www.new advent.org/summa.

48　Aristotle, *Nicomachean ethics*, 10.6, 2.4.

49　Arcangeli (2003), *Recreation in the Renaissance*, 114.

50　Aquinas, *Summa theologica*.

51　Aquinas, *Summa theologica*.

52　Arcangeli (2003), *Recreation in the Renaissance*, 62, 114.

53　Arcangeli (2003), *Recreation in the Renaissance*, 112; R. Renson (1976), Juan Luis Vives and the moral aspects of play, in J. D. Massicotte and C. Lessard (Eds.), *History, games and sports in Canada. Games and sports 1776–1876; Mutual influences between America and other countries.* Proceedings of an International Seminar, Trois-Rivieres, 4, 1–18.

54　Arcangeli (2003), *Recreation in the Renaissance*, 54.

55　Henderson (2001), *Ball, bat and bishop*, 39.

56　G. R. S. Mead (1913), Ceremonial game-playing and dancing in medieval churches, *Quest: A Quarterly Review*, 4, 91–123.

57　Henderson (2001), *Ball, bat and bishop*, 37.

58　Mead (1913), Ceremonial game playing, 105–6; Henderson (2001), *Ball, bat and bishop*, 37.

CHAPTER 3

1　T. Johnston (2000), The reformation and popular culture, in A. Pettegree (Ed.), *Reformation world*, 545–58 (London: Taylor and Francis Routledge).

2　H. R. Van Til (1959), *The Calvinistic concept of culture* (Philadelphia: The Presbyterian and Reformed Publishing Company), 132; C. G. Coulton (1945), *Medieval panorama* (Cambridge: Cambridge University Press), 613; A. Arcangeli (2003), *Recreation in the Renaissance: Attitudes towards leisure and pastimes in European culture: 1425–1675* (New York: Palgrave Macmillan).

3　M. Luther, quoted in H. Barnard (1878), *German teachers and educators*, trans. from Karl von Raumer's *Geschichte der pedagogic* (London: Hodder and Stoughton), 158. M. Luther (1914), *Werke, kritische gesamtausgabe, Tischreden 3rd band* (Weimar: Hermann Bohlaus Nachfolger), 339, quoted in B. Bennett (1970, September), The curious relationship of religion and physical education, *Journal of Health, Physical Education and Recreation*, 69.

4　U. Zwingli ([1526] 1899), *The Christian education of youth*, trans. Alcide Reichenback (Collegeville, Pa.: Thompson Brothers), 90–91.

5　On Calvin and dancing, see F. L. Battles (1996), *Interpreting John Calvin* (Grand Rapids: Baker Books), 338–39.

6   J. Calvin, *Institutes of the Christian religion*, book 3, chapter 10, How to use the present life, and book 2, chapter 19, Of Christian liberty, in *Christian Classics Ethereal Library*, http://www.ccel.org/ccel/calvin/institutes.v.xx.html; C. Hill (1964), *Society and Puritanism in pre-revolutionary England* (London: Secker & Warburg), 171.

7   On darts, see R. N. C. Hunt (1933), *Calvin* (London: Centenary), 186. On quoits and clef, see W. Walker (1906), *John Calvin* (New York: G. P. Putnam & Sons), 433. On Calvin's bowling on Sunday, see Hill (1964), *Society and Puritanism*. On golf, see Van Til (1959), *Calvinistic concept of culture*, 104.

8   D. Brailsford (1969), *Sport and society: Elizabeth to Anne* (London: Routledge), 38; P. Smith (1920), *The age of the Reformation* (New York: Henry Holt), 171.

9   E. Jaceline (1632), The mother's legacie to her unborne child, 27–29, quoted in Hill (1964), *Society and Puritanism*, 124; Baxter, quoted in Arcangeli (2003), *Recreation in the Renaissance*, 70.

10   M. Oriard (1991), *Sporting with the gods* (Cambridge: Cambridge University Press), 361–63.

11   J. Bunyan (1962), *Grace abounding to the chief of sinners*, Roger Sharrock (Ed.) (Oxford: Clarendon Press), 10.

12   Oriard (1991), *Sporting with the gods*, 363.

13   P. Stubbes ([1583] 1877), *Anatomy of the abuses in England in Shakespeare's youth, AD 1583*, part 1, F. J. Furnivall (Ed.) (London: New Shakespeare Society), 174; Burkitt (1725), *The poor man's help and the young man's guide* (Boston), 32–33, quoted in H. P. Wagner (1982), *Puritan attitudes towards recreation in early seventeenth-century New England* (Frankfurt: Verlag PeterLang), 46.

14   Burkitt (1725), *Poor man's help*, quoted in Wagner (1982), *Puritan attitudes*, 50.

15   Packer quoted in R. Baxter ([1693] 1997), *A Christian directory* (Morgan, Pa.: Soli Deo Gloria Ministries), 6.

16   Quoted in R. Baxter (1693), *A Christian Directory,or, a sum of practical theologie and cases of conscience*, *Early English Books Online*, 387, 388, http://eebo .chadwyck.com/home.

17   M. Weber (1958), *The Protestant ethic and the spirit of capitalism* (New York: Scribner's Sons), 167; Baxter (1693), 387.

18   Wagner (1982), *Puritan attitudes*, 62.

19   Stubbes ([1583] 1877), *Anatomy*, 174.

20   Brailsford (1969), *Sport and society*, 130; J. Bunyan (1853), *The pilgrim's progress* (Buffalo: George Derby and Company), The Fifth Stage, *Christian Classics Ethereal Library*, www.ccel.org/ccel/bunyan/pilgrim.toc.html

21. E. Dunning & K. Sheard (1979), *Barbarians, gentlemen and players* (Oxford: Martin Robertson), quoted in E. Cashmore (1990), *Making sense of sports*, 2nd ed. (New York: Routledge), 72.

22   Stubbes ([1583] 1877), *Anatomy*, 184.

23   Oriard (1991), *Sporting with the gods*, 363.

24   Hill (1964), *Society and Puritanism*, 174.

25   G. A. Hakehill (1641), *A short, but cleare, discourse of the Lords-day*, 36; quoted in Hill (1964), *Society and Puritanism*, 173.

26 F. F. White (1635), *A treatise of the Sabbath day* (London: Richard Badger), 234, available in the *Early English Books Online* database.

27 N. Bownde (1959), *The true doctrine of the Sabbath* (London: F. J. Porter), 142; L. Bayley (1723), *The practice of piety*, 55th ed., 270–72, quoted in Hill (1964), *Society and Puritanism*, 171, 174, 182.

28 Calvin (1967), *Institutes*. See Hill (1964), *Society and Puritanism*, 170 n. 4 for Calvin and Sunday play.

29 Hill (1964), *Society and Puritanism*, 189.

30 R. Gabriel (1929), *The pageant of America* (New Haven, Conn.: Yale University Press), 2.

31 B. Daniels (1995), *Puritans at play* (New York: St. Martin's), 168. This section relies heavily on Daniels' excellent summary of Puritans and play.

32 J. Sewall (1728), He that would keep God's commandments must renounce the society of evil doers: A sermon preached at the public lecture in Boston, July 18, 1728 after a bloody and mortal duel, in *Early American Imprints I: Evans, 1639–1800*, iii, iv, http://www.readex.com/readex/product.cfm?product=247.

33 Oriard (1991), *Sporting with the gods*, 359; J. A. Lucas & R. A. Smith (1978), *Saga of American sport* (Philadelphia: Lea & Febiger), 12–13, 24; W. Baker (1988), *Sports in the western world*, rev. ed. (Champaign: University of Illinois Press), 83.

34 Wagner (1982), *Puritan attitudes*, 96.

35 R. J. Higgs (1995), *God in the stadium* (Lexington: University of Kentucky Press), 23; Daniels (1995), *Puritans at play*, 168.

36 T. B. Macaulay (1849), *History of England*, vol. 1 (New York: Harper & Brothers); Oriard (1991), *Sporting with the gods*, 363.

37 W. Gladden (1885), Christianity and popular amusements, *Century Magazine*, 29, 387; Arcangeli (2003), *Recreation in the Renaissance*, 113.

38 Arcangeli (2003), *Recreation in the Renaissance*, 52; B. Colman (1707), *The government and improvement of mirth, according to the laws of Christianity, in three sermons*, Early American Imprints, Series I: Evans 1631–1800, 100–108, http://www.readex.com/readex/product.cfm?product=247.

39 Colman (1707), *Government and improvement*, 19ff.

40 Oriard (1991), *Sporting with the gods*, 363; Colman (1707), *Government and improvement*, 46–47.

41 Weber (1958), *Protestant ethic*, 37.

42. Daniels (1995), *Puritans at play*, 22.

43 A. Guttmann (1985), English sport spectators: The restoration to the early nineteenth century, *Journal of Sport History*, 12(2), 103–25; Daniels (1995), *Puritans at play*, 172.

44 Daniels (1995), *Puritans at play*, 172.

45 Gladden (1885), Christianity, 387.

46 J. Buckley (1898, July 7, 14, 21, 28, August 4, 11), Psychology, hygiene, and morality of the bicycle, *New York Christian Advocate*, quoted in W. R. Hogan (1967), Sin and sports, in R. Slovenko & J. A. Knight (Eds.), *Motivations in play, games and sports*, 121–47 (Springfield, Ill.: Charles C. Thomas), 122.

47   Hogan (1967), Sin and sports, 123.

48   J. Wesley, quoted in Hogan (1967), Sin and sports, 121.

49   H. A. Graves (1890), *Andrew Jackson Potter: The noted parson of the Texan frontier* (Nashville: Southern Methodist Publishing House), 448; C. Putney (2001), *Muscular Christianity: Manhood and sports in Protestant America, 1880–1920* (Cambridge, Mass.: Harvard University Press), 52; Hogan (1967), Sin and sports, 122.

50   Has it about gone far enough? (1867, August 19), *Boston Congregationalist and Recorder*; J. T. Crane (1869), *Popular amusements* (New York: Carlton & Lunahan), 80–85; *Little Rock Arkansas Baptist* (1891, September 10), quoted in Hogan (1967), Sin and sports, 129; E. L. Frazier (1885, August 22), Baseball, *Cincinnati Christian Record*, quoted in Hogan (1967), Sin and sports, 129.

51   Hogan (1967), Sin and sports, 122; Amusements, *New Englander*, 355.

52   W. Gladden (1866), *Amusements: Their uses and their abuses* (North Adams, Mass: James T. Robinson), 14–15; *Richmond Religious Herald* (1897, February 25), quoted in Hogan (1967), Sin and sports, 129.

53   A. Doyle (1997), Foolish and useless sport: The southern evangelical crusade against intercollegiate football, *Journal of Sport History*, 24(3), 333, 324; P. Miller (1997), The manly, the moral, and the proficient: College sport in the New South, *Journal of Sport History*, 24(3), 307–8.

54   Amusements, *New Englander*, 350–51.

55   Headington (1878, September 24), *American Christian Review*, quoted in Hogan (1967), Sin and sports, 127.

56   M. Lee & B. Bennett (1960), This is our heritage, *Journal of Health, Physical Education and Recreation*, 31, 27–28.

57   Amusements, *New Englander*, 347; L. R. Yoder (1907, October 30), Sabbath desecrations, *Gospel Witness*, 482–83.

58   Amusements, *New Englander*, 347.

59   J. Taylor (1831), The rules and exercise of daily living, in T. Hughes (Ed), *The works of Jeremy Taylor* (London) in 5 vols., quoted in Wagner (1982), *Puritan attitudes.*

60   Daniels (1995), *Puritans at play*, 217–18.

61   Oriard (1991), *Sporting with the gods*, 360.

CHAPTER 4

1   W. J. Baker (1988), *Sports in the Western world*, rev. ed. (Champaign: University of Illinois Press); J. C. Harris (2000), History of physical activity, in S. J. Hoffman & J. C. Harris, *Introduction to kinesiology* (Champaign, Ill.: Human Kinetics), 195.

2   R. H. Davis (1893, December 9), The Thanksgiving Day game, *Harper's Weekly*, 37, 1169–71.

3   R. Boyle (1963), *Sport: Mirror of American life* (Boston: Little, Brown), 37.

4   C. H. Watson (1887), The proper attitude of the church toward amusements, *Sixth Annual Baptist Congress, Proceedings*, 6, 120; S. Beach (1892, October), The church and popular amusements, *Presbyterian and Reformed Review*, 3,

710; R. A. Swanson (1967), *American Protestantism and play: 1865–1915* (Ph.D. dissertation, Ohio State University), 116–17.

5   Boyle (1963), Sport, 18; R. S. Lynd & H. M. Lynd (1929), *Middletown* (New York: Harcourt & Brace), 340; S. D. McConnell (1900, June 2), The moral side of golf, *Outlook*, 301.

6   F. Sawyer (1847), *A plea for amusements* (New York: D. Appleton), 139; Davis (1893), Thanksgiving Day game, 1171.

7   P. B. Miller (1997), The manly, the moral, and the proficient: College sport in the new South, *Journal of Sport History*, 24(3), 295–96; A. Doyle (1997), Foolish and useless sport: the southern evangelical crusade against intercollegiate football, *Journal of Sport History*, 24(3), 333.

8   *New York Christian Advocate* (1924, July 10), quoted in W. R. Hogan (1967), Sin and sports, in R. Sovenko & J. A. Knight (Eds.), *Motivations in play, games and sports*, 121–47 (Springfield, Ill.: Charles C. Thomas), 135; *Baptist Student* (1925), 3, 2–3, quoted in Hogan (1967), Sin and sports, 135–36.

9   The "great reversal" is a term coined by historian Timothy L. Smith to refer to the decline in evangelical interest in social concern during the early twentieth century in favor of individualism; the term was popularized in D. Moberg (1972), *The great reversal: Evangelism versus social concern* (Philadelphia: Lippincott); F. W. Cozens, & F. S. Stumpf (1953), *Sports in American life* (Chicago: University of Chicago Press), 93; H. Gates (1917), *Recreation and the church* (Chicago: University of Chicago Press), 21.

10 R. Dickinson (1741), *The true-scripture-doctrine concerning some important points of Christian faith* (Boston: D. Fowle), 217; M. A. Noll (2002), *America's God* (Oxford: Oxford University Press), 102; Rules to be followed by those who redeem the time (1802, January 1), *Beauties of the Evangelical Magazine*, 1, 256.

11 N. Fiering (1981), *Jonathan Edward's moral thought and its British context* (Chapel Hill: University of North Carolina Press), 6–7; A. Alexander (2001), Nature and evidence of truth, in M. Noll (Ed.). *The Princeton Theology, 1812–1921*, 2nd ed. (Grand Rapids: Baker Academic), 63–65.

12 T. L. Smith (1957), *Revivalism and social reform in mid-nineteenth century America* (Nashville: Abingdon), 7.

13 W. Arthur (1880), *The tongue of fire* (New York: Harper & Brothers), 92–93.

14 On amusements (1886, December), *Blackwood's Edinburgh Magazine*. The comparison of play to gardening is from W. Spiegelman (1995), *Majestic indolence, English romantic poetry and the work of art* (New York: Oxford University Press). Spiegelman's book shows how poets from Coleridge to Frost have tended to link play with beauty rather than external purposes.

15 H. A. Atkinson (1915), *The church and the people's play* (New York: Pilgrim), 40.

16 Atkinson (1915), People's play, 28. Atkinson's ideas were by no means novel. Perhaps the earliest book to mark the liberalization of church attitudes toward play was *A Plea for Amusements*, written in 1847 by Frederic Sawyer.

17 H. Bushnell (1864), Work and play, in H. Bushnell (Ed), *Literary varieties* (New York: Charles Scribner), 18, 29, quoted in M. Oriard (1991), *Sporting with the gods* (Cambridge: Cambridge University Press), 379.

18   H. Bushnell (1861), *Christian nurture* (New York: Charles Scribner), 389.

19   Bushnell (1861), *Christian nurture*, 339–40.

20   W. Gladden (1866), *Amusements: Their uses and abuses* (North Adams, Mass.: James T. Robinson), 8.

21   Gladden (1866), *Amusements*, 23.

22   Gladden (1866), *Amusements*, 15, 20.

23   Culture of social life in the churches (1864, November), *Boston Review*, 4, 545, quoted in Swanson (1967), *American Protestantism*, 144–45; M. C. Tyler (1869), *The Brawnville papers* (Boston: Fields, Osgood and Company), 20; W. W. Patton, (1868, September), Amusements and the Church, *Hours at Home*, 7, 423, quoted in Swanson (1967), *American Protestantism*, 144–45.

24   Swanson (1967), *American Protestantism*, 56; Cozens & Stumpf (1953), *Sports in American life*, 103.

25   J. Strong (1900), *Religious movements for social betterment* (New York: Baker & Taylor), 27–28, 13.

26   N. Richardson (1922), *The church at play* (New York: Abingdon), 19; H. B. Stowe (1866, September), The chimney corner for 1866, *Atlantic Monthly*, 340; C. A. Dickinson (1889, October), Problems of the modern city church, *Andover Review*, 367.

27   W. F. Forbush (1901), *The boy problem: A study in social pedagogy*, 5th ed. (Boston: Pilgrim), 46–47.

28   C. Kingsley, quoted in B. Haley (1978), *The healthy body and Victorian culture* (Cambridge, Mass.: Harvard University Press), 119.

29   D. Cavallo (1981), *Muscles and morals* (Philadelphia: University of Pennsylvania Press), 33; H. F. Ward (1914), The church and recreation, in Proceedings (National Conference of Charities and Correction), quoted in Swanson (1967), *American Protestantism*, 372.

30   J. Royce, quoted in Cavallo (1981), *Muscles and morals*, 96.

31   Cavallo (1981), *Muscles and morals*, 4–5; H. Braucher (1910), *Miscellaneous writings*, Braucher Papers, National Recreation and Parks Association, quoted in Cavallo (1981), *Muscles and morals* , 99.

32   J. Addams (1930), *The second twenty years at Hull House* (New York: Macmillan), 265–67.

33   A. Hoben (1912), *The minister and the boy* (Chicago: University of Chicago Press), 68.

34   Richardson (1922), *The church at play*, 19.

35   R. G. Walters (1978), *American reformers 1815–1860* (New York: Hill & Wang), 149–50.

36   C. Putney (2001), *Muscular Christianity: Manhood and sports in Protestant America, 1880–1920* (Cambridge, Mass.: Harvard University Press); H. Green (1986), *Fit for America: Health, fitness, sport and American society* (New York: Pantheon), 182.

37   H. B. Smith (1905, January), Every church work, *Munsey's*, 32, quoted in Cozens & Stumpf (1953), *Sports in American life*, 95; Athletics and Religion (1914, May 23), *Outlook*, 107, 151–52; Gladden (1866), *Amusements*, 9–10.

38 Richardson (1922), *The church at play*, 43.

39 L. Gulick, quoted in Putney (2001), *Muscular Christianity*, 71, 69. See C. H. Hopkins (1951), *History of the YMCA in North America* (New York: Association Press), for an exhaustive account of the development of the YMCA in North America.

40 T. Ladd & J. A. Mathisen (1999*), Muscular Christianity: Evangelical Protestants and the development of sport* (Grand Rapids: Baker), 42, 63.

41 Hopkins (1951), *History of the YMCA*, 518, 520.

42 Hopkins (1951), *History of the YMCA*, 520.

43 D. Newsome (1961), *Godliness and good learning* (London: John Murray), 209.

44 T. Hughes, quoted in Newsome (1961), *Godliness*, 203.

45 T. Hughes (1894), *The manliness of Christ* (London: Macmillan), 26.

46 T. W. Higginson (1858, March), Saints and their bodies, *Atlantic Monthly*, 584; Hughes (1894), *Manliness of Christ*, 5; G. Lewis (1966, May), The muscular Christianity movement, *Journal of Health, Physical Education and Recreation*, 42, 27–28.

47 Forbush (1901), *The boy problem*, 37–38; Hoben (1912), *Minister and the boy*, 45; R. Whitaker (1915), *Laughter and life: A Christian view of amusement* (Philadelphia: American Sunday School Union), 23–25.

48 Richardson (1922), *The church at play*, 33; Atkinson (1915), *People's play*, 29; Gladden (1866), *Amusements*, 10.

49 Whitaker (1915), *Laughter and life*, 134; W. Gladden (1885), Christianity and popular amusements, *Century Magazine*, 28, 389.

50 Miller (1997), College sport, 303.

51 Miller (1997), College sport, 304; S. Mathews, quoted in J. R. Betts (1974), *America's sporting heritage* (Reading, Mass: Addison-Wesley), 127.

52 Alabama Christian Advocate (1896), *16* editors quoted in Doyle (1997), Foolish and useless sport, 318.

53 Cavanaugh, quoted in Betts (1974), *America's sporting heritage*, 129; Modern sport symbolized (1929, January 9), *Sportsmanship*, quoted in Cozens & Stumpf (1953), *Sports in American life*, 104.

54 Betts (1974), *America's sporting heritage*, 355–56.

55 Pastors advocate boxing at hearing (1920, May 21), *New York Times*, 13.

56 W. Rainsford (1922), *The story of a varied life* (Garden City, N.Y.: Doubleday, Page), 302.

CHAPTER 5

1 R. Whitaker (1915), *Laughter and life: A Christian view of amusement* (Philadelphia: American Sunday School Union), 134.

2 In *Fundamentalism and American culture*, George Marsden points out that social class was not in itself predictive of liberal or fundamentalist predilections. G. Marsden (1980), *Fundamentalism and American culture* (New York: Oxford University Press).

3 P. Scott (1970), Cricket and the religious world of the Victorian Period, *Church*

Quarterly, *3*, 137–39. For an in-depth account of the events surrounding the call of these men to the mission field, see: J. C. Pollock (1955), *The Cambridge seven* (London: Inter-Varsity Fellowship).

4   W. C. McLoughlin (1959), *Modern revivalism* (New York: Ronald Press), 399, 410–12, 429, 437.

5   W. C. McLoughlin (1955), *Billy Sunday was his real name* (Chicago: University of Chicago Press), 185, 171.

6   McLoughlin (1955), *Billy Sunday*, 175–79, 141–42, 187. G. Loud (1928), *Evangelized America* (New York: Dial Press), 302.

7   B. Sunday (1893, July 27), Why I left professional baseball, *Young Men's Era*, *19*(30), 1; T. Ladd & J. A. Mathisen (1999), *Muscular Christianity: Evangelical Protestants and the development of sport* (Grand Rapids: Baker).

8   B. Sunday (1913, October 18), My all-star nine, *Collier's*, 30; W. Knickerbocker (2000), *Sunday at the ballpark: Billy Sunday's professional career* (Lanham, Md.: Scarecrow), 146.

9   W. R. Hogan (1967), Sin and sports, in C. Slovenko & J. A. Knight (Eds.), *Motivations in play, games and sports*, 121–47 (Springfield, Ill.: Charles C. Thomas), 134.

10 R. J. Higgs (1995), *God in the stadium* (Lexington: Kentucky University Press), 191, 264–65; H. J. Dawson (1989), Veblen's social satire and Amos Alonzo Stagg: Football and the American way of life, in J. Salzman (Ed.), *Prospects: An Annual of American Cultural Studies* (New York: Cambridge University Press), *14*, 278 n. 23, 280 n. 31.

11 Higgs (1995), *God in the stadium*, 92–93; Dawson (1989), Veblen's social satire, 280 n. 31.

12 E. Lucia (1970), Mr. Football: Amos Alonzo Stagg (South Brunswick, N.J.: Barnes); Higgs (1995), *God in the stadium*, 192; Dawson (1989), Veblen's social satire, 282; P. B. Iverson (1996), *A mission on the midway: Amos Alonzo Stagg and the gospel of American football* (Ph.D. dissertation, Michigan State University).

13 M. Frady (1979), *Billy Graham: Parable of American unrighteousness* (Boston: Little, Brown), 174, quoted in Ladd & Mathisen (1999), *Muscular Christianity*, 96; G. Farmer (1948), Best indoor mile, *Life*, *24*(7), 95–96, 98.

14 See Ladd & Mathisen (1999), *Muscular Christianity*, for a detailed account of the history of these and other sport evangelism organizations.

15 B. Glass (1981), *Expect to win* (Waco, Tex.: Word), 81; B. Glass & W. M. Pinson (1972), *Don't blame the game* (Waco, Tex.: Word), 27; Glass (1981), *Expect to win*, 28; B. Glass (1965), *Get in the game* (Waco, Tex.: Word), 67–68; C. Flake (1985), *Redemptorama* (New York: Penguin), 94.

16 J. Meroney (2000), Sports city, *American Enterprise*, *11*(7), 40–45.

17 Flake (1985), *Redemptorama*, 111; S. Bayless (1990), *God's coach: The hymns, hype and hypocrisy of Tom Landry's Cowboys* (New York: Simon & Schuster), 17, 19.

18 J. Churdar, former head of the Department of Exercise and Sport Science, Bob Jones University, telephone conversation, February 20, 2007; That boxing match (1921), *Moody Bible Institute Monthly*, *22*(1), 548; Clergymen and base ball (1921), *Moody Bible Institute Monthly*, *22*(12), 1155.

19 Taylor University Website, Venture for victory, http://www.taylor.edu /athletics/mbasketball/vv.shtml; Ladd & Mathisen (1999), *Muscular Christianity*, 129; FCA Website (2008), Annual impact report, http://www.fca.org /DonatetoFCA/AnnualImpactReport.1sp (accessed November 18, 2008).

20 Athletes in Action Website, http://www.aia.com (accessed January 29, 2007); G. Warner (1979), *Competition* (Elgin, Ill.: David C. Cook), 169.

21 Ladd & Mathisen (1999), *Muscular Christianity*, 139; Pro Athlete Outreach Website (2007), PAO: History, http://www.pao.org/who/history.cfm (accessed May 14, 2009); Are sports good for the soul? (1971), *Newsweek*, 77(2), 51–52.

22 D. Collins (1978, November 19), Nearer my God to the goal line, *Washington Post*, 12, 15–19; R. Blount (1976, December), Temple of the playing fields, *Esquire*, 111–13, 198.

23 Ladd & Mathisen (1999), *Muscular Christianity*.

24 United Press International (1979, July 6), Arkansas floor coach rejects Oral Roberts, *Pittsburgh Press*; Flake (1985), *Redemptorama*, 98; S. Jenkins (1985, October 5), Liberty U Hits First, Saves Later, *Washington Post*, B1.

25 Liberty University Website, About Liberty: Athletics, http://www.liberty.edu /index.cfm?PID=6912; M. Bechtel & S. Cannella (2005), For the record, *Sports Illustrated*, 103(22), 31.

26 J. Kasai (2000), *The book of Landry: Words of wisdom from and testimonials to Tom Landry, former coach of America's Team* (Nashville: Towle House); J. Gibbs (2003), *Racing to win* (Sisters, Ore.: Multnomah); B. McCartney (1995), *From ashes to glory* (Nashville: Thomas Nelson); D. Branon (1998), *Competitor's edge: Women athletes talk about sports and their faith* (Chicago: Moody). Basketball is represented by a book published as part of the Role Model Series by the FCA: C. Ward (1998), *Winning by his grace* (Champaign, Ill.: Sagamore); M. Littleton (2002), *Extreme sports* (Grand Rapids: Zondervan).

27 B. Schaller (2002), *Faith of the Sooners: Inspiring Oklahoma sports stories of faith* (Kearney, Neb: Cross Training); W. Atcheson (2000), *Faith in the Crimson Tide: Inspiring Alabama sports stories of faith* (Kearney, Neb.: Cross Training); G. Thiessen & M. Todd (1999), *Lessons from Nebraska football: Inspirational stories and lessons from the Gridiron* (Kearney, Neb.: Cross Training); D. Branon (2000), *A sports fan's guide to Christian athletes and sports trivia* (Chicago: Moody); J. Hillman & K. Hillman (1998), *Devotions from the world of sports* (Colorado Springs, Colo.: Chariot Victor); D. Branon (2002), *Sports devotional Bible* (Grand Rapids: Zondervan).

28 J. A. Mathisen (1992, November), *The rhetoric of modern "muscular Christianity": Taking a second look at Sports Spectrum* (paper presented at the annual meeting of the Society for the Scientific Study of Religion, Washington, D.C.).

29 R. Quebedeaux (1973), *The worldly evangelicals* (New York: Harper & Row), 76.

30 J. Garner (2003), *Recreation and sports ministry* (Nashville: Broadman & Holman).

31 Ultimate Goal Ministries Website, About us, http://www.ultimategoal.net; Sports Ministries, Inc. Website, http://www.sm-inc.org; Upward Website, History, http://www.upward.org/about.aspx?id=50; L. McCown & V. J. Gin (2003), *Focus on sport ministry* (Marietta, Ga.: 360° Sports).

CHAPTER 6

1 C. Clark (1977), *Misery and company* (Chicago: University of Chicago Press), 3, 112.

2 R. E. O. White (1979), *Biblical ethics* (Atlanta: John Knox), 106; C. F. H. Henry (1957), *Christian personal ethics* (Grand Rapids: Baker), 479.

3 N. Mills (1997), *The triumph of meanness: America's war against its better self* (New York: Houghton Mifflin), 11.

4 R. J. Mouw (1973), *Political evangelism* (Grand Rapids: Eerdmans), 44; emphasis added.

5 C. S. Lewis (1955), *Surprised by joy* (New York: Harcourt, Brace & World), 129.

6 Novak (1976), Joy of sports (New York: Basic Books), 312.

7 (1995), The cutthroat within, *Women's Sports and Fitness*, 17(4), 122; Hodges, quoted in They said it, *Sports Illustrated*, 39(10), 18. Description of killer instinct is psychiatrist Arnold Beisser's in A. R. Beisser (1967), *The madness in sports: Psychosocial observations on sports* (New York: Appleton-Century), 157, 161. J. Gruden, ABC Sports interview, January 7, 2006.

8 S. Walker (1980), *Winning: The psychology of competition* (New York: W. W. Norton), 46–47; Novak (1976), *Joy of sports*, 162.

9 T. Owens, quoted in J. Macur (2004, November 28), *New York Times*, D-1, D-10; Rich Seubert, quoted in W. C. Rhoden (2008, February 3), Two personalities: One for game day, one for every other day, Sports Sunday, *New York Times*, 6.

10 Nothstein quoted in D. Becker (1996, June 4), Fearlessness a must at win-or-else trials, *USA Today*, 9C; M. Clarkson (1999), *Competitive fire* (Champaign, Ill.: Human Kinetics); Van Dyken quoted in Clarkson (1999), *Competitive Fire*, 116.

11 P. Finney (1989, October 16), McNeil mourns debilitating hit, *Sporting News*, 54; B. Newman (1989), Remorse: Not in the NFL, *Sports Illustrated*, 71(16) 112.

12 Rhoden (2008, February 3), Two personalities, 6.

13 Cain and Schloder quoted in Clarkson (1999), *Competitive fire*, 140, 115–16; M. Winkeljohn (2001, December 7), Serious routine: Falcon players prepare in different ways as they seek the edge of mayhem on Sunday, *Atlanta Constitution*, 15F.

14 M. Wilbon (1992, September 16), Bring back the Gipper, *Washington Post*, C1; M. Silver (2000), Do or die, *Sports Illustrated*, 93(25), 115; A. Guttmann (1978), From ritual to record (New York: Columbia University Press), 75.

15 H. G. Bissinger (1990), *Friday night lights* (Reading, Mass.: Addison-Wesley), 154.

16 M. Lucas (2004, May 21), Guns loaded? War? Cassell, Garnett need to face reality, 1D; Eisenhower quoted in G. Warner (1979), *Competition* (Elgin, Ill.: David C. Cook).

17 Kush Puts the kibosh on camaraderie (1973, December 19), *Pittsburgh Post-Gazette*, B2; Hurricane bad boys part II: The dinner (1986, December 29), *News-Press* (Cape Coral, Fla.), 3C.

18 Boys' night out (1993, May 18), *Greensboro News & Record*, C-4.

19 Friendly rivals (2000, December 31), *Greensboro News & Record*, C-5. Official is quoted in E. Stark (1984, July), Women's tennis: Friends and foes, *Psychology Today*, 17.

20   S. Michaux quoted in R. Shattuck (1996), *Forbidden knowledge* (New York: Harcourt Brace), 151.

21   L. Keech (2001, March 17), Fine line drawn today between friend and foe, *Greensboro News & Record*, C1–C2.

22   J. Macur (2007, June 11), Masters of clay, Nadal and Henin win 3rd, *International Herald Tribune*, 20; J. Stein (2001), Power game, *Time*, *158*(9), 54; C. Clarey (2006, June 29), All in a day's work for leading women, *International Herald Tribune*, 23; Roddick puts friendship aside, heads for semis (2007, January 24), *Greensboro News & Record*, C3.

23   M. Fuchs (2006, November 29), Thomas says outburst and ejection a "fluke," *New York Times*, D9; I. Thomsen (2004, December 20), Inside the NBA, *Sports Illustrated*, *101*(24), 92; NBA Draft Website, Kevin Durant, http://www.nbadraft .net/admincp/profiles/kevindurant.html.

24   R. Hoffer (2006), No more Mr. Nice Guy, *Sports Illustrated*, *104*(21), 18–19; Relentless Blue Devils force Temple to crack (1988, March 27), *Greensboro News & Record*, B1, B14.

25   D. Hyland (1978), Competition and friendship, *Journal of the Philosophy of Sport*, 5, 36

26   Henry (1957), *Christian personal ethics*, 416.

27   H. Slusher (1967), *Man, sport and existence* (Philadelphia: Lea & Febiger), 148. D. Scarton (1991, September 8–13), The New Testament: Christianity's march on sports, *Pittsburgh Press*, 31; Strawberry's teammate quoted in L. Rotenberk (1988, August 22), Pray ball, *Chicago Sun-Times*, A11.

28   R. Dunn & C. Stevenson (1994), The paradox of the church hockey league, unpublished paper, University of New Brunswick, Canada.

29   On positive deviance, see J. J. Coakley (1994), *Sport in society*, 5th ed. (St. Louis: Mosby), 136, 143; and A. Kohn (1986), *No contest: The case against competition* (New York: Houghton Mifflin), 161.

30   B. Bright (1984), That winning spirit, *Athletes in Action Magazine*, 6, 21.

31   A. Wolters (1985), *Creation regained* (Grand Rapids: Eerdmans), 73.

32   Wolters (1985), *Creation regained*, 86.

33   D. Reisman (1953), Football in America: A study in cultural diffusion, in *Individualism reconsidered and other essays* (Glencoe, Ill.: Free Press), quoted in Kohn (1986), *No contest*, 25, 30.

34   P. McIntosh (1979), *Fair play: Ethics in sport and education* (London: Heinemann), 30; Reagan quoted in B. J. Bredemeier & D. L. Shields (1985, October), Values and violence in sports today, *Psychology Today*, *19*(10), 23–32.

35   Bright (1984), That winning spirit, 21.

36   D. Gerdes (2003), *Coaching for character* (Mobile, Ala.: Evergreen), 116; R. Simon (2004), *Fair play*, 2nd ed. (Boulder, Colo.: Westview), 17.

37   B. Williams (n.d.), Competing rightly: Applying Christian ethical thinking to sport competition, unpublished paper, Wheaton College, Wheaton, Ill. (unpublished).

38   "Triumph of the therapeutic" is Philip Rieff's term: P. Reiff (1987), *The triumph of the therapeutic* (Chicago: University of Chicago Press). It is related to

modern evangelicalism by Dennis Hollinger in D. Hollinger (2002), *Choosing the good* (Grand Rapids: Baker Academic), 118; J. D. Hunter (1983), *American evangelicalism* (Piscataway, N.J.: Rutgers University Press), 99; A. Wolfe (2003), *The transformation of American religion* (New York: Simon & Schuster), 83.

39   R. Robbins (1995, March), Flip turn, *Sports Spectrum*, 26.

40   N. J. Watson & J. White (2007), Winning at all costs in modern sport, in J. Parry, S. Robinson, N. J. Watson, & M. Nesti (Eds.), *Sport and spirituality*, 61–79 (London: Routledge), 70. "Crucible of sanctification" is Andrew Murray's term: A. Murray (2001), *Humility* (Grand Rapids: Bethany House), 63.

41   C. Flake (1985), *Redemptorama* (New York: Penguin), 111, 101; H. R. Niebuhr (1951), *Christ and culture* (New York: Harper & Bros.), 109–10.

42   K. Lindskoog (1976, January), Making it big, *Reformed Journal*, 4.

43   D. Hiebert (1984, February 24), Sport: Competitive relationships, *The Messenger*, 4. This is part 3 of a three-part series by Hiebert on sport and faith; parts 1 and 2 were published in *The Messenger* on January 27 and February 10, respectively.

44   Why Jaeger left the court (2007, February 2), *The Week*, 8; W. Coffey (2006, December 10), Former tennis sister act II: Former tennis great Jaeger sporting a new habit, *USA Today*, 98.

CHAPTER 7

1   M. Miles (2006), *Fullness of life: Historical foundations for a new asceticism* (Eugene, Ore.: Wipf & Stock), 45; J. Calvin, *Institutes of the Christian religion*, book 3, chapter 10, How to use the present life, and book 2, chapter 19, Of Christian Liberty, in *Christian classics ethereal library*, http://www.ccel.org/ccel/calvin/institutes.v.xx.html, 1.15.3; K. G.Vanderpool (1973), The attitude of selected nineteenth-century disciples of Christ leaders regarding physical activity (Ph.D. diss., Temple University), 100–101, 136–37.

2   D. E. H. Whiteley (1974), *The theology of St. Paul* (Oxford: Blackwell); D. Hiebert (1985), Glorifying God in the body, *Dialog*, 24, 133–35.

3   Hiebert (1985), Glorifying God.

4   S. Grentz (1997), *Moral quest* (Downers Grove, Ill.: InterVarsity), 263; Thou shalt get in shape: Pastor is personal trainer (2005, February 21), *St. Louis Post Dispatch*, 55.

5   K. Cooper (1965), *It's better to believe* (Nashville: Thomas Nelson), 14.

6   R. M. Griffith (2004), *Born again bodies* (Berkeley: University of California Press), 241.

7   Cooper (1965), *It's better to believe*, 20.

8   C. Edgely, B. Edgely, & R. Turner (1981), The rhetoric of aerobics: Fitness as a religion, *Free Inquiry in Sociology*, 10, 188; L. F. Winner (2000, September 4), The weigh and the truth, *Christianity Today*, 50–58; J. Stein (2005, April 18), Body work, *Los Angeles Times*, F1.

9   Winner (2000), Weigh and the truth, 50; Churches stressing health and fitness (2004), *Christian Century*, 121(7), 13; A. Leichman (2004, December 23), Faith-based fitness: A body and soul connection, *The Record* (Bergen County, N.J.), L6; K. Ferraro (1998), Firm believers? Religion, body weight, and well being, *Review of Religious Research*, 39(3), 238.

10 R. Pitter (1998), *Sport delivery within the urban voluntary sector: Locating church-based sport and recreation in Memphis*, unpublished manuscript, University of Memphis, Tenn.; Dunwoody Baptist Church Sports and Fitness Centers, http://www.dbc.org/sportsfitness.

11 Victoria Johnson Fitness Ministries, Gospel aerobics directory, http://www.victoriajohnson.com/Ministry/gad.shtml.

12 Griffith (2004), *Born again bodies*, 241.

13 T. Elkins (1985, September 20), The body spiritual, *Christianity Today*, 29(11), 24.

14 Putney (2001), *Muscular Christianity*, 62; M. A. Zuidema (1999), Developing an aim-centered K–12 physical education program based on Christian tenets, in J. Byl & T. Visker (Eds.), *Physical education and wellness: Looking to God as we look at ourselves*, 99–126 (Sioux City, Iowa: Dordt College Press), 107, 101; J. Byl (1977), *Fitness and sport within a Christian lifestyle*, unpublished manuscript, Redeemer University, Ancaster, Ont., Canada, 56; J. White (1981, October), Running to win, *Christian Herald*, 79.

15 J. Huizinga (1950), *Homo ludens* (Boston: Beacon), 2; S. Kretchmar & W. Harper (1979), Why does man play, in E. W. Gerber & W. J. Morgan (Eds.), *Sport and the body: A philosophical symposium*, 2nd ed., 204–6 (Philadelphia: Lea & Febiger).

16 See R. S. Paffenbarger, R. T. Hyde, A. L. Wing, & C. H. Steinmetz (1984), A natural history of athleticism and cardiovascular health, *Journal of the American Medical Association*, 252(4), 491.

17 H. Pierce (1974, August 2), Team trailing, he breaks arm on fast pitch, *Pittsburgh Post-Gazette*, 1.

18 T. Weir (1983, August 11), Rotator cuff: Strike three for pitchers, *USA Today*, C1; J. McCloskey & J. Bailes (2005), *When winning costs too much* (Lanham, Md.: Taylor Trade), 191; emphasis added.

19 CDC (2002), Nonfatal sports- and recreation-related injuries treated in emergency departments—United States, July 2000–June 2001. *Morbidity and Mortality Weekly Report 2002*, 51, 736–40, also reported in the *Journal of the American Medical Association*, 288(16), 1977–79; Concussion: hazardous to heads (1999), Scorecard, *Sports Illustrated*, 90(14), 30; J. M. Conn, J. L. Annest, & J. Gilchrist (2003), Sports- and recreation-related injury episodes in the US population, 1997–1999, *Injury Prevention*, 9, 117–23.

20 J. Hoberman (1992), *Mortal engines: The science of performance and the dehumanization of sport* (New York: Free Press), 110.

21 Rebel neurologists say boxing can be safe (1990, May 22), *New York Times*, C1.

22 For the record (2005), *Sports Illustrated*, 103(13), 31; J. Eligon (2005, September 23), 5 days after title bout, fighter dies of injuries, *New York Times*, D6.

23 B. P. Bodden, R. L. Tacchetti, R. C. Cantu, S. B. Knowles, & F. O. Mueller (2007), Catastrophic head injuries in high school and college football players, *American Journal of Sports Medicine*, 35(7), 1075–81; M. Kram (1992, January), No pain no game, *Esquire*, 75; T. Layden (2007), The big hit, *Sports Illustrated*, 107(4), 52–62, quotation from p. 53.

24 Mandell quoted in D. Ateyo (1979), *Blood and guts: Violence in sports* (New York: Paddington), 13; emphasis in original.

25 T. P. Dompier, J. W. Powell, M. J. Barron, & M. T. Moore (2007), Time-loss and non-time-loss injuries in youth football players, *Journal of Athletic Training*, 42(3), 395–402.

26 B. Vastag (2002), Football brain injuries draw increased scrutiny, *Journal of the American Medical Association*, 287(4), 437–39; J. Leiber (1996, January 5), True grit at quarterback, *USA Today*, 3C; M. W. Collins, S. H. Grindel, S. H. Lovell, et al. (1999), Relationship between concussion and neuro-physiological performance in college football players, *Journal of the American Medical Association*, 282(10), 964–70.

27 Associated Press (2005, September 14), Coroner: Ex-Steeler died from brain injury, *Charlotte Observer*, 3C; A. Schwarz (2007, January 18), Expert ties ex-player's suicide to brain damage from football, *New York Times*, A1, A29.

28 A. Schwarz (2007, February 2), Dark days follow hard-hitting career in NFL, *New York Times*, C1, C16; J. Lloyd (2009, May 5), High school athletes face serious concussion risks, *USA Today*, 7D; A. Schwarz (2007, September 15), High school players stay silent on concussions, raising risks, *New York Times*, A1, A10.

29 Layden (2007), The big hit; Ateyo (1979), *Blood and guts*, 221; D. Haase, personal communication (2008, February 12, telephone conversation); Fox, quoted in P. King (2004), Painful reality, *Sports Illustrated*, 101(14), 60–63.

30 W. Nack & L. Munson (2001), The wrecking yard, *Sports Illustrated*, 94(19), 60–71; Center for the Study of Retired Athletes, Current research, http://www.csra.unc.edu/statistics.htm; J. Jares (1981, August 16), Unitas quoted in W. Nack & L. Munson (2001), 61. Football's pain a reminder to Jim Otto, *New York Times*, S8.

31 McGlockton, quoted in J. Battista (2003, August 17), McGlockton is ready for action, *New York Times*, 3; R. O'Halloran (2006, December 6), In the NFL everybody hurts, *Washington Times*, C2.

32 Brenly, quoted in Masked masochists (1985, May 14), *American Way*, 51–55.

33 L. Peterson, A. Junge, J. Chomiak, T. Graf-Baumann, & J. Dvorak (2000), Incidence of football injuries and complaints, *American Journal of Sports Medicine*, 28(suppl. 5), S51–S57; Headers face scrutiny in soccer (1999, November 5), *USA Today*, 3C; E. J. T. Matser, A. G. H. Kessels, M. D. Lezak, B. D. Jordan, & J. Troost (1999), Neuropsychological impairment in amateur soccer players, *Journal of the American Medical Association*, 282(10), 971–73; C. F. Babbs (2000), Brain injury in amateur soccer players, *Journal of the American Medical Association*, 283(7), 16.

34 L. Y. Griffin, J. Agel, M. J. Albohm, et al. (2000), Non-contact anterior cruciate ligament injuries: Risk factor and preventative strategies, *Journal of American Academy of Orthopedic Surgeons*, 8(3), 141–50.

35 S. Eitzen (1999), *Fair and foul* (Lanham, Md.: Rowman & Littlefield); S. Stevensen (1997, September 7), Here's the painful truth: Injuries nagging juniors, *New York Times*, Y27.

36 A. Gluklich (1999), Self and sacrifice: A phenomenological psychology of sacred pain, *Harvard Theological Review*, 92(4), 491.

37. P. Safai (2003), Healing the body in the "culture of risk," *Sociology of Sport Journal*, 20(2), 127–46; S. Walk (1997), Peers in pain: The experience of student athletic trainers, *Sociology of Sport Journal*, 14(1), 22–56.

38 S. Ward (1959, January), Some observations on athletes, *Psychiatric Communications*, 60, quoted in R. Boyle (1963), *Sport: Mirror of American life* (Boston: Little, Brown).

39 K. Young, P. White, & W. McTeer (1994), Body talk: Male athletes reflect on sport, injury, and pain, *Sociology of Sport Journal*, *11*(3), 186.

40 Meredith, quoted in J. Meroney (2000, October/November), Sports city, *American Enterprise*, 40.

41 C. Jones, M. Strahan, & J. Cuneo (2002, November), Be happy for this man, *Esquire*, *1*(5), 62.

42 Nightmare in the backfield (2006, November 17), The Last Word, *The Week*, 53.

43 P. Conroy (1987), *The prince of tides* (New York: Bantam), 384; T. Dowling (1970), *Coach: A season with Lombardi* (New York: Popular Library), 132. See also: J. Kramer (1970), *Lombardi: Winning is the only thing* (New York: Pocket); and J. Kramer (1969), *Instant replay* (New York: Signet).

44 E. Reid (1997), My body my weapon my shame, *GQ*, 67, 360–67.

45 H. G. Bissinger (1991), *Friday night lights* (New York: Harper Collins), 167–68.

46 Pistons lose Wallace, game to Spurs 89–83 (2003, April 7), *USA Today*, 13C.

47 M. Bechtel, Sports Beat (2004), *Sports Illustrated*, *100*(26), 25; M. Orecklin (2002), Gross anatomy, *Time*, *159*(21), 81. As soon as the bone chip listing was discovered by eBay employees, it was removed.

48 Hoberman (1992), *Mortal engines*, 159.

49 K. Vaux (1985, September 20), How do I love me? *Christianity Today*, 26; M. Chass (2005, January 2), A pitcher hopes to come off the injury treadmill, Sports Sunday, *New York Times*, 3; J. Sire (1997), *The universe next door* (Downers Grove, Ill.: InterVarsity), 194.

50 B. Richardson (1993, December 8), If human dartboards thrill you, be sure to catch this show, *Wall Street Journal*, 1.

51 L. Ryken (1987), *Work and leisure in Christian perspective* (Portland, Ore.: Multnomah), 223; A. F. Holmes (1981), Towards a Christian play ethic, *Christian Scholars Review*, *11*(1), 41–48; T. Campolo (1988), *20 hot potatoes Christians are afraid to touch* (Dallas, Tex.: Word), 1988.

52 Meroney (2000), Sports city, 41 (1979, Fall).

53 H. Oriel & B. Plaschke (1991, May 29), Shouldering a heavy burden, *Los Angeles Times*, C1, C5.

54 D. Dravecky & T. Stafford (1991), *Comeback* (Scranton, Pa.: HarperCollins).

55 B. Glass & W. M. Pinson (1972), *Don't blame the game* (Waco, Tex.: Word), 24.

56 M. Silver (2002), American beauty, *Sports Illustrated*, *97*(11), 40; K. Seitzer (1995), Fear strikes back, *Sports Illustrated*, *83*(4), 118.

57 M. Galli (2005, October), Should we ban boxing? *Christianity Today*, 49 (web only), http://www.christianitytoday.com.

58 J. D. Lawson, M. J. Sleasman, & C. A. Anderson (2007), The gospel according to Safeway, in K. J. Vanhoozer, C. A. Anderson, & M. J. Sleasman, *Everyday theology* (Grand Rapids: Baker Academic), 73.

59 A. Wolfe (2003), *The transformation of American religion* (New York: Free Press); W. Neal (1975), *The handbook of athletic perfection: A training manual for Christian athletes* (Prescott, Ariz.: Institute for Athletic Perfection), 62–64.

CHAPTER 8

1 They said it (2000, January), *Sports Illustrated*, 92(3), 12; This week's sign of the apocalypse (2007), *Sports Illustrated*; 10(4), 18; A. Camus (1961), *Resistance, rebellion and death* (New York: Alfred A. Knopf), 242.

2 J. A. Mangan (1986), *The games ethic and imperialism* (New York: Viking), 65.

3 D. Cavallo (1981), *Muscles and morals* (Philadelphia: University of Pennsylvania Press), 100; L. Gulick, Fundamental basis of the Young Men's Christian Association, typescript [ca.1890], Archives, Babson Library, Springfield College, Springfield, Mass., 1–3, quoted in C. Putney (2001), *Muscular Christianity: Manhood and sports in Protestant America, 1880–1920* (Cambridge, Mass.: Harvard University Press), 69; L. Merrill (1908), *Winning the boy* (New York: F. H. Revell), 132.

4 G. R. Ford (1974), In defense of the competitive urge, *Sports Illustrated*, 41(2), 16–23; President's Council on Physical Fitness and Sports, Department of Health and Human Services, www.fitness.gov (accessed November 11, 2003).

5 W. J. Bennett (1976, February), In defense of sports, *Commentary*, 68–70; M. Novak (1976), *The joy of sports* (New York: Basic Books), 43.

6 Pope John Paul II (1984, November 24), Beloved young athletes (speech given to athletes from the Olympic Games, Los Angeles, Calif.), reproduced on Apple Seeds, http://www.appleseeds.org/JP-2_Sports.htm; Vatican announces setting up of sports desk (2004, August 5), *Cath News*, http://www.cathnews.com/news/408/26.php; M. Marty (2005), Good sports, *Christian Century*, 122(7), 5.

7 Falwell, quoted in D. Lederman, *Chronicle of Higher Education* (1989, March 15), "Liberty U Seeks Success in Football to Spread Fundamentalist Message," A29; Oral Roberts University, ORU athletics mission statement, http://www.orugoldeneagles.com.

8 S. Hauerwas (2002), Foreword, in C. H. Evans & W. R. Herzog, *The faith of fifty million: Baseball, religion and American culture* (Louisville, Ky.: Westminster John Knox), xvii.

9 R. White (January, 1995), Jeremy's Hero, interview, *Sports Spectrum*, 15; G. Warner (1979), *Competition* (Elgin, Ill.: David Cook), 62.

10 Westmont College, The mission of Westmont athletics, http://blogs.westmont.edu/athletics/mission; Wheaton College, Alumni: Our mission in real life, http://www.wheaton.edu.

11 Dallas Theological Seminary, How have sports influenced your life? http://www.dts.edu.

12 C. S. Lewis (1967), Christianity and culture, in W. Hooper (Ed.), *Christian reflections*, 12–36 (Grand Rapids: Eerdmans), 22–23.

13 C. S. Lewis (1955), *Surprised by joy* (New York: Harcourt, Brace & World), 129.

14 C. S. Lewis (1955), *Surprised by joy*, 130.

15 L. B. Smedes (1975), Theology and the playful life, in C. J. Orlebeke & L. B. Smedes (Eds.), *God and the good* (Grand Rapids: Eerdmans), 55.

16　D. Sabo, M. J. Melnick, & B. E. Vanfossen (1993), High school participation, *Sociology of Sport Journal*, 10(1), 47–49; S. L. Hanson & R. S. Kraus (1999), Women in male domains: Sport and science, *Sociology of Sport Journal*, 16, 104.

17　I. Murdoch (1971), *The sovereignty of good* (New York: Shocken), 89. The connection is underscored and given amplification in R. Feezell (2002), *Sport, play and ethical reflection* (Urbana: University of Illinois Press), 147.

18　R. Bellah, R. Madsen, W. Sullivan, A. Swidler, & S. Tipton (1985), *Habits of the heart: Individualism and commitment in American life* (New York: Harper & Row), 9; B. A. Broh (2002), Linking extracurricular programming to academic achievement: Who benefits and why? *Sociology of Education*, 75, 78–79; P. Zimmerman (2001), Boston Patriots, *Sports Illustrated*, 95(9), 162–63; M. Felger (2000, October 2), Dawn of a new day, *Boston Herald*, http://www .bostonherald.com (accessed July 18, 2006).

19　A. Rudd (2005), High school coaches' definitions of character (1999), unpublished paper, quoted in A. Rudd (2005), Which "character" should sport develop? *Physical educator*, 62(4), 206.

20　Historians now believe Wellington was referring to the number of officers in his army who had graduated from Eton rather than to the effects of sports in particular.

21　K. Lorenz (1966), *On aggression* (New York: Harcourt, Brace & World), 260.

22　W. Schmidt (1987, May 25), For town and team, honor is its own reward, *New York Times*, 1.

23　A. Gumbel (2007, October 6), Batting for Jesus, *Independent* (London), 48.

24　I. Maisel (1997), Hallowed be his name, *Sports Illustrated*, 87(20), 63; Staff and wire reports (1997, November 13), Player's admission takes the kick out of Nebraska's miracle, *Greensboro News & Record*, C5.

25　W. F. Reed (1990), A loser in victory, *Sports Illustrated*, 73(19), 96; J. Terry (1990, October 31), It's only wrong if you get caught, *St. Louis Post-Dispatch*, 3B. Stroud received the Jack Kelly Fair Play Award in 1987 from the U.S. Olympic Committee.

26　A. Chiu (1999, October 28), Untruths are often the sporting thing, *Greensboro News & Record* (AP), B4; S. Carter (1996), *Integrity* (New York: Harper Perennial), 7.

27　National Collegiate Athletic Association, NCAA Sportsmanship Awards: Recipients, http://www.ncaa.org.

28　M. Feldman (1969), *Some relationships between specified values of student groups and interscholastic athletics in selected high schools* (Ph.D. dissertation, University of Massachusetts); J. Webb (1969), Professionalization of attitudes toward play among adolescents, in G. Kenyon (Ed.), *Aspects of contemporary sport sociology* (Chicago: Athletic Institute), 178; R. C. Mantel & L. Vander Velden (1974), The relationship between the professionalization of attitude toward play of preadolescent boys and participation in organized sport, in G. Sage (Ed.), *Sport and American society*, 172–78 (Reading, Mass.: Addison-Wesley); R. A. McAfee (1955), Sportsmanship attitudes of sixth, seventh and eighth grade boys, *Research Quarterly*, 26(2), 120.

29　R. F. Priest, J. V. Krause, & J. Beach (1999), Four-year changes in athletes' ethical value choices in sport situations, *Research Quarterly for Exercise and Sport*, 70(2), 170–81; D. E. Richardson (1963), Ethical conduct in sport situations, in *Proceedings of the National College Physical Education Association for Men* (Washington, D.C.), 103–4.

30 G. Pilz (1979, February), Attitudes toward different forms of aggression and violent behavior in competitive sports: Two empirical studies, *Journal of Sport Behavior*, 3; P. McIntosh (1979), *Fair play: Ethics in sport and education* (London: Heinemann), 130–31 (the research reported by McIntosh was carried out by Professor K. Heinila at University of Jyvaskyla in Finland); J. M. Silva (1983), The perceived legitimacy of rule violating behavior in sports, *Journal of Sport Psychology*, 5(2), 438–66.

31 Report reveals propensity of high school athletes to lie and cheat when the stakes are high (2007, February 16), Josephson Institute: Center for Sport Ethics, http://josephsoninstitute.org/sports/programs/survey/index.html.

32 B. J. Bredemeier & D. L. Shields (1985, October), Values and violence in sport, *Psychology Today*, 19(1), 23–32; D. L. Shields & J. L. Bredemeier (1995), *Character development and physical activity* (Champaign, Ill.: Human Kinetics), 188.

33 B. Wolverton (2006, August 4), Morality play, *Chronicle of Higher Education*, 52(48), 260; S. K. Stoll & J. M. Beller (1992), *Division I athletes: Sportsmanship qualities*, unpublished manuscript, Center for Ethical Theory and Honor in Competitive Sports, University of Idaho; S. K. Stoll (1992), *Sportsmanship: Dead or alive?* unpublished manuscript, Center for Ethical Theory and Honor in Competitive Sports, University of Idaho; S. K. Stoll & J. M. Beller (1993), Sportsmanship: An antiquated concept? *Journal of Health, Physical Education, Recreation and Dance*, 64(6), 74.

34 J. M. Beller, S. K. Stoll, & I. Sumanik (1992), Moral reasoning of elite Canadian and American athletes and coaches, unpublished manuscript, Center for Ethical Theory and Honor in Competitive Sports, University of Idaho; S. Ruibal (2004, December 3), Steroid case takes on new life, *USA Today*, C1.

35 A. Huxley (1947), Education, in C. Fuess & E. S. Basford, *Unseen hunter* (New York: Macmillan), 500–501; D. S. Eitzen (1999), *Fair and foul* (London: Rowman & Littlefield), 44; B. Glass & W. M. Pinson (1972), *Don't blame the game* (Waco, Tex.: Word Books).

36 D. Brooks (2007, October 16), A still small voice, *New York Times*, A23.

37 T. Verducci (1997), No relief in sight, *Sports Illustrated*, 87(7), 45–49; K. Moore (1989), Bionic man, *Sports Illustrated*, 71(17), 84; S. L. Price (2001), Semi-tough, *Sports Illustrated*, 94(4), 76; They said it (1982), *Sports Illustrated*, 57(12), 14; S. Roberts (2007, April 8), The road to success is paved by cheating, *New York Times*, 8-1, 8-3; T. Ringolsby (2006, June 4), Rockies try to "dirty up their image," *Pittsburgh Post-Gazette*, C1.

38 B. J. Bredemeier & D. L. Shields (1986), Moral growth among athletes and non-athletes: A comparative analysis, *Journal of Genetic Psychology*, 147(1), 7–18; D. L. Shields & B. J. Bredemeier (1995), *Character development and physical activity* (Champaign, Ill.: Human Kinetics); C. R. Rees, F. M. Howell, & A. W. Miracle (1990), Do high school sports build character? A quasi-experiment on a national sample, *Social Science Journal*, 27(3), 303–15; W. Kroll & K. H. Petersen (1965), Study of values test and collegiate football teams, *Research Quarterly*, 36(4), 446.

39 J. Ford (2007), Substance use among college athletes: A comparison based on sport/team affiliation, *Journal of American College Health*, 55(6), 367–73; D. A. Yusko, J. F. Buckman, H. R. White, & R. J. Pandina (2008), Alcohol, tobacco, illicit drugs, and performance enhancers: A comparison of use by college student athletes and non-athletes, *Journal of American College Health*, 57(3), 281–90; H. Wechsler, A. E. Davenport, G. Dowdall, B. Moeykens, & S. Castillo (1994), Health and behavioral consequences of binge drinking in college: A national survey of students at 140 campuses, *Journal of the American Medical Association*, 272(21), 1672–77; A. E. Davenport (1977), Binge drinking, tobacco and illicit drug use and involvement in college athletics: A survey of students at 140 American colleges, *Journal of American College Health*, 45(5), 195–200; S. B. Boereinger (1999), Associations of rape-supportive attitudes with fraternal and athletic participation, *Violence Against Women*, 5(1), 81–90.

40 T. Tutko & B. Olgivie (1971, October), If you want to build character try something else, *Psychology Today*, 5, 60–63.

41 Rob Miller (2008, November 18), telephone conversation.

42 J. Devaney (1964), A bible in the bullpen, *Saturday Evening Post*, 237(17), 28–29.

43 M. B. Scott (1973), A man on the horse, in J. T. Talamini & C. H. Page (Eds.), *Sport and society*, 336–54 (Boston: Little, Brown).

44 B. Glass & W. M. Pinson (1972), *Don't blame the game*, 27.

45 C. L. Stevenson (1997), Christian athletes and the culture of elite sport: Dilemmas and solutions, *Sociology of Sport Journal*, 14(3), 259.

46 Official quoted in G. Vecsey (1999, August 8), When is it gamesmanship, and when is it cheating? *New York Times* (Sports Sunday), 30.

47 D. F. Wells (1998), *Losing our virtue: Why the church must recover its moral vision* (Grand Rapids: Eerdmans), 63–64.

48 R. B. Frost & E. J. Sims (Eds.) (1974), *Development of human values through sport* (Washington, D.C.: American Alliance for Health, Physical Education, and Recreation), 89.

CHAPTER 9

1 W. A. Moore (2007, February 6), Super Bowl is a super pulpit, *St. Petersburg Times*, 1B; emphasis added.

2 A. Stricklin (2007, January 22), Super Bowl coaches, Dungy, Smith known for Christian testimony, *Baptist Press*, http://www.sbcbaptistpress.org/bpnews.asp?ID=24811; R. Stroud (2007, March 1), Grateful Dungy back in Bay Area, *St. Petersburg Times*, 1C.

3 H. R. Niebuhr (1951), *Christ and culture* (New York: Harper & Row); S. J. Grentz (2000, June), What does Hollywood have to do with Wheaton? The place of (pop) culture in theological reflection, *Journal of the Evangelical Theological Society*, 309; K. H. Sargeant (2000), *Seeker churches* (Piscataway, N.J.: Rutgers University Press), 42; C. Colson (2000, August 7), Salad-bar Christianity, *Christianity Today*, http://www.christianitytoday.com/ct/2000/009/31.80.html; M. Shibley (1999), *Resurgent evangelicalism in the United States* (Columbia: University of South Carolina Press), 109.

4 Augustine, *On Christian doctrine*, 9.4.24; A. Wolfe (2004, April 30), interview

by J. Sheler, *Religion & Ethics Newsweekly*, PBS, http://www.pbs.org/wnet /religionandethics/week735/interview.html.

5   D. Thompson, comments on Bride Website, http://www.bridepub.com /bridem4.htm; Lifeway: Biblical Solutions for Life, http://www.lifeway.com; J. Ellul (1986), *The subversion of Christianity* (Grand Rapids: Eerdmans), 18; B. Stone (2008, April 8), telephone conversation.

6   V. S. Owens (1980), *The total image* (Grand Rapids: Eerdmans), 11; Art thou ready for some football? (2006, April 21), *Greensboro News & Record*, C2; J. Dodderidge quoted in C. Smith (1997, July 27), God is an .800 hitter, *New York Times*, SM26.

7   R. Wuthnow (1988), The restructuring of American religion (Princeton, N.J.: Princeton University Press), 108; T. Ladd & J. A. Mathisen (1999), *Muscular Christianity* (Grand Rapids: Baker), 136.

8   In His Grip Golf Association, http://www.inhisgripgolf.com/pages .asp?pageid=54620; J. Dotson (2002, October 7), Sports evangelism called bridge to reaching 96% of population, *Baptist Press*, http://www.bpnews.net /bpnews.asp?ID=14393.

9   J. Gardner quoted in R. H. Bork (1996), *Slouching toward Gomorrah* (New York: Regan), 129.

10   P. Heinegg (1976), Philosopher in the playground: Notes on the meaning of sport, *Southern Humanities Review*, 10(2), 155; B. Pascal (1965), *Pensées* (New York: Washington Square), 46.

11   K. Lorenz (1966), *On aggression* (New York: Bantam), 271; Sports: Are we overdoing it? (1972, August 11), *Christianity Today*, 11; C. Detweiler & B. Taylor (2003), *A matrix of meaning: Finding God in popular culture* (Grand Rapids: Baker Academic), 255.

12   M. Noll (1986), As we see it, *Reformed Journal*, 36(1), 2–3; D. Jenkins (1982), *Christian maturity and success* (Philadelphia: Fortress), 113; A. Wolters (1985), *Creation regained* (Grand Rapids: Eerdmans), 84.

13   R. G. Sipes (1973, February), War, sports and aggression: A test of two rival theories, *American Anthropologist*, 75(1), 64–86; R. G. Sipes (1976), Sports as a control for aggression, in T. T. Craig (Ed.), *Humanistic and mental health aspects of sports, exercise and recreation* (Chicago: American Medical Association), 373; J. McMurtry (1971, October), Kill 'em! Crush 'em! Eat 'em raw! *Macleans*.

14   J. Nuechterlein (1998, June/July), The weird world of sports, *First Things*, 84, 8–9, 11–12. See, e.g., L. R. Sloan (1989), The motives of sports fans, in J. D. Goldstein (Ed.), *Sports games and play: Social and psychosocial viewpoints*, 2nd ed., 175–240 (Hillsdale, N.J.: Lawrence Erlbaum); D. L. Wann, M. J. Melnick, G. W. Russell, & D. G. Pease (2001), *Sport fans: The psychology and social impact of spectators* (New York: Routledge); W. A. Harrell (1981), Verbal aggressiveness in spectators at professional hockey games: The effects of tolerance of violence and amount of exposure to hockey, *Human Relations*, 34(8), 643–55.

15   Asbury College, athletics Website, http://www.asbury.edu/athletics. Baylor University pledges an athletic program that is "consistent with the overall mission of the university," which is "to educate men and women for worldwide leadership and service by integrating academic excellence and Christian

commitment within a caring community." Baylor University, mission statement, http://baylorbears.cstv.com/school-bio/bay-mission-statement.html. J. Mathisen & R. Burwell (2001), *Intercollegiate athletics at consortium institutions: More than mere fun and games*, unpublished manuscript, Messiah College, Grantham, Penn., 6; J. Mathisen & R. Burwell (2002, August), *About the role of intercollegiate athletics at conservative Protestant colleges* (paper presented at the annual meeting of the American Sociological Association, Chicago), Wheaton College, Wheaton, Ill.

16 Wolfe (2004, April 30), PBS interview; P. J. Schroeder & J. P. Scribner (2006), To honor and glorify God, *Sport Education and Society*, *11*(1), 39–54.

17 I. Thomsen (2004), Higher calling, *Sports Illustrated*, *100*(25), 56–59; W. Neal (1998), *Total release performance* (Grand Island, Neb.: Cross Training), 23; Schroeder & Scribner (2006), To honor, 49.

18 J. M. Gustafson (1981), *Ethics from a theocentric perspective* (Chicago: University of Chicago Press), 180; B. Stone (2007), *Evangelism after Christendom* (Grand Rapids: Brazos), 21.

19 J. R. W. Stott (1978), *Christian counter-culture* (Downers Grove, Ill.: InterVarsity), 17.

20 M. McLuhan (1964), *Understanding media: The extensions of man* (New York: McGraw-Hill), 17; R. Gruneau (1977), *Making spectacle: A case studying televised sports production*, in L. A. Wenner (Ed.), *Media, sports and society* (London: Sage), 134–56; P. Comisky, J. Bryant, & D. Zillman (1977), Commentary as a substitute for action, *Journal of Communication*, *27*(3), 150–53; J. Bryant & D. Zillman (1983), Sports violence and the media, in J. H. Goldstein (Ed.), *Sports violence*, 154–221 (New York: Springer Verlag).

21 Gordon quote from B. Lipsyte (2001, February 23), NASCAR and religion, *Religion & Ethics Newsweekly*, PBS, http://www.pbs.org/wnet/religionandethics/week426/feature.html; D. Alford (2008, August), Racing for Jesus, *Christianity Today* (online), 23–27.

22 T. Krattenmaker (2006, May 10), Going Long for Jesus, *Salon.com*, http://www.salon.com/news/feature/2006/05/10/ministries/index.html; R. Word (2005, February 5), Super Bowl a marriage of parties, religion in buckle of the Bible Belt, Associated Press.

23 B. Giamatti (1989), *Take time for paradise: Americans and their games* (New York: Summit), 44.

24 B. Miller-McLemore (2001), Through the eyes of Mircea Eliade: United States football as a religious rite de passage, in J. L. Price (Ed.), *From season to season* (Macon, Ga.: Mercer University Press).

25 J. Michener (1976), *Sports in America* (New York: Random House), 383.

26 J. Coakley (2001), *Sport in society*, 7th ed. (New York: McGraw-Hill), 94.

27 P. Tickle (1997), *God-talk in America* (New York: Crossroad), 128.

28 S. Zucker & M. McCarthy (2008, February 5), MVP Eli poised to score on Madison Avenue, *USA Today*, 1C.

29 L. Ries (2007, July 2), Origin of brands blog, http://ries.typepad.com/ries_blog/2007/07/celebrity-endor.html; M. Roll (2008, February 7), Branding and celebrity endorsements, *Venture Republic*, http://www.venturerepublic.com

/resources/Branding_celebrities_brand_endorsements_brand_leadership
.asp; S. J. Gilbert (2007, October 29), Marketing Maria: Managing the athlete
endorsement, *Working Knowledge* (Harvard Business School), http://hbswk
.hbs.edu/item/5607.html.

30 D. Ribadeneira (1996, January 25), They play and pray, *Boston Globe*, SP22; F.
Deford (1976), The word according to Tom, *Sports Illustrated*, 44(17), 54–60;
Owens (1980), *Total image*, 28.

31 M. Tierney (2008, February 17), Next big thing still has room to improve, *New
York Times*, SP4.

32 H. S. Slusher (1967), *Man, sport and existence* (Philadelphia: Lea & Febiger),
167; Blessed are the pass-catchers (2000, September), *Focus on the Family Citizen*, 6–9.

33 Owens (1980), *Total image*, 29.

34 M. A. Kellner (1999, November 15), God on the gridiron, 76.

35 C. E. Zylstra (1999), Christian sports and leisure: Oxymoron or redundancy,
in J. Byl & T. Visker (Eds.), *Physical education, sport and wellness: Looking to God as we look to ourselves*, 167–77 (Sioux City, Iowa: Dordt College
Press), 170.

36 God is my quarterback: NFL chaplains help players battle self doubt, *Athletes in
Action*, http://www.bloomberg.com/apps/news?pid=newsarchive&sid=aBmsB
k5mJuXE; Yoder (1984), *The priestly kingdom* (Notre Dame, Ind.: University of
Notre Dame Press), 138.

37 J. Smalley (1983), *Heroes of the NFL: Exciting stories of faith from football's top
superstars* (San Bernardino, Calif.: Here's Life Publishers), 25–28.

38 Smalley, *Heroes of the NFL*, 27.

39 J. Posnanski (2001, August 19), Paths of sports and religion often cross, *Kansas
City Star*, B2.

40 D. J. Bosch (1979), *A spirituality of the road* (Scottsdale, Pa.: Herald), 78–81.

41 Football and religion (2004, December), NFL Films, Show 18, Tape ID 137444.

CHAPTER 10

1 J. A. Marbeto (1967), *The incidence of prayer in athletics as indicated by selected
California collegiate athletes and coaches* (Master's thesis, University of California, Santa Barbara).

2 D. Reed (1995, September 1), Falwell seeks to block NCAA no-gloating rule,
Patriot News (Harrisburg, Pa.), A8.

3 NCAA clarifies prayer stance (1995, September 2), *Charleston Daily Mail*
(W.Va.), 2B; S. Grossfeld (2006, November 7), An issue of fair pray: Disagree-
ment sends coach, school to court, *Boston Globe*, 5C.

4 K. King (2002), Winning ugly, *Sports Illustrated*, 97(21); J. Rowe (1996, November 23), You guys are so on! Cats in hats, *Greensboro News & Record*, D3.

5 D. Firestone (2000, August 27), South's football fans stand up and pray, *New
York Times*, 1; FCA president Dale Sheehy's comments on FCA Website, http://
www.fca.org (accessed 2000, July 25).

6 No comment department (1993, January 27), *Christian Century*, 76; Excerpts

from Supreme Court opinions on prayer (2000, June 20), *New York Times*, A22.

7   Allen, quoted in A. Levitt (1972), *Somebody called Doc* (Carol Stream: Ill.: Creation House), 33; N. Armour (2005, December 1), Disagreements remain on what place prayer has in sports, *The Associated Press State and Local Wire*; M. A. Murray, A. B. Joyner, K. L. Burke, M. J. Wilson, & A. D. Zwald (2005), The relationship between prayer and team cohesion in collegiate softball teams, *Journal of Psychology and Christianity* 24(3), 233–39.

8   See, e.g., N. J. Watson & M. Nesti (2005), The role of spirituality in sport psychology consulting: An analysis and integrative review of literature, *Journal of Applied Sport Psychology*, 17, 228–29; R. B. Douglass (1991, June 14), Keep your prayers to yourself? *Commonweal*, 118(12), 395; D. Zirin (2006, June 11), Good arm, good speed . . . and he's born again!: Is this any way for the Colorado Rockies to pick a baseball team? *Chicago Sun Times*, B3; Amid sex scandals, one Aussie football team turns to God (2004, March 17), Agence France-Presse.

9   H. G. Bissinger (1990), *Friday night lights* (Reading, Mass.: Addison-Wesley), 273–74.

10 P. Conroy (1987), *The great Santini* (New York: Bantam), 251; P. Gent (1973), *North Dallas forty* (New York: William Morrow), 247–48.

11 Dale Earnhardt Jr. in his own words (2005, April 10), *Roanoke Times*, Martinsville Speedway race insert, 4; S. J. Hoffman (1985), Evangelicalism and the revival of religious ritual in sport, *Arete: The Journal of Sport Literature*, 2(2), 67.

12 O. Hallesby ([1931] 1994), in John W. Harvey (Trans.), *Prayer* (Minneapolis, Minn.: Augsburg), 18; R. Otto (1923), *The idea of the holy* (Oxford: Oxford University Press).

13 T. Boswell (1978, October 6), Reggie's fate: Bluster takes luster off work at plate, *Washington Post*, E1.

14 L. Montville (1989), Thou shalt not lose, *Sports Illustrated*, 71(20), 87.

15 Baylor Institute for Studies of Religion (2006, September), American Piety in the 21st century: New insights into the depth and complexity of religion in the US, Selected findings from the Baylor religion survey, Baylor University, http://www.baylor.edu/content/services/document.php/33304.pdf.

16 K. Schmitz (1979), Sport and play: Suspension of the ordinary, in E. W. Gerber & W. J. Morgan (Eds.), *Sport and the body: A philosophical symposium*, 2nd ed. (Philadelphia: Lea & Febiger), 22–29; B. Giammati (1989), *Take time for paradise* (New York: Summit), 71; E. Fink (1979), The ontology of play, in Gerber & Morgan, *Sport and the body*, 73–83.

17 W. J. Morgan (2006), *Why sports morally matter* (New York: Routledge), 19.

18 J. L. Price (2009), Playing and praying, sport and spirit: The forms and functions of prayer in sports (manuscript copy of the forthcoming article in the inaugural issue of the *International Journal of Religion and Sport*, in press (2009), 22; Wood, quoted in W. Nack (1998), Does God care who wins the Super Bowl? *Sports Illustrated*, 88(3), 46.

19 P. Yancey (2006), *Prayer: Does it make any difference?* (Grand Rapids: Zondervan), 222.

20 Prayer and school football (editorial) (1999, November 26), *New York Times*, A42; J. Pieper (1963), *In tune with the world: A theory of festivity* (New York: Harcourt, Brace & World), 34.

21 K. Eisner (1906), *Feste de Festlosen* (Dresden: Kaden), 9; quoted in Pieper (1963), *In tune*, 62.

22 Soccer: Steaua paymaster calls religious tune (2007, June 7), *International Herald Tribune*, 20.

23 E. Sherman (1990, September 27), Holt's logic on God's role more holey than holy, *Chicago Tribune*.

24 D. Warner (1978, December 1), Wayne Alderson, Oilers huddle with God for extra point, *Pittsburgh Post-Gazette*, 2; Area man's praying scores with Oilers (1979, January 6), *Pittsburgh Press*, 5; Yancey (2006), *Prayer*, 222.

25 Bailar's prayer is contained in J. Michener (1976), *Sports in America* (New York: Random House), 384.

26 Collingsworth, quoted in M. A. Kellner (1999, November 15), God on the gridiron, *Christianity Today*, 76; Bradshaw's comments in Football and religion (2004, December), NFL Films, Show 18, Tape ID 137444; T. Landry (1990), *Tom Landry: An autobiography* (Grand Rapids: Zondervan), 293. On criticism of prayers, see R. Reilly (1991), Save your prayers please: Organized worship has no place at football games, *Sports Illustrated*, 74(4), 8; and R. B. Douglass (1991, June 14), Keep your prayers to yourself? *Commonweal*, 395–98.

27 C. Smith (1997, July 27), God is an .800 hitter, *New York Times*, SM26; Stone (2007), *Evangelism after Christendom* (Grand Rapids: Brazos), 284.

28 "Righteousness of ostentation," from C. F. H. Henry (1957), *Christian personal ethics* (Grand Rapids: Baker), 575; Reed (1995, September 1), Falwell seeks to block.

29 K. Walker (1997, November/December), Feel the REAL power, *Today's Christian*, 15, http://www.christianitytoday.com/tc/7r6/7r6015.html.

30 J. Kelly (1997, April), Keep God out of the big leagues, *U.S. Catholic*, 62(4), 26; R. Mouw (2007), *Praying at Burger King* (Grand Rapids: Eerdmans), 4.

31 D. Bonhoeffer (1978), *The cost of discipleship* (New York: Macmillan), 181.

32 D. R. Czech, C. A. Wrisberg, L. A. Fisher, C. L. Thompson, & G. A. Hayes (2004), The experience of Christian prayer in sport: An existential phenomenological investigation, *Journal of Psychology and Christianity*, 23(1), 3; R. Bentz (2000, May 3), Survival of the fittest, *Sports Spectrum* (online), http://www.sportsspectrum.com; R. Orozco (2007, August 4), Prayer a pre-race ritual for some race car drivers, *Star News* (Wilmington, N.C.), 7D.

33 R. E. O. Smith (1979), *Biblical ethics* (Atlanta: John Knox Press), 70.

34 S. Kelley (2001, November 4), One year later, one bad hit later, teams had vision of Williams again, *Seattle Times*, C1; K. Armstrong & N. Perry (2009, February 15) To Husky fans a tragic hero, to the courts a wanted felon, *Seattle Times* (online), http://seattletimes.nwsource.com/html/localnews/2004150796_rbwilliams 281.html.

35 L. Truss (2007, July 18), Have faith in the power of prayer (and a good putter), *The Times*, 64.

36 L. Kee (1998, August 10), Lions and Christians, *The Nation*, 267(5), 37; G. J. Mac-Donald (2004), In Boston, some see hand of higher power, *Christian Century*, 121(23), 39.

37 J. Blank (1997), The greater struggle, *U.S. News and World Report*, 122(25), 9; W. Nack (1998, January 26), Does God care? 88.

38 D. Plotz (2000, February 4), The God of the gridiron: Does he care who wins the Super Bowl? *Slate*, http://www.slate.com/id/74294/.

39 Nack (1998, January 26), Does God care? 46.

40 C. H. Evans & W. R. Herzog (2002), *The faith of fifty million: Baseball, religion and American culture* (Louisville, Ky.: Westminster John Knox), 218.

41 J. Price (2009), Playing and praying, 22; J. J. Huizinga (1955), *Homo ludens: A study of the play element in culture* (Boston: Beacon), 205.

42 R. Smith (1979, August 26), They heard the cheers, *New York Times*, S3.

43 R. Rosenblatt (2001, November 11), Highs and lows from Saturday's games, Associated Press; A. Kreider (2003), Prayers for assistance as unsporting behavior, *Journal of the Philosophy of Sport*, 30(1), 17–25.

44 Nack, Does God Care? 49.

45 C. F. H. Henry (1957), *Christian personal ethics*; Evans & Herzog (2002), *Faith of fifty million*.

46 "Relentlessly plural" is R. E. O. Smith's description: Smith (1979), *Biblical ethics*, 69; Henry (1957), *Christian personal ethics*, 577.

47 Notebook: Yesss, it's another year (2001, January 15), *Time*, 21; K. Kennedy, P. King, A. White, R. Deitsch, & A. Kim (2002), Curses! *Sports Illustrated*, 96(21), 21; N. A. Scotch (1961), Magic sorcery, and football among urban Zulu: A case of reinterpretation under acculturation, *Journal of Conflict Resolution*, 5(1), 70–74; D. Hack (2007, July 25), Garcia bemoans bounces that didn't go his way, *New York Times*, C15.

48 J. McCallum (1988), Green cars, black cats and lady luck, *Sports Illustrated*, 68(6), 88–93; H. G. Buhrmann & M. K. Zaugg (1981), Superstitions among basketball players, *Journal of Sport Behavior*, 4(2), 4; H. G. Buhrmann & M. K. Zaugg (1983), Religion and superstition in the sport of basketball, *Journal of Sport Behavior*, 6(3), 14.

49 J. G. Frazier (1922), *The golden bough* (New York: Macmillan); B. Malinowski (1954), *Magic, science and religion* (Garden City, N.Y.: Doubleday).

50 M. Isaacson (2002, February 2), Religion looms as part of Rams' team spirit, *Chicago Tribune*; K. Kennedy & B. J. Schecter (2005), Doing it my way, *Sports Illustrated*, 103(2), 48; D. Tom (1990, January 18), Superstition bowl, *USA Today*, D1.

51 J. R. W. Stott (1978), *Christian counter-culture* (Downers Grove, Ill.: InterVarsity), 142–52; Smith (1979), *Biblical ethics*, 69; Marbeto (1967), *The incidence of prayer in athletics*, 67; M. Winkeljohn (2001, December 7), Pro football: Serious routine: Falcons players prepare in different ways as they seek the edge of mayhem on Sunday, *Atlanta Constitution*, 15F.

CHAPTER 11

1   Cultural religion: C. L. Albanese (1981), *America: Religions and religion* (Belmont, Calif.: Wadsworth), 321–22; Natural religion: M. Novak (1976), *The joy of sports* (New York: Basic Books); Civil religion: J. W. Loy, B. D. McPherson, & G. Kenyon (1978), *Sport and social systems* (Reading, Mass.: Addison-Wesley); Folk religion: J. A. Mathisen (1992), From civil religion to folk religion: The case of American sport, in S. J. Hoffman (Ed.), *Religion and Sport*, 17–33 (Champaign, Ill.: Human Kinetics), 22.

2   J. R. W. Stott (1978), *Christian counter-culture* (Downers Grove, Ill.: InterVarsity), 40.

3   J. Pieper (1962), *Leisure: The basis of culture* (New York: Pantheon), 153.

4   A. B. Giamatti (1989), *Take time for paradise* (New York: Simon & Schuster), 81; G. Dahl (1972), *Work, play, and worship in a leisure oriented society* (Minneapolis, Minn.: Augsburg), 70–71.

5   E. Shaughnessy (1976), Santayana on athletics, *Journal of American Studies*, *10*(2), 180; K. L. Schmitz (1979), Sport and play: Suspension of the ordinary, in E. W. Gerber & W. J. Morgan (Eds.), *Sport and the body*, 2nd ed., 22–29 (Philadelphia: Lea & Febiger), 26.

6   T. Veblen ([1899] 1953), *The theory of the leisure class* (New York: New American Library), 172.

7   S. Culin (1974), *Games of the North American Indians* (New York: Dover).

8   R. Mandell (1984), *Sport: A cultural history* (New York: Columbia University Press), 5.

9   A. Guttmann (1978), *From ritual to record: The nature of modern sports* (New York: Columbia University Press), 55.

10 Restoration of the created order is a key component of Reformed theology; see, e.g., A. Wolters (1985), *Creation regained* (Grand Rapids: Eerdmans); H. Rahner (1972), *Man at play* (New York: Herder & Herder), 7–8.

11 J. Nuechterlein (1995, January), The wide world of sports, *First Things*, *49*, 8–9.

12 Novak (1976), *The joy of sports*, 21.

13 C. Prebish (1984), Heavenly Father, divine goalie: Sport and religion, *Antioch Review*, *42*(3), 306–18; G. Sheehan (1978), *Running and being* (New York: Warner), 230.

14 R. J. Higgs (1983), Muscular Christianity, holy play, and spiritual exercises: Confusion about Christ in sport and religion, *Arete: The Journal of Sport Literature*, *1*(1), 59–85; R. J. Higgs & M. C. Braswell (2004), *Unholy alliance: The sacred and modern sports* (Macon, Ga.: Mercer University Press), 183; D. Watson (1978), *I believe in the church* (Grand Rapids: Eerdmans), 194.

15 L. Smedes (1975), Theology and the playful life, in C. Orlebeke & L. Smedes (Eds.), *God and the good*, 46–62 (Grand Rapids: Eerdmans), 58.

16 C. S. Lewis (1965), *The weight of glory* (Grand Rapids: Eerdmans), 4.

17 H. M. Best (1981), Christian responsibility in music, in L. Ryken (Ed.), *The Christian imagination*, 401–14 (Grand Rapids: Baker), 409.

18 J. Wilson (1986, October 6), Dilemmas of the Christian college athlete (lecture at symposium titled Who's on first? Liberal arts, Christianity, and sports,

Hillsdale College, Hillsdale, Mich.), published May 1987 as Dilemmas of the Christian college athlete, *Imprimis* (Hillsdale College), 1–2, available at *Imprimis Archive*: http://www.hillsdale.edu/news/imprimis/archive/author.asp.

19 N. Pearcey (2004), *Total truth: Liberating Christianity from its cultural captivity* (Wheaton, Ill.: Crossway), 40.

20 Pearcey, *Total truth*, 40.

21 Giamatti (1989), *Take time for paradise*, 33–34; J. Leonard (1979, August 15), Private Lives, *New York Times*, C10.

22 L. Kliever (2001), God and games in modern culture, in J. L. Price (Ed.), *From season to season: Sports as American religion* (Macon, Ga.: Mercer University Press), 42.

23 M. Galli (2005, April 8), The prodigal sports fan, *Christianity Today*, *49* (online only), http://www.christianitytoday.com/ct/2005/114/53.0.html.

24 W. J. Morgan (2000), *Why sports morally matter* (New York: Routledge), 200.

25 R. K. Johnston (1983), *The Christian at play* (Grand Rapids: Eerdmans), 45.

26 R. Callois (1961), *Man, play and games*, trans. M. Barash (Glencoe, Ill.: Free Press); D. Siedentop (1980), *Physical education: An introductory analysis*, 3rd ed. (Dubuque, Iowa: W. C. Brown), 247–48.

27 S. Kretchmar (1973), Ontological possibilities: Sport as play, in R. G. Osterhoudt (Ed.), *The philosophy of sport* (Springfield, Ill.: Charles C. Thomas), 64.

28 Smedes (1975), Theology, 50; R. Feezell (2006), *Sport, play and ethical reflection* (Champaign: University of Illinois Press), 74–75.

29 "Paramount reality" is Alfred Shutz's term and appears in Peter Berger (1980), *Heretical Imperative*, (New York: Doubleday), 35. P. Weiss (1971), *Sport: A philosophic inquiry* (Carbondale: Southern Illinois University Press), 148.

30 "Asylum of time" is from E. Fink (1968), The oasis of happiness: Toward an ontology of play, in J. Ehrmann (Ed.), *Games, play, literature* (Boston: Beacon), 21; P. L. Berger (1969), *A rumor of angels* (New York: Doubleday), 57–60.

31 Rahner (1972), *Man at play*, 26.

32 D. Hyland (1990), *A philosophy of sport* (New York: Paragon House), 134.

33 R. Neale (1969), *In praise of play* (New York: Harper & Row), 78.

34 J. Esposito (1979), Play and possibility, in Gerber & Morgan, *Sport and the body*, 106.

35 Pieper (1962), *Leisure*, 13.

36 Pieper (1962), *Leisure*, 31.

37 Hyland (1990), *Philosophy of sport*, 141.

38 J. Gustafson (1981), *Ethics from a theocentric perspective*, vol. 1 (Chicago: University of Chicago Press), 195.

39 Rahner (1972), *Man at play*, 58, 65.

40 A. F. Holmes (1982), Towards a Christian play ethic, *CMS Journal*, *13*(4), 9–12.

41 Lewis (1965), *Weight of glory*, 7; C. S. Lewis (1967), *Christian reflections* (Grand Rapids: Eerdmans), 23.

42 R. Caspar (1978), Play springs eternal, *New Scholasticism*, *52*(2), 197.

43 Johnston (1983), *The Christian at play*.

44 D. Naugle (1995, September 15), A biblical philosophy of sport and play, unpublished paper, Department of Philosophy, Dallas Baptist University, available at: http://www.dbu.edu/Naugle/pdf/sport_play.pdf; Johnston (1983), *The Christian at play*, 74, 80.

45 W. Neal (1981), *The handbook on coaching perfection*, 3rd ed. (Grand Island, Neb.: Cross Training), viii.

46 R. Stark (1971), *Wayward shepherds* (Harper & Row), 102–3; M. Galli (2005, February 18), Salt and light in the arena, *Christianity Today*, 49 (online only), http://www.christianitytoday.com/ct/2005/februaryweb-only/53.0b.html?start=2.

47 M. Galli (2005, March 5), The grace of sports, *Christianity Today*, 49 (online only), http://www.christianitytoday.com/ct/2005/marchweb-only/52.0.html?start=1.

48 Galli (2005, March 5), Grace of sports.

49 Feezell (2006), *Sport*, 67, 69, 74–75.

50 Feezell (2006), *Sport*, 78.

51 A. Guttmann (1986), *Sport Spectators* (New York: Columbia University Press), 184.

52 Schmitz (1979), Sport and play, 28–29.

53 G. Vecsey (2008, April 30), An act of sportsmanship that touched 'em all, *New York Times*, C13.

54 Rahner (1972), *Man at play*, 33.

INDEX